ANTISOCIAL BOYS

Other volumes in this series:

VOLUME 1: *Families with Aggressive Children*
Patterson, Reid, Jones, and Conger (1975)

VOLUME 2: *Observation in Home Settings*
John B. Reid, Editor (1978)

VOLUME 3: *Coercive Family Process*
Gerald R. Patterson (1982)

ISBN for the series: 0-916154-10-6

A Social Interactional Approach

VOLUME 4

ANTISOCIAL BOYS

Gerald R. Patterson, Ph.D.
John B. Reid, Ph.D.
Thomas J. Dishion, Ph.D.

Oregon Social Learning Center
Eugene, Oregon

Castalia Publishing Company
P.O. Box 1587
Eugene, OR 97440
(503) 343-4433

1992

ISBN 0-916154-03-3
Printed in the United States of America
Copies of this book may be ordered from the publisher.

Editorial and Production Credits
Editor-in-Chief: Scot Patterson
Associate Editor: Margo Moore
Copy Editor: Steven Summerlight
Tables and Page Composition: Margo Moore
Figures and Illustrations: Will Mayer
Cartoon: Cheryl Reed

Dedication

This volume is dedicated to our editor, Scot Patterson, who not only seduced us into rewriting this book but also had the temerity to require us to live up to *his* standards!

Table of Contents

Acknowledgments

We consider ourselves privileged to be working in a society that is willing to provide support for a lifetime of research on a clinical problem such as children's antisocial behavior. Each of our careers has represented a full-time commitment to building both a clinical and empirical base for understanding antisocial children and their families. As research scientists, our existence is precarious because we depend on "soft money" awarded by funding agencies such as the National Institutes of Mental Health (NIMH), the National Institutes of Child Health and Development (NICHD), and the National Science Foundation (NSF).

Fifteen years of NIMH-supported intervention studies have preceded the work described in this volume. We gratefully acknowledge the long-standing support for these clinical studies. The decision to translate our clinical experience into a measurable model has received enduring support primarily from the NIMH. Grant number MH32857 provided funding for four absolutely crucial years that allowed us to gain experience in recruiting families, build an assessment battery, and develop constructs to test the model. The Oregon Youth Study was initiated in 1982 with five years of support provided by grant number MH37940. It allowed us to rebuild our assessment battery, recruit families of at-risk boys, and carry out the first two waves of assessments.

At several points in the development of this book, the NIMH section on Crime and Delinquency convulsively cut our budgets. The first of these cuts made it almost impossible for us to continue working on the complex modeling studies that were in progress. This, in turn, placed OSLC and its entire staff in jeopardy because the new models were needed for the next round of research proposals. The administrative officer at OSLC, Gerry Bouwman, came up with a brilliant solution that gave us an additional six months to carry out analyses. The proposal involved taking money from our retirement pool and vacation time, which required the unanimous consent of our entire staff. That consent was given by the following OSLC staff members who, in a very real sense, have made this book possible: I. August, L. Bank, G. Bouwman, D. Capaldi, P. Chamberlain, L. Crosby, J. P. Davis, K. Douglass, L. Edwards, J. Evitt, B. Fagot, B. Fetrow, C. Flagg, D. Ford, M. Forgatch, J. Frey, K. Gardner, K. Greenley, N. Groutage, B. Higgins, K. Jordan, K. Kavanagh, S. Kelley, D. Larsen, M. Lathrop, W. Mayer, M. McKean, M. Nygaard, M. Perry, A. Prescott, J. Ray, L. Reed, M. Skinner, S. Spyrou, J. Trombley, M. Welge, G. Wiemann, and M. Yamamoto.

The Oregon Youth Study reflects the efforts of many individuals, but a few stand out in particular. Deborah Capaldi has supervised the longitudinal project since its inception. She is responsible for the high-quality data generated by the study, which required day-to-day cleanup and reorganization. One outcome of her meticulous labor is a slim volume with the engaging title, *Psychometric Properties of Fourteen Latent Constructs from the Oregon Youth Study* (Capaldi & Patterson, 1989).

She has recently added a new dimension to her role by writing several first-rate papers on different aspects of the coercion model itself.

Another pivotal presence, Lew Bank, joined the staff just as we were beginning the complex multivariate analyses of our first wave of data. Under his aegis, and with the able assistance of Martie Skinner, the entire staff has become immersed in the arcane mysteries of structural equation modeling and canonical and discriminative analyses. The exchanges between the statistician and our clinical theorists have gradually led to a new series of methodological papers on the perplexities of the "glop" problem, the generalizability of models, factor invariance, and stationarity. Mike Stoolmiller, a recent addition to our staff, reanalyzed all of the modeling data to make sure the facts fit the figures; currently he is leading us through the arcane mysteries of latent growth modeling in preparation for our next round of studies on process and change. The efforts of Bank, Capaldi, and Stoolmiller have made a profound difference in the content and scope of this book.

We gratefully acknowledge the Sisyphean labors of Kate Douglass and Will Mayer. They have responded with patience and humor to our endless requests for help in verifying references, turning cryptic notes into new versions of chapters, and creating new figures and tables. Our special thanks to Will Mayer for his masterful rendering of the various figures that appear throughout the book and for his illustrations of the elephant(s) that provide a memorable beginning and ending.

Preface

This volume builds on the theory of children's aggression that was outlined in the three earlier volumes in our social learning approach series. The earlier books described family intervention procedures, observation techniques, and a theoretical formulation of children's antisocial behavior. In this volume, we present the substantive findings for that theory. Although the theory focuses on antisocial behavior, it also addresses attendant problems in the areas of peer relations, school failure, self-esteem, and depression. The perspective has been expanded to take into account the impact of contextual factors such as social disadvantage and divorce on family process. This broader perspective pulls together a wide range of findings that have been reported in the research literature. For example, it organizes the variables traditionally emphasized in "multiple causation" statements about delinquency into a single meaningful pattern. The theoretical model seems to fit the majority of chronic offending delinquents and accounts for most of these causal variables. The fact that the model is being used by our therapists and other investigators to design prevention programs for conduct disorders, substance abuse, and child adjustment problems encountered by single mothers attests to the practical utility of looking at aggression in this way. The focus reflects our general commitment to clinical issues, although the findings also have many implications for developmental psychologists.

Building the theoretical model has led us down some strange paths and byways. Along the way, we encountered some very complex methodological problems related to measuring family process. It also was inevitable that we would run into questions about how to integrate the enormous mass of data that we had collected. Our insights regarding these issues may turn out to be the be the most important contribution of this volume. To understand something as complicated as family process, the data set and analytic strategies must be of comparable complexity. For this reason, the present volume draws the reader into the arcane mysteries of structural equation modeling, mediational models, progressions, and multimethod, multiagent definitions of key constructs.

Coercive Family Process (Patterson, 1982) presents a detailed analysis of family interaction sequences. The title of the book emphasizes the significance of aversive exchanges among family members in the development of antisocial behavior. Because aversive events seem to play a key role, the theory was labeled the *coercion model*. Considerable effort was devoted to identifying the contingencies thought to determine children's aversive behavior. The primary focus of that book, which was based on two decades of field observations in homes and classrooms, was on the problems encountered in applying contingency concepts such as positive reinforcement, punishment, and negative reinforcement to family interaction sequences. We advise careful reading of Chapters 4 through 7 in that volume (Aversive Events, Positive Reinforcement for Aggression, Punishment for Aggression, and Negative Reinforcement and Escalation, respectively). Those chapters (and Chapter 7 in particular) provide the theoretical background necessary to understand the material presented here.

Our long-term goal at the Oregon Social Learning Center always has been to develop an empirical base for understanding children's aggression and to build a theory that can be used to design effective prevention programs. *Coercive Family Process*, however, did not provide satisfactory answers to several crucial questions that a "practical" theory of children's antisocial behavior must address. Although a compelling case was made for the effects of contingencies on children's antisocial behavior, data were not available to adequately specify the relation between parenting practices and children's antisocial behavior. The present volume addresses two core issues: (1) *How much of the variance in child adjustment is accounted for by measures of parenting practices?* and (2) *Which families are most likely to fail in their efforts to control coercive behaviors?* This second question leads us to consider the contribution of contextual variables such as socioeconomic status, stress, parental personality traits, and marital discord. The earlier studies noted that many antisocial boys tend to be unskilled; thus, the third major issue addressed here is *How is it that antisocial behaviors function as a key determinant for academic and peer relational skill deficits?* Models are presented that show that antisocial behaviors are directly and indirectly related to both of these skill deficits.

Background Considerations

Our discussion begins in Chapter 1 with a review of the social interactional underpinnings of the coercion model, a consideration of its main assumptions, and a description of how this perspective differs from other social learning models. Also included is an overview of how we propose to develop a dynamic model that explains changes in the adjustment of the child over time.

In designing the assessment batteries for our current studies, we have attempted to operationalize the key concepts by using multimethod, multiagent measures. The procedures for doing this are outlined in Chapter 2 (and Appendix 1). Building constructs based on data from multiple methods and agents gives the investigator some control over the complex problem of shared method variance. We consider this approach to be a precondition for developing a generalizable model of antisocial behavior.

The coercion model relies heavily on an updated definition of antisocial behavior as a trait. Data are presented in Chapter 3 that demonstrate that antisocial behavior is stable across both time and settings, which satisfies the basic requirements for a trait. A central hypothesis is that the juvenile forms of this trait are prototypes of later delinquency and adult criminal behavior.

The coercion mechanism and negative reinforcement are briefly reviewed in Chapter 4, and findings are presented from our recent studies on aversive events in families. It is suggested that the coercion mechanism relates to measures of aggressive response strength in children and to a wide range of adult pathology as well (e.g., depression, schizophrenia, and marital conflict). The implications of the cognitive revolution and the relevance of recent social cognition studies are also discussed. *Coercive Family Process* presents data that demonstrate that social behaviors adjacent in time are functionally related. In Chapter 4, we develop the idea that as a family becomes involved in the coercion process, the basic structure of the interactions between its members changes.

It is our position that *molar* family management skills (i.e., parental monitoring, discipline, problem solving, involvement, and positive reinforcement) control ongoing *microsocial* exchanges among family members. *Coercive Family Process* outlines our speculations about the contribution of each of these parenting practices. It also reviews pilot data that show that most of the family management constructs are significantly correlated with antisocial behavior. Now we are able to take these speculations much further. The parent training model presented in Chapter 5 describes how these measures of parenting practices covary with a wide spectrum of child adjustment outcomes.

Our attempts to measure positive parenting and its impact on child adjustment are described in Chapter 6. The underlying hypothesis is that parental positive reinforcement, dyadic problem solving, and parental involvement covary with children's prosocial skills. The relation among family management skills is also examined.

Chapter 7 focuses on the relation between child adjustment and both static and dynamic contextual variables. Static variables include social disadvantage and parental personality characteristics. Dynamic contextual variables such as stress, transitions, and marital conflict are considered to be more likely to change over time. The working hypothesis is that the effects of these variables are largely, but not entirely, mediated through parenting practices.

The coercion model is defined by a network of connections among key concepts. Part of the network defines the relation between parenting practices and antisocial child behavior. Another part describes the connection between parenting practices and children's prosocial skills such as peer relations and academic achievement. Other networks examine hypotheses about children's self-esteem, depression, deviant peers, drug use, and delinquency. Structural equation models define each of these networks. Chapter

8 addresses these issues. Many of the correlational matrices have been included for those courageous individuals who may be interested in reproducing the models.

Intended Audience

It is our impression that many authors set out to write the book they wanted to find in the library when they were graduate students. For the senior author, this is such a book. As a speech therapist trainee and later as a probation officer, I encountered many antisocial children. The best treatments available did not seem to help, and the prevailing explanations of antisocial behavior essentially were untestable. The only contribution to understanding children's antisocial behavior that had *any* empirical base was the classic book *Patterns of Childrearing* by Sears, Maccoby, and Levin, (1957). At that time, it was the most exciting book I had read in the field of child clinical psychology. It presented data relevant to important concepts in both developmental and clinical psychology.

It is our hope that the present volume follows in the same tradition and that the perspective it offers is exciting and helpful to the next generation of therapists and scientists. Our goal is to provide an empirical base for a theory of children's antisocial behavior. To understand the coercion model, some background is necessary in reinforcement theory, sequential analysis, and learning theory. This volume builds on the concepts presented in *Coercive Family Process*; these concepts require some familiarity with personality theory, structural equation modeling, and multivariate analyses. Most graduate students in the social sciences should be able to comprehend all of the material presented here; undergraduates should be able to grasp the main ideas.

Therapists working in residential settings, juvenile courts, and outpatient clinics — and school psychologists and guidance counselors who routinely encounter antisocial children — should find many sections of this volume relevant to their work (e.g., Chapters 1, 3, 4, 5, and 8). Our greatest hope is that the present volume will become a cornerstone in the future edifice that describes empirically based prevention programs for antisocial children.

Chapter 1

A Social Interactional Stage Model

If you would understand something, try to change it.
— Dearborn's dictum (cited in Bronfenbrenner, 1977)

Our research facility, the Oregon Social Learning Center (OSLC), currently has more than 100 staff members. We began as a small group some 20 years ago and have supported ourselves since then by competing for research grants. From the beginning, we have been intrigued by the same two questions: *What causes children's antisocial behavior? What can be done to help families change these problem behaviors?* Although these questions have always determined the course of our programmatic studies, the specific focus has shifted almost cyclically over the years. Through several long periods, our primary objective was to develop better interventions for families with oppositional children, stealers, abused children, or multiple-offender delinquents. Interspersed with these clinical studies were efforts to design better measures of family process and treatment outcome.

In the 1980s a third area of interest emerged. A group of sociologists who were on a site visit from our funding agency asked, "Where are your theories?" and "Where are your models?" Our answer was that we were behaviorists and that our strategy was to obtain data first and then develop a theory if one were justified. Their response was terse and to the point: "As sociologists, this is our territory. If you want to collect any data at all, you must first show us a model." The resulting proposal that was funded, in fact, did have an *a priori* model. This volume is about that model.

With pleasure, we acknowledge that our sociologist colleagues were right. Having an *a priori* model has forced us to tailor the assessment battery carefully so that key concepts can be defined properly. In our enthusiasm, we have embedded the model in several other OSLC studies, and several key components of the model already have been replicated. Such replication is itself a cause for celebration here at OSLC, but the cumulative findings, which carry their own special message, are beginning to form a pattern. Now we often can predict what the next finding will be, and it appears that we can understand children's antisocial behavior with a relatively small number of interrelated concepts. We can use these concepts to accurately predict which boys are most at risk for later juvenile delinquency and to develop integrated prevention strategies. This is extremely gratifying because previous investigators who claimed to understand could not predict, and those who predicted often contributed little to understanding.

This chapter begins with a discussion of the context in which the coercion model was developed. The section on context relates the current work to the genealogy of social learning theories; the clinical chronology that led to our current focus on parenting practices also is summarized. The last section of this chapter defines models in general and provides a broad outline of the coercion model. Because a theory of antisocial behavior eventually must explain why some individuals enter the process early and continue while others enter late and soon drop out, special attention has been given to the development of a stage model perspective that can be used to study changes that unfold over time.

A Context for the Coercion Model

The coercion model is based on more than 20 years of work devoted to understanding and helping families with antisocial children. The clinical trials were behavioral in orientation with strong social learning overtones. The perspective that has emerged from this fusion of ideas is what we call the social interactional point of view. Before we describe this new perspective, we will review the history of each contributing theory. These theories have influenced the way in which we have defined clinical problems, and they have determined the *kind* of data we collect to measure family process.

The Clinical Beginnings

Our first contacts with antisocial children revealed that they lived in multiple-problem families (Patterson & Brodsky, 1966). The clinical symptoms were readily observable. Most of the boys lacked one or more of the skills that are necessary for building good relationships with others and being successful in school. As we worked with hundreds of these families, some of the variables that we thought would be important proved to be of only secondary significance. At the same time, certain contextual variables that we had been ignoring moved to the forefront. For example, we spent several years training parents to reinforce prosocial behaviors that would "compete" with antisocial behaviors (e.g., cooperation and compliance). This approach simply did not work. Even though the children became slightly more cooperative, they still hit others and had temper tantrums. It became clear that variables such as negative reinforcement and punishment, which were given little attention by B. F. Skinner and other 1960s theorists, were core considerations for changing antisocial behavior. As it turned out, it also was necessary to teach parents to reinforce positive behaviors, such as doing chores or homework, when they did occur. Two important themes emerged from our clinical work: (1) Parents of antisocial children were noncontingent in their interactions with their problem children (they failed to use effective punishment for deviant behaviors and reinforcement for prosocial behaviors), and (2) they tended to be irritable in their exchanges with family members in general.

By working with these families, we learned what was effective and what was not. Ten years of clinical contacts and treatment outcome studies emphasized the importance of teaching parents specific family management practices such as monitoring, discipline, positive reinforcement, problem solving, and parental involvement (Patterson, 1974a, 1974b, 1976; Patterson & Reid, 1970).

These variables define key constructs for specific components of our current model.

In retrospect, learning how to intervene with clinical cases may not have been the best way to begin our study of families. Knowing what changes something is not a *sufficient* basis for understanding the initial cause of the problem. As the clinical studies continued, it became clear that the therapists and parents did not function in a social vacuum. The families were constantly disrupted by a variety of stressors. Parents lost their jobs, separated, divorced, and became acutely depressed. Working with troubled families in their homes was not a controlled laboratory experience. Our staff therapists adapted by learning how to alternate between teaching parenting skills and working on problems such as stress, marital discord, and depression, among others. As a group, we were forced to consider the effects of context on family interactions. By the 1970s, when we encountered Urie Bronfenbrenner's (1977) elegant statements, we already had adopted his position.

Our treatment orientation was strongly behavioral, which meant that considerable attention was given to the contingencies provided by parents for children's behaviors. Gradually, observation data collected in the home became the standard for evaluating treatment outcome. Our clinical impression was that there seemed to be little correlation between what parents claimed they were doing and what we actually observed them doing in the home. In a similar vein, their reports about child behavior — particularly about *changes* in behavior — were highly reactive. Their statements seemed to reflect how they felt rather than what they had observed the child doing.

In our first clinical studies, the ratio of boys to girls referred for treatment of antisocial behavior was approximately 5:1. This referral ratio has been relatively stable, although an increasing number of girls are referred to us who meet most of the criteria for classification as antisocial. Our initial research strategy was to focus only on boys. This was based on the belief that a single model or theory would not be able to account for antisocial behavior in both boys and girls. In retrospect, this was a sound decision. It is our impression that there is a fundamental difference in the antisocial behavior patterns and theoretical models for boys and girls. Two staff members at OSLC, Kathryn Kavanagh and Beverly Fagot, have recently submitted a proposal to study antisocial behavior in girls.

Fourth-Generation Social Learning Theory

Cairns (1979), in his characteristically systematic mode, examined the evolution of theoretical perspectives and traced the genealogy of social learning theories. His summary, shown in Figure 1.1, includes developments through the 1970s. We have extended his interpretation

Figure 1.1
Third Generation Social Learning Theories and Beyond (from Cairns, 1979)

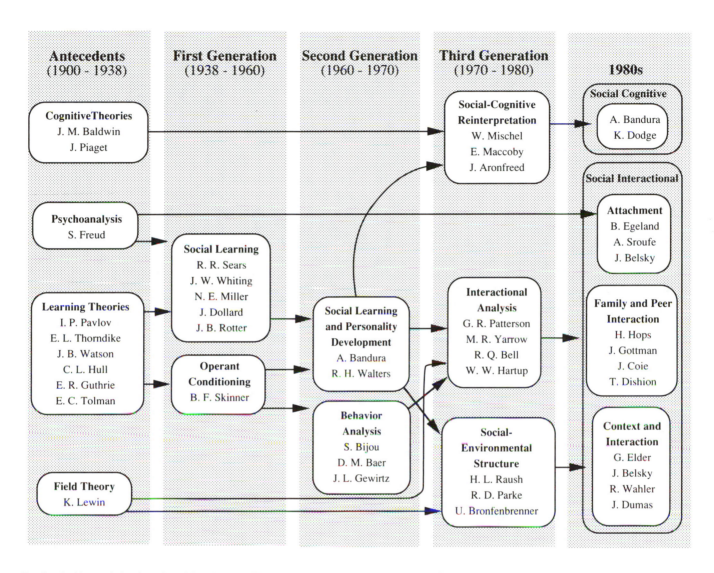

Reprinted with permission from *Social Development: The Origins and Plasticity of Interchanges.* Copyright 1979 by W. H. Freeman and Company.

by adding theories developed during the 1980s to the extreme right side of the figure.

Four contemporary themes seem to be emerging from the research of the 1980s. The social cognitive perspective has become a major social learning theme. The key assumption is that children's social behaviors are mediated by their expectations, attributions, and social cognitions. Recent laboratory studies have focused on identifying the parameters that control children's social cognitions. For example, Dodge (1980) found a significant covariation between children's attributions and their aggressive behaviors. The current studies are designed to test for the causal status of these attributions and cognitions. Under

what conditions do negative attributions about others determine antisocial behaviors in natural settings?

Another major theme that has emerged in the 1980s is a blend of three different theoretical perspectives: *attachment, family–peer interaction,* and *context and interaction.* All three perspectives assume that observed parent–child and child–peer interactions are key determinants for the socialization process. When these perspectives are combined, they form what we have labeled the *social interactional perspective.*

The attachment group seems to have made its contribution to the social interactional approach during the 1980s. Attachment theorists such as Belsky, Egeland, and Sroufe have suggested that the effect of the parent–child interaction on child adjustment is mediated by the child's attachment to the mother. This model is being tested by a series of carefully designed studies. What is particularly striking is that each of the three variables — interaction, attachment, and adjustment — usually is measured by a different method.

The family–peer interaction group was identified earlier by Cairns. This group now includes some productive investigators who are pursuing Hartup's perspective on the contribution of the peer group. To have a comprehensive theory, we need to understand the unique contribution of family and peers to the process of child adjustment. Bierman, Coie, Dishion, Dodge, Gottman, Parke, Putallaz, and Suomi are some of the major proponents of this perspective.

The third group that has contributed to the social interactional perspective has focused on the relation between social structure, or context, and family interaction patterns. The label *context and interaction* seems to be appropriate for this group. Just as the writings of Bowlby and Ainsworth set the stage for the empirical studies on attachment, Bronfenbrenner's articulate statements served a similar function for the context and interaction group. He contended that parent–child interactions are embedded in a larger matrix: that is, the context in which the child and the family live. The context is defined by variables such as social status, employment, poverty, prolonged illness, neighborhood, ethnic status, cultural beliefs, and attitudes. Contextual variables influence social interactions, and social interactions may in turn alter context. Complex interactional and bidirectional models are the hallmark of contemporary studies that represent this point of view. Studies by Elder, Caspi, Wahler, and our own group exemplify this perspective.

The boundaries that separate attachment variables from family–peer interaction or contextual variables are becoming increasingly obscure. Most investigators who study parent–child interactions are including analyses on the impact of context. There seems to be a congenial amalgam of metaphors provided by Kurt Lewin with earlier models of social learning. Current longitudinal studies will determine whether the attachment construct will be a defining characteristic of the approach. Do current measures of attachment contribute to predictions about *future* antisocial behavior beyond what can be predicted from the parent–child interaction variables? Similarly, longitudinal studies will clarify whether children's social cognitions make a unique contribution to the prediction of later antisocial behavior. Do current measures of social cognitions predict future antisocial behavior after measures of current antisocial behavior are partialled out?

The composite of the three themes has been labeled *social interactional* to emphasize the central role of the child's interactions with family members and peers. As we have pointed out in some detail (Patterson & Reid, 1984), this focus is intended to be a research strategy rather than an end goal. There is a general consensus among modern investigators that the real task for developmental theories of social behavior is to integrate children's social interaction sequences with their ongoing social cognitions and emotions. This new generation is concerned with how behavior comes about (i.e., a performance theory). There are few heated debates about whether behavior is determined by environmental contingencies *or* genes *or* cognitions *or* emotions. The implicit assumption is that all of these variables influence ongoing streams of social behavior. The question is, how do they interact to determine these processes?

It has been a strange experience to be immersed in the research that eventually led us to label ourselves and others as social interactional psychologists. It is a little like having an elephant back slowly into your living room. When the process began in 1970, we exclaimed, "That's what social interactional psychology is!" Little did we know that we had just caught a glimpse of the elephant's tail (see Figure 1.2). Later, it became apparent that social sequences were structured in interesting ways. Then we realized that a whole new process was initiated when children's problem behaviors were observed in settings outside the family. At that point, the elephant had backed farther into the room. Now we recognize that context is a major determinant of what goes on in the family and that there may be many spinoffs that contribute to the long-term maintenance of various processes. The elephant has finally backed completely into the room.

The social interactional perspective has strongly influenced the way we define and conceptualize the nature of antisocial behavior. Instead of focusing on how children *learn* antisocial behavior, we are interested in identifying the variables that determine why children *perform* antisocial behaviors. These issues will be considered in detail in the next two sections.

The Definition of Antisocial

A variety of terms have been used to describe children with behavior problems: *conduct disorder*, *acting out*, *hyperactive*, *aggressive*, and *antisocial* are among them. Each term has a history associated with its usage. This is a problem for investigators: There is simply no way to measure every aspect of the definition for each term. Initially, we used the words *antisocial* and *aggressive* interchangeably, but that caused some confusion. Finally, we agreed to use the term *antisocial* because it seemed to be the least controversial and it described the nature of the behavior.

The definition of antisocial offered by Patterson (1982) is a good beginning. The focus is on describing what an antisocial *event* is rather than on what an antisocial *person*

Figure 1.2

An Emerging View of Social Interactional Psychology

is. The definition is based on two criteria that apply to both family and peer interaction sequences. Events that are both aversive *and* contingent are considered antisocial. Our studies are concerned with the subset of antisocial events that occur within family and peer interactions. We generally use the term *coercive* to describe these events.

The advantage of starting with this definition is that both of the key terms can be operationalized. For example, parents, psychologists, and children all seem to agree about which behaviors are aversive and which are not

(Hoffman, Fagot, Reid, & Patterson, 1987). The rankings assigned by parents in clinical samples of the aversiveness of children's behaviors correlated .80 with rankings by parents of normal children (Patterson, 1982). The term *contingent* refers to the connection between the behavior of one family member and another. The statistical interdependencies that describe these connections have become commonplace in social interactional studies of families experiencing problems with antisocial children, marital conflict, and depression. The research findings relevant to a theory of aggression in children are summarized in Patterson (1982).

Presumably, all antisocial events are aversive, but not all aversive events are antisocial. To be classified as antisocial, the occurrence of the aversive event must be contingent on the behavior of other family members. Observation studies from several laboratories have shown strong support for the idea that some aversive events occur contingently. For example, children's whining, hitting, and yelling appear to be strongly tied to certain antecedent behaviors of other family members (Patterson, 1982).

Although the definition of antisocial behavior provided a starting point for our investigations, it also introduced several problems. If family interactions are coded and then analyzed, how is it possible to determine whether the occurrence of an aversive event is contingent on the behavior of other family members? Does this mean it is necessary to show that one family member *intended* to inflict an aversive event on the other? With the exception of Bandura (1973), most major theorists include the concept of intent in their theories. As yet, however, there is no satisfactory way to measure a child's intentions as they occur in natural settings. This dilemma can be resolved by thinking about the problem in another way. If it can be shown that an antisocial event reliably follows specific behaviors of family members, then the action–reaction patterns probably would be isomorphic with measures of intent (if they could be measured). Because the sequences are patterned, the possibility that the aversive event is accidental can be ruled out. For example, an older brother might say that he did not mean to push his sister, but if the data show that he is more likely to push during play with his sister than at any other time, then the validity of the boy's statement is questionable.

The original definition presents another problem. Most aversive events in family interactions consist of behaviors such as whining, yelling, teasing, threatening, and occasional hitting. These events seem to be trivial examples of what is usually meant by antisocial behavior; they are not as dramatic as events such as fighting, stealing, mugging, car theft, and burglary. The definition also does not apply to victimless crimes usually classified as antisocial (e.g., curfew violations, drunkenness, drug use, and truancy).

It is a primary hypothesis that the seemingly trivial examples of coercive acts observed in the home and at school are *prototypes* of adolescent delinquent behaviors. Several sets of data are required to support this hypothesis. First, a significant covariation must be demonstrated between contemporaneous observations of coercive events and more extreme forms of antisocial behavior (e.g., fighting and stealing) as reported by teachers, peers, and parents. Second, it is necessary to explain *why* the relatively trivial antisocial events em-

bedded in social interaction might eventually lead to high amplitude, low baserate events such as assault or substance abuse. These key issues will be addressed in later chapters.

The coercive acts observed in the home and at school closely resemble the DSM-III-R category of Oppositional Defiant Disorder (ODD). Child noncompliance and temper tantrums are central components of both categories of behavior. In fact, there is a significant progression from ODD behaviors observed in the home to the more extreme antisocial acts that define the DSM-III-R category of Conduct Disorder (Bank, Duncan, & Fisher, 1991). Spending time in the coercive process allows the child's oppositional defiant problems to become conduct disorder problems. As noted above, the term *antisocial* applies to the entire progression. Chapter 4 discusses the reinforcement mechanisms that are thought to account for the progression. The concept of aversive stimuli plays a key role in understanding these mechanisms (i.e., the contingent reinforcement is provided by the child's escape from or avoidance of aversive stimuli).

Learning Versus Performance

Almost all children in our culture have learned a variety of antisocial behaviors by the time they are 3 or 4 years old (Patterson, 1982). The learning reflects exposure to hundreds of antisocial episodes in which the child was at least an observer or, more likely, was involved personally in the episodes. Extensive exposure to television violence and aggression have undoubtedly enhanced the extent of this learning in modern times. In a sense, all children have *learned* about antisocial behavior. From a social interactional standpoint the question is, why do some children *perform* antisocial behaviors at higher rates than do others?

The coercion model represents a performance theory at two levels. At one level, the model specifies the variables that determine the level of performance for a particular behavior. For example, why do some children whine more often than they hit? Why do some children hit more often than do other children? Because the theory identifies some of the main contingencies that determine such outcomes, it should be classified as a performance theory.

The coercion model is a performance theory at a second level in that it is evaluated by examining the variance accounted for in measures of children's antisocial behavior. We propose that 30% of the variance is an acceptable minimum value. As pointed out by Forgatch (1991) and others, there is much more to establishing the validity of a theory than just demonstrating that the correlates account for substantial amounts of variance in the criterion measures. For example, the model also needs to be replicated and subjected to *experimental* tests.

Correlations derived from data sets in which a single agent provides ratings for both dependent and independent variables are not an acceptable means for evaluating a performance theory. For example, asking the mother to describe her parenting practices *and* her child's antisocial behaviors may produce correlations that would satisfy the requirements for a performance theory, but such a design would make it impossible to partial out the confound of shared method variance. The problem of shared method variance and several methods of circumventing it are discussed elsewhere (Bank, Dishion, Skinner, & Patterson, 1990; Reid, Bank, Patterson, & Skinner, 1987). All of the solutions emphasize the need for multiagent, multimethod assessments for each concept in a model.

Model Building

This section begins by defining what a model is and then briefly discusses how to build and evaluate models in general. Because the coercion model is designed to explain changes that take place over time, the key concepts that define the content of the model also must describe a sequence of developmental stages that characterize a child's antisocial career.

We begin with theoretical or clinical hunches about the determinants for certain kinds of antisocial behaviors. At this stage, the connections between variables are entirely speculative. Once an *a priori* web of relationships is in place, we can move on to the second step, which is to define the methods for measuring each concept. We accept the position advanced by Bentler (1980), Sullivan (1974), and others that *all* measures used in the social sciences are biased estimates of the concept being evaluated. The measures may be perfectly reliable, but they are still biased in the sense that they are distorted or incomplete. Presumably, using more than one indicator for the same concept would address the problem of incomplete measures, particularly if they are based on different methods of assessment or on different agents. Some of the details involved in designing such indicators are covered in Chapter 3. If multiple indicators are used to define a construct, what should be done with the resulting nomological network? Typically, the solutions offered have been some variation on the theme of factor analysis. We use a principal components factor analysis constrained to a single solution to delete inappropriate indicators.

Now we can ask a new question. Is the concept discriminately different from some other concept? We can use a confirmatory factor analysis to address this question. Before the construct can be considered to be defined, the nomological network must converge (i.e., the intercorrelation between indicators must be at least .2) *and* it must be differentiated from other constructs. This approach is a variation on the multimethod, multitrait problem posed by Campbell and Fiske (1959).

Once the construct is defined, we can use our clinical and theoretical hunches to specify how it should relate to other constructs in the model. The model gives a precise estimate of the structural relations among the set of constructs. Correlations or path coefficients are a convenient method of specifying these relations; one example is the path analytic format introduced by Duncan (1975).

A model specifies the means by which concepts are to be measured. It also specifies the structural relations among the concepts. One might attempt to meet these two requirements in many different ways. We decided to use structural equation modeling (SEM) because it has several obvious advantages (Bentler, 1980; Dwyer, 1983; Pedhazur, 1982). The foremost advantage is that it allows the investigator to estimate simultaneously the factor structures that define the constructs and the structural relations among the constructs. This will be discussed in more detail later; most of the empirical modeling studies can be found in Chapter 8.

Bootstrapping a Model

We do not think it is desirable, or possible, to develop a complex clinical model in a single study. The typical sequence of steps is summarized in Figure 1.3; a more detailed discussion is available in Forgatch (1991). Essentially, the sequence consists of replicating the measurement model and then using the final correlational model to design experimental manipulations that test for the causal status of the variables.

The first step, field observation and clinical experience, already has been discussed. We view this as an essential part of the social interactional approach. It provides the breeding ground for hypotheses about child behavior.

The necessity for designing customized multiagent, multimethod indicators became apparent early on. It was a lesson learned from developmental psychology. Previous efforts to relate childrearing practices to measures of child behavior had not been successful (Schuck, 1974). For instance, even when both the independent and dependent variables were generated by the same data source, such as the parent interview (Sears, Maccoby, & Levin, 1957), the correlations were disappointingly low (typically in the .2 to .3 range). Worse yet, a systematic effort to replicate these results failed (Schuck, 1974; Yarrow, Campbell, & Burton, 1968).

Given this state of affairs, it seemed unlikely that we would achieve our goal of building a performance model that would account for 30% to 40% of the variance in measures of child behavior. We assumed that one of the fundamental problems with the earlier studies was that measurement issues had not been given enough attention. Our hunch was that a single rating from one family member does not provide an adequate measure of a com-

Figure 1.3
To Build a Model

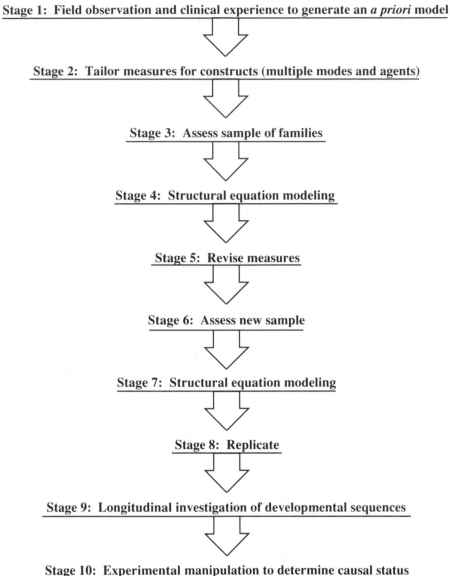

Stage 1: Field observation and clinical experience to generate an *a priori* model

Stage 2: Tailor measures for constructs (multiple modes and agents)

Stage 3: Assess sample of families

Stage 4: Structural equation modeling

Stage 5: Revise measures

Stage 6: Assess new sample

Stage 7: Structural equation modeling

Stage 8: Replicate

Stage 9: Longitudinal investigation of developmental sequences

Stage 10: Experimental manipulation to determine causal status

plex concept such as children's antisocial behavior or parental discipline practices.

The National Institutes of Mental Health (NIMH) agreed to support a four-year Planning Study to test this hunch. It included funds to develop an assessment battery that would measure both the parent and child behaviors thought to be central to the coercion model. Details of the research strategy and measures and the characteristics of the Planning Study sample are provided in Chapter 2. Once the constructs were assembled, they were tested in the various models for which they had been designed. SEM was used to examine the factor structures for the constructs, the overall fit of the data to the model, the significance of the specified *a priori* path coefficient, and the amount of variance accounted for in criterion measures. For example, a model for physical fighting for the younger boys was examined (Patterson, Dishion, & Bank, 1984), as was a general model for delinquent behavior for the adolescent samples (Patterson & Dishion, 1985). Things seemed to work out as expected. The fit to the data was good, and the key path coefficients were significant in both instances. Both models accounted for more than 50% of the variance in the criterion constructs.

These results were promising, so we began the replication phases (stages 5 through 9) of model building. Based on the results from the Planning Study, we submitted a proposal to NIMH to start the current longitudinal study (the Oregon Youth Study). We were very excited by the results of the Planning Study and wanted to continue improving the model. Several key constructs had not been assessed adequately in the Planning Study. We also had failed to include several important concepts such as child depression and self-esteem. We spent six months revising the assessment procedures and two more years training our assessment staff and collecting the first of five waves of data. We needed to get the model ready for a 10-year study.

The general strategy was in keeping with Meehl's 1954 bootstrapping metaphor. First, clinical hunches are translated into variables that can be measured. The empirical analyses tell us what to improve next. Then we collect more data and revise our ideas again. In this way, the clinician pulls him- or herself up by the empirical bootstraps.

Replicated correlational models are helpful in establishing causal status for the variables believed to function as determinants. Critics of the literature on SEM have pointed out that some investigators who employ this method have been careless in their use of causal language (Freedman, 1983; Ling, 1982). It is clear that the fit of the data to a model, the significance of path coefficients, and variance accounted for do not provide a test for the causal status of a construct such as parental discipline. In our view, the current studies and analyses are a convenient way to identify the variables worthy of experimental manipulation. The experimental manipulations that we have completed are reviewed in Chapter 5.

A Stage Model

This section begins with a brief review of some of the variables used to explain delinquent behavior. The variables were selected because they had been shown to be significantly correlated with delinquency. It is argued that only one or two of these variables actually play a causal role; the rest are by-products of the process that generates antisocial behavior or of the problem behaviors themselves. A stage model is used to describe the orderly manner in which these variables become part of the process.

The Causal Wheel

The empirical literature on antisocial and delinquent youth is replete with examples of correlated variables being reified and given causal status. Some of the more salient ones are summarized in Figure 1.4; each has been cited as a major determinant for delinquency or antisocial behavior. For example, Wilson and Herrnstein (1985) reviewed hundreds of studies of academic deficiencies among delinquent youth and found a consistent covariation between poor school performance and delinquency. These correlations have led some psychologists to conclude that academic failure might be one of several causes of delinquency. It also has been hypothesized that children act out because they have low self-esteem resulting from negative experiences such as academic failure. Still others have emphasized the significance of being labeled as a failure (Cohen, 1955; Schur, 1973). Finding consistent correlations between low self-esteem, academic failure, and antisocial traits has led many investigators to focus on remediating academic deficiencies as an intervention for both delinquency and low self-esteem. These studies are popular despite the failure of large-scale programmatic efforts, such as that of Cohen (1973), to demonstrate an impact on delinquent behavior even though the boys were able to improve their academic skills. Wilson and Herrnstein reviewed two large-scale projects that employed random assignment and long-term follow-up that also failed to demonstrate that skill training had a significant effect on delinquent behavior. As we shall see in later discussions, it is not low self-esteem that immediately causes low achievement or antisocial behavior. In fact, the studies suggest it is just the opposite: Social and academic failure leads to low self-esteem.

Many investigators have noted the relation between peer rejection and antisocial behavior for adolescents (Roff, 1961, 1972) and preadolescents (Hartup, 1982). Several investigators have assumed that peer rejection causes antisocial behavior. Essentially, this is an update of the frustration–aggression hypothesis. Two experimental studies have demonstrated that it is not rejection by normal peers that causes antisocial behavior; rather, it is antisocial behavior that leads to peer rejection (Coie & Kupersmidt, 1983; Dodge, 1983).

One current theory advanced by sociologists emphasizes that it is the peer group and not the family that teaches and supports antisocial behavior (Elliott, Huizinga, & Ageton, 1985). The child's lack of commitment to parental values, along with academic incompetence, places the child at risk for involvement in a deviant peer group. Their data showed a strong covariation between involvement in a deviant peer group and both substance abuse and delinquent behavior.

Clinical and empirical studies agree on the consistent relation between delinquent behavior and frequent use of physical punishment by parents (Glueck & Glueck, 1968; Wilson & Herrnstein, 1985). Reid, Taplin, and Lorber (1981) found that approximately one-third of the antisocial boys referred for treatment to OSLC were known by community agencies to have been physically abused. The

Figure 1.4
The Causal Wheel

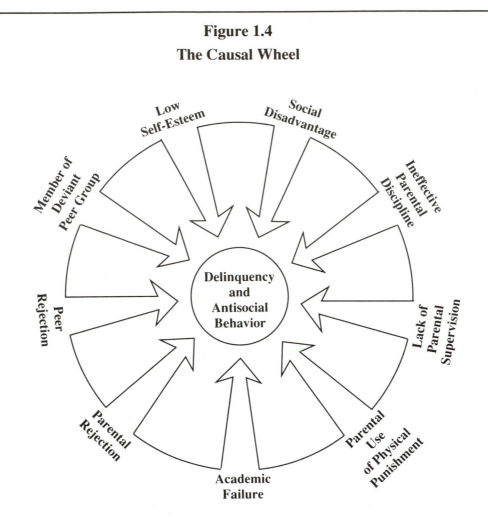

consistency of these findings has led some writers to assume that parental modeling of assaultive, violent behavior in punishment practices is a sufficient cause for antisocial behavior (Welsh, 1976). Lorber, Felton, and Reid (1984) trained parents to use more effective discipline approaches and other family management skills. After treatment, child antisocial behavior and parental assaults were reduced. The findings were consistent with the idea that occasional parental assaults were the outcome of desperate but ineffective efforts to stem the rising tide of child antisocial behavior. It was not so much that parental violence during discipline caused the antisocial behavior, but that the parents simply did not know how to use effective discipline.

The variables listed in Figure 1.4 are important in the sense that they are consistently associated with the antisocial process. Nevertheless, consistent covariation does not automatically imply causal status. Each variable listed in the causal wheel serves as an important step in the sequence. Unfortunately, most of the extremely antisocial boys move through all of the steps in the sequence.

The Four Stages

Retrospective accounts of problem children's development have suggested a patterned sequence of effects that seem to be repeated in many cases. The parents usually described the child's preschool years as difficult, and they mentioned that he was noticeably different from his siblings. The label we have given to this developmental milestone is *basic training*. The parents often commented that they didn't think the child was "disturbed" or "in need of help" until he started school. Within a few months, the parents began to receive telephone calls from distraught school personnel who reported that he was disruptive in class. Later still, the parents were told that the child was not acquiring academic skills. This is the second stage in the development of coercive behaviors. The hypothesis is that the child's abrasive behavior leads to peer rejection and academic skill deficits. In effect, *the social environment reacts*. The child's failures at stage 2 limit the social experiences available to him, and he begins to seek out a

10

supportive environment. This places the child at risk for involvement with *deviant peers and polishing antisocial skills*, which is the third stage. Each small step increases the risk that the child will fail as an adult in the areas of work and human relationships. We believe that the eventual outcome is *the career antisocial adult*.

The four stages have been arranged in what is basically an action–reaction sequence. The child's coercive actions initiate stage 1, the social environment reacts in stage 2, and so on. The following section briefly reviews the empirical findings and hypotheses that relate to each of the four stages.

Stage 1: Basic Training

The key hypothesis is that the basic training for patterns of antisocial behavior prior to adolescence takes place in the home, and family members are the primary trainers. It begins with a breakdown of parental effectiveness in disciplinary confrontations. This breakdown permits an increase in coercive exchanges between the target child and all other family members. The target child finds that aversive behaviors such as whining, crying, yelling, hitting, or having temper tantrums are effective. Typically, the training involves a "dance" of at least three steps that changes the behaviors of both participants over time. We use the term *process* to describe these gradual changes. The details of the training process are presented in Patterson (1982) and briefly reviewed in Chapter 4. Essentially, the child learns that his own aversive behaviors turn off the aversive behaviors of other family members and may also directly produce positive reinforcers.

After several hundred trials, we hypothesize that the coercive exchanges increase in duration. Studies have shown that these extended exchanges are accompanied by commensurate increases in amplitude (e.g., the likelihood of hitting increases). We call this *escalation*. The escalation is dyadic in the sense that, as might be expected, it occurs not only for the target child but also for siblings and parents.

It is difficult to monitor the whereabouts of a child who is extremely coercive. The child literally coerces the rest of the family into allowing additional unsupervised street time, which leads him to a deviant peer group. The child's patterns of antisocial behavior then include both overt (e.g., fighting, temper tantrums) and clandestine acts (Loeber & Schmaling, 1985a, 1985b). This coercive process characterizes approximately two-thirds of the families referred to OSLC for treatment. The children in these families are most at risk for arrest during early adolescence.

The training trials occur dozens of times every day, but they go unnoticed because they are embedded in the daily stream of interactions among family members. Why is it that the training process begins and continues in some families and not others? We believe that ineffective

parenting practices are the primary (but not the only) determinants. For the younger child, ineffective parental discipline seems to be the primary determinant, and the child's temperament is a secondary determinant (Bates & Bayles, 1988). For the adolescent, a combination of ineffective discipline and a lack of parental monitoring seems to characterize the coercive process in the home. Ineffective discipline consists of scolding and nagging about relatively trivial matters and threatening to use punishment without following through. A lack of monitoring means that the parent often doesn't know where the child is, who the child is with, what the child is doing, or when the child will be home. If these parenting skills are suspended for weeks, months, or years, the natural contingencies found in coercive exchanges will prevail, and there will be a steady increase in antisocial behavior. On the other hand, increasing the effectiveness of parental monitoring and discipline reduces the rate of antisocial behavior.

It is hypothesized that three other parental family management skills relate to the child's social competence: (1) the contingent use of positive reinforcement, (2) group problem-solving skills, and (3) parental involvement. The models presented in Chapter 8 describe the relation between parenting practices and child adjustment. Figure 1.5 summarizes the relations between parenting skill variables and child adjustment variables. Each concept is measured with multiagent, multimethod indicators. The arrows in Figure 1.5 represent path coefficients that describe the connection between two concepts. For example, the correlations between measures of parental family management skills and child behavior (i.e., outcome) are expected to be significant.

The basic training concept includes the idea that family process occurs within a context, which has a significant impact on what happens within the family. Figure 1.5 summarizes some of the contextual variables we have examined in the past few years. These variables and their relation to family process are discussed in greater detail in Chapter 7. Each variable has been identified as having some relation to poor child adjustment. For example, families with lower socioeconomic status and those coping with divorce or high levels of stress are at risk for producing antisocial boys.

The figure summarizes the expected relations among three sets of variables. It shows that the relation between context and child adjustment is thought to be indirect. The *a priori* model indicates that the effect of context on child problem behavior is mediated by its disruptive effect on childrearing practices. Most children who live in ghettoes or in divorced families do not become chronic delinquents, but the child who lives in a ghetto with parents who are marginal in their family management practices is at much greater risk for becoming delinquent.

Parents with a difficult infant may be at least margin-

Figure 1.5
The Effect of Context on Child Adjustment

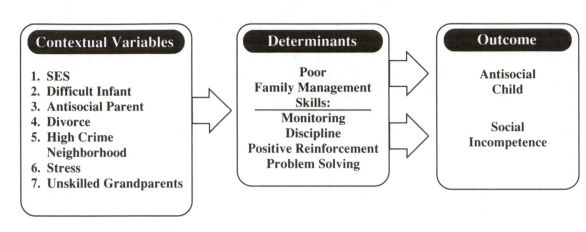

ally skilled in raising their other children, but they may find that they are unable to discipline the difficult child as he grows older. Similarly, parents may do quite well in raising several children and then have their parenting skills seriously disrupted by marital conflict or other major stressors.

The relations specified in Figure 1.5 would require significant correlations between measures of risk variables and measures of parental family management skills. Substance abuse, marital conflict, or changes in parental stress level would be followed by corresponding changes in the family management skills.

Stage 2: The Social Environment Reacts

Stage 2 describes the outcome of the child's efforts to cope with a major developmental hurdle. When he enters school, will he be able to relate to normal peers and develop at least minimal academic skills? Failure at these two developmental tasks presumably has profound implications for the child's adjustment as an adolescent and as an adult. The hypothesis is that coercive or antisocial behaviors learned in the home place the child at grave risk for dual social failure. In response to our request to translate the stage model into something more organic, Will Mayer has illustrated the sequence in Figure 1.6.

The abrasive style of these children in their interpersonal exchanges at home places them at serious risk for rejection by their parents (Patterson, 1986a). It is difficult to teach these children social or academic skills. Their explosive tempers and refusal to accept negative feedback eventually make them spectators, rather than participants, in peer group activities. Their status as relatively unskilled youngsters becomes more pronounced as the gap between them and their normal peers widens over time.

These children avoid difficult tasks and demanding

settings by coercing those who try to teach them to be "responsible." They soon learn to evade doing homework and chores. They eventually learn to avoid school and all its demands, and they are often tardy or truant. Even when they are in the classroom, they spend little time on task. It is not surprising, then, to find that they tend to be identified early on as problem children at school. The literature and empirical findings that relate to this stage are reviewed in Chapters 6 and 8.

We hypothesize that rejection by peers and parents contributes to recurring bouts of sadness in the child and that by age 10 or 11 the dysphoria is acute enough to be noticed by adults who interact with the child at both home and school.

Stage 3: Deviant Peers and Polishing Antisocial Skills

Stage 3 describes the probable outcome of stages 1 and 2. Recurring academic failure and rebuffs by parents, teachers, and normal peers induce unskilled children to seek out peers who are mirror images of themselves. By the time the children are 12 or 13 years old, parents and teachers can readily identify which peer groups are deviant. They are characterized by negative attitudes about school and adult authority. Recent studies have strongly implicated the contribution of a deviant peer group to increases in later delinquency and substance abuse (Elliott et al., 1985). We hypothesize that the problems associated with antisocial children and the failure of their parents to discipline and monitor them provide a basis for identifying which boys are at risk for membership in deviant peer groups. This involvement increases the risk for substance abuse, truancy, and delinquency later in adolescence (Patterson & Yoerger, 1991). One hypothesis to be tested with the longitudinal data set

12

Figure 1.6
The Vile Weed: Stages in the Coercion Model

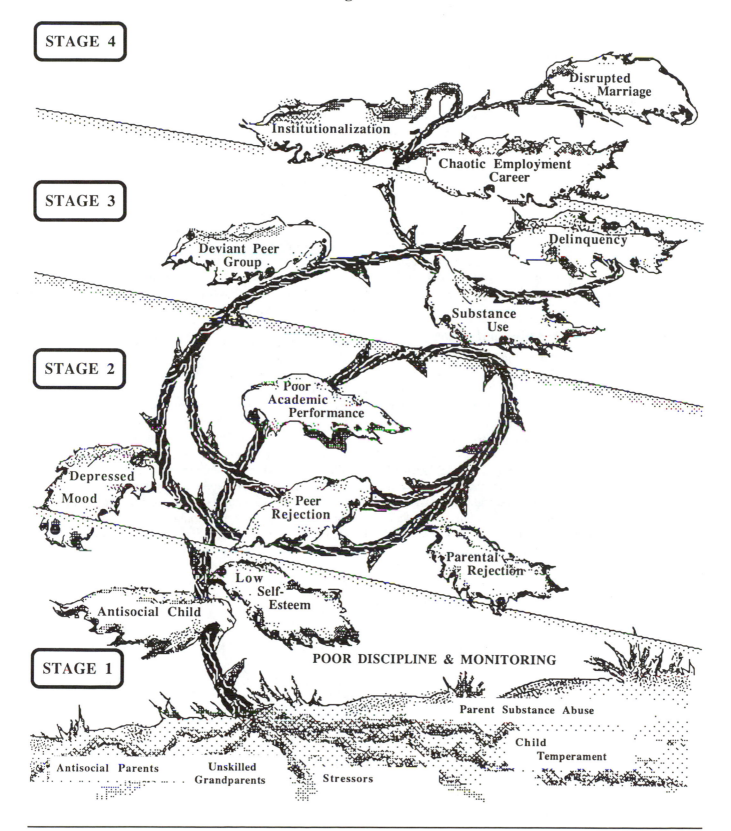

STAGE 4

STAGE 3

STAGE 2

STAGE 1

Disrupted Marriage

Institutionalization

Chaotic Employment Career

Deviant Peer Group

Delinquency

Substance Use

Poor Academic Performance

Depressed Mood

Peer Rejection

Parental Rejection

Low Self-Esteem

Antisocial Child

POOR DISCIPLINE & MONITORING

Parent Substance Abuse

Child Temperament

Antisocial Parents

Unskilled Grandparents

Stressors

13

now being collected is that boys who are antisocial at age 10 are at greater risk for involvement in a deviant peer group two to four years later.

Although the stages of the coercion process seem to define a progression, we are not suggesting that *all* antisocial children move through each stage in succession. We view the connection between adjacent stages as transitive in a probabilistic sense. This implies that if a child is at a particular stage, there is a strong likelihood that he has already moved through the previous stage(s). The coercion process is a flexible, probabilistic sequence that applies to many extremely antisocial children. The progression concept will be presented at several different points in this volume. In the present context, it suggests that many boys who are failing in school and have been rejected by peers also will be identified as antisocial at home. On the other hand, not all boys who are antisocial fail in school, nor are they all rejected by peers. Each stage is more extreme in terms of risk, but the number of children at each successive stage is commensurately smaller. Those children who are at the more advanced stages are at increased risk for status as career antisocial adults.

Stage 4: The Career Antisocial Adult

This stage reflects the findings from several longitudinal studies of antisocial individuals that include their overall adjustment as adults (Caspi, Elder, & Bem, 1987; Huesmann, Eron, Lefkowitz, & Walder, 1984; Magnusson, 1984; Robins & Ratcliff, 1978–1979; West & Farrington, 1977). The studies consistently indicate a marginal existence in adulthood. Antisocial children often have trouble staying employed as adults, and they tend to be downwardly mobile. Caspi and his colleagues also showed that unhappy marriages and higher risk of divorce are in store for antisocial children. Robins and Ratcliff found the same combination of erratic employment and marital difficulties in adulthood, as well as a higher risk for alcohol and drug problems and multiple arrests, for antisocial children. Their lack of social skills leads them to an increasingly marginal existence characterized by a constant stream of crises, many of which are of their own making. Antisocial children are at more serious risk than any other subgroup (with the possible exception of autistic and schizophrenic children) for a wide spectrum of adult adjustment problems such as substance abuse, institutionalization for crimes or mental disorders, disrupted marriages, and marginal employment records (Caspi, Bem, & Elder, 1989; Robins, West, & Herjanic, 1975). Antisocial people tend to be lonely and loved by few.

One could attempt to romanticize such children as being the stuff of which cultural rebels are formed. Nevertheless, theirs is not the selective resistance to authority that characterizes the effective rebel. Instead, they defy all authority figures and rules that restrict them. They are not even very good at fighting or stealing. These boys are losers. It is the combination of extremely high rates of antisocial behavior and incompetence that places them at risk for being arrested as preadolescents (Hood & Sparks, 1970).

A primary objective for our programmatic intervention and modeling studies has been to provide a solid empirical base for preventing antisocial problems in children. One basic requirement is to develop a long-range method of identifying the children who are at risk for becoming chronic delinquent adolescents. This critical prerequisite for effective prevention was considered carefully by Loeber and Dishion (1983) and Loeber, Dishion, and Patterson (1984). This again emphasizes the importance of developing models, because the ability to predict is determined by the adequacy of the underlying model.

The processes relating to coercion seem to be as ubiquitous as the common cold. From one month to the next, minor fluctuations probably occur in this process all the time. This volume is not designed to address the important topic of maintenance; that requires a systematic study of longitudinal data. The focus is on evaluating the coherence of the structure within stages and, in so doing, to establish a solid empirical foundation for the process studies that are now in progress.

Chapter 2

Strategies and Methodology

Primary Goals

The Oregon Youth Study (OYS) was designed to achieve three primary goals: (1) to build a family-based theory that would explain how antisocial behavior is maintained, (2) to identify the problems that emerge over time because of the antisocial behavior, and (3) to predict which fourth-grade boys would become chronic offenders by the age of 18. This chapter examines several issues associated with these goals: the considerations involved in selecting the samples used in the OYS and the rationale for assessing the samples in such detail.

At-Risk Samples

As a starting point, it seemed reasonable to study samples in which the incidence and prevalence of antisocial behavior would be at least moderately high (i.e., at-risk samples). If the antisocial behavior occurred infrequently, the distribution for our dependent variable would be negatively skewed. Such distributions violate the basic assumptions necessary for the parametric statistical analyses we had planned for model building.

Families were recruited from areas of the city with high crime rates. The details of the recruitment procedures are outlined in Appendix 1. The boys are now 15 years old, and 37% of them already have been arrested at least once. This suggests that the strategy for selecting the sample has been successful. It should be kept in mind, however, that the findings presented in this volume are not repre-

sentative of the findings that might be obtained from a random stratified sample of boys in the same metropolitan area.

Inspection of the distributions for variables used in the analyses indicates that most of the measures of skewness and kurtosis are within acceptable limits (Capaldi & Patterson, 1989). Of course, a few exceptions can be expected when assessing variables such as substance use during preadolescence.

Limited Generalizability

The sociologists who served as consultants and site visitors were quick to point out the weaknesses of this design. The fact that *all* of the families in the sample were from one small metropolitan area severely limited the generalizability of the findings. The alternative is to employ probability sampling in which families that are representative of age, sex, ethnic background, community size, and geographic region are studied.

For many purposes, the representative sampling approach seems to be ideal. Large-scale surveys such as the Philadelphia Cohort Studies (Wolfgang, Figlio, & Sellin, 1972) and the National Youth Survey (Elliott, Ageton, Huizinga, Knowles, & Canter, 1983) have made important contributions to our knowledge of the incidence and prevalence of delinquent behavior, but the size and complexity of these samples severely limit the extent and types of assessments that can be carried out.

The coercion model requires precise measures of parents' reactions to specific child behaviors. Our assessments of parenting practices in families with preadolescents involved several hours of interviews with the parents and the child, three hours of home observation, and six telephone interviews with the parents and the child. In contrast, a representative survey usually can support only one or two hours of interviews or administering a brief set of questionnaires. In these studies, information on parenting practices and the child's adjustment is obtained from a single agent (i.e., the parent *or* the child).

Limited assessment imposes severe restrictions on the kind of models that can be built. For example, without observation data it would not be feasible to build a model that emphasizes the importance of parental discipline practices. The large-scale survey makes it possible to specify precisely how the findings generalize to various subgroups, but a model based on data from a single agent may not generalize to models generated by other agents. Studies at OSLC have compared single-agent models to multiagent, multimethod models; in both instances, the single-agent models were found to be extremely limited (i.e., nongeneralizable) (Bank & Patterson, 1989; Bank & Patterson, in press; Reid, Bank, Patterson, & Skinner, 1987).

Like most other investigators, we assume that each agent and each method of assessment has its own unique distortions and biases. The measures can be highly reliable but extremely biased. Data from parent interviews are no exception. Reid et al. (1987) used SEM to define both parenting practices and child adjustment based on multiple maternal reports. The chi-square showed that the mothers' perceptions of parenting practices were significantly related to their perceptions of their boys' adjustment. Not only did the chi-square show a good fit ($p = .40$), but the model accounted for 35% of the variance in the mothers' ratings of antisocial behavior.

The mothers' ratings formed a coherent picture of parenting practices and child adjustment, but the model was not generalizable. When Reid et al. (1987) used maternal ratings of the independent variables to predict the antisocial construct defined by teachers and the child, the chi-square indicated that the data fit the *a priori* model. However, all of the path coefficients were *nonsignificant*, and the model accounted for only 15% of the variance. The mothers' ratings generated a very limited model. Bank and Patterson (1989) obtained similar results when they used mothers' ratings of a set of independent variables to predict their sons' delinquency. In both studies, when the multiagent, multimethod procedure was used to define the constructs on both sides of the equation, all path coefficients were significant and the models accounted for two or three times more variance in the criteria being predicted. In several of the generalizability studies, the variables thought to be causal were quite different from those identified in multiagent, multimethod models. We are not suggesting that *all* single-agent studies are useless, but it would be prudent for each investigator to demonstrate the generalizability of a single-agent model *before* embedding it in a large-scale national survey.

We propose that studying a small number of families in depth is a prerequisite for generating a theory of children's aggression. Such in-depth studies may reveal one model for small metropolitan areas and other models for specific subgroups (e.g., black families living in ghettoes). This first step might generate more than one theory; it may indicate that a set of theories is required, each tailored to a specific subsample.

Once we have a set of theories and each has been replicated, and it has been shown that we are on reasonably solid empirical ground, we would expect to find considerable overlap between the models in the determinants that have been identified for antisocial behavior. Presumably, the models also would differ along meaningful dimensions. For example, a model for families living in ghettoes might specify an earlier involvement with deviant peer groups. Once it has been established that a model is robust, it is possible to determine how the parametric values change as a function of the size of metropolitan area, ethnicity, and so on. This would require embedding key constructs and indicators from the model in national surveys that sample society at large. Epidemiologists have come up with cost-effective techniques that make this enterprise feasible. For example, current studies by Sheppard Kellam and James Anthony randomly select from the larger sample a subset of 100 to 200 families that will be intensively assessed for key indicators from the OSLC models. This means that we eventually will have the parametric values of key indicators for the coercion model.

The approach outlined here addresses the concept of generalizability in two different ways. Both are necessary, but neither is sufficient by itself. The in-depth assessment takes into account the generalizability of the model across agents and methods. Embedding the key parameters in a subset of a national probability sample addresses the issue of whether the derivation sample is representative (i.e., the extent to which the model is generalizable across different segments of our society).

Replication Design

Using SEM to simultaneously estimate the factor structures and the relations among them requires reasonably large samples. Because knowledge about the measurement of children's aggression is limited, there is no systematic way to specify in advance what the sample size should be. When we were designing the longitudinal study, the estimates we were given ranged from 100 to 300. The exigencies of budget and funding led us to select approximately 100 families for each cohort. After working with these data sets for several years, we seem to have made a reasonable guess. We have been able to obtain significant path coefficients and factor loadings for a majority of the models with this sample size. Most of the models seem to replicate from one cohort to the other, although it has been necessary to combine the data from both cohorts to make some of the weaker or more complex models "work." In those instances, we would feel more comfortable if the samples were larger — a minimum of 125 to 150 families.

Because previous efforts to replicate major findings relating parent behavior to child aggression have failed, we decided to rely heavily on replication designs. Baldwin and Skinner (1989), Patterson and Dishion (1985), and Patterson and Stouthamer-Loeber (1984) noted that although the key models worked well enough, certain changes should be made in the measurement models. Strictly speaking, the current analyses are not replications of those studies. We spent the first year of the OYS improving the measurement models, and much of the assessment battery was changed in the process.

Our efforts to carry out more tightly controlled replication studies have relied on the use of one cohort for a derivation sample and the other cohort for replication. Cohort I constitutes the derivation sample; if this is successful, the model is reevaluated using the data set from Cohort II. The same assessment procedures were used to recruit both cohorts, and the assessments were only one year apart. We assume that a failure to replicate would result from flaws in either the measurement models or the underlying theory. Eventually, we will carry out a systematic study of the contributions of cohort differences to the models. In the meantime, our working hypothesis is that the differences between cohorts are minimal.

Multiagent, Multimethod Indicators

As we noted in Chapter 1, the use of multiple indicators in conjunction with SEM makes it possible to sort out the contribution of shared method when estimating the relations between variables. However, two problems are associated with using "heteromethod" indicators to define concepts: (1) How can the different types of data be combined into a single score? (2) How can the indicators that will contribute be differentiated from those that will not? The following section provides a brief discussion on building latent constructs.

Building a Construct

We generally follow the same sequence of steps in building a construct. These steps and the rationale for using them are outlined in Patterson and Bank (1989). The psychometric properties of most of the constructs used in this volume are described in Capaldi and Patterson (1989). The present discussion provides only a brief overview of the procedure.

The general goal in building a construct is to meet four criteria: (1) Each construct should be defined by a minimum of three indicators, (2) it must be demonstrated that each indicator is reliable (i.e., internally consistent or significant test–retest reliability), (3) each indicator must show a significant factor loading (.30 or more for our sample size) when it is included in a principal components factor analysis, and (4) the structure must be sufficiently robust to survive replication.

Sampling Indicators

The aspect of the procedure that we understand the least is the process of selecting indicators. The population of measures is described in Figure 2.1. Ideally, the third dimension would describe settings within the home, school, and community. In the OYS it was not possible to systematically sample this dimension. However, we went to considerable effort to obtain measures from both home and school. The approach is consistent with the theoretical assumptions underlying generalizability theory (Cronbach & Gleser, 1965; Wiggins, 1973). Ideally, we would select a random sample from all possible indicators that relate to a specific construct. In the Brunswickian sense (Petrinovich, 1979), the more representative the sample is across settings or agents, the more generalizable the resulting definition of the latent construct. The approach is in keeping with the principle of aggregation in personality theory; it clearly has been shown that aggregated measures have increased predictive validity (Buss & Craik, 1983; Epstein, 1979).

In actuality, we do not know how to select a representative sample of indicators. Furthermore, the pragmatics of construct building usually force us to develop our own indicators. The indicators we have created can be organized along a continuum from molar to molecular. The term *molar* implies a broad spectrum of assessment (e.g., global judgments that sample across time and settings), and the term *molecular* describes the sampling of events from more restricted time intervals. Molecular indicators often include action–reaction sequences observed in natural settings.

The Child Antisocial construct is one of the most molar constructs in the model. It includes home observation plus global impressions from individuals about the child's antisocial traits across two settings: home and school. To enhance generalizability, the measures sampled across settings and from multiple agents within each setting (i.e., peers and teachers at school; mother, father, and child at home).

On the other hand, when action-reaction patterns are required (as in the Discipline construct), the indicators are based on molecular measures (i.e., sequential data that describe the mother's reaction to the child). It has been our experience that parents' global ratings do not ac-

Figure 2.1

A Multiagent, Multimethod Strategy for Sampling Indicators for Theoretical Constructs

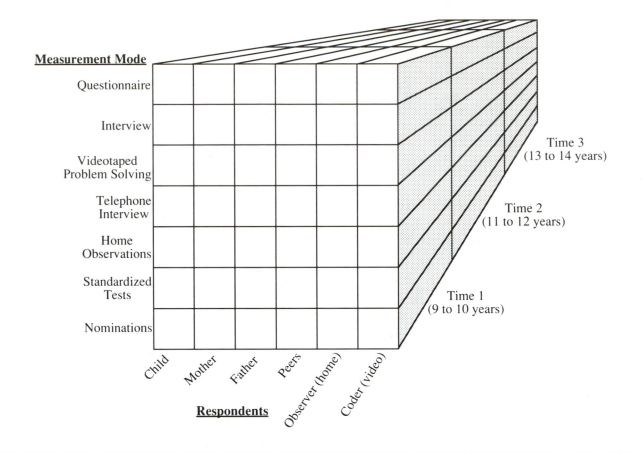

curately reflect what is occurring in these action–reaction sequences. We have repeatedly tried to develop interview measures that describe the reactions of parents to children's deviant behaviors. Although it is possible to obtain a reliable scale from such data, the indicator typically does not converge with the other measures.

Perhaps we eventually will discover how to use molar indicators to sample sequential patterns. Meanwhile, it is imperative to develop new, less expensive ways to sample interaction sequences. Our current feeling is that two kinds of constructs require molecular measures as indicators: those designed to *measure* changes in behavior and those that attempt to *explain* changes in behavior. These issues are discussed in more detail in Chapter 8, where the actual models are presented.

Building an Indicator

The definition of a construct often suggests the kind of indicator that would be most suitable. In the case of the Child Antisocial construct, for example, the definition indicated that the measures must sample both overt and clandestine antisocial acts. The definition also designated which acts were considered overt and covert (details are provided in Chapter 3).

The other part of the definition specified that we wanted to explain events that occurred not only in the home but also in the school and community. This meant developing separate scales or item sets for use by fathers, mothers, teachers, peers, and the target children. Items within each scale were analyzed for internal consistency. Individual items that generated item-total correlations of less than .20 were dropped from the scale. Scales that produced alphas (Cronbach, 1951) of less than .60 were excluded from further analyses.

Convergence

The next issue involves the question of whether the set of indicators measures the same thing. The OSLC studies have used a principal components factor analysis constrained to a single solution as a preliminary means of dealing with this issue. As a rule of thumb, those indicators with factor loadings of less than .30 are dropped from the construct definition. It is our impression that a median convergence correlation of .20 or less among the indicators creates a borderline situation. It means that either the definition is weak or the measures are faulty. If the construct is weak, there is a good chance that the model will not work (i.e., the model will not fit the data set). The modeling proceeds more smoothly when the correlations among the indicators are in the .30 to .40 range.

The "Glop" Problem

We have referred repeatedly to the issue of shared method variance as a problem in theory building. Many of the models published in the literature are based on reports from a single agent. This approach makes it impossible to partial out the shared method variance when estimating the structural relations among the constructs. The "monomethod bias" problem was discussed by Cook and Campbell (1979). This section briefly outlines some of the issues and literature that relate to what we affectionately refer to as the "glop" problem.

Dawes (1985) discussed this problem in terms of the theory-based schema that functions as a filter for the individual's global judgments about self and others. Given that the schema is essentially negative, the individual's global statements regarding expectations about self and others or about past and future events are likely to be highly correlated. In effect, the person is reporting that he or she is a sad, angry, and unhappy individual who is surrounded by people who have these negative qualities. Watson and Tellegen (1985) extensively reviewed and reanalyzed the self-report studies and developed a reformulation that is very much in keeping with Dawes's formulation. Traits such as anxiety, guilt, anger, and depression are all considered to be components of a broader trait, *negative affectivity*. The disposition to be particularly sensitive to minor irritations and failures of everyday life has been shown to have a high stability correlation of approximately .65 over two years (Watson & Clark, 1984).

Dawes (1985) implied that the negative–positive filters that apply to various dimensions of self-reports also might generalize to descriptions of others. Griest, Wells, and Forehand (1979) and Patterson (1982) showed that mothers of oppositional children had significantly higher depression scores. Griest et al. and Lobitz and Johnson (1975) found that maternal depression scores based on self-reports correlated significantly with maternal reports of deviant child behavior. In keeping with the idea that distressed mothers might have a negative bias that distorts their descriptions of their children's behavior, Griest et al., Lobitz and Johnson, and Patterson found *no significant correlations* between observations of deviant behavior in the home and maternal depression scores. The implication

is that mothers' reports regarding the behavior of their children may be influenced heavily by their mood.

As Fiske (1974) pointed out, each report of behavior by each observer using each mode has unique distortions and biases. The idea that an indicator can be *reliable* (or unreliable) but distorted or biased is one of the central issues addressed by SEM (Bentler, 1980; Dwyer, 1983). This assumption led to an extensive emphasis on the use of multiple indicators in the early publications describing SEM (Sullivan, 1974).

When a model fails to fit the data, it may result from the problem of convergent and discriminant validity (Campbell & Fiske, 1959). A cursory review of the literature confirmed that few investigators had been able to demonstrate both convergent and discriminant validity (Fiske, 1987). There was one interesting exception. Waksman (1978) used two very different assessment methods — telephone interviews and home observations — and six traits. Three traits met the criteria for convergent validity; one (whine) also met the criteria for discriminant validity.

Practically speaking, we have found three different methods that are useful in coping with the glop problem. They are described in detail by Bank, Dishion, Skinner, and Patterson (1990). Of the three, the one we prefer is *indicator mismatching*. If global judgments based on questionnaires from teachers, mother, and father define three indicators for one child trait, then the second construct should be identified by three indicators from, for instance, home observers, ratings from videotapes of family problem solving, or child self-report. Another possibility would be to have the same agents provide data defining the indicators for the two traits, while ensuring that they are based on different assessment methods.

Another method currently being explored at OSLC is to extract the method factors and then estimate the residual loadings of latent constructs on indicators and structural equations relating one construct to another (Bank et al., 1990). This approach was originally recommended by Jöreskog and Sörbom (1983), but it has been difficult to implement. A more useful version of this same solution would be to specify correlated residuals for those indicators that have common agents, methods, or repeated measures.

The third method we have used is to collapse a perfectly respectable construct into a single risk score. The Stress construct has been used (and misused) in this way. We do not yet know why this method works, but it does.

The method-variance problem will be addressed in the present volume primarily by the use of mismatching indicators and by specifying correlated error terms.

Details regarding sample characteristics and assessment procedures are provided in Appendix 1. Readers who want to examine those issues should turn to the appendixes. Others who are more interested in following the concepts outlined in the first two chapters should proceed to Chapter 3.

Summary

In many ways this book is about the problems involved in measuring clinically based concepts. It is clear that we have invested an enormous effort in tailoring assessments for the multitude of concepts that make up the clinical model. Will it provide a basis for describing and predicting long-term changes in the boys and their families? The chapters that follow will provide a partial answer to this question. Our own feeling after the first few years of data analysis is that the models are working better than we had expected. We credit much of the success to the extensive support provided by the National Institutes of Mental Health (NIMH) for the development of the assessment battery.

Chapter 3

The Antisocial Trait

The social interactional perspective emphasizes the delicate mechanisms that produce changes in behavior (Patterson, 1986b). Therefore, it may seem somewhat contradictory to introduce the concept of a trait for antisocial behavior. We agree with Allport (1937) that a trait score represents a disposition to respond that is stable across both time and settings. In this chapter, we examine the empirical findings to determine whether the data support the two hypotheses about stability for the antisocial trait.

From a social interactional perspective, prosocial and deviant child behaviors are direct by-products of social exchanges, particularly those with family members and peers. In a probabilistic sense, these behaviors are elicited by observable stimuli in the immediate social environment. The rates of occurrence vary as a function of the density of controlling stimuli. By the time children are five or six years old, the critical interaction patterns have stabilized within the family. And shortly after that, the patterns stabilize with members of the peer group as well. The effect of these highly predictable action–reaction patterns is to produce equally stable perceptions of the problem child by peers, teachers, and parents.

In a sense, the trait score is a macrosummary of small shifts that are occurring all the time. For most of us, these microshifts do not "go" anywhere: They simply fluctuate around a mean value. As we shall see later in this volume, a profound disruption in parental discipline can amplify the microshifts and lead to increases over time that are quite noticeable to outside observers. In keeping with Sameroff's (1981) speculations about systems theory, the trait score could be thought of as reflecting a dynamic underlying process.

Deviance as a Developmental Process

We view deviance as a developmental process in which one type of deviant act is a prelude to more extreme acts. In families, the progression moves from high rates of noncompliance and temper tantrums to increases in hitting and physical attacks. Probably, only the latter more extreme acts would be labeled as aggressive. But as the child becomes more proficient in the use of coercion techniques, he is reinforced for an increasing array of antisocial acts. Gradually, there is a shift from coercive acts to antisocial acts. As this occurs, only some of the child's antisocial acts would fit the definition of coercive. For example, hitting would be coercive and antisocial, while stealing or fire setting would be thought of as antisocial but not necessarily coercive. The child's skillful use of coercion makes it possible to reach for a new set of reinforcers for a new set of antisocial acts. If he wants money, he simply takes it from his mother's purse (positive reinforcement for stealing). If his mother notices the money has been taken, he simply lies and she lets it go (escape conditioning for lying). If school is boring, he avoids the unpleasantness by not going at all (avoidance conditioning for truancy). This key to the child's success is his proficiency in controlling parents, teachers, and people in general with his abrasive and explosive interpersonal style.

Our position is similar to the quantitative developmental hypothesis put forth by Robins and Wish (1977). There are two parts to this hypothesis. The longer a child remains in the coercion process, the higher the overall frequency of antisocial acts. The higher the overall frequency of antisocial acts, the greater the likelihood that extreme acts also will be involved. In spite of these developmental changes, the *core* of the antisocial trait changes very little over time. Eddy (1991b) asked mothers of toddlers and mothers of fourth-grade boys to describe the antisocial trait in their children by responding to a 12-item scale. The most frequently checked item consisted of noncompliance and the least frequent was hitting. But the correlation between item frequencies checked at 18 months and those checked at age 10 was .79. The core of what we mean by the trait is highly stable; more extreme acts such as fire setting, substance abuse, truancy, and vandalism are added to the child's repertoire later on.

Robins and Wish (1977) collected retrospective data by interviewing adult black males about earlier deviant behaviors and the age at which the acts were committed. They obtained a correlation of -.70 between the average age of initiation for 13 deviant acts and the frequency of occurrence. This supports the hypothesis that high frequency antisocial acts occur at an early age, and low baserate deviant acts tend to be added at a later age.

It is hypothesized that as children move from antisocial acts that are frequent and relatively trivial to acts that are infrequent and more serious, the progression is transitive (Guttman, 1944). That is, all boys who engage in the most serious acts also engage in more common ones as well. This implies that all of the steps leading to extreme acts may reflect the same underlying process. Before we examine the data related to this issue, we will consider the implications that this kind of progression might have for the trait concept.

Let us assume that we could observe a large sample of boys and count all of their antisocial acts every day for a month. The score for each boy would probably include many trivial acts (e.g., disobedience) and several relatively serious acts (e.g., fighting and stealing). In a large sample, a few boys might even be engaged in fire setting or cruelty to animals. Each boy's total score for antisocial acts (i.e., the *trait score*) would describe individual differences in the frequency of antisocial acts. According to our hypothesis, the higher the frequency of antisocial acts, the longer the child has been involved in the process. Frequency and extreme acts are related ideas. If we know the most extreme antisocial act a child commits, we should be able to estimate the overall frequency of his general repertoire of antisocial acts. We assume that macromeasures based on ratings by teachers, parents, peers, and the child's self-report are a crude estimate of the hypothetical measure of total antisocial acts.

A Definition of the Antisocial Trait

The antisocial trait consists in part of *a stable disposition to use aversive behaviors contingently*. Antisocial boys use aversive behavior to shape and manipulate their social environment. Although everyone uses aversive behaviors occasionally, an antisocial individual engages in these behaviors at significantly higher rates. The trait also consists of behaviors that signify a tendency to avoid responsibility (e.g., chores and schoolwork) and to maximize immediate self-gratification (e.g., stealing and using drugs).

Because of the well-known problems in measuring *intent*, this concept has not been included in our definition. There is no way to determine whether a child intended to use aversive behavior contingently by looking at an individual act. However, we can examine his behavior and determine that he reacts contingently with aversive behaviors. We also can show that the rate of occurrence is significantly higher than his peers.

There are many individuals in our culture whose behavior is aversive to others, but we would not label them as antisocial. Dentists, for example, inflict high rates of aversive stimuli on their patients, but it is not contingent on the behavior of the other person. Some examples, however, challenge our definition of an antisocial individual. Football players, boxers, soldiers, and judges fulfill both requirements — they use aversive stimuli at high rates *and* their behavior is contingent on the behavior of the other person — but we do not ordinarily view these people as antisocial. Because these individuals only dispense aversive stimuli in specific settings as part of their occupations and they must follow explicit rules, it is not difficult to distinguish them from the antisocial adults discussed in this book.

What Is Antisocial Behavior?

Coercive behaviors are functional for children. They are a primitive but effective means for changing the social environment. They are used in some form by infants and all primates (Patterson, 1982). Almost all children occasionally use aversive behaviors contingently to alter the behavior of a parent, a sibling, or another child. If an infant is cold or hungry, a brief crying spell will prompt his or her caretaker to take appropriate action. The crying usually stops when the parent attends to the infant's needs. The infant uses aversive contingencies to train new parents *when* to respond and *what* to do. When the toddler is older, he or she may learn that temper tantrums produce desirable outcomes. Most children eventually learn to use language to communicate their wants, needs, and feelings. The problem child stands out because he or she continues to use coercive techniques that other children gave up when they were toddlers.

Problem children use aversive behavior to maximize immediate gratification and to deflect or neutralize requests and demands made by others. The coercive child's motto seems to be a rephrasing of Caesar's famous dictum: "I see it, I want it, I'll take it." Most preschoolers eventually learn to take turns, share toys, and cooperate with others. Some, however, find that taking what they want has its own immediate rewards. It eliminates the need for waiting, sharing, or cooperating. These are the ultimate "here and now" children: They are not concerned about long-term consequences or the feelings of others who get in their way.

Some parents also practice coercion. For these adults, how they react depends on their mood. Many of the parents who bring their children to OSLC for treatment are extremely irritable; their reactions seem to be thoughtless, angry reflexes rather than responses that will help socialize their children.

Trait Characteristics

Is the trait score stable across both time and settings? Should the trait be conceptualized as a single dimension such as frequency? What are the relations among age of onset, frequency, and prognosis for treatment? Is there an identifiable progression from common to uncommon antisocial acts? The rest of this chapter examines the empirical findings relevant to these and other issues associated with the antisocial trait.

As with most models in the social sciences, many of the studies needed to confirm a specific hypothesis have not yet been completed. Our goal in writing this book is to use existing studies to make a reasonable case for a set of interrelated hypotheses. In a sense, our concern with the antisocial trait in children represents an attempt to push the coercion model to its limits. The utility of the model will be evaluated in terms of how well it organizes the vast array of information about children's problem behaviors, its effectiveness in accounting for significant proportions of variance in composite measures of children's antisocial behavior, and its ability to stimulate future research.

Stability Across Time

To determine how stable a trait is across time, we need to measure the same sample of subjects at two different points in time. Because our current studies assume that children's antisocial behavior is prototypic of adult antisocial behavior, two different sets of longitudinal data will be examined. The first set describes the stability of antisocial behavior from childhood to adolescence; the second set examines the stability from adolescence to adulthood. Some evidence is also presented for continuity across generations. The underlying assumption is that even though the manifestation of antisocial behavior changes somewhat with age, its function remains basically the same. Therefore, we would expect to find high stability correlations across substantial time intervals. An important implication of the continuity hypothesis is that adolescent delinquency simply represents one point on a lifelong continuum. Antisocial behavior at one age is thought to be the developmental precursor for behaviors that occur later.

Continuity from childhood to adolescence. Olweus (1979, 1980) reviewed 16 longitudinal studies on aggression in children and adolescents. The intervals for these studies varied from one to 18 years. Olweus found an average stability correlation of .63 between measures of aggression obtained at one point in time and those obtained at follow-up. As he pointed out, the stability correlations for this trait are comparable to those obtained for measures of IQ. As might be expected, Olweus also found that the magnitude of the correlation decreased as the time interval was increased. However, even for an interval of 10 to 18 years, the average test–retest correlation was .49!

Continuity is apparent at a surprisingly early age (Loeber, 1982; Olweus, 1979, 1980). For example, in an observation study of mother–infant interactions, a stability correlation of .49 was obtained for infant coerciveness measured at 22 months of age and again at 42 months (Martin, 1981). A follow-up study by West (1969) showed that 49% of boys who were identified by their teachers in grade 3 as troublesome were later identified as adolescent delinquents. Although teacher ratings identified many of the delinquent adolescent boys, they also overlooked a large number as evidenced by the false-negative error of 63%. The findings suggest that many chronic offender adolescents can be identified by grade 3 or 4. This means that prevention programs could be implemented for at-risk children at least as early as grade 4; we assume that the earlier these programs are implemented, the greater the chance for successful intervention. Ideally, such a program would begin in kindergarten.

Continuity from adolescence to adulthood. Robins (1966) and Robins and Ratcliff (1978–1979) found that 70% of antisocial adults were antisocial as children. In those studies, the *frequency* of antisocial acts was the best single predictor of adult antisocial behavior. When antisocial behavior was accompanied by additional risk factors, the chance of becoming an antisocial adult was considerably higher. In the latter study, three risk factors were particularly important: poverty, separation from both parents, and the frequent absence of both parents from the home. If a child was antisocial and was characterized by

"Like grandfather, like father, like son…"

all three factors, the likelihood of becoming an antisocial adult was .89. Of course, only a small percentage of the sample met these criteria.

In a review of 23 follow-up studies of antisocial children, Robins (1974) concluded that all of the adult sociopaths had started their careers by age 18. However, follow-up studies from the Cambridge sample showed that a considerable number (20% to 30%) did not start their criminal careers (first arrest) until they were well into their adult years (Farrington, Gallagher, Morley, St. Ledger, & West, 1988). A review of three longitudinal studies by Blumstein, Cohen, Roth, and Visher (1986) showed an almost linear relation between the number of juvenile arrests and the risk of arrest as an adult. For example, given four arrests as a juvenile, the risk of arrest as an adult was in the range of .7 to .9.

Antisocial children are at considerable risk for adjustment problems as adults. In a follow-up study of 524 children referred to child guidance clinics, Robins (1966) was able to compare children referred for antisocial behaviors to those referred for other reasons. As adults, the antisocial children were characterized by more arrests, marginal employment records, and frequent heavy drink-

ing; 44% had been convicted of a major crime, compared to 3% of the other clinical group. As might be expected, the antisocial group tended to be less involved in community affairs. They also had a higher rate of dishonorable discharge from the armed forces; a similar finding was reported in the follow-up study by Roff (1972). In the Robins study, *only 16% of the antisocial sample were classified as well-adjusted as adults*; this is in contrast to 52% of those in the nonclinical comparison group. It is interesting to note that approximately one in seven of the antisocial children also were diagnosed as neurotic as adults.

In another study by Robins (1984), several thousand adults participated in a diagnostic interview that included a set of questions about their recollections of childhood antisocial behavior. Two-thirds of those who reported one or two clinically significant conduct-problem behaviors before age 15 were diagnosed as having a psychiatric problem as adults. Only 7% of those who were antisocial as adolescents had no psychiatric diagnoses as adults. The most common disorders included alcohol and drug abuse; for women who had been antisocial children, phobias and depression also were common.

The reanalysis of the Berkeley follow-up data by Caspi, Elder, and Bem (1987) showed an equally distressing outcome. Children who were characterized as irritable (i.e., had frequent temper tantrums) tended to have stormy marriages as adults. The men had more arrests and marginal employment records, and the women were described by their children as irritable and explosive. Similarly, Huesmann, Eron, Lefkowitz, and Walder (1984) found a correlation of .27 between peer-nomination scores for aggression in grade 3 and spouse-abuse ratings obtained 30 years later.

Irritable–coercive individuals follow dismal life courses, even by their own accounts. They seem continually caught off balance by each transitional challenge. Lacking essential skills at one stage of life, they are pushed unprepared into the next, and they seem more off balance at each juncture. They inflict pain, misery, and sorrow on the people who are close to them. They tend to have low self-esteem and rely increasingly on drugs and alcohol to fill the gaps in their lives.

Continuity across generations. There is increasing evidence that the thread of continuity is not only apparent within the life of the individual, but also across generations. Huesmann et al. (1984) found a correlation of .24 between individuals' childhood antisocial behavior and later self-reported use of physical punishment with their own children. Interestingly enough, the subjects' early aggression was more highly correlated with the aggression of their children 30 years later than with their own aggression at follow-up.

In a study of black urban families, Robins, West, and Herjanic (1975) found that having antisocial grandparents was significantly related to the likelihood that the parents would be arrested; this also was highly related to the likelihood that the grandchildren would be delinquent. The effect of the grandparents' antisocial conduct on the behavior of the grandchildren was mediated primarily by its impact on the parents. Nevertheless, the findings provided strong support for the hypothesis of stability across generations.

Elder, Caspi, and Downey (1983) examined mechanisms that might account for the stability across generations. They showed that the explosive, irritable discipline practices of the father, and to a lesser degree of the mother, interacted to produce an antisocial child. There was a direct relation between the antisocial behavior of the grandparents and that of the grandchildren. This time, the mediating variables were the father's discipline practices and aggressive personality traits.

In a structural modeling study of intact families from the OYS samples, Patterson and Dishion (1988) replicated two of the effects obtained by Elder et al. (1983). Retrospective data provided by the parents showed a significant correlation between reports of *their parents'* irritable, explosive reactions in the home and their own antisocial traits. Furthermore, the effect of parental antisocial traits on the children's antisocial behavior was mediated by parental discipline practices.

The findings from these studies are consistent with the hypothesis that discipline practices may be the mediating mechanism for the maintenance of antisocial traits from one generation to the next. This hypothesis is examined in more detail in Chapter 5.

How Stable Are the Extremes?

The high stability correlations for the antisocial trait suggests that extreme scores might be quite stable. Are the extreme scores more or less stable than other scores in the distribution? Why is the antisocial trait score stable? This section examines the data relevant to these questions.

Data from a follow-up study in Illinois (Eron, Walder, & Lefkowitz, 1971) consisted of aggression scores for boys in grade 3 and comparable data obtained 10 years later. The stability correlation for the two aggression scores was .38. Patterson (1982) reanalyzed the data for boys in grade 3 at the 85th, 90th, and 95th percentiles 10 years later. The data showed that boys at the extremes were very likely to remain at an elevated ranking for aggression. Of the boys at the 95th percentile in grade 3, 38% were at or above that percentile 10 years later. Almost all of the boys at or above the 85th percentile were perceived to be above the median for aggression 10 years later.

A stronger version of the hypothesis suggests that the extreme antisocial scores are actually *more stable* than scores at the middle of the distribution or those at the opposite extreme (i.e., not aggressive). Although this variation on the hypothesis is not crucial to the model, it is of interest because it contradicts the conventional wisdom that extreme scores tend to regress to the mean. There has been only one test of the hypothesis that antisocial scores are more stable at the extreme. Loeber (1982) analyzed the self-report data collected in the National Youth Survey (Elliott & Huizinga, 1980) and concluded that the data support the hypothesis of greater stability at the extreme. However, a recalculation of his published data revealed an unfortunate error in his analysis. Of the 252 youths whose self-report data indicated they were extremely delinquent at Time 1, only 73 were at the extreme a year later, which yields a stability coefficient of .28. The stability coefficient for youths who reported that they were not delinquent at Time 1 was .68. Thus, the findings from these self-report data are not consistent with the hypothesis that youngsters at the extreme for antisocial behavior are *more* stable across time than are youngsters at other points in the distribution.

However, as we shall see in a later section, extremely antisocial boys tend to be arrested earlier and are at risk for becoming chronic offenders. The stabilities are of a very high magnitude. We have not checked the official record data to determine whether the extremes are more stable. We need to review this data before we can make any definitive statements about greater stability at the extremes.

Why Is the Antisocial Trait Stable?

Patterson (1982) suggested that the stability of the antisocial trait across time provided indirect support for the hypothesis that extremely aggressive children tend to program their own social environments. They are highly selective about whom they interact with and the settings in which the exchanges take place. Their behavior elicits predictable reactions from others. The effect is to keep the children locked into the coercion process. It was also assumed that the parents' lack of family management skills was highly stable over time. In an analysis of the Oakland and Berkeley longitudinal studies, Elder et al. (1983) found that disruptions in parental discipline were highly stable (.63) over an interval of three to five years. There seems to be support for the idea that childrearing practices, as well as attitudes about childrearing, are stable across time (Roberts, Block, & Block, 1984).

Patterson and Bank (1989) tested the hypothesis about parallel continuities in children's antisocial behavior and parental family management practices. The path coefficients for the Child Antisocial construct and for the Parental Monitoring and Discipline constructs from grades 4 to 6 were highly significant and of approximately the same magnitude.

Stability Across Settings

Our position is that deviant individuals are, almost by definition, less sensitive to subtle variations in the demands associated with different settings. Problem children are labeled as deviant because they are out of control in setting after setting. Jones, Reid, and Patterson (1975) found indirect support for this idea in a three-faceted generalizability design. Regular and calibrating observers collected data in the home as one facet (with two conditions). Separately scheduled visits to the home constituted the second facet, and the subjects constituted the third facet (with two conditions: normal and clinical samples). In the analysis of variance for the Total Aversive Behavior (TAB) scores, the subject-by-occasion interaction term accounted for most of the variance (81.4%) for the normal subjects, and deviant status accounted for most of the variance (79.4%) for the clinical subjects. The implication is that normal boys tend to be much more responsive to occasions than are problem children, who tend to behave in much the same way regardless of the occasion.

Reviews by Mischel (1968) and others have concluded that there is a lack of stability across settings. We believe these findings reflect faulty data more than anything else. Many of the earlier studies were based on one variable assessed at a single point in time from one agent. The alternative is to aggregate trait measures across time within settings. One approach, for example, would be to collect data from several agents in each setting (Epstein, 1979).

Wright (1983) has provided what we feel is an adequate test for the across-settings stability hypothesis. He trained 74 counselors at a children's summer camp to function as participant observers. Eighty-nine children were involved in the study; they were rated on nine traits, including physical and verbal aggression. The children could be observed in more than a dozen settings on a regular basis. The observers were rotated through settings so that each child received a minimum of four ratings for each activity. Observers rated the children on each trait in each setting. The data were collected in such a way that both temporal and setting stabilities could be estimated. When trait scores were based on assessments in a single setting or from a single occasion, only modest stability was found. For example, ratings sampled on only one occasion for the aggression trait correlated .33 with the summed ratings across time and settings. The split-half correlation across settings and time was .71. When ratings were aggregated within settings (across raters and across time), however, the across-setting correlation for the traits was in the .5 to .6 range. A single rating from a single setting is clearly an inadequate assessment for aggression or, for that matter, any trait.

Relevant data also are available from clinical studies of problem children. Patterson (1982) reviewed three studies that included data on the children's status as deviant or nondeviant at home and at school. The studies were small-scale, but the findings were consistent. Children viewed by adults as deviant in one setting also were viewed as deviant in a second setting. The overlap between settings ranged from 20% to 52%. To put this into perspective, let us assume that the baserates for conduct problems at school and at home are both 10%. If there is no trans-situational consistency for the trait (i.e., status in one setting is *independent* of status in the other), the expected overlap would be $(.10)^2$, or 1%.

Loeber and Dishion (1984) reanalyzed the observation data collected by Bernal, Delfini, North, and Kreutzer (1976) and found that *all* boys who exhibited deviant behavior at school also showed high rates of deviant behavior at home. Incidentally, the reverse was not necessarily true; not all boys who were deviant at home were deviant at school. Ramsey, Patterson, and Walker (1990) provided an elegant test for the stability-across-settings hypothesis. A latent construct was built for the antisocial trait consisting of indicators for the home setting assessed at grade 4. A year later, a second construct was built based on indicators from the school. There was no overlap in method or agents in defining the two constructs. In the SEM, the path coefficient was .73! The findings provided strong support for the hypothesis that antisocial behavior is stable across both time and settings, which satisfies the requirements for status as a trait.

Generalization across settings and risk. Patterson (1979b, 1982) hypothesized that boys who are deviant at home *and* at school would be at greater risk for chronic delinquency than would boys who are deviant in only one setting. Mitchell and Rosa (1981) provided substantive support for this aspect of the multiple-setting hypothesis. They found that the recidivism rate for children identified as stealers by parents was 14.3%, and the comparable rate for children identified as stealers by teachers was 45.5%. The recidivism rate for children identified as stealers in both settings was 71.4%. We found that 53.8% of the boys in our Planning Study who were described only by their mothers as fighters (at home) had one or more police contacts, 12.8% of those identified as fighters only by teachers had police contacts, and 66.7% of those identified as fighters by mothers *and* teachers had police contacts.

Parenting skills and generalization across settings. We assume that the stability of antisocial behavior across settings results from primarily the parents' failure to discourage antisocial behavior and promote prosocial behavior. This suggests that children who are antisocial in a variety of settings have been exposed to more pathogenic family management practices. Loeber and Dishion (1984) addressed this question using data from the Planning Study. They examined the family correlates of boys who had a tendency to be aggressive in more than one setting. Greater disruptions were noted in the parents' childrearing practices for children who fought at home *and* at school than for children who fought in only one setting. The findings indicate that disruptions in family management practices is associated with consistency in children's antisocial behavior across settings.

Measuring the Antisocial Trait

Children's antisocial behavior seems to be relatively stable across time and settings, which satisfies the basic requirements for a trait. The next question is, how do we measure this trait? We believe that the antisocial trait score should sample behavior across more than one setting and include information from more than one agent in each setting. It also should include both common and uncommon antisocial acts.

Building the Child Antisocial Construct

The details of the psychometric studies of the Child Antisocial construct are presented in Capaldi and Patterson (1989). The item pools from the Child Behavior Checklist (CBC) (Achenbach & Edelbrock, 1979) were examined *a priori* to form scales that assessed our definition of antisocial behavior. Separate scales were used for overt and clandestine items, and analyses were carried out separately for mothers, fathers, and teachers. A questionnaire that sampled these items even more intensively was filled out by both parents. To balance the distortions introduced by questionnaire data, telephone interviews and standard intake interviews were conducted with the mother, father, and target child. During the telephone interview, the parents were asked to describe the antisocial events that had occurred within the preceding 16 hours. A telephone interview and a standard interview were used to obtain self-report data from the target child regarding antisocial acts (overt and clandestine). A peer-nomination scale also was included as a potential indicator of the target child's antisocial behavior. These methods and agents are summarized in Figure 3.1.

Each of the 12 potential indicators was examined for internal consistency. In our initial review of the data, the scales measuring the child's clandestine and overt antisocial behavior were analyzed separately. First, the items with a correlation of less than .20 with the corrected total scores were dropped; then the scales with alphas of less than .6 were dropped. The 11 indicators that survived these tests were used in a principal components factor analysis to demonstrate that each indicator had a significant loading on the Child Antisocial construct. Only those variables with a loading of .30 or more were retained; nine indicators survived that test. The three indicators that had to be dropped were scales based on interviews with the mother, father, and child.

The first wave of analyses was based on the data from Cohort I. To balance the contribution of settings and agents, the indicators were grouped as shown in Figure 3.1. Two agents were used to report on antisocial acts (overt and clandestine) both at school and at home. The factor loadings are provided for Cohort I and Cohort II. The findings show a moderately stable factor structure for the two samples.

We thought that the factor structure might change as a function of the age of the child. Baldwin (1987) provided the first clue in a modeling study of six- to eight-year-old boys from single-parent families. The numbers in parentheses in Figure 3.1 are from that study; notice that the loading for teacher ratings was considerably lower. This difference could result from the nature of the sample (single-parent families) or the age of the child. Analyses from other samples suggest that the age of the child is the critical factor. We have found that it is difficult to get convergence for parent–teacher data for children in grades 1 and 2; there seems to be a developmental shift in factor structure for the antisocial trait at that age. Patterson and Yoerger (1991) found that other developmental shifts may occur during adolescence. In that study, the change was not in the contribution of parents or teachers, but in the kind of antisocial behavior. During adolescence, both police arrest and substance abuse become significant

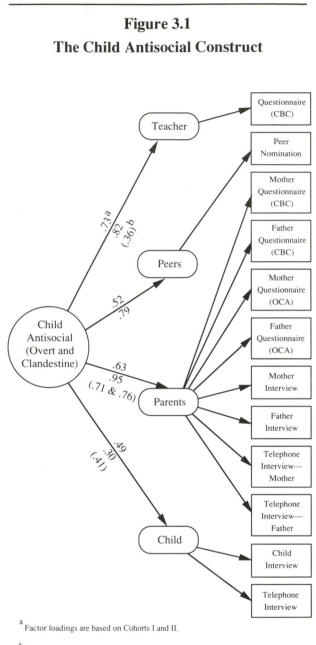

Figure 3.1
The Child Antisocial Construct

.73 ᵃ
.82
(.36) ᵇ

.52
.79

.63
.95
(.71 & .76)

.49
.30
(.41)

Teacher

Peers

Child Antisocial (Overt and Clandestine)

Parents

Child

Questionnaire (CBC)

Peer Nomination

Mother Questionnaire (CBC)

Father Questionnaire (CBC)

Mother Questionnaire (OCA)

Father Questionnaire (OCA)

Mother Interview

Father Interview

Telephone Interview— Mother

Telephone Interview— Father

Child Interview

Telephone Interview

ᵃ Factor loadings are based on Cohorts I and II.

ᵇ Numbers in parentheses are from Baldwin (1987).

additions to the core definition of the term *antisocial*.

It is an implicit assumption throughout this volume that direct observation is the preferred assessment method for aggression in children. The TAB score is a summary of all categories of coercive behaviors coded during three or more observation sessions in the home. The TAB score is computed by dividing the total time spent engaging in coercive behaviors by the total time spent interacting with others (Reid, 1978). When TAB was included as an indicator for the Child Antisocial construct in a clinical sample, it provided one of the highest loadings (.67) with parent report (.73), teacher report (.58), and child self-

report (.54) (Patterson & Chamberlain, 1988). Ideally, observation data should be collected in both the home and school settings. Bank and Patterson (in press) analyzed the data for a subset of OYS boys observed in both settings when they were 10 and 11 years old. The SEM showed that the composite measures were powerful predictors of delinquency rates for the next five years. In fact, the observation-based measures predicted as well as the composite measure based on parent, teacher, peer, and child reports. In our experience, when the TAB score is based only on home observation data, the loading for the latent construct is modest (in the .3 to .4 range).

Validity. The fact that different measures of the trait converge suggests a kind of validity by consensus. A more direct test would be to examine the utility of the construct when it is employed in the modeling studies summarized in Chapter 8. Suffice it to say here that the construct relates to an impressive array of models that includes future delinquency. Walker, Shinn, O'Neill, and Ramsey (1987) examined the implications of high and low antisocial scores for school-related behavior. The score significantly predicted the amount of time on task in the classroom, grades repeated, tardiness, truancy, disciplinary contacts, and referral for remedial work. The score also predicted rates of aversive exchanges with peers on the playground. When the construct score assessed at grade 4 was used to predict school adjustment at grade 5, it functioned as a powerful psychological instrument. It seems reasonable to assume that the construct score is a valid measure of antisocial behavior.

From Common to Uncommon Antisocial Acts

Do a significant number of children who perform uncommon acts also perform all of the more common ones? According to the trivial–serious hypothesis, all youths who engage in serious offenses should engage in high rates of trivial offenses as well. On the other hand, not all boys who engage in trivial acts move on to more serious acts (i.e., the progression is transitive). It seems to be the norm in our culture for boys to engage in moderate rates of trivial antisocial acts. In fact, it has been shown that normal children of all ages in all cultures engage in *some* coercive behaviors (Whiting & Whiting, 1975). Our field studies suggest that it would be abnormal for a child in our community to engage in a zero rate of coercive behavior. The data indicate that a normal preschool boy will yell, tease, or whine approximately once every three minutes, and a normal 10-year-old boy will engage in the same behaviors once every 10 minutes (Patterson, 1982). According to the self-report data reported by Elliott and Voss (1974), 34% of normal adolescents engage in at least one minor delinquent act per year.

As the first step in testing the trivial–serious

hypothesis, adults were asked to categorize behaviors using a 34-item checklist of child problem behaviors (Patterson, 1979a). Twenty-nine police officers and 18 OSLC staff members rated each of the problem behaviors using a three-category scale that ranged from trivial to serious. The agreement in ratings between the two groups was very good. The scores then were used to classify the Parent Daily Report (PDR) data for child problem behaviors obtained from telephone interviews. Presumably, children who engaged in higher rates of trivial acts (based on telephone interview reports) also would be at risk for engaging in more serious acts such as fighting. Fighting was measured by a composite of questionnaire ratings by mothers, teachers, and peers (Patterson, Dishion, & Bank, 1984). It also was rated as a serious antisocial act by all of the adults. The correlation between the mean frequency of trivial items with the total fighting score was .39 ($p <$ .001). The frequency of trivial items also correlated significantly (.32, $p < .05$) with a composite score for stealing. The results are not compelling, but they are consistent with the trivial–serious hypothesis.

In a second test of the hypothesis, the boys in the Planning Study were divided into three groups: nondelinquents, minor delinquents (one or two police contacts), and multiple offenders. The multiple offenders engaged in roughly twice as many trivial antisocial acts as the boys in the other two groups ($F[2, 120] = 5.83$), $p < .004$. The studies in the next section provide a more direct test of the same hypothesis.

A Progression for the Child Antisocial Trait

Given the right environment and perhaps a difficult temperament, some toddlers are at significant risk for engaging in high rates of coercive acts. The more often a child uses coercive–avoidant behaviors, the more likely it is that the child will learn new variations and become more proficient at using them. A parent who is continually defeated in face-to-face discipline confrontations with a child will begin to feel there is no way to control the child's behavior. Eventually, the parent will stop monitoring what the child is doing. When the child's behavior is no longer being monitored by parents and teachers, the stage is set for learning about clandestine acts such as stealing, lying, truancy, experimenting with drugs, and spending time with antisocial peers.

Our position is that behaviors such as disobedience, temper tantrums, and fighting define a single transitive progression. The behaviors reflect a common underlying coercion mechanism that determines the initiation and maintenance of each step in the progression. The coercion mechanism takes over when disruptions in parenting practices allow escape–avoidance learning to occur. The coercion mechanism will be discussed in more detail in the next chapter.

For problem children, clandestine acts such as stealing

are an outgrowth of the same underlying process that produced the overt acts. First the child learns to be very noncompliant and have frequent temper tantrums backed up with hitting. This sets the stage for learning to steal and lie at high rates, followed by truancy and dropping out of school. We are not suggesting that every child moves through all prior steps in the progression, but we do believe that the progression describes three out of four cases. It also has been shown that the further the youth moves into the progression, the greater the risk for later delinquency (Patterson & Bank, 1989).

Our first studies of coercive progressions used frequency estimates based on observations in the home (Patterson & Dawes, 1975) and in the school (Harris & Reid, 1981). These studies used Guttman's coefficient of reproducibility as an index for the transitive progression. However, Robinson (1973) showed that some problems with this analytic format could not be solved. There does not seem to be a satisfactory single index that can summarize all the information in a progression. At this point, we use several probability statements to describe each shift from one stage to another. This is not an elegant solution, but it provides a good description of what is going on.

The data from the OYS samples have been used to define a progression that begins with the child's disobedience in the home, followed by temper tantrums and then teacher reports of fighting and stealing. For disobedience or temper tantrums to be identified as problem behaviors, both parents from intact homes had to report that the problem occurred at least once a week. The results of the sequence of analyses are provided in Figure 3.2. The four antisocial traits are ordered from most common (disobedience, which characterizes approximately 50% of the boys) to least common (stealing, which characterizes only 12.5% of the boys). The baserate values for both cohorts are presented in the lower part of each box. Note that these values appear to be reasonably stable from one sample to the other. Ideally, each step down in the progression should be of the same magnitude (i.e., we think that the baserates should decrease in even steps). However, the step from disobedience to temper tantrums is larger than the other two, so our progression is somewhat unbalanced.

Is there a constant that describes the risk of moving from one step to the next? In other words, is the progression really a kind of Markov process? It is hard to say — there may be a constant, but the value is determined by how we set the baserates. In any case, the data presented here do not support the idea of a constant. For example, two-thirds of the disobedient boys have temper tantrums, but only one-third of the boys described by parents as having temper tantrums are labeled by teachers as fighters.

To us, the most interesting data are those that specify the *probability of an alternative path*. This value

Figure 3.2

The Progression from Overt to Clandestine Antisocial Behaviors

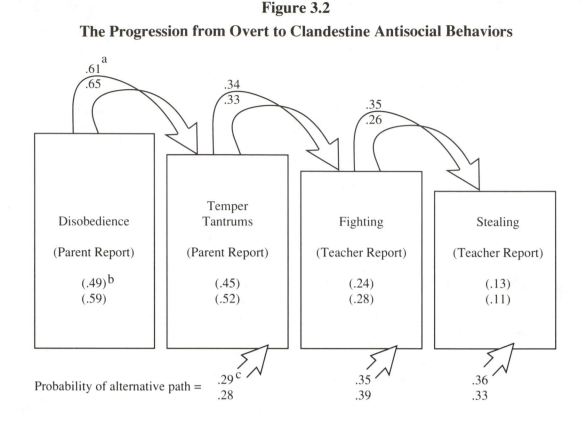

.61 [a]
.65
.34
.33
.35
.26

Disobedience	Temper Tantrums	Fighting	Stealing
(Parent Report)	(Parent Report)	(Teacher Report)	(Teacher Report)
(.49) [b]	(.45)	(.24)	(.13)
(.59)	(.52)	(.28)	(.11)

Probability of alternative path =
.29 [c]
.28
.35
.39
.36
.33

[a] The proportion of boys in Cohort I who disobey and have temper tantrums.

[b] The baserate of occurrence for the target behavior for Cohorts I (upper values) and II (lower values).

[c] The proportion of boys not fitting the hypothesized progression for Cohorts I (upper values) and II (lower values).

describes the percentage of children at a given stage who *did not* go through the preceding stage (i.e., they are not involved in a transitive progression). For example, roughly one-third of the temper tantrum group did not seem to fit the coercion model. We are not sure exactly what this means. One possibility is that we need an additional model; some boys who steal do not fit the coercion model. A more likely possibility is that the values for alternate paths simply reflect the level of noise in the data.

Currently, the fit of the data to the *a priori* progression cannot be tested. However, a comparison of the baserate value to the probability of an alternate path may be a reasonable way to describe the movement from one stage to the next. The crucial matter is how the progression changes over time. The coercion model proposes that children move increasingly to the extremes as they spend more time in the process. Thus far, there has been only one test of the hypothesis (Patterson & Duncan, 1991). Mothers' ratings of their sons at ages 18, 36, and 56 months served as the data base. The descriptive study

showed a definite movement over time from disobedience to temper tantrum to hitting. The data support the progression hypothesis that developmental changes occur over time.

The transitive progression concept seems appropriate for many clinical problems such as depression (Forgatch, Patterson, & Duncan, 1990; Patterson & Forgatch, 1990b). It may be particularly useful for clinicians who are interested in studying low baserate events such as acute depression, hallucinations, and so on. If a low baserate act is the last stage in a unidimensional process, then it is possible to work backward to identify its common manifestations. In other words, studying common acts may provide an understanding of less common acts.

One Path or Two to Stealing?

An early study of treatment referrals showed that approximately 25% of the antisocial boys were pure stealers. This group did not fit the coercion model based on escape–avoidance mechanisms (Patterson, 1982). The intake symptoms for these boys consisted only of clandestine behaviors, and the home observation data showed normal rates of coercive behaviors (Reid & Hendriks, 1973). These findings led us to speculate that this group might represent a second path to antisocial behavior. The boys in this group also seemed more socially skilled: They tended to get along better with peers and performed reasonably well in school. What makes these initial speculations particularly interesting is the finding that roughly one-third of the stealers in the OYS samples did not seem to fit the coercion model. Perhaps there is more than one path to clandestine acts.

Loeber and Schmaling (1985b) analyzed the data for the adolescent samples in the Planning Study. They showed that the police contact rate was 60% for the adolescents who were mixed stealers and coercers, 13% for the pure stealers, and 17% for the pure fighters. It was interesting to note that the pure stealers were more likely to come from intact homes (75%) and from homes of higher social status than were the adolescents in the clinical and normal samples. These differences may have been confounded by the fact that the adolescents in the mixed sample were significantly older. We believe that the mixed cases are at an advanced stage in the coercion progression and at greatest risk for early arrest and for becoming chronic offenders.

The Antisocial Trait: One Dimension or Two?

The progression metaphor suggests that overt and clandestine acts reflect a single underlying process, which implies that the acts may be organized along a single dimension. However, earlier reviews of factor analytic studies of antisocial behavior (whether based on referral symptoms, self-report, or observer ratings) generally reported two factors. The two-factor findings were based on both normal and clinical populations (Patterson, 1982; Quay, 1965). As Quay pointed out, however, the factors were invariably intercorrelated. He cited three different investigators who attempted to classify antisocial children using factor scores. These investigators found that most of the children were elevated on more than one factor and therefore could not be classified as pure cases. To us, this suggests that the two factors may simply reflect a single, or second-order, dimension.

Loeber and Schmaling (1985a) reviewed 22 published factor analytic studies of children's referral symptoms. In their multidimensional scaling of 34 different problem behaviors, they found that a single, bipolar dimension provided the best fit to the data. Clandestine behaviors were at one end of the dimension, and overt aggressive behaviors were at the other end. The former included behaviors such as truancy, gang membership, running away, associating with deviant peers, stealing, fire setting,

and using alcohol or drugs. The children who behave in this manner are very much like the "rowdies" identified by Pulkkinen (1983), that is, they are committed to their peer group and have some social skills. The data from the Planning Study showed that children who were identified as clandestine also tended to be socially competent. The other end of the bipolar dimension included the behaviors typically included in the coercion model: poor peer relations, arguing, screaming, moodiness, stubbornness, demanding behavior, teasing, impulsiveness, sulking, jealousy, attacking others, temper tantrums, threatening, fighting, cruelty, irritability, showing off, bragging, swearing, blaming others, and sassiness.

Confirmatory Factor Analysis

The idea that children's referral symptoms can be organized along a single dimension can be tested within the context of a confirmatory factor analysis. To improve the measurement fidelity of the Clandestine and Overt Antisocial constructs, multiagent, multimethod indicators were used from the Planning Study. The question is, do measures of clandestine and overt antisocial behavior form one construct or two?

Measures of overt antisocial behavior included reports of fighting from parents, peers, and teachers. Ratings from parents regarding arguing and disobedience were used to define a category of overt aggression. The multitrait and multimethod correlation matrices for the measures of the two constructs are provided in Table 3.1 for both grades 4 and 7. It is apparent that the correlation between constructs (discriminant validity) often exceeded the correlation within constructs (convergent validity). For example, at grade 4 the median correlation among the clandestine indicators was only .24, but the median correlation between constructs was .31! These correlations provide additional support for the idea of a single dimension.

In a more formal test of the single dimension concept, a confirmatory factor analysis was performed using the LISREL VI approach to SEM. First, the two-factor model was analyzed with the clandestine and overt antisocial acts representing two dimensions, as shown in Table 3.1. The two-factor model yielded an adequate fit to the data, as shown by the overall test of significance (chi-square [5, $N = 126$] = 4.79, $p < .44$). The indicators loaded significantly on the method factors (teacher, peer, parent) and on both of the latent constructs. In this approach to data analysis, however, it is necessary to examine more than just the overall fit of the model to the data. The correlation between overt and clandestine antisocial behavior in this model was estimated to be approximately 1.0. In other words, a child's score on the overt factor could be perfectly predicted from his score on the clandestine factor or vice versa. A test of a single-content factor solution was run on the model; as might be expected, it

Table 3.1

Correlational Matrix for Measures of Child Antisocial Behavior in Planning Study Sample

	Clandestine Antisocial Behavior			Overt Antisocial Behavior		
	Peer: Dishonesty	Teacher: Dishonesty	Parent: Clandes.	Peer: Fighting	Teacher: Fighting	Parent: Overt
Grade 4						
Peer Nomination: Dishonesty	1.0					
Teacher Rating: Dishonesty	.27**	1.0				
Parent Rating: Clandes. Behavior	.12	.24*	1.0			
Peer Nomination: Fighting	.64***	.31**	.24**	1.0		
Teacher Rating: Fighting	.45***	.62***	.31**	.57***	1.0	
Parent Rating: Overt Behavior	.23*	.29**	.36***	.35***	.35**	1.0
Grade 7						
Peer Nomination: Dishonesty	1.0					
Teacher Rating: Dishonesty	.32**	1.0				
Parent Rating: Clandes. Behavior	.30**	.32**	1.0			
Peer Nomination: Fighting	.79***	.36***	.26**	1.0		
Teacher Rating: Fighting	.65***	.59***	.33***	.60**	1.0	
Parent Rating: Overt Behavior	.41***	.52***	.55***	.42***	.56**	1.0

*$p < .05$ **$p < .01$ ***$p < .001$

was found to provide an equally satisfactory fit to these data. To test this further, the chi-square value of the two-factor solution is subtracted from that of the more parsimonious single-factor solution; the significance of this difference is then tested in any standard chi-square table (Bentler & Bonnett, 1980). The difference in the two chi-squares for this analysis was not statistically significant.

We retested the hypothesis using data from Cohort I of the OYS sample to eliminate the possibility that the results of the analysis reflected a failure to measure adequately clandestine behavior. The clandestine behavior data for the OYS sample were very complete and included information on stealing, lying, and cheating from all sources. Table 3.2 provides the multitrait and multimethod correlation matrix for both OYS cohorts combined. Again, the between-construct correlations were equal to or surpassed the magnitude of the within-construct correlations. The results of the confirmatory analysis were replicated (i.e., the single-factor solution provided the same fit to the observed data as the two-factor solution). In the two-factor solution, the correlation between the Overt Antisocial and Clandestine Antisocial constructs approached 1.0. The findings support the concept that the antisocial trait reflects a single dimension.

We believe that this, in turn, reflects a single underlying reinforcement process.

Developmental Perspective

In this section we review the empirical findings relevant to two key questions: (1) Are there changes in rates or types of antisocial behavior as a function of age? (2) What are the variables that relate to early arrest?

Changes in Rates and Types

Systematic observation data collected in the homes of both normal and oppositional conduct-disordered children showed marked decreases in rates of coercive behavior from ages 2 to 15 (Patterson, 1982). Loeber (1982) reviewed data from several studies and found a reliable increase in clandestine antisocial acts during the same time span. He also found a steady decrease in the incidence of overt behavior from ages 6 to 16. Changes of this kind in the occurrence of antisocial behavior have major implications for model building, particularly the models for longitudinal studies.

Data from the Planning Study were analyzed to examine age differences in clandestine and overt antisocial behavior. Several scores were used for both criterion

Table 3.2

Correlational Matrix for Measures of Child Antisocial Behavior in OYS Samples (Cohorts I and II)

	Clandestine Antisocial Behavior				Overt Antisocial Behavior			
	Child Interview	Parent Report	Teacher Report	Peer Report	Child Interview	Parent Report	Teacher Report	Peer Report
Child Interview	1.0							
Parent Report	.11[†]	1.0						
Teacher Report	.16**	.36***	1.0					
Peer Report	.10[†]	.42***	.58***	1.0				
Child Interview	.64***	.18**	.05	.11*	1.0			
Parent Report	.14*	.64***	.36***	.34***	.32***	1.0		
Teacher Report	.15**	.35***	.75***	.58***	.04	.38***	1.0	
Peer Report	.12*	.38***	.53***	.84***	.09[†]	.33***	.60***	1.0

[†] $p < .10$ *$p < .05$ **$p < .01$ ***$p < .001$

variables. The overt antisocial score was based on child self-report data and ratings by teachers and peers. Among the items included were provoking conflict, physical fighting, and threatening others. Each item was standardized for the combined sample of boys in grades 4, 7, and 10. The standard scores for overt antisocial behavior (normed across the age groups) from peer ratings declined from 1.35 at grade 4 to .054 at grade 7 and -.32 at grade 10. Both child self-report data and teacher report data showed an increase from grade 4 to grade 7 and then an abrupt drop at grade 10. The means for the teachers were .047 at grade 4, 2.40 at grade 7, and -.27 at grade 10; the means for child self-report at grades 4, 7, and 10 were 1.43, 1.84, and .70, respectively. Information provided by parents on the CBC indicated some variation in developmental trends depending on the specific antisocial behavior. For example, parental reports of child disobedience at home showed a very marked and steady decrease between the ages 4 and 5 (59%) to age 16 (30%) for boys in a nonclinical sample. In a sample of children referred to mental health clinics, 90% of the 4- to 5-year-olds and 70% of the 16-year-olds were reported to be disobedient at home. Obviously, disobedience is a factor that distinguishes maladjusted from adjusted children; it is also one of the most common reasons parents bring children to mental health professionals. Parental reports of children's fighting indicated a stable pattern for boys 4 to 12 years of age (20%) and an abrupt decrease to almost no fighting by age 16. The percentage of clinically referred youths reported to be fighters varied widely across age levels, but remained basically the same from age 4 (45%) to age 16 (39%).

Elliott, Ageton, Huizinga, Knowles, and Canter (1983) obtained teacher, parent, and self-report data consistent with ours. They sampled more extreme forms of overt antisocial behavior: aggravated assault; gang fighting; hitting teachers, parents, or students; disorderly conduct; and strong-arming of teachers, students, and others. The mean rates found in that study were as follows: .46 for 11-year-olds, 1.36 for 13-year-olds, and .68 for 16-year-olds.

We also examined data on the frequency of clandestine antisocial behaviors (e.g., lying, stealing, and truancy) for different age groups of children. Ratings by both peers and teachers indicated that the frequency of clandestine behavior did not change as a function of age. Child self-report data, however, showed an exponential increase; the standard scores were .19 at grade 4, .46 at grade 7, and 2.58 at grade 10. Elliott et al. (1983) obtained similar findings; they examined self-report data (e.g., damaging property at home and school, cheating, stealing at home or at school, and breaking and entering) and found a rate of .50 at age 11, 1.02 at age 13, and 1.58 at age 16. The epidemiological study by Achenbach and Edelbrock (1981) also provides relevant data. Parents of boys in the clinically referred sample reported marginal increases in stealing (both at home and outside) with age. For example, 20% of the 4-year-olds and 30% of the 16-year-olds were reported to be stealers at home. Roughly 30% of the 4-year-olds and a similar percentage of 16-year-olds were stealing outside the home. Truancy and drug use were the behaviors that showed the most striking developmental increase in the clinically referred sample; approximately 50% of the 16-year-olds engaged in these behaviors, but practically none of the boys younger than age 12 were reported to do so. It is interesting to note that almost all clandestine acts are rare at all age levels for children not referred for treatment.

The frequency of overt antisocial behavior seems to decrease across childhood and adolescence, but the frequency of clandestine antisocial behavior increases steadily after grade 4. Although the topography changes, the overall rate of antisocial behavior appears to be relatively constant as children mature. These developmental changes must be taken into account in longitudinal models. For example, stealing becomes a frequent problem (based on self-report data) at about the time the peer group begins to have more influence on the child; this also is the time when the family begins to have less influence. These two trends strongly suggest that any longitudinal model of antisocial behavior should include constructs that measure peer contacts and the interface between parental supervision and peer group influence as the child enters adolescence (Elliott, Huizinga, & Ageton, 1985).

Predicting Early Arrest

We hypothesized that the extremely antisocial boy would be at greatest risk for early arrest (Patterson, De-Baryshe, & Ramsey, 1989). It seemed likely that these boys would overpower parental efforts to monitor them, which would mean they would be out on the streets at an early age. In that setting, the high rate at which they perform antisocial acts would place them at risk to be the first boys in the peer group to be arrested. Empirical studies of delinquency have emphasized the correlation between early onset and increased risk of offending as an adult (Farrington, 1983; Glueck & Glueck, 1959; Wadsworth, 1979).

Comparison studies of prison populations have shown that most recidivists were arrested for the first time by the age of 14 or 15. One-time offenders usually were arrested for the first time at a later age (Gendreau, Madden, & Leipciger, 1979; Koller & Gosden, 1980; Mandelzys, 1979; Mannheim & Wilkins, 1955). Farrington, Gallagher, Morley, St. Ledger, and West (1988) studied the average number of convictions as a function of the age of onset. For boys between 16 and 18 years of age, the youngest starters (those who began between the ages of 10 and 12) averaged almost twice as many convictions as did the late starters (those who began between the ages of 13 and 15). The boys who started at a younger age continued committing crimes at a higher rate throughout adolescence and early adulthood. Even when they were 22 to 24 years old, their average conviction rate was twice that of men who first committed crimes between the ages of 19 and 21. Early onset seems to be associated with higher rates of delinquent behavior and greater risk of becoming a chronic offender. By implication, the findings

for chronic offenders serve as a major indictment of the deterrent effects of our criminal justice system.

The early onset hypothesis was tested by Patterson, Crosby, and Vuchinich (1991) using OYS data sets. The antisocial trait assessed at grade 4 and a measure of social disadvantage correlated .57 with age of first arrest through age 15. For those arrested during this interval, the average annual arrest rate was a surprisingly high .93, which is roughly once every 13 months! The boys who are arrested early are, indeed, at risk for becoming chronic offenders. The finding for OYS early starters is very close to the figure of .80 reported by Blumstein et al. (1986) for the Cambridge sample. The findings strongly support the idea that the more antisocial the boy, the greater the likelihood of an early start and later becoming a chronic juvenile offender.

Heritability for the Antisocial Trait

The coercion model assumes that genetic predisposition and environment both contribute to the development of the antisocial trait in children. For example, the combination of a marginally skilled mother and a biologically at-risk infant represents a high-risk sample for involvement in the coercion process. It is too early to say just what the key biological risk variables are, but there are some promising leads. Several variables thought to reflect genetic influence were discussed in Patterson (1982). It is possible that some children are hyporesponsive to social reinforcers. This might explain why they are more difficult to socialize. However, as pointed out in the earlier review, hyporesponsiveness may be the result of either a noncontingent social environment or a biological predisposition. It also seems possible that a successful outcome for coercive exchanges may be more reinforcing for some children than for others. A third possibility is that children who are excitement seekers might find some types of delinquent activities more arousing than do normal children. The fourth and perhaps most plausible explanation is that some children have a predisposition to be hyporesponsive to aversive contingencies. Some laboratory studies of children and adults have suggested that antisocial individuals are less responsive to aversive contingencies. This is consistent with the reports by many parents that punishment seems to have less impact on the behavior of antisocial children than on that of normal children. Again, note that individuals who live in environments where aversive consequences are delivered frequently and noncontingently would be likely to become less responsive to punishment.

Snyder and Patterson (1986) provided a promising lead for the study of heritable responsiveness to both reinforcers and aversive contingencies for aggression. They developed an assessment procedure for reinforcement and

34

punishment effects that can be applied to interaction sequences in natural settings. The procedure detects the effect of a reinforcer or a punishment for aggression at Time 1 on the likelihood of the same aggressive response at Time 2, given the same stimulus. Presumably, reinforcement for aggressive responses strengthens the stimulus–response (S–R) connection more for children with fathers who have criminal histories than for children with noncriminal fathers. In addition, aversive contingencies may have less effect in weakening the S–R connections for children with fathers who have criminal records. To date, however, the procedure has not been used directly to test these ideas about heritability.

Quay (1965, 1982), Lykken (1957), and Mednick and Christiansen (1977) made a reasonable case for the empirical studies that relate hyporesponsiveness to adults with criminal records. They argued that hyporesponsiveness to aversive contingencies is likely to be heritable. Quay (personal communication, 1980) felt that heritable hyporesponsiveness to aversive contingencies might characterize in particular the early starter delinquents identified by the coercion model.

Temperament

Our impression is that temperament is the most promising candidate as a biological risk factor. However, it is difficult to untangle biological and environmental causes. Thomas, Chess, and Birch (1968) reported that child temperament was an important variable in the prediction of later child adjustment. In that study, 10% of the infants were classified by their mothers as difficult. When followed up 10 years later, 75% of the difficult infants had become problem children; 25% of the infants not described as difficult also had become problem children. The investigators assumed that some unspecified heritable mechanism(s) accounted for status as a difficult infant. Although the study had several methodological problems, results from other investigators have clarified and supported the general findings. For example, Korner, Zeanah, Linden, Berkowitz, Kraemer, and Agras (1985) showed significant correlations between activity levels measured during the first three days of life and activity levels measured five years later. Electronic activity monitors were used to collect both sets of data. The measure of infant activity also correlated significantly with parental ratings of child temperament at 5 years of age.

Lee and Bates (1985) cited several studies that demonstrated a correlation between mothers' ratings of how difficult their infants were during the first six months of life and problem behaviors at 3 and 4 years of age. They found modest but significant correlations between maternal ratings of temperament and observed mother–child interactions. Dunst and Lingerfelt (1985) found that 2-

and 3-day-old infants with disrupted cycles of waking and sleeping (one of the dimensions in the study by Thomas et al., 1968) were less likely to show a learning effect in an operant-conditioning task.

The question is, how much of the apparent continuity in temperament during early childhood is a function of the mother's perceptions of the child and how much is a function of the child's behavior? The convergence between observation data and maternal ratings is generally positive and significant, but the magnitude of the correlations is disappointingly low (Lee & Bates, 1985). It also is difficult to separate the contribution of maternal reactions to infant behavior from the biological components. In fact, there is mounting evidence that maternal negative affect (e.g., anxiety and depression) is a prime determinant for maternal ratings of child temperament (Sameroff, Seifer, & Elias, 1982).

The joint contribution of genes and environment to children's social behavior and temperament is becoming increasingly apparent (Scarr, 1985b). Goldsmith (1983) reviewed two major studies of twins; the data provide a strong case for some heritable components of child sociability, emotionality, and activity. He pointed out that the problem of estimating the extent of genetic or environmental effects rests on the ability to provide molecular (rather than global) measures of child behavior that are both reliable and valid. He cited as an example the Lytton twin study (e.g., Lytton, 1977, 1980), in which the observation data for child compliance showed a heritability quotient of .36 and an environmental quotient of .26. Obviously, both factors make a contribution, but nonshared experiences (by siblings) also are important.

Twins and Adoptees

Pollock, Mednick, and Gabrielli (1983) noted that at least eight studies of criminality in twins were conducted between 1929 and 1962 in the United States, Europe, and Japan. The results showed that between 60% and 70% of the monozygotic twins and 15% to 20% of the dizygotic twins were concordant for adult criminality. These early studies tended to be based on somewhat biased samples, but current studies in Norway and Denmark involve the entire population of twins in those countries. In a review of these twin studies, Cloninger and Gottesman (1987) found concordance rates of 41% and 51% for the Norwegian and Danish samples of monozygotic twins and 26% and 30% for the dizygotic twins. These researchers estimated that the heritability of *adult* criminal behavior was 54%. They pointed out that primary alcoholism and adult antisocial personality are not genetically related, even though each is in part genetically determined. Their analysis showed that crimes against persons often are associated with alcohol abuse, whereas crimes committed in the absence of alcohol seem to be directed more against property. They estimated that the heritability of crimes against property was 75% and the comparable figure for crimes against persons was 50%.

An analysis of concordance rates for twins again raises questions about inferring causality from correlational data. A more convincing test of causal status is provided by experimental manipulation. Pollock et al. (1983) cited five cross-fostering studies that meet the requirements for such a design. In the U.S. studies by Cadoret (1978) and Crowe (1975) and the European studies by Bohman (1978), Hutchings and Mednick (1977), and Schulsinger (1977), children were placed in adoptive homes and then were followed up. The incidence of adult criminal behavior was calculated as a function of the criminality of the biological and foster parents. Each study supported the idea of a genetic factor in adult criminality. The results of a large-scale adoption study by Mednick, Gabrielli, and Hutchings (1982) emphasized the contribution of genetic factors (and, to a lesser extent, environmental factors) to adult crime. When neither the biological parents nor the foster parents were criminal, 13.5% of the adoptees had criminal records; when the adoptive parents were criminal but the biological parents were not, the figure was 14.7%; when the biological parents were criminal but the foster parents were not, the rate was 20%; and when both sets of parents had criminal records, 24.5% of the adoptees had criminal records.

One of the most puzzling findings in this series was presented by Cloninger and Gottesman (1987). They reviewed the five twin studies focusing on juvenile delinquency. Although only a small number of twin pairs were involved, the results suggested that the concordance rates did not differ as a function of zygosity. If one child was delinquent, the sibling tended to be involved regardless of genetic relatedness. The results somewhat resemble those that would be obtained in a study of twins with infectious diseases. We assume that biological variables are probably involved for only a small subset of delinquents. These would be the early onset chronic offenders.

Another Possible Mechanism

It is extremely unlikely that a single gene is responsible for adult antisocial behavior. Furthermore, the criminality of a biological parent is only a crude indication of the presence of heritable characteristics. Many individuals could carry the characteristics and pass them on to their progeny without having criminal records themselves. In spite of these problems, however, there has been considerable interest in the relation between physiological mechanisms and the heritable features of antisocial behavior. Pollock et al. (1983) provided a useful, albeit brief, review of the studies relating to this issue.

One line of research has explored a cortical-immaturity hypothesis that seems to be a variant of the hypoarousal concept discussed previously. The studies have shown that incarcerated individuals tend to have a higher incidence of abnormal electroencephalograms (EEGs) than do individuals in the general population (approximately 50% and 10%, respectively). Excessive slow-wave EEG activity is the most frequent of these abnormal patterns. As individuals mature from infancy to adulthood, the wave rates generally increase. Two studies cited in the review used longitudinal designs to demonstrate a significant relation between slow-wave EEG in childhood and later delinquent or criminal behavior.

The other primary line of research has focused on autonomic activity measured through skin conductance as it relates to the hypoarousal hypothesis. The studies have demonstrated a weak relation between baseline conditions of hypoarousal and criminal behavior (Siddle, 1977). Lykken (1957) and Schmauk (1970) demonstrated that adult psychopaths profit less from pain-avoidant contingencies than do normal adults. According to Siddle, the adult criminal or psychopath tends to show consistent underarousal in response to aversive stimuli. Quay (1990) recently reviewed data from five studies that support this hypothesis.

These findings are critical to the formulation of self-control as postulated by Mednick and Christiansen (1977). They assumed that adult criminals profit less from avoidant contingencies because of their hyporesponsiveness to such contingencies. Included in this formulation is an assumed slow autonomic nervous system (ANS) recovery following aversive stimuli, which determines the individual's failure to control his or her antisocial behavior. Pollock et al. (1983) reported that three longitudinal studies have demonstrated a significant relation between slow ANS recovery and later antisocial behavior.

Although the findings from the two series of studies are impressive, a detailed review of relevant studies is needed. For example, we need to examine the details of studies that failed to replicate. The abbreviated reviews do not provide information about the reliability of the findings. Genetic variables deserve a place in the existing models of adult criminal behavior, but the next generation of studies should be designed to provide more information about the parameters (e.g., the amount of variance accounted for by any given heritable mechanism).

Important new developments in psychophysiology have paralleled the findings of behavioral geneticists. Gray (1978) postulates two motivational systems that coordinate ongoing behavior and environment: a *behavioral activation system* and a *behavioral inhibition system* (BIS). Aversive motivational states involve the BIS. For example, the shy, withdrawn persona would be characterized by a dominant BIS, whereas the BIS is not dominant in antisocial behavior. This line of reasoning suggests that antisocial children would respond well to rewards but not to punishment. A BIS deficit is associated with reduced sensitivity to threatening stimuli. Fowles

(1984) deduced that measures of electrodermal recovery, not measures of heart rate, differentiate normal individuals from antisocial individuals.

Summary

The antisocial trait composite score is viewed as a crude summary of an entire set of habits or dispositions. These habits are not salient for the normal child because the behaviors associated with them rarely occur. For the problem child, however, there seems to be a trend toward increases in the frequency and seriousness of the antisocial behaviors over time. The longer the child remains in the coercion process, the greater the risk that the child will engage in more serious acts.

Several studies were reviewed that support the hypotheses that the antisocial trait is stable across time and settings. Parallel disruptions in parental discipline and monitoring practices seem to be major contributors to stability. Extremely antisocial boys are most likely to be arrested early and are at risk for becoming chronic offenders. The vast majority of antisocial children are severely maladjusted as adults.

It was suggested that there may be a developmental progression of antisocial acts from common to relatively uncommon. A trait progression was presented using disobedience as a common trait; less common traits included temper tantrums, fighting, and stealing. The hypothesis was that most of the boys at any particular stage have gone through the previous stage(s). The findings from factor analytic studies of antisocial behaviors offer moderate support for the idea of a single dimension implied in the progression metaphor.

It seems likely that antisocial behavior has some heritable components. Five areas of relevant research were discussed: hyporesponsiveness to punishment, temperament, excitement seeking (hyporesponsiveness to stimuli in general), hyper-responsiveness to the reinforcers associated with coercive exchanges, and slow electrodermal activity.

Chapter 4

The Coercion Mechanism, Aversive Events, and Cognitive Processing

The antisocial trait was described in the previous chapter as a stable disposition to use aversive behaviors to manipulate the social environment. The trait includes overt antisocial acts that are contingent on the behavior of another person and covert acts that are used to avoid unpleasant experiences and maximize immediate self-gratification. Escape contingencies are the primary determinants for overt behaviors, and avoidance contingencies are the primary determinants for covert behaviors. Positive reinforcement makes an important contribution to both overt and covert antisocial behavior. The focus of this chapter is on escape conditioning as it relates to overt antisocial behaviors. Coercion theory describes how these contingencies work in the context of family interactions.

As noted earlier, the term *coercive* refers to the use of an aversive stimulus by one member of a dyad that is contingent on the behavior of the other person. For example, a mother turns off the television and her child begins to whine, or a little sister takes the last cookie and her big brother hits her. From our perspective, contingencies supplied by the social environment maintain these coercive behaviors. Escape contingencies and positive reinforcement are the payoffs for overt antisocial behaviors such as whining, teasing, temper tantrums, and hitting.

The coercion mechanism is thought to play a central role in understanding how families train children to be antisocial. This has led us to focus on the escape conditioning paradigm for the last decade, somewhat to the exclusion of positive reinforcement and avoidance con-

tingencies. In the long run, we may find that all three contingencies are equally important, but we currently assume this not to be the case. The empirical findings that support this assumption are reviewed later in this chapter.

Patterson (1982) discussed the findings that relate positive reinforcement to children's aggressive behavior. We still believe positive contingencies make an important contribution to some coercive and antisocial behaviors. We also believe that clandestine acts such as stealing, lying, and truancy are governed by a powerful combination of positive reinforcement and avoidance learning. In that the empirical studies testing these hypotheses have not advanced beyond the review presented in *Coercive Family Process*, they will be mentioned only in passing here.

Given that coercion is the key mechanism, aversive events become the focus of investigation. This concern prompted us to spend several years developing a new coding system for observing aversive events: the Family Process Code (FPC). The coding system has two major advantages: (1) It samples events in real time and (2) it records the emotional valence of each episode. Our data on aversive events now include information on duration and emotional intensity. These data are reviewed in a later section of this chapter.

The Coercion Mechanism

As mentioned earlier, the coercion model maintains that escape contingencies are the primary determinants for overt antisocial behaviors. This section begins with an overview of how escape conditioning works in social interaction sequences. In a later section, we speculate about how it might apply to adult depression and schizophrenia.

We assume that the reader is familiar with the principles of negative reinforcement and escape conditioning as they apply to social interaction sequences. *Coercive Family Process* reviews the issues involved in applying these principles to dyadic exchanges. The empirical base for these concepts consists primarily of laboratory studies with animals as subjects. The book by Domjan and Burkhard (1986) provides a good introduction to the experimental literature. Our interpretation of what happens in family interactions is closely related to the operant perspective on negative reinforcement (Hineline, 1977).

Social exchanges that include aversive behaviors are very likely to contain escape-conditioning sequences. For example, if one person says something sarcastic, the other person may simply walk away or counter with a devastating rejoinder that leaves the attacker speechless. An older brother might stop his younger sister's teasing by hitting her. All of these interactions contain a three-step escape-conditioning sequence: Person A acts aversively toward person B, and the reaction of person B is followed by a termination of the aversive behavior presented by person A. Because person B's reaction "worked," it is more likely to occur again in future exchanges. Socially skilled people learn to use prosocial techniques to neutralize or deflect unpleasant intrusions of this kind. However, parents and children from clinical samples rely almost exclusively on aversive behaviors in such situations. They also have learned that *escalating the amplitude* of an aversive response works even better. The daily routine in such households consists of a steady torrent of low-intensity aversive exchanges punctuated by occasional high-amplitude explosions.

Most of the time, aversive initiations (start-ups) are simply ignored by other family members. However, when a family member responds aversively (counterattacks), the coercion mechanism comes into play. Depending on which family members are involved and the type of start-up, the likelihood of a counterattack is estimated to be 20% to 30% (Patterson, 1982). The type of counterattack is related in a predictable way to the type of antecedent. For example, teasing is most likely to produce teasing as a reaction, but the response also may involve hitting. Both outcomes are possible, which means that teasing is risky. On the other hand, scolding or disapproval are most likely to produce disapproval as a reaction. Most parents are familiar with how these dyadic dances are performed in their own families. Both the action and reaction segments of the dance represent overlearned behaviors that are executed as quickly and smoothly as a well-rehearsed arpeggio.

Whether the two-step exchange becomes a three-step escape-conditioning sequence depends on what happens next. Does the initiator continue being aversive (continuance) or terminate his or her aversive behavior? The probability of continuance depends on the type of sample (e.g., normal, clinical) and who is involved (e.g., siblings, mother–child, father–child) If two aversive events occur in sequence in normal families, there is roughly a 50% chance that the conflict will continue (Patterson, 1982). This also means there is a 50% chance that the initiator will terminate the conflict at step 3 by responding with a neutral or prosocial behavior. When this happens, the resulting sequence satisfies our definition of escape conditioning (the issues associated with interpreting interactional sequences in this way are reviewed in *Coercive Family Process*).

A Closer Look

So far, we have discussed how an aversive event might lead to a three-step escape-conditioning sequence that strengthens the connection between the first and second events. But the potential effects of an aversive event are *much* broader than that. A closer look reveals that the behaviors of both members of the dyad are being altered and that one episode may have as many as four different outcomes.

Figure 4.1 illustrates a typical four-step interaction and the immediate and long-term outcomes for a mother and her son. The exchange begins when the mother finds the boy watching television instead of studying, even though he is failing in school. The mother scolds him, "You're flunking out of school, but there you sit watching TV. Why aren't you doing your homework?" The boy responds with the classic arguments: School is boring, the teachers are stupid, and he doesn't have any homework anyway.

The boy's reaction is a negative consequence for his mother's scolding. In effect, his response functions as a punishment that suppresses her immediate behavior (scolding); it also may have the long-term effect of reducing the likelihood that his mother will try to do something about his problems with homework and school.

The mother allows herself to be mollified by the boy's claim that he does not have any homework, and she shifts to a conversational mode: "Does everyone still go to sleep during Mr. Bailey's history class?" Her reaction completes the three-step escape-conditioning sequence. This interaction has increased the likelihood that the next time she makes an issue of homework, the boy will respond by arguing; over time, he also may learn to escalate the intensity of his counterattack by yelling and throwing things.

The fourth event in the sequence is somewhat surprising: The boy stops arguing and his next behavior is neutral or positive. As soon as the initiator removes the aversive

Figure 4.1
A Four-Step Escape-Conditioning Sequence

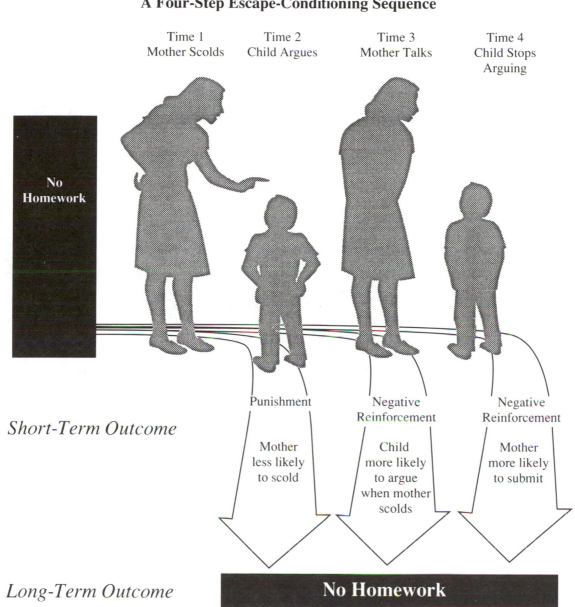

Time 1	Time 2	Time 3	Time 4
Mother Scolds	Child Argues	Mother Talks	Child Stops Arguing

No Homework

Short-Term Outcome

Punishment — Mother less likely to scold

Negative Reinforcement — Child more likely to argue when mother scolds

Negative Reinforcement — Mother more likely to submit

Long-Term Outcome — **No Homework**

---

stimulus, the other person often will stop his or her counterattack — and sometimes so abruptly that it is startling. Dengerink, Schnedler, and Covey (1978) found something analogous to this using a Buss-type shock situation. When one member terminated the attack, the other person quickly reduced his or her level of aggression. Patterson (1982) found a similar effect for mother–child dyads. Across a series of home observations, the mean duration for the child's whining in the home was 28 seconds. However, if the whining was preceded by an aversive stimulus and was followed by maternal compliance, the child stopped whining with an average laten-

cy of 4.6 seconds. Obviously, experienced coercers are sensitively tuned in to their social environment. In this case, variations in the duration of an aversive child behavior could function as a reinforcer for strengthening maternal submission.

The complexity of these effects is of particular relevance to social cognitive theories that suggest that such behavioral events have little effect on behavior unless they are mediated by thoughts or cognitions about what is happening. Given that we have a limited capacity for processing information, it is very unlikely that we could track and store these minuscule shifts in probability.

In the above examples, three simultaneous shifts would have to be identified and remembered. We believe that coercion patterns consist of well-rehearsed action–reaction sequences that are performed without the conscious awareness of the people involved. Over the long run, however, coercive individuals find themselves trapped by the consequences of their own behavior, which is why we call this *the reinforcement trap.*

Coercion training requires frequent interactions with people who consistently do two things: (1) They initiate aversive interactions at a high rate, and (2) they have a reliable disposition to withdraw once the other person counterattacks. In effect, *the initiator trains the other family member to use reactions that terminate the unpleasant intrusions.* In most families, each person develops a unique variation on what is probably a familial style of handling such situations. Humor is the preferred style in some families. In other families, aversive behavior may be politely ignored or lead to arguing. It is interesting to note that escape (and avoidance) conditioning may contribute as much as does positive reinforcement to the development of high-level prosocial skills such as these.

Why do the initiators in some families make the termination of their aversive behavior contingent on the counterattacks of others? Although we have not systematically studied this component of the coercive mechanism, it is our impression that coercive exchanges are most likely to occur in families in which either the rules for child behavior or the roles of family members are not clearly defined. Parents and children in at-risk families often have relatively equal power. In these families, the parents and children alternate in assuming the roles of victim and aggressor. Equal power also means that the parents allow their children to "win" about as often as they do when they initiate or counterattack with aversive behaviors. In normal families, it is generally the parent who wins.

Aversive Events in Family Interactions

The content of most social exchanges consists of relatively prosaic behaviors that would be classified as either neutral or positive. Only a fraction of social exchanges would be considered aversive. When observers go into homes or other social settings, most of what they report consists of give-and-take statements such as "Hi, how are you?", "Have you seen the...?", or "Do you want some...?" When we first developed the FPC and looked at the data, it was as though we had gone on a fishing trip and returned empty-handed. We were interested in recording both the content and emotional accompaniments of social interactions, but the data showed that roughly 90% of family exchanges were relatively neutral. There was not much anger — and very little laughing or loving

either. Most of the aversive events that did occur were not emotionally charged.

Although aversive events had a profound effect on family process and functioning, it was difficult to observe how they worked in natural settings. It was clear that large amounts of sequential data would be needed to study the coercion mechanism and that we would have to learn where to look for these critical events. Families with high densities of aversive exchanges were also at risk for producing problem children, which meant the issue was clinically important as well.

Our studies indicated that the density of aversive events seemed to be a function of certain characteristics of the parents and the status of the family itself. As might be expected, aversive events occur at much higher rates in large families or families that have been referred for treatment than in normal families (Patterson, 1982). Socially disadvantaged families are characterized by higher densities of aversive exchanges than are middle-class families. The parental characteristics most clearly associated with high densities of aversive behaviors are the antisocial trait, irritability, and depressed mood. In the OYS, for example, the correlation between the Parental Antisocial construct score (based on self-report, police arrests, and traffic violations) and nattering was .41 ($p <$ .0001) for mothers and .24 ($p < .02$) for fathers (Patterson & Dishion, 1988). As we shall see in Chapter 7, both stressors impinging on the family and parental depression are associated with parental irritability, which also increases the density of aversive exchanges (Patterson, 1983; Patterson & Forgatch, 1990b; Snyder, 1991).

There is an interesting paradox in these findings. Irritable parents permit their children to use aversive behaviors at rates that match their own. This is somewhat surprising. One would think that a highly practiced, irritable parent would win in all of his or her encounters with a preschool child. However, irritable parent–child exchanges have a thoughtless, reflexive quality. No one seems to be keeping score. Each person simply tries to maximize immediate gains by turning off the aversive behavior of the other person as quickly as possible. This is analogous to the automatic-processing model in cognitive psychology put forth by Reed (1982). The exchange consists of over-learned sequences that each family member can perform without thinking about them. Many of the exchanges that strengthen specific behaviors would not be thought of as heated conflicts because they are not accompanied by strong emotional overtones.

Based on earlier findings, we expected the FPC data to show that mothers and target children from clinical samples had higher rates of aversive behaviors than did those from nonclinical samples (Patterson, 1982; Reid, 1978; Snyder, 1977). In addition, we expected longer *durations* of aversive behaviors and more frequent bouts of negative emotions in the clinical samples. We also

Table 4.1

Target Child: Mean Duration and Frequency of Aversive Behaviors

FPC Categories	At-Risk Sample ($N = 104$)				Clinical Sample ($N = 48$)			
	Frequency		Duration (seconds)		Frequency		Duration (seconds)	
	Mean	SD	Mean	SD	Mean	SD	Mean	SD
Negative Verbal	16.87	13.70	65.03	60.67	21.93	20.16	74.19	65.95
Tease	4.64	5.17	15.89	16.81	2.63	3.52	8.77	12.09
Verbal Attack	2.76	3.48	10.25	13.83	5.23	12.64	18.56	44.11
Command	10.40	7.75	36.60	31.37	13.96	15.60	46.06	52.38
Coerce	.05	.22	.22	1.05	.19	.49	.79	2.34
Command Ambiguous	4.13	4.49	14.64	16.94	5.42	6.16	16.90	20.34
Coerce Ambiguous	.03	.17	.24	1.77	.08	.28	.44	1.53
Refuse	1.73	2.00	5.91	7.30	—	—	—	—
Negative Nonverbal	3.13	3.29	10.73	12.37	5.04	6.21	16.65	19.99
Physical Aggression	1.63	2.76	6.57	10.90	2.52	2.66	10.79	13.59
Physical Attack	.00	.00	.00	.00	.85	1.80	14.35	36.16
Noncomply	3.26	3.58	10.44	12.29	.69	1.60	2.94	7.03
Sum of Means	48.63		176.52		58.54		210.44	
Mean Frequency[a]	465.51				359.81			
Mean Duration[b]			1640.14				1339.10	
% Aversive	10.4		10.76		16.3		15.7	

[a] Mean total frequency of interactions when target boy was focus of observation.

[b] Mean total duration of interactions when target boy was focus of observation.

assumed that some activities or settings in the home would be characterized by higher frequencies and longer durations of aversive behaviors than others, although there was no theoretical basis for classifying settings *a priori*. We decided to investigate this issue because the information would be clinically useful and it was in accord with contemporary theories regarding the effect of context on interactions (Bronfenbrenner, 1988).

Findings for Target Children

Data were collected for both cohorts of the OYS. Because of a misunderstanding, however, the target children in wave 1 of Cohort I were the focus of observation for only *one* 10-minute interval, while the target children in Cohort II were the focus for *two* 10-minute intervals. Therefore, the data from Cohort I were not included in the present analysis. A second sample consisted of the first 48 families with antisocial children referred to OSLC for treatment. The sample included 13 girls and 35 boys who were 6 to 12 years of age; the demographic characteristics are summarized in Patterson and Stoolmiller (1990). Using the data from these two samples, we can make simple comparisons between at-risk and clinical families.

Because the target children in the samples differed by age and sex as well as by clinical status, no attempt has been made to test for the significance of these differences. The mean frequency and duration for the 12 aversive code categories for the target children in the two samples are summarized in Table 4.1. The mean values sum across events that occurred during different activities or settings. The data also are summed across events that vary in affective tone (i.e., negative, neutral, or positive).

Frequency. In the at-risk sample, there was an average of 465 exchanges between target boys and other family members when the target boys were the focus of observation. The comparable figure for target boys in the clinical sample was 360 exchanges. As shown in Table 4.1, there was a corresponding difference in the amount of time the target children spent interacting with other family members.

The findings for these samples are consistent with findings from earlier OSLC studies in that only a small proportion of social exchanges were aversive (10% for boys in the at-risk sample and 16% for boys in the clinical sample). Previous studies using the less-sensitive FICS observation procedure showed that approximately 1% to 2% of the responses of normal 10-year-old boys and 8% of the responses of 10-year-old socially aggressive boys in clinical samples were aversive (Patterson, 1982). The data are consistent with the hypothesis that children in clinical samples have the highest rates of aversive behaviors. Data from a *normal* comparison sample are needed to put these findings into perspective. The rate of aversive behavior should be considerably lower in normal samples than in at-risk samples.

The samples differed in the *proportion* of aversive events, but notice that the *types* of events were similar. The most likely event for both samples was some form of verbal behavior (e.g., Negative Verbal, Command, Tease). Nonverbal aversive events (e.g., Physical Aggression, Attack) were the least likely to occur. A rank ordering of the aversive categories by frequency of occurrence showed a high order of consistency between the samples; the *rho* was -.79 ($p < .01$).

Duration. Our interest in testing the escalation hypothesis was the primary impetus for developing a coding system that measured events in real time. According to that hypothesis, there is a covariation between the duration of coercive episodes and the likelihood of escalation in *amplitude*. Reid (1986) showed that high-amplitude behaviors such as hitting were more likely to occur during aversive dyadic exchanges that lasted more than 18 seconds. This raises an important question concerning which aversive behaviors are associated with long durations. We will consider the findings separately for problem children and mothers.

The data showed that verbal aversive events tended to have longer durations than did nonverbal aversive events. For example, the average duration of verbal negative events was 65 to 74 seconds, and the duration of physically aggressive events was 6 to 11 seconds (the events consisted primarily of low-amplitude behaviors such as slapping or pinching). These data suggest that prolonged aversive exchanges are relatively common, particularly in the clinical sample. Each exchange represents an opportunity for escalation in amplitude.

Aversive behaviors by setting. Ecological studies by Barker (1963) and others have reported that different settings within the home and school impose their own unique constraints on the types of behaviors most likely to occur there. Snyder (1987a) found that various settings within the home were associated with differential rates of coercive and prosocial behaviors for a sample of preschool children. In the present context, we will examine the possibility that different kinds of activities constitute a setting variable. The data summarized in Table 4.2 represent some of the first descriptive information avail-able on the effect of various activities on preadolescent aversive behaviors.

It is immediately apparent that the overall rate of social interaction varies dramatically from one activity (setting) to the next. During the observation sessions, most of the interactions occurred while family members were playing, working, eating, or doing other miscellaneous activities; this is not surprising in that the sessions usually were conducted just before or after family dinners.

We tested two hypotheses about the effect of settings on aversive child behaviors. On one hand, the likelihood of aversive behaviors might be constant regardless of the setting, which would mean that the settings with the highest rates of social interaction would have the highest rates of aversive behavior. On the other hand, some settings may be programmed in such a way that aversive behaviors are more or less likely to occur. Parents might relax the rules and reduce negative sanctions for aversive behavior in some settings and strictly enforce them in others; for example, there might be an implicit rule that "Quarreling is not allowed at the dinner table." If this rule is enforced in most families, that setting would be characterized by lower rates of aversive behavior even though the overall rate of interactions is high.

The data at the bottom of Table 4.2 provide little support for the hypothesis that some settings are uniquely programmed for the occurrence of aversive events. The settings in which most of the social interactions occurred also had slightly higher proportions of aversive behaviors. The correlation between frequency of social interaction and proportion of aversive child behaviors was .73 (N.S.). It seems reasonable to conclude that an "aversive event constant" holds across settings (and perhaps across time) for families that engage in coercive interactions.

Findings for Mothers

We expected the data to show that the rates of aversive behavior were higher for mothers in the clinical sample than for mothers in the at-risk sample. Previous comparisons indicated that problem children in clinical samples were only slightly more coercive (.98 response per minute, or RPM) than their mothers (.87 RPM). In normal families, mothers were significantly more coercive (.45 RPM) than the children (.27 RPM) (Patterson, 1982). In effect, we hypothesize that the person who is most coercive controls the social setting. For normal families this is the mother, while in clinical samples it is the problem child. Many clinicians have speculated that there is a role reversal in families with antisocial boys in that *the problem child runs the family*!

Previous studies of clinical samples have shown that most of the parents' aversive behaviors occur during interactions with the problem child and that their interactions with siblings are in the normal range (Patterson,

Table 4.2

Boys: Effect of Setting on Aversive Behaviors

FPC Categories	Setting											
	Work		Play		Read		Eat		Watch		Misc.	
	Mean	SD	Mean	SD	Mean	SD	Mean	SD	Mean	SD	Mean	SD
Neg. Verbal	2.78	4.29	8.75	10.45	.48	1.28	1.72	3.13	.21	.62	2.62	5.87
Tease	.75	1.77	2.05	3.86	.14	.40	.84	1.92	.03	.17	.83	1.46
Verbal Attack	.29	.62	1.80	3.16	.04	.19	.14	.45	.03	.22	.46	1.39
Command	1.83	3.03	5.21	5.86	.39	1.08	.97	1.59	.16	.56	1.73	2.85
Coerce	.00	.00	.03	.17	.00	.00	.00	.00	.00	.00	.02	.14
Comm. Ambig.	.64	1.69	2.44	3.60	.10	.36	.25	1.17	.09	.34	.58	1.21
Coerce Ambig.	.01	.10	.02	.14	.00	.00	.00	.00	.00	.00	.00	.00
Refuse	.39	1.02	.63	1.09	.07	.32	.21	.69	.02	.14	.39	.83
Neg. Nonverbal	.40	.98	1.61	2.68	.07	.29	.27	.73	.06	.34	.68	1.35
Physical Aggr.	.12	.35	.93	2.08	.01	.10	.05	.22	.00	.00	.52	1.38
Physical Attack	.01	.10	.09	.28	.00	.00	.00	.00	.00	.00	.00	.00
Noncomply	.64	1.25	1.40	1.92	.07	.25	.39	1.21	.04	.19	.66	1.37
Sum of Means	7.86		25.00		1.35		4.85		.64		8.48	
Mean Social Exchanges[a]	84.62		220.53		15.33		57.02		9.53		72.92	
% Aversive	9.3		11.3		8.8		8.5		6.7		11.6	

[a]Mean total frequency across settings.

1982, 1986a). Although we have not tested this relation in the current samples, these findings suggest that the problem child has a unique status with regard to parent–child exchanges.

Frequency. The findings summarized in Table 4.3 show that mothers in the clinical and at-risk samples engaged in about the same number of interactions and that the mean duration of the exchanges was approximately the same as for normal families. However, some dramatic differences are immediately apparent between the mothers in the two samples. Those in the clinical sample engaged in roughly twice as many aversive behaviors as did the mothers in the normal sample. In the clinical sample, approximately one maternal behavior in three was coded as aversive. The mothers differed most in their rates of Negative Verbal, Command Ambiguous, Negative Nonverbal, Physical Aggression, and Physical Attack.

The findings are consistent with the hypothesis that the mothers in both samples were more aversive than were their sons. The proportions of aversive behaviors for mothers and sons in the clinical sample were 31.1% and

16.3%, respectively; the comparable figures for mothers and sons in the at-risk sample were 16.5% and 10%, respectively. Obviously, mothers are actively involved in the coercion training that takes place in families with problem children. In fact, Patterson (1982) found that parents were involved in some aspect of 80% of problem children's aversive episodes.

Duration. The mean durations of aversive behaviors for mothers in the clinical sample were roughly twice those of their problem children and also twice those of mothers in the at-risk sample. In the at-risk sample, the mean durations for mothers were a little more than 1.5 times those of their children.

The descriptive data in Table 4.3 suggest that long chains of aversive interactions are initiated by verbal exchanges. The average durations for maternal Negative Verbal (116.17 seconds), Command (173.92), Command Ambiguous (81.15), and Noncomply (45.10) in the clinical sample all exceed the 18-second escalation threshold established by Reid, Patterson, and Loeber (1982) and Reid, Taplin, and Lorber (1981). It is easy to imagine a scene in which a mother issues one command after

Table 4.3
Mothers: Mean Frequency and Duration of Aversive Behaviors

FPC Categories	At-Risk Sample (N = 104)				Clinical Sample (N = 48)			
	Frequency		Duration		Frequency		Duration	
	Mean	SD	Mean	SD	Mean	SD	Mean	SD
Negative Verbal	17.97	16.73	68.78	68.33	29.98	19.60	116.17	85.48
Tease	3.66	4.59	12.27	15.88	2.40	3.22	8.48	11.09
Verbal Attack	1.89	3.28	8.13	13.60	1.90	2.56	7.52	9.19
Command	26.14	18.57	86.46	66.00	55.98	43.39	173.92	134.17
Coerce	.14	.47	1.00	3.43	.56	1.27	2.83	6.04
Command Ambiguous	12.17	10.42	44.85	38.56	23.63	20.38	81.15	64.09
Coerce Ambiguous	.26	.98	1.40	5.28	.40	.79	2.43	5.03
Refuse	2.63	2.45	7.36	7.81	—	—	—	—
Negative Nonverbal	2.32	3.04	7.92	10.84	6.48	5.82	10.60	15.49
Physical Aggression	.92	2.06	3.13	6.46	3.77	4.03	11.79	11.86
Physical Attack	.07	.60	.18	1.68	1.81	2.20	90.04	214.40
Noncomply	1.19	1.42	3.73	4.91	5.06	5.68	45.10	82.39
Sum of Means	69.36		245.21		131.97		550.03	
Mean Frequency[a]	418.84				423.77			
Mean Duration[b]			1529.76				1588.57	
% Aversive	16.5		16.0		31.1		35.1	

[a] Mean total frequency of interactions when mother was focus of observation.

[b] Mean total duration of interactions when mother was focus of observation.

another in a desperate attempt to control a child who is both noncompliant and argumentative. Mothers of normal children tend to issue one or two commands and then ignore the outcome if the issue is not important; when they are concerned about the outcome, they use an effective negative sanction to interrupt their children's ongoing behavior. In either case, the mothers' behavior reduces the likelihood that aversive interactions will continue. The most ominous finding presented in Table 4.3 is the extended duration of mothers' high-amplitude physical attacks. When the mothers in the clinical sample engaged in such behavior, it tended to persist for 90.04 seconds. The label *out of control* often is used to describe the behavior of antisocial children. Based on the findings presented here, it is the problem child who must learn to cope with an out-of-control parent.

Negative Affect

It can be argued that family members are more likely to respond to the negative affect than to the aversive content of one another's behavior. Gottman's recent work with children and married couples emphasizes the regula-

tion of negative emotion as a key issue for effective adjustment (Gottman, 1983; Gottman & Levenson, 1984).

Even in our earliest home observation studies, it was apparent that most aversive behaviors were performed reflexively and were accompanied by little discernible negative affect. These affectless irritable behaviors seemed to be inserted into interaction sequences like punctuation marks in a sentence. On the other hand, some families communicated negative affect through facial expressions or voice inflections even though the *content* of the interaction was coded as neutral. Before the FPC was developed, we could not investigate these different styles of using aversive behaviors. We assumed that although measures of aversive content and negative affect may covary, there also would be important differences among families that would contribute to our understanding of interaction sequences.

The FPC has allowed us to examine aversive exchanges in more detail. For each interaction, the observer rates the affect of the target person. A five-point scale is used to assign ratings to facial expressions, voice tone,

Table 4.4

Target Child: Mean Frequency and Duration of Negative Affect

| | At-Risk Sample (N = 104) | | | | Clinical Sample (N = 48) | | | |
| | Frequency | | Duration | | Frequency | | Duration | |
FPC Categories	Mean	SD	Mean	SD	Mean	SD	Mean	SD
Negative Verbal	5.55	6.48	22.60	30.10	11.08	13.52	38.38	45.39
Tease	.24	.76	.84	2.57	.52	1.22	1.63	3.56
Verbal Attack	.75	1.25	2.92	5.31	2.67	7.46	9.50	25.92
Command	1.56	2.12	5.86	7.77	4.40	6.62	16.21	23.71
Coerce	.02	.14	.12	.84	.08	.35	.40	1.76
Command Ambiguous	.88	1.70	3.01	5.45	2.00	3.28	6.85	10.90
Coerce Ambiguous	.00	.00	.00	.00	.04	.20	.23	1.12
Refuse	.48	.86	1.73	3.54	—	—	—	—
Negative Nonverbal	.81	1.48	2.61	4.59	2.44	4.21	8.48	14.54
Physical Aggression	.30	.71	1.36	3.30	1.10	1.70	4.85	10.93
Physical Attack	.00	.00	.00	.00	.02	.14	.02	.14
Noncomply	.20	.79	.66	2.15	.23	.81	.92	3.40
Sum of Means	10.79		41.71		24.58		87.47	
% Aversive	2.3		2.5		6.8		6.5	

and gestures. The ratings are coded as negative, neutral, or positive affect. The data in Table 4.4 summarize the frequency and duration of events coded as negative affect. The content may or may not have been coded as negative by the FPC. The data were taken from exchanges involving the target child. As might be expected, most of the negative events were verbal rather than physical. Only a small percentage of the child's interactions were classified as negative (2.3% for the at-risk sample and 6.8% for the clinical sample). Negative affect was associated with physical aggression more than three times as often in the clinical sample as in the at-risk sample.

The Structure of Social Behavior

We view reinforcement and punishment contingencies as primary determinants for the functional relations between social behaviors. Over time, such contingencies establish predictable interaction sequences. To examine these social interaction sequences, we must go back to the idea that an antecedent stimulus (Ai) immediately precedes a given response (Rj). When a response is reinforced, it increases the likelihood that the same antecedent will elicit the same response in the future. Because the probabilistic connections between one behavior and another tend to be small, the underlying *structure* can be difficult to detect.

Social behaviors have a web like structure that repre-

sents the probabilistic connections between the antecedents and responses. For example, Patterson (1982) studied boys from normal and clinical samples and found a web of nine behaviors of other family members that significantly increased the probability of teasing as a response. A five-strand web described the likelihood of hitting; there were three strands for the likelihood of disapproval. Several responses shared major components of the web of controlling stimuli and, in this sense, could be thought of as a class of functionally equivalent responses. Patterson (1985) found a similar structure for maternal behaviors. For example, each of three child behaviors (Noncomply, Hit, and Tease) exerted significant control over three maternal behaviors (Command, Command Negative, and Disapproval).

These structures impart a predictable quality to social exchanges. In fact, if a person's behavior is not predictable in this low-level sense, it is a cue that something is wrong. Patterson (1979b) reviewed studies of monkeys, peer groups, and families and found that the predictability of social interactions was relatively universal. In one study, knowing the behavior that immediately preceded the response accounted for 30% of the variance in predicting the next event in the sequence. In another study, 50% of the events shown to control children's behavior were found in the event that immediately preceded the sequence. These data indicate that people are delicately tuned in to their social environment. If a person reacts

47

Table 4.5

Means and Standard Deviations for Microsocial Variables
(Target Child's Reactions to Family Members)

more single parent

	Cohort I		Cohort II		Clinical Sample	
	Mean	SD	Mean	SD	Mean	SD
Child to Mother	(N = 97)		(N = 96)		(N = 48)	
Start-Up	.036	.026	.056	.053	.104	.062
Negative Synchronicity	.081	.081	.118	.102	.250	.127
Continuance	.076	.149	.121	.180	.103	.051
Child to Father	(N = 70)					
Start-Up	.030	.031	.047	.039	.041	.062
Negative Synchronicity	.079	.118	.095	.096	.086	.136
Continuance	.051	.146	.072	.155	.074	.091
Child to Siblings						
Start-Up	.042	.044	.055	.041	.067	.063
Negative Synchronicity	.103	.138	.128	.110	.126	.128
Continuance	.057	.132	.134	.194	.098	.120

more to his or her own inner thoughts and emotional states than to the social environment, that person is labeled as "schizoid" or deviant.

Antecedents, responses, and reactions to responses seem functionally related, but in what sense are these structures the outcomes of contingencies embedded in social interaction? Experimental studies have provided indirect evidence that the escape contingencies supplied by family members strengthened children's aversive or prosocial behaviors. Patterson (1982) summarized the findings from three sets of experiments that lend support to the hypotheses.

The key idea is that escape conditioning is the mechanism that generates the web structures that characterize so much of social interaction. Chapter 8 in *Coercive Family Process* presents a detailed discussion of these structures. Integrating the information from these web structures will build, in turn, the foundation for a microsocial theory of aggression.

The structure of coercive exchanges also can be defined using the structural variables of start-up, negative synchronicity, and continuance. These are discussed in the section that follows.

Structural Variables for the Coercion Process

As family members become involved in the coercion process, the basic structure of their interactions changes; the further they move into the process, the greater the

structural changes. Given that the changes follow a recognizable sequence, an analysis of the structures could function as a psychological litmus test that indicates how far a particular dyad has moved into the coercion process.

We believe that reinforcing contingencies alter both the *content* and *structure* of ongoing interaction sequences. For example, reinforcement might increase the likelihood that a child will whine (content); the same contingency also might increase the likelihood that the child will initiate negative contacts (structure) with the mother even though her interactions with the child are neutral or positive.

The structural changes produced by the coercion process can be defined by three variables: *start-up*, *negative synchronicity*, and *continuance*. The first two variables describe a reaction that is conditional on what the other person is doing. The third variable is an estimate of the likelihood that the person will continue to be aversive, regardless of the other person's behavior. The means and standard deviations for the three variables are summarized in Table 4.5.

Because we are interested in coercion, each structural variable includes a conditional probability value that involves an aversive behavior. If we were studying friendship, we might be interested in structural variables that would include an estimate of positive affect and prosocial behavior instead.

Start-Up. The first structural variable, start-up, is defined as the likelihood that one member of a dyad will initiate an aversive behavior when the other person is engaged in neutral or prosocial behavior. The data in Table 4.5 are based on the FPC, which records interaction sequences in real time. If the target person initiated an aversive behavior concurrently or during the six seconds following the other person's prosocial or neutral behavior, the reaction was classified as start-up.

Data from three samples were used to estimate the means and variances listed in Table 4.5. The at-risk samples included data collected at grade 4 from Cohorts I and II of the OYS and the clinical sample described earlier. We expected the clinical sample to demonstrate somewhat higher mean rates than the at-risk samples. Because we did not have a normal sample, no systematic comparisons were made. The means and variance estimates are intended to serve a purely descriptive function.

In all three samples, there was a trend for target boys to initiate more conflicts with their mothers than with their fathers. Patterson (1982) noted a similar trend in the comparisons of clinical and normal samples. Mothers were the preferred victims in the clinical sample, while victim preference was not as clear in the at-risk sample. This is in agreement with findings from earlier studies of *normal* families that showed no significant differences among family members in the likelihood of start-up (Patterson, 1982).

Why are mothers the preferred victims of start-up for target children in *distressed* families? We hypothesize that mothers in clinical samples are more likely to reinforce coercive attacks. In keeping with Herrnstein's (1961) formulation of the matching law, the relative frequency of start-up by the target child should match the relative frequency of maternal reinforcers for start-up. Patterson (1985) tested this hypothesis in analyses of home observation data. The study was based on a comparison of the relative frequency of conflicts between the target child and his mother and siblings. There was a very close match between the relative frequency of attacks and positive outcomes for attacks. The data are consistent with the idea that mothers provide more discriminative stimuli for start-up and a rich schedule of reinforcement when it does occur. Another possible explanation is that the child is more likely to read hostile intentions into his mother's behavior than into the behavior of other family members. Subtle nuances in the mother's behavior not detected by the coding system might be involved in the child's negative attributions.

In an analysis of the impact of residential treatment on aggressive boys, Raush (1965) found a significant decrease in the likelihood of aggressive acts after a friendly act by another person. This sequence fits our definition of start-up. Hahlweg, Reisner, Kohli, Vollmer, Schindler, and Revensdorf (1984) carried out an interesting comparison of pre- and posttreatment measures of start-up for distressed couples in marital therapy. The behavioral treatment effectively reduced the likelihood of fights being started; but once a fight began, it tended to run its course.

Negative synchronicity. The second structural variable, *negative synchronicity*, was designed to assess events that seem to keep things going. It is defined as the likelihood that a person will respond aversively immediately following the aversive behavior of the other member of the dyad. This variable has been useful in the assessment of social exchanges in studies of both marital conflict (Gottman, 1979; Hahlweg et al., 1984) and children with conduct disorders (Patterson, 1982).

Aversive behaviors occur occasionally in every relationship, but they usually are isolated events that are deflected or ignored by the other person. Even in clinical samples, coercive overtures usually do not lead to more conflict. In fact, they are ignored roughly 90% of the time. These nonsynchronous reactions are essential for having close, nondefensive relationships.

The other person's negative synchronous reaction is what determines whether simple aversive overtures become active conflicts. Nondistressed married couples (Gottman, 1979, 1980; Margolin, 1977) and families (Patterson, 1982; Snyder, 1977) tend to let most aversive overtures go by. In clinical samples, however, there is a significant risk that the other person will respond in kind to an aversive overture. The probability of negative synchronous reactions also differentiates distressed families from normal families. In previous studies of normal families, mothers and siblings were more likely than fathers to react in a negative synchronous fashion to the target child (Patterson, 1982); a comparative analyses showed that members of clinic-referred families were roughly *twice as likely* as members of normal families to react in a negative synchronous fashion (Patterson, 1982). The data for both cohorts in Table 4.5 show only moderate differences among family members in negative synchronous reactions.

The findings for marital interactions are similar. Distressed married couples were significantly more likely than their normal counterparts to engage in negative synchronicity (Gottman, 1979). In fact, Gottman found that an aversive behavior by one spouse can significantly alter the other spouse's *next four reactions*. This ripple effect was replicated by Margolin and Wampold (1981); they showed a significant reciprocity for negative events at lag one and lag two for distressed couples, but not for nondistressed couples. They also found a significant correlation between reciprocity for negative events and self-reports of marital satisfaction.

Continuance. The third variable describes the likelihood that once a person reacts aversively, he or she will continue to be aversive regardless of the other person's reaction. *Continuance* is an action–action variable. In keeping with Reid (1986), continuance represents an extended coercive chain and therefore is associated with an increased risk of escalation. We also assume that families characterized by high rates of continuance are further into the coercion process than are families that exhibit lower rates of continuance.

The following would be an example of continuance as recorded by FPC data: The target person yells at Time 1 and then either yells again or engages in some other aversive behavior at Time 2. The denominator for continuance is the frequency of the target person's aversive actions toward another specified person. The numerator is the frequency of episodes in which one aversive behavior is immediately followed by another.

The findings in Table 4.5 show that when the target child was aversive at Time 1, the likelihood that he would continue to be aversive at Time 2 was 7% to 10% for the clinical sample and 5% to 13% for the at-risk samples. Patterson (1982) showed that continuance was significantly more likely for clinical samples than for normal samples. The risk for continuance is greatest when the target child is interacting with his mother and siblings and least when he is interacting with his father. This was also the case in earlier studies.

A Progression in Structure?

When all of the structural variables are products of the same underlying process, they might form a transitive progression from most frequent to least frequent. If the various points along this progression can be identified, they could be used to define a family's movement into the coercion process (i.e., families further along on the progression are further into the process). The more extreme structural variables should covary with the high-amplitude, low-baserate products of the coercion process such as physical attack.

Data from three home observation sessions collected at grade 4 served as the data base to test the progression hypothesis. The data were analyzed separately for Cohorts I and II in a replication design. The coercion model emphasizes the joint contribution of the mother and siblings in training the target child to use coercive behaviors. For this reason, the analysis included only those families in which the siblings of the target child were at least 3 years old. The resulting sample sizes were 86 for Cohort I and 82 for Cohort II. The baserate values showed that 71% of the boys in Cohort I and 73% in Cohort II initiated one or more start-ups. In both cohorts, approximately 50% of the boys engaged in a negative synchronous reaction and 36% in a continuance; approximately 20% were observed engaging in physical aggression.

Assuming that these events form a transitive progression in which all of the boys who practiced the least frequent reactions also performed the most frequent reactions (earlier in the progression), the majority of boys who

hit also should engage in continuance, negative synchronicity, and start-up. A strong test of the transitivity hypothesis requires a longitudinal study of younger subjects who are just entering the coercion process. The hypothesis implies a developmental sequence that unfolds over time. Because we do not have such a data set, the following analyses are presented more for illustrative purposes than for hypothesis testing. At this time, the transitivity question can be answered only indirectly. First, we must determine whether knowing that some boys are characterized by all three structural variables provides a better basis for prediction than just knowing the baserate value for hitting. In Cohort I, 56% of the boys who hit also engaged in start-up, negative synchronicity, and continuance. The baserate for hitting was .21. The findings for Cohort II were comparable.

If a child is at a particular stage in the progression, what is the likelihood that he arrived there by way of the previous stage? As shown in Figure 4.2, more than 80% of the boys in the negative synchronicity stage also engaged in start-up (subtract the probability of an alternate path from 100%). Roughly 60% of the boys who engaged in continuance also engaged in negative synchronicity. Approximately one-half to two-thirds of the fighters also engaged in continuance. The findings are consistent with the idea of a transitive progression.

A regular sequence of steps seems to lead to physical aggression. High-amplitude aggression in families is an important issue for several reasons. Straus (1978) commented that "the family [is] the most violent of all civilian institutions" (pp. 450–451). His findings for a national probability sample showed that 28% of couples engaged in violent acts during interactions with each other. In fact, self-report data indicated that wives engaged in violent acts *more often* than did their husbands; over a 12-month period, 3.8% of the wives reported one or more physical attacks against their spouses (e.g., throwing objects, slapping). Women are reported to be as aggressive as men in these studies, but their aggression results in fewer injuries. Presumably, this parity is the result of the coercion process itself; there seem to be no gender differences in terms of being controlled by the coercion mechanism.

In the analysis of a clinical sample, Patterson (1985) showed that 48% of the target children's hitting was directed at male siblings, 20% at female siblings, 23% at mothers, and 9% at fathers. This was in direct contrast to the findings from a normal sample in which more than 90% of the target children's hitting was directed at siblings.

Convergence

As discussed earlier, Guttman (1944) postulated that if a progression were found, the variables that defined it would be the products of a single underlying process or dimension. If the structural variables form a progression,

Figure 4.2

A Progression for Structural Variables

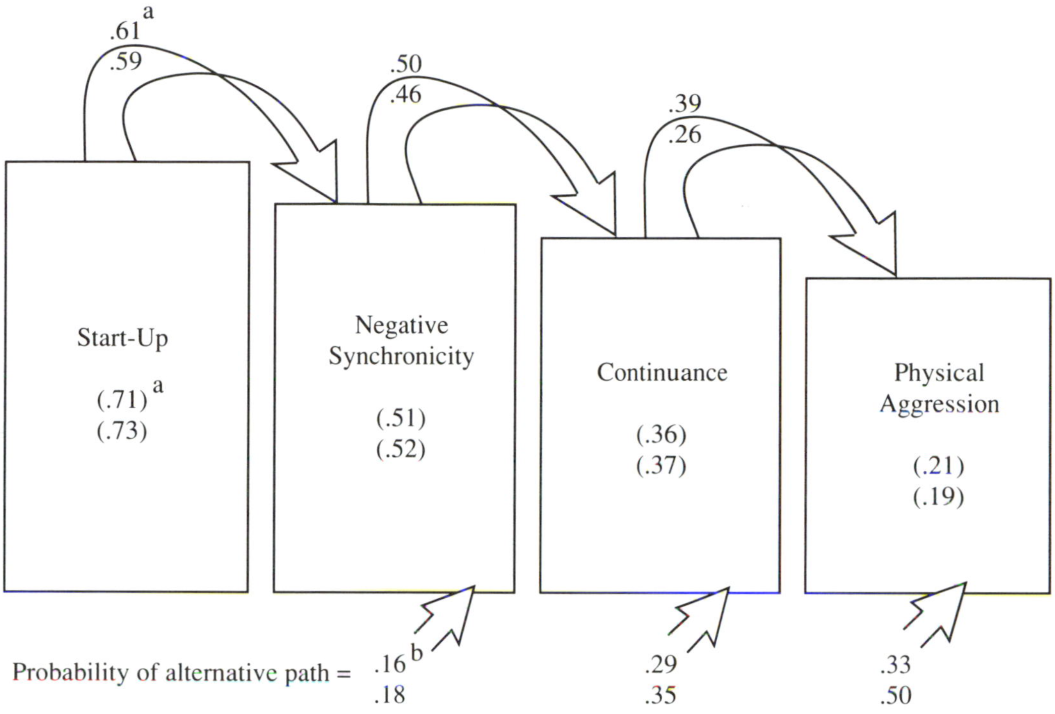

.61[a]
.59

.50
.46

.39
.26

| Start-Up (.71)[a] (.73) | Negative Synchronicity (.51) (.52) | Continuance (.36) (.37) | Physical Aggression (.21) (.19) |

Probability of alternative path = .16[b]   .29   .33
.18   .35   .50

[a] The baserate of occurrence for the target behavior for Cohorts I (upper values) and II (lower values).

[b] The probability values for Cohorts I (upper values) and II (lower values).

---

then they also must intercorrelate, that is, form a single cluster or factor. Of course, convergence by itself is not a test for the presence of a single underlying process, but a failure to converge indicates that the progression is flawed.

The correlational findings for the target child's reactions to his mother, father, and siblings are summarized in Table 4.6 for Cohorts I and II combined. The correlations show convergence; the variables form a reasonably well-delineated cluster that describes the boys' reactions to mothers, siblings, and fathers. The target child's reactions to his mother, father, and siblings constitute a low-level generalized trait (or style) for coping with family members.

Theory Building

To understand children's antisocial behavior, we may need to develop two theories: one at a microsocial level and the other at a macrosocial level. At a microsocial level, it is necessary to demonstrate that the reinforcing

contingencies found in natural settings account for most of the variance in children's antisocial behavior. At a macrosocial level, parenting practices are thought to control the reinforcing contingencies. Therefore, it should be possible to build a theory of antisocial behavior that is concerned only with the effect of parenting practices on children's behavior. In a sense, the data from the microsocial theory would explain why the macrosocial model of parenting works. For example, we assume that information about the relative rates of reinforcement and punishment for coercion could account for the magnitude of the path coefficient from the Discipline construct to the Child Antisocial construct.

Building a microsocial model would require a substantial data set based on observations at home and at school. We are attempting to build the macrosocial model first because the data can be collected at relatively low cost. Notice, however, that even the macrosocial parent training model presented in Chapter 5 requires some observation data. Our long-term goal is to develop two parallel theories that define the relation between microsocial and

Table 4.6

Intercorrelations Among Indicators of Microsocial Structure for Boy's Reactions to Family Members (Cohorts I and II Combined)

	Boy to Mother			Boy to Father			Boy to Siblings		
	Start-Up	Neg. Syn.	Contin.	Start-Up	Neg. Syn.	Contin.	Start-Up	Neg. Syn.	Contin.
Boy to Mother									
Start-Up	1.0								
Negative Synch.	.54***	1.0							
Continuance	.46***	.46***	1.0						
Boy to Father									
Start-Up	.45***	.20**	.15*	1.0					
Negative Synch.	.33***	.06	.05*	.50***	1.0				
Continuance	.29***	.14	.15	.38***	.67***	1.0			
Boy to Siblings									
Start-Up	.26***	.16	.31***	.37**	.43***	.40***	1.0		
Negative Synch.	.32***	.25***	.23***	.27***	.12*	.07	.23***	1.0	
Continuance	.29***	.16*	.29***	.28***	.19*	.20*	.36***	.57	1.0

$*p < .05$ $**p < .01$ $***p < .001$

---

macrosocial variables. It probably will take another decade of studies to achieve that goal. In the meantime, we have assembled enough pieces of the macrosocial model to know what it is and evaluate its utility.

Four Theories of Aggressive Behavior

The prevailing theories that have been developed to account for human behavior are based on laboratory analogues. None of them, however, has been able to explain adequately or to predict how specific behaviors work in the real world. The four most plausible contenders for a theory of aggression are: *cognition*, *imitation*, *frustration*, and *contingency*. Cognitive models of antisocial behavior are based on the assumption that crimes are the result of social cognitions about relative payoffs (Wilson & Herrnstein, 1985) or negative attributions about people in the social environment (Dodge, 1980). Bandura (1973) argued that children learn aggressive behavior by imitating aggressive models. The venerable frustration–aggression theory (Dollard, Doob, Miller, Mowrer, & Sears, 1939) has the longest history of the four. Our position is based on Skinner's (1969) theory that all social behaviors, including antisocial acts, are controlled by immediate contingencies. Each of the four theories is appealing in its own way and has its own tradition of laboratory studies. The findings for each theory support the mechanisms thought to be determinants for aggres-

sion. The question is, does each analogue also work in natural settings?

The first requirement in evaluating such theories is to find a way to measure the incidences of cognition, imitation, frustration, and contingencies in natural settings. Dodge (1980) developed an analogue procedure for measuring children's cognitions and attributions about aggressive behavior. Efforts to code imitation in natural settings have not been successful. Fawl (1963) has developed a method for coding frustration events in natural settings. Currently, several investigators have built observational coding systems to measure the contingencies for children's antisocial behaviors in natural settings.

The second requirement is to demonstrate that measures of cognition, frustration, imitation, and contingency covary with adequate measures of aggression in children. Fawl's (1963) measures of observed frustrations did not covary with observed aggression. Dodge, Bates, and Pettit (1990) have demonstrated that measures of social cognition correlate with future measures of aggression. The data outlined in this chapter show a similar successful effort to correlate reinforcement schedules with the strength of aggressive responses. Later chapters in this volume offer strong support for the idea that specific parenting practices are correlated with children's aggressive behavior. Even at the correlational level, only two of the original analogue theories are viable.

The third requirement is to conduct *in vivo* experiments to show that manipulating reinforcing contingencies or the child's negative attributions will produce changes in aggression. The manipulations would be clinical trials in which the child's attributions and cognitive processes are changed or the parent alters the reinforcing contingencies. The extensive review by Kazdin (1985) showed that experiments involving the manipulation of social cognitions have not been successful in reducing aggressive behavior in the natural environment. The cognitive processes change, but the aggressive behavior does not. The review by Kazdin (1985) and Wilson and Herrnstein (1985) did show that training parents to alter reinforcing contingencies does produce predictable changes in aggressive behavior.

A Microsocial Theory of Children's Aggression

This section examines how negative reinforcement relates to measures of aggressive response strength. Specifically, the microsocial theory should explain why some aggressive responses occur more often than others (i.e., it should account for variance associated with differences among responses). It also should account for differences among individuals in the rates at which they perform aggressive behaviors.

Differences among aversive responses. Why are most children more likely to argue or disapprove than they are to hit? We believe that children are most likely to use the response that works the best. The utility of the response should be determined by the likelihood of negative reinforcement, positive reinforcement, and punishment. So far, we have examined primarily the contribution of negative reinforcement to the differences in response strength.

The studies reviewed by Patterson (1982) showed that the hierarchy of antisocial responses for an individual are surprisingly stable across settings. This suggests that the most frequent response should have the highest density of negative reinforcement, and the least frequent response should have the lowest density. For each individual, it would be possible to rank aggressive responses by baserates and the density of negative reinforcement. Then we could either correlate the rankings separately for each individual and take the mean or take the mean of the rankings and correlate that. This approach would not be influenced by the fact that the overall level of reinforcement for one individual might be 10 times the level of reinforcement for another.

Patterson (1979b) examined data for the seven coercive responses previously shown to fit a Guttman scalogram progression. The correlation between the ranking for rate and the ranking for reinforcement was .59 (N.S.) for one sample and .93 ($p < .05$) for the other. A comparable analysis was carried out for the OYS data collected with the new code. Response strength was defined by the baserates for the target child's coercive reactions to all other family members. The rank order correlation between the rankings for response rate and reinforcement density was .90 ($p < .05$).

These findings are consistent with the hypothesis that the antisocial acts with the highest rate of payoff occur most frequently. However, the findings also lead to new questions. For example, why is there more than one form of antisocial behavior? The simplest model of reinforcement econometrics would predict that the individual will always use the antisocial response with the highest payoff. We suspect that future studies will demonstrate that context determines which response works best. In settings such as the playground, for example, the preferred response to being pushed may be hitting because it produces a better outcome. At home, siblings involved in a conflict may find that whining produces a better outcome than does hitting. We need to study the relation between settings and payoff utilities. Until we do this, there will be a fundamental sense in which we do not truly understand aggression.

The Snyder technique. Snyder (1987b) used an elegant design to account for differences among a single child's social behaviors as they related to one kind of positive reinforcement provided by the mother. The same design could be applied to study the effects of positive and negative reinforcement for aversive behaviors. Snyder's first study was based on more than 20 hours of observation data collected from a single dyad. He analyzed the web of responses controlled by each of seven stimuli presented by the mother. For example, maternal *negative verbal stimuli* were followed by any one of nine child reactions. However, the analyses showed that only three child reactions were *reliably* controlled by this single maternal antecedent.

Next, Snyder calculated the likelihood that the mother would provide a positive consequence for each reaction to the antecedent. Like Watson (1979), he described the likelihood of a reinforcer being contingent on the target response. He directly compared this to the likelihood that the same class of reinforcers was contingent on all other responses. This is a variation on Herrnstein's (1961) *matching law*, which is based on the assumption that the child tends to match his or her actions to whatever the environment offers. In other words, the response that works best in that setting is used the most. Snyder reported a correlation of .82 between the relative strength of the nine responses and their relative rates of positive consequences. For example, child *compliance* was the behavior most likely to elicit a positive reaction from the mother; it was also the response most likely to occur. For each of the controlling stimuli, the child matched the relative occurrence of his or her behaviors to the relative payoffs provided by the mother.

Snyder is currently making a comparable analysis of the effect of negative reinforcers. His work illustrates what could be accomplished by the next generation of studies. He also has developed a technique for demonstrating that in a natural setting reinforcers affect the future probability that the response will occur given the same stimulus (Snyder & Patterson, 1986). Again, this procedure requires large amounts of observation data.

Snyder's techniques make it possible to systematically delineate the web of antecedents that control children's aversive behaviors. They also can be used to identify the consequences that are functionally related to these responses. Analyses such as these are necessary to explain differences among baserates for antisocial responses.

Differences among children. Why is one child more aggressive than another? The coercion model provides two different ways to approach this question. One approach examines individual differences in relative payoffs for aggression, and the other examines individual differences in the density of stimuli that control aggressive behavior.

Snyder and Patterson (1986) collected intensive data in the homes for a small sample of children. For each child, the relative likelihood was calculated both for payoffs for deviant behavior and for the relative likelihood that deviant behavior would occur. The correlation between the two variables was .73! Boys who received the highest relative payoffs were more likely to perform deviant than prosocial behaviors. This is striking confirmation for a microsocial theory of children's aggression. Children are delicately tuned in to their social environment and learn to match their behaviors to the contingencies provided by those around them.

It follows that children receiving massive reinforcement for aggression would come under the control of an array of discriminative stimuli. If the strength of the connection between the network of stimuli and the behavior were known, then the density of occurrence for these stimuli should provide a basis for predicting individual differences. The child with the strongest web and the most frequently occurring controlling stimuli would be the highest rate aggressor.

The density of controlling stimuli also should explain why a particular child is more aggressive on one day than another. Thus far, only one study has examined this hypothesis. Extensive observations were carried out for a single subject before and after treatment. The baseline data (50 sessions) showed the expected covariation between the density of controlling stimuli and rates of aggression (Patterson, 1979c). The density of controlling stimuli accounted for 37% of the day-to-day variations in antisocial behavior. After a parent training treatment program, the analyses of observation data from 22 sessions showed that *fewer* antecedents reliably controlled aversive child behaviors (Patterson, 1973). Furthermore, the events that did control aversive behaviors occurred less often. As the density of controlling stimuli was reduced, the overall rate of the child's aversive behavior also was reduced.

The work completed thus far shows that, in principle, a microsocial reinforcement theory could be constructed that would explain differences among children in their aggressiveness *and* differences among aggressive responses. The current findings offer strong support for a contingency-based theory of aggression.

Aversive Events and Adult Pathology

The coercion mechanism seems to be implicated in a wide range of adult pathology. For example, aversive events embedded in family interaction seem to play a significant role in the maintenance of marital conflict, adult depression, and schizophrenia. This section briefly examines the hypothesis that escape- and avoidance-conditioning mechanisms relate to some of the behaviors of disturbed adults and their family members.

Aversive behaviors are a ubiquitous feature of the social environment. Although some people are exposed to higher rates of aversive events than others, everyone must learn to deal with the unpleasant intrusions of others in some way. It requires a high level of skill to deflect or minimize the impact of these events. Some individuals find themselves in situations in which the skills they possess are no match for the daily flood of aversive events, and they resort to extreme measures. Over time, their coping behaviors may become so salient that they are given clinical labels such as depressive, schizophrenic, and so forth.

Maternal Depression

The stress and aversive events that are part of family life take their greatest toll on mothers, who often are directly in the line of fire. At least a dozen longitudinal studies have shown that the first year or two after the birth of a child is associated with maternal depression (Patterson, 1980). Even under the best conditions (i.e., normal mother, intact family, normal infant), raising an infant exposes the mother to massive increases in aversive events and reductions in positive reinforcement. This seems to be a well-kept secret, or perhaps it is considered unimportant because most adults have accepted the fact that parents must endure a high density of aversive events while they are raising infants and young children.

A normal mother will experience a mildly aversive event about once every three minutes when she is interacting with family members; the rates are even higher for mothers with young children or large families. Even young housewives *without* children report several unpleasant experiences each day with their husbands; again, most of these are trivial. However, they also report that more serious conflicts occur about once a week. In addition, families experience recurring nonsocial stressors at a rate of approximately two per week, such as car trouble and bills that cannot be paid (Patterson & Forgatch, 1990a). We think it is the daily round of aversive events, punctuated by minor daily conflicts and major weekly conflicts, that lead twice as many mothers as fathers to report being depressed.

The social interactional analysis of adult depression was initiated by Coyne (1976). He showed that interacting with depressed adults on the telephone led to significant increases in self-report ratings of hostility, anxiety, and depression. The ratings also implied rejection of the depressed person. These findings strongly suggest that depressive behaviors have a significant impact on others in the social environment.

Hops, Biglan, Sherman, Arthur, Friedman, and Osteen (1987) and Hops, Sherman, and Biglan (1990) demonstrated that depressive behavior also may be *functional* in that it has a significant impact on the social environment. These researchers hypothesized that depressed mothers live in families characterized by high levels of aversive events. Hops et al. (1987) cited four sets of findings, including their own, that were consistent with this hypothesis. In all of the studies, husbands were more negative in their marital interactions if their wives were depressed. Home observations for the same samples showed higher rates of children's aversive behaviors in families with depressed mothers.

Although it seems likely that family members would be negative and irritable in response to depressive behaviors, Hops et al. (1990) showed quite the reverse. Maternal behaviors coded as depressive were significantly more likely to be followed by a *reduction* in negative–aversive behaviors by family members. It appears that a depressed individual is less likely to be the target of familial discontent, at least during the intervals immediately following depressive behaviors.

These findings can be interpreted in several ways. We initially thought this was an example of escape conditioning, but that formulation did not seem to fit the data. Hops et al. (1987) showed that mothers were *less likely* to exhibit depressive behaviors following the negative–aversive behaviors of family members. In a negative reinforcement arrangement, we would expect to find that depressive behaviors were more likely to follow aversive events than were nondepressive behaviors. A more viable interpretation is that these sequences represent avoidance conditioning. For example, depressive reactions might suppress negative intrusions by others, which would increase the interval between negative intrusions. The longer the reprieve, the greater the reinforcement effect. To date, this possibility has not been tested.

Aversive events play another role in maternal depression. Forgatch, Patterson, and Duncan (1990) conducted systematic studies of the effects of aversive events on problem solving and the relation of disrupted problem solving to the maintenance of depression. They found that irritable single mothers tend to select friends who also are irritable. When these irritable dyads were observed in a problem-solving situation, the outcome was poor. In addition, limited problem-solving skills were directly related to increased depression and indirectly related to further stress and loss of support.

Evidence suggests that aversive events are intimately related to both the initiation *and* maintenance of maternal depression. The beginning of the depression process appears to be somewhat different for mothers from intact families than for single mothers. For mothers and fathers from intact families, financial problems and ill health or a death in the family were associated with depression (Patterson, 1991b). For single mothers, the antecedent seems to be the conflicts surrounding separation, and the situation is exacerbated for a year or two by financial problems and loss of support (Patterson & Forgatch, 1990b).

In conclusion, it seems that aversive events are the key to understanding the onset of depression. The findings also suggest that depressive behaviors may be functional in that they are a means for controlling a chaotic and aversive social environment.

Schizophrenic Adults

We hypothesize that aversive events play an important role in the development of schizophrenia and that the aversive behaviors of family members is significantly related to recidivism for treated schizophrenic adults.

The general consensus is that if one parent is schizophrenic, the likelihood that the child will develop a schizophrenic condition is roughly .10; if both parents are schizophrenic, the likelihood is still not significant (roughly .20). Why are these probability values so low? We hypothesize that the effect of genetic risk is much greater if family interactions are characterized by extremely high rates of aversive behavior. Rodnick and Garmezy (1957) and others have suggested that schizophrenic individuals are particularly disrupted by the aversive reactions of others. The most compelling data set describes the functional relation between a high density of aversive behavior in the family and recidivism for schizophrenic adults. Several very different measures of aversive family interactions have shown such variables to be significantly related to increased risk for either exacerbation of schizophrenic symptoms or relapse (Doane, Falloon, Goldstein, & Mintz, 1985; Leff & Vaughan, 1985; Vaughan & Leff, 1981).

Because consistent findings have been reported by different investigators using a variety of measures, the hypothesized covariation seems quite robust. One possible explanation is that the schizophrenic individual causes an increase in aversive family interactions, and this forces the family to return the individual to the hospital. However, the studies by Doane et al. (1985) refuted this hypothesis. These researchers randomly assigned families of stabilized, medicated schizophrenic patients to intensive individual therapy or experimental group therapy. Family members in group therapy were given extensive information about the course of schizophrenia. They also were taught behavioral approaches to problem solving and communication skills that were designed to reduce their aversive interactions with the patient (Falloon, 1988). All of the families selected for the study had been shown to have high rates of aversive interactions, and the risk of recidivism for the schizophrenic patients was therefore very high. The results showed that problem-solving skills were significantly altered for the experimental subjects but not for the control subjects. The changes were accompanied by a steady decline in schizophrenic symptoms for the family therapy group but not for the comparison group. The patients in the experimental group doubled the amount of time they spent engaging in constructive social activities; the family members also reported increased satisfaction with the patients. The results of this experimental study offer strong support for the hypothesis that high rates of aversive behavior directed at the schizophrenic patient by family members aggravate his or her clinical condition, and reduced rates are associated with a better prognosis.

Although our clinical experience with adult schizophrenics is limited, it seems possible that schizophrenic behavior may be functional in terms of directing family interactions. The behavior may be maintained by escape and avoidance contingencies in much the same way as are children's aggressive behavior. Extensive, fine-grained observations of family interactions are not currently available, so the hypothesis is entirely speculative. The schizophrenic distancing and strange talk may "turn off" the relentless intrusions by irritable family members. This would increase the likelihood that the schizophrenic behavior would occur again in the same situation in the future. This hypothesis suggests that aversive behaviors of family members increase the likelihood of an immediate schizophrenic reaction.

Only careful microsocial analyses will determine the extent to which such mechanisms can be generalized to the full range of adult pathology and perhaps certain prosocial behaviors as well. We are convinced that examining the role of aversive events in social exchanges from the escape–avoidance perspective will prove to be a powerful analytic tool. For example, Gottman (1981) described the techniques that skilled married couples use to *soothe* each other. If a spouse makes an irritable initiation, the other person has learned how to respond to terminate the behavior. In effect, escape-conditioning arrangements may strengthen behaviors such as soothing that build satisfactory adult relationships.

The studies reviewed in this section emphasize the importance of regulating the aversive behaviors and negative emotions that occur in daily life. Increases in the density of aversive events place everyone in the immediate social environment at risk for exposure to escape and avoidance contingencies that may produce outcomes that are both dramatic and disruptive.

Implications of the Cognitive Revolution

In the last decade, we have witnessed what has been called the cognitive revolution. This has been accompanied by renewed interest in the study of cognitive processes. The revolution also has generated new data and concepts about the nature of human rationality. The implications of these new developments for the social interactional perspective are discussed in the section that follows.

The idea that aversive family exchanges represent overlearned patterns has important implications for how we think about the role of social cognitions in human behavior. Coercive patterns are analogous to the overlearned behavior of the musician or the highly trained athlete. The events in the patterns are performed too quickly to be mediated by cognitive processes. As we shall see in the discussion that follows, the concept of overlearned behavior highlights the differences between the social cognitive and social interactional perspectives.

The Limits of Rationality

Our Aristotelian heritage reifies the idea that human beings are rational decision makers. In fact, the concept of the rational man is the capstone of our legal, educational, and religious beliefs. Rational thinking is considered a natural state, and any deviation from it is attributed to conflict, unconscious processes, or disruptions resulting from biological or learned motives (Dawes, 1976, 1981). According to this view, negative affect disrupts rational processes such as family problem solving (Forgatch, 1989). However, the picture of human nature that is now emerging suggests that *even under ideal conditions, human rational capacities are quite limited.* Dawes (1976) concluded that:

> Our cognitive limitations are greater than we believe them to be, that we insist in the face of contradictory evidence that we can do more than we do…. Not only may dysfunction and conflict arise from cognitive limitations, therefore, but our inability to grasp the role of such limitations may itself result from our limited cognitive capacity…. To paraphrase: Conscious judgment — as opposed to automatic processing based on vast experience — is feeble. Yet it is precisely this sort of feeble conscious processing on which most people rely when attempting to solve most interpersonal and intrapersonal problems. This

feebleness alone — without the help of motivational factors — may account for many of our disasters. (pp. 10–11)

The studies reviewed by Dawes (1976, 1981) included those from behavior-decision theory, which is a relatively new field. Slovic, Fischhoff, and Lichtenstein (1977) showed that under conditions of uncertainty, the decision-making processes of most individuals do not follow Bayesian processes. In study after study, people consistently violated the principles of rational decision making. This is only one dimension of the limitations in human cognitive capacity. A more fundamental limitation is the inability to track and remember the myriad of complex stimuli that impinge upon us at any given moment. It is possible to process only a few channels of information at the same time (Howard, 1983; Reed, 1982). Given the complexity of most social interaction sequences, the limitations in tracking and memory force each individual to be selective about what he or she attends to. For example, the observation study by Reid (1978) showed that 2,400 events were recorded per hour for a family dyad! This figure illustrates the complexity of ongoing social interaction even in simple settings such as the home. How much of this avalanche of input does a parent attend to and commit to long-term memory? It could only be a tiny portion at best.

Automatic Processing

In a discussion of automatic processing, Howard (1983) suggested that some overlearned activities, such as driving a car or walking, require very little access to working memory. Howard stated:

> Complex motor skills are particularly obvious examples. For the adult, driving, typing, and playing tennis all require controlled processing at first try…. After varying degrees of practice, many components of these skills seem to become automatic…. For the person who has been driving for many years, it is easy to carry on a conversation while driving as long as no emergencies arise…. Such development of automaticity doesn't only occur for motor skills…[it also] develops even for extremely complex tasks. (pp. 83–84)

Kanfer (1987) and Langer (1984) underscored the importance of this concept as it applies to the complex matrix of social interaction. They both pointed out that controlled cognitive processing is most likely to occur in the early stages of learning, and they postulated that the amount of attention (or awareness) required is directly related to the amount of experience we have had with an activity. Langer concluded that most complex social behavior involves relatively little attentional capacity. Our position is in accord with Langer, and both positions differ markedly from the stand taken by cognitive behaviorists such as Bandura (1985), who stated: "People are not simply reactors to their immediate environment or steered by remnants of the past. Most of their behavior, being purposeful, is under forethought control." (p. 87).

During the past decade, social psychologists have shown that even in carefully controlled laboratory studies in which the complexity of stimuli was restricted, subjects' self-reports about the immediate causes of (and changes in) their behavior were surprisingly distorted (Wilson & Nisbett, 1978). Although the subjects may have let many events slip by unnoticed, when asked about the events they could nevertheless construct a causal theory about them.

Because events that occur during automatic processing do not require access to memory, most of the details concerning such ongoing social interactions do not find their way into long-term memory. We have emphasized that aversive exchanges in families represent overlearned coercive patterns. These patterns are an important part of each family member's repertoire of behaviors. Because the aversive chains are overlearned, they can be performed automatically. When asked to describe what happens in exchanges with other family members, a parent or child is not able to produce an accurate account of past events. His or her reports are intriguing examples of heuristic and representational thinking, rather than an accurate account of past events (Nisbett & Wilson, 1977; Tversky & Kahneman, 1974). This means that the usefulness of traditional interview and questionnaire forms of assessment may be extremely limited for understanding microsocial exchanges among family members. For example, we have consistently found that parents are not able to accurately describe their discipline practices in interviews.

Tversky and Kahneman (1974) described the heuristics that individuals use to reduce complex processing problems to simplified judgmental operations. Like Nisbett and Wilson (1977), they emphasized that many of the details of incoming information simply are not processed. In other words, individuals often form judgments about social exchanges without processing all of the information. Instead, they tend to use simplifying heuristics that provide a basis for making complex judgments about social behavior. However, as Tversky and Kahneman pointed out, each of these heuristics may carry a unique set of biases.

Changes in Coercive Behavior Without Awareness

Much of the ebb and flow of conditional probability values that describe shifts in response rates or the likelihood of reinforcement and punishment is *permanently lost* (i.e., it is not tracked and stored in long-term memory in the first place). Our hypothesis is that the contingencies associated with the coercion process are embedded in social interaction sequences that simply are not processed for the most part. A computer analysis of the outcome of these contingencies would reveal the day-to-day shift in probability values for $p(R_j|A_i)$. However, it is doubtful that the individual would be able to report daily shifts or monthly trends, even if the probability values changed dramatically from one point in time to another.

We assume that the effects of reinforcement and punishment contingencies found in family interaction sequences are *automatic*, that is, they are not necessarily mediated by thoughts or expectations. This is in contrast to the position taken by Bandura (1981). In the verbal conditioning studies of the 1960s, two people were placed in a room in which there was little activity aside from an occasional "uh-huh" or "good" from the experimenter. As Nisbett and Wilson (1977) pointed out, those studies seemed to be designed to elicit accurate reports by subjects about reinforcing contingencies. Our assumption is that the complexity of coercive exchanges in natural settings places severe restrictions on the ability of the participants to accurately track and report on the ongoing stream of events.

This position is supported by the findings from double-agent studies, in which reinforcing contingencies are manipulated to effectively alter behavior. In each instance, carefully designed interview probes carried out at the end of the sessions failed to show a correlation between awareness of the contingencies and changes in behavior. The reason for the lack of awareness in such studies is that the reinforcers are embedded in ongoing social interaction (Gewirtz & Boyd, 1977; Rosenfeld & Baer, 1969). It should be noted that these findings are based on only a small number of subjects. We need to know more about the variables involved in the double-agent effect. For example, a recent effort to extend the earlier findings to 12 new subjects showed that the contingencies used in that study produced experimental control for only half of the subjects and incomplete control for the other half (Rosenfeld & Gunnell, 1985).

Some social learning theorists (e.g., Bandura, 1985; Dodge, Pettit, McClaskey, & Brown, 1986) postulate that internal cognitions play a central mediational and causal role in determining how the behavior of one person is functionally related to the behavior of others. In the case of maladaptive or destructive behavior such as depressive or antisocial patterns, it is assumed that the individual is making wrong decisions because he or she has failed to process information about ongoing interactions correctly. In his *information-processing model* of social behavior, Dodge argues that antisocial individuals have a paranoid bias. This means that ambiguous initiations from others tend to be perceived as threats, which justifies a counterattack. The implicit (and often explicit) assumption is that the cognitive functioning of such an individual is malfunctioning. Given this assumption, the focus of treatment should be on the antisocial individual's faulty information processing and inability to make correct decisions.

We are not convinced that antisocial children process information about social interactions incorrectly. Indeed, it appears that their cognitions are an accurate representation of their social experiences. Most socially aggressive boys live with parents who initiate negative interactions (start-up) with them at more than twice the rate of parents with well-socialized boys. Siblings initiate negative exchanges with these boys at more than three times the rate of siblings of well-socialized boys (Patterson, 1982). In school, the peer group systematically rejects the antisocial boy (Dodge, 1980). Even when an antisocial boy is taught to reduce his negative behavior toward peers, there is little change in the rate at which his peers direct negative behavior toward him (Bierman, Miller, & Stabb, 1987). The paranoia of the aggressive boy reported by Dodge may not be paranoia at all, but an accurate cognitive representation of the way his peers react to him and his response to those reactions.

We agree with Bandura (1985) that repeated exposure to success experiences will give the antisocial child a sense of self-efficacy about the power of positive social behavior. However, changing the child's cognitive processes would require an environment that consistently provided positive responses to the child's prosocial overtures. The aggressive boy accurately perceives that he is academically incompetent and socially rejected; his low self-esteem reflects a history of failure. In addition, the boy's family *does not* reinforce prosocial behavior. Most antisocial individuals do not consider the long-term consequences of their coercive actions until they are forced into group therapy in prisons or group homes. As children, they need caring adults to provide consistent feedback and immediate consequences until positive responses become overlearned. A reduction in the child's antisocial behavior and the development of positive social skills and good work habits will enhance the child's sense of self-efficacy. We assume that increasing the child's sense of efficacy or self-esteem will not, by itself, reduce his antisocial behavior. For the moment, we will maintain the position that self-esteem, self-efficacy, and current measures of social cognitions are phenomena that are correlates of but not causes of antisocial behavior.

As we learn more about how to study cognitions embedded in ongoing social interactions we undoubtedly will have to revise our position. The creative approach taken in Gottman's (1991) studies of emotion and cognition seems to be the wave of the future. In his studies, the multidimensional stream of thoughts, feelings, and overlearned patterns of social behavior is measured in real time with great precision. The technology is currently available to collect this kind of data. To make things even more complicated, many of the relationships among the various dimensions of this continuous stream are probably bidirectional. This is the next level of complexity for sampling social interactions. During the next stage in the development of the coercion model, we will focus on the nature of these continuous streams of behavior. We plan to begin with sequential studies of the interaction between the content of behavior and emotion. As we begin to understand that, we will add data on cognitions. After all, it is the combination of these three things that psychology is all about.

Summary

"Why is this child antisocial?" We are convinced that microsocial analyses of the contingencies found in social interactions will provide part of the answer. Another part of the answer will be derived from macrosocial analyses such as those presented in Chapter 5 for the contribution of parenting practices to children's antisocial behavior. In both instances, aversive events play a central role. Escape from aversive events seems to be the mechanism that drives antisocial behavior in both the microsocial and macrosocial theories of the coercion mechanism. Our brief review suggested that the same mechanism may contribute to depression, schizophrenia, and perhaps marital conflict as well.

The cognitive revolution has given us a new perspective on the nature of human thought processes. In light of recent findings, our cultural fascination with the purported rationality of the human mind seems misplaced. Even under ideal conditions, our cognitive abilities are limited. As Dawes (1976) pointed out, the cumulative technological advances our society has made have led us to overestimate the rational powers of a single human mind. It also seems reasonable to assume that most of the action–reaction themes within social interaction are overlearned and therefore represent an automatic process. We need to establish how overlearned chunks of social behavior interact with social cognitions to determine ongoing social exchanges.

One of the first questions many parents ask after their children acquire language skills is: "Why are you doing that?" Most of the time, the child will not be able to answer this question. Even as adults, we simply don't know *why* we do what we do. After years of socialization, most of us become adept at generating a coherent story about our behavior. Although the story may be satisfying, it probably is not accurate. This poses more of a problem for those of us who study people than it does for the individuals directly involved. The information required to answer causal questions either is not tracked in the first place or it is lost as soon as it fades from short-term memory.

Future research may unravel the fascinating interplay between thoughts and feelings on the one hand and automatic social behaviors acquired outside of awareness on the other. The question is, "What is the nature of the equations that define the interactions among these three sets of variables?" Our current work on microsocial analyses of escape sequences constitutes a crude beginning in the development of a more interesting and sophisticated approach to psychology.

Authors' Note

We wish to acknowledge the contributions of Professor Mark Rilling to this chapter. Because of his familiarity with recent developments in learning theory in general and negative reinforcement in particular, he kindly agreed to serve as consultant. His response to an earlier version of this chapter was overwhelming: 19 pages of typewritten suggestions, a new book to read, and three reprints from recent publications. Many of his comments and suggestions were incorporated in this chapter. The resulting changes make this a stronger, and we think more understandable, presentation. The perspective is not always in agreement with Professor Rilling's position, but this is in keeping with our original request that he keep us from making the more egregious errors to which clinicians are prone when discussing theories of learning.

Chapter 5

The Parent Training Model

This chapter assembles the pieces for a macrosocial theory of children's antisocial behavior. The underlying assumption is that parenting practices defined by macrosocial variables (ratings and composite observation scores) control the microsocial sequences discussed in previous chapters. Five key questions will be addressed: (1) How can we measure parenting practices? (2) Do the measures of parenting variables covary with measures of child adjustment? (3) How much variance is accounted for? (4) Can the effect be replicated with data from other samples? and (5) What are the findings from experiments that have tested for the causal status of parenting variables?

The Preschool Model

The preschool model describes how we think the process starts. During those years, when the socialization process takes place primarily within the home, we had expected to find a set of relationships similar to those presented in Figure 5.1. One key feature of this model is the bidirectional relation between the Coercive Child and Discipline constructs. Presumably, the failure to use effective discipline would result in high rates of coercive child behaviors (as indicated by the structural variables start-up, negative synchronicity, and continuance). It was thought that these behaviors, in turn, would cause further disruptions in parenting practices.

The other important feature of this model is the path from the Coercive Child construct to the antisocial trait.

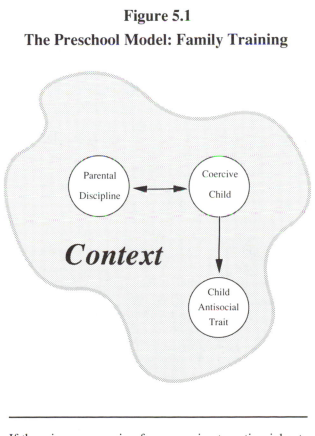

Figure 5.1

The Preschool Model: Family Training

If there is a progression from coercive to antisocial acts in the home, this path should be significant. Eddy (1991a) demonstrated in an SEM for a sample of normal preschool boys and girls that there is a strong path (.56) between observed coercive child behavior and parents' discipline practices. The measures of child antisocial behavior were related to parenting practices, but the connection to coercive child behaviors was weak. Notice that the model did not address the problem of the bidirectional relation between parental discipline and coercive child behavior. Bidirectional effects can be estimated only under restrictive conditions that could not be satisfied by the Eddy data set.

It is difficult to estimate bidirectional effects. Even if the right kind of data are available, it is unlikely that there are enough degrees of freedom to define the model. Estimating the bidirectional effect simply requires many more degrees of freedom than most models have available. We tried to get around this problem by assuming that the bidirectional effects were *equal* (Baldwin & Skinner, 1989; Patterson, Dishion, & Bank, 1984). This was not satisfactory, however, because there was no theoretical basis for the equality assumption. Our colleague Sam Vuchinich has recently proposed an elegant solution that uses measures collected within a longitudinal design to estimate each effect separately (Vuchinich, Bank, & Patterson, in preparation).

At this point, we have not carried out a direct test of the preschool model with the Coercive Child construct as the core component. Such a test would require a longitudinal study that started when the children were toddlers and continued through the first or second grade. The study would have to include observations of parenting practices. It also would be important to sample children's coercive behaviors within the home at *different* times and settings than those used to define parental discipline practices. If both the Coercive Child and Discipline constructs were defined using data from the same times and settings, the errors of measurement would be hopelessly entangled. Our preliminary efforts to examine the preschool model have been based on inadequate data sets. We now understand how to design data collection procedures to test the model, and the Vuchinich solution describes how to analyze the data. For the time being, however, Coercive Child is viewed as a hypothetical construct in our modeling studies.

The Parent Training Model

For samples of older boys, the Coercive Child construct would have to be expanded to include observations of start-up, negative synchronicity, and continuance for interactions with peers (because they make an important contribution to the socialization process). Provisions were not made for this in the design for the OYS. We were disappointed to find that our data sets were not sufficient to define the Coercive Child construct. However, we discovered that the parent training model would work

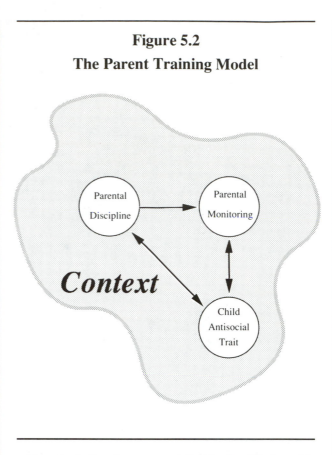

Figure 5.2
The Parent Training Model

without including the construct. In this simplified model, the path coefficient from Discipline goes directly to Child Antisocial. For samples of older boys, it also was necessary to add the Parental Monitoring construct. The relation between the constructs is illustrated in Figure 5.2.

This section examines the utility of including both the Parental Monitoring and the Discipline constructs in the parent training model for older boys. The resulting model has proven to be so robust that we call it *basic black*; it is simple, elegant, and seems appropriate for more than one setting.

Monitoring

When boys are allowed to have more unsupervised time at age 9 or 10, the risk of engaging in antisocial activities increases. The implication is that, by early adolescence, parental monitoring determines the amount of unsupervised street time the child is allowed. Parents of fourth-grade boys in the Planning Study sample reported that their sons spent an average of .78 hours per day in settings in which they were not supervised by adults (Patterson & Stouthamer-Loeber, 1984). Unsupervised time increased to 1.02 hours at grade 7 and to 2.06 hours at grade 10. Parents are faced with the problem of deciding how much unsupervised time to allow when their sons reach adolescence and begin spending more time with peers (including deviant peers). In our society, there is no clear consensus about how much structure should be imposed by adults during the developmental period from pre- to midadolescence. The data from the Planning Study showed that the highest monitoring score was for the fourth-graders, and the lowest score was for the tenth graders. The mean was .89 at grade 4, .50 at grade 7, and -1.24 at grade 10 (the F value of 11.40 was significant at $p < .0001$). We feel it is extremely important for parents of early and midadolescents to continue monitoring where their children are, who they are with, and what they are doing. As we shall see in later sections, lack of monitoring places a child at serious risk for involvement with deviant peers, antisocial activities, and substance abuse.

The hypothesis that follows from the considerations just outlined is that during adolescence there will be a direct and significant path from Parental Monitoring to Child Antisocial. In the multiple-regression analyses of data from the OYS samples, Patterson and Bank (1989) showed that the Discipline and Parental Monitoring constructs made significant contributions at grade 4 and again at grade 6. Using data from the Planning Study, Patterson and Dishion (1985) found that parental monitoring practices seemed to have both a direct and an indirect effect on delinquency. The indirect effect was mediated by involvement with deviant peers. We have not identified the precise point in the developmental sequence at which parental monitoring becomes important.

Developmental Shifts

We anticipate other developmental shifts in the model (Patterson, DeBaryshe, & Ramsey, 1989). Involvement in a deviant peer group is thought to play a crucial role in the development of late-starter adolescents who begin their careers as delinquents after the age of 15. Stressors impinging on the parents such as unemployment or divorce are thought to be followed by disruptions in monitoring, which places the child at risk for spending time with a deviant peer group.

In our treatment studies, we have found that most parents of antisocial children have little information about where their children are, who they are with, what they are doing, or when they will be home. If parents do not know that the child is doing something wrong, they cannot provide negative sanctions. Early in the treatment of such families, we tried to teach the parents to track their children more carefully. Typically, our attempts to improve the level of tracking in the home were met with considerable resistance by the children. The parents had been defeated repeatedly in their efforts to discipline their children for misbehavior that occurred right in front of them. Requesting information about where the child was going, who he would be with, and what he was going to do meant having a series of intense confrontations with the child. Often, the child would assert that the parent had

no right to ask for such details.

This group of parents seemed to feel that it would be pointless to call the school to find out about truancy or discipline problems. Even if they had the information, these parents knew they would not be able to do anything about it. Many of the parents said they did not trust these sources of information anyway because the school and community were "out to get their child." These assumptions seemed to provide a convenient rationale for not even attempting to monitor their children.

Another group, the *unattached parents*, resisted tracking activities because they were deeply committed to their own pursuits (Patterson, 1982). Some of these parents were so unmotivated to help their children change that we had to pay them a salary to get them to complete their homework assignments.

The data show that parents who are socially unskilled or antisocial are at risk for disruptions in monitoring and discipline (Patterson & Capaldi, 1991a). The data also show that sudden increases in stressors (e.g., unemployment, prolonged illness, the onset of their children's pubescence, and divorce) are associated with disruptions in parental monitoring and discipline (Patterson, Bank, and Stoolmiller, 1990). These hypotheses are examined in detail in Chapter 7.

Parents must learn effective monitoring skills if they want their children's behavior to improve, but this is not enough by itself. Blechman (1980) showed that training parents to increase the monitoring of their children did not reduce deviant child behavior. However, the combination of parental monitoring *and* providing appropriate contingencies for deviant and prosocial behaviors was effective. Bien and Bry (1980) showed that simply having the teacher, child, and parent track behavior effectively did not produce significant increases in target behaviors.

Empirical Literature

Parental supervision has been identified as an important variable by researchers using both retrospective and prospective longitudinal designs to study delinquents. These studies have consistently found that parents of delinquent youths have limited awareness of where their children are, who they are spending their time with, and what they are doing (Farrington, 1982; Hirschi, 1969; McCord, 1979; Wilson, 1980a). For example, in a follow-up study of the Cambridge–Somerville sample, McCord found that poor parental supervision was related to youths committing offenses against both property and persons. Farrington found that one of the best predictors of teachers' ratings of troublesomeness for 8- to 10-year-old boys was a lack of parental supervision. An earlier analysis of data from that study had shown that a lack of parental supervision of preadolescent boys correlated significantly with the incidence of violent crimes at age 21 (Farrington, 1978). In a questionnaire study of children and delinquents in grade 7, Schaefer (1965) found that delinquents agreed that the following statements described their parents: "Allows me to go out as often as I please," and "Lets me go anyplace I please without asking."

We hypothesized that the impact of poor monitoring is greater for adolescents than for preadolescents and younger children. We also assume that as early as age 9 or 10 an extremely antisocial boy will overcome parent strictures and spend as much time on the street as he wants. It should be the case then that monitoring effectiveness determines the amount of street time. This idea is supported by data from the Planning Study that showed a correlation of .43 ($p < .001$) between disruptions in Parental Monitoring (construct score) and the mean number of hours of unsupervised street time (Patterson & Stouthamer-Loeber, 1984).

For older children and adolescents, parental monitoring seems to be a mediating mechanism for many of the forces that impinge upon the family from the outside. Children who live in high-delinquency neighborhoods are at considerable risk for antisocial behavior, but children who live in the same type of neighborhood *and* have parents whose monitoring skills are meager or disrupted are most at risk. This was strongly supported by the elegant study of families living in a ghetto by Wilson (1980b). Those parents who closely supervised their sons had very low baserates of delinquency compared to those families who did not. If ghetto life is considered to be a risk factor, it is clear that effective monitoring reduces the degree of risk. In an analysis of a national probability sample of 12- to 17-year-olds, Goldstein (1984) found that youths from father-absent families had more police contacts than those from intact homes. With adequate supervision, however, youths from father-absent families were no more likely than those from intact families to have conduct problems. Again, this suggests that monitoring plays a key role in mediating the impact of such variables as social status, neighborhood, and family structure on antisocial behavior in older children and adolescents.

Measurement of the Parental Monitoring Construct

The Parental Monitoring construct has been measured by combining data from both traditional interviews and telephone interviews. The latter is considered to be a more microsocial measure of supervision. In our first investigation of monitoring during the Planning Study sample, we tried to develop items that effectively described parental efforts to supervise children and track their activities outside the home (Patterson & Dishion, 1985; Patterson & Stouthamer-Loeber, 1984). Because it was our first attempt, the assessment devices were rather primitive. For example, the interview scale for the parents was based on

only two items, and the child-interview scale had five items. The third indicator was a single global rating by the person who interviewed the child: "Did the child seem well-supervised by the parents?" The fourth indicator was based on an interesting approach to collecting telephone interview data. In each of six telephone calls to the parents and the child, family members were asked whether the child had engaged in any of six deviant behaviors during the previous 16 hours. The difference between parent and child reports defined the score; the mean for the six calls defined the indicator. Based on the data from the Planning Study sample, the convergence correlations for the Parental Monitoring construct were quite low (the mean was .153) (Patterson & Dishion, 1985). Nevertheless, the convergence was sufficient to produce a construct that made significant contributions to the other latent constructs for delinquency and membership in a deviant peer group.

Prior to the assessment of the OYS samples, we spent several weeks creating better indicators for the Parental Monitoring construct. The therapists and interviewers participated in brainstorming sessions to generate new examples of effective and ineffective monitoring. As a result, several items were added to the original scales, and some entirely new scales were invented. The scales that were successful in the Planning Study were retained and, if possible, expanded and strengthened. The distributions for each indicator and the itemetric and factor analyses are described in Capaldi and Patterson (1989).

The interviewer impressions rating also was revised to include scores from the child's interviewer as well as scores from the father's or mother's interviewer or both. The telephone interview format was expanded to include a report by the parent on how many hours he or she had spent with the child the previous day. The present study employed the same six items used in the Planning Study to generate a score based on interviews with the child, even though the alpha was rather low (.59). The difference score that performed so well for the adolescent sample in the Planning Study did not converge with other monitoring indicators when assessed for an at-risk sample of fourth-grade boys. We were unsuccessful in our attempts to develop a telephone interview scale for the child's report of parental supervision during the previous 16 hours. An intensive effort to expand an interview-based scale for assessing parent reports of monitoring was also unsuccessful. The details are summarized in Capaldi and Patterson (1989).

Three of the indicators survived the principal components factor analyses. The results of the principal components factor analyses (constrained to a single solution) for the two OYS samples are shown in Figure 5.3A. The combined interviewer-impressions ratings had the strongest loading. The supervision scale from the child interview formed a strong indicator. The contribution of the parent telephone indicator was borderline; its

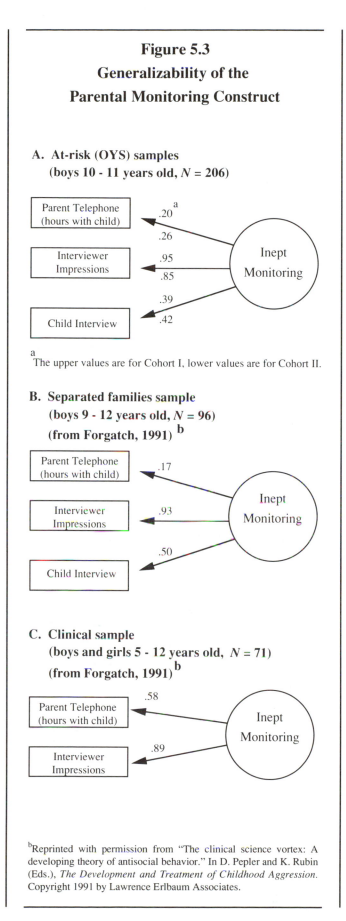

Figure 5.3

Generalizability of the

Parental Monitoring Construct

A. At-risk (OYS) samples

(boys 10 - 11 years old, *N* = 206)

a
The upper values are for Cohort I, lower values are for Cohort II.

B. Separated families sample

(boys 9 - 12 years old, *N* = 96)

(from Forgatch, 1991) [b]

C. Clinical sample

(boys and girls 5 - 12 years old, *N* = 71)

(from Forgatch, 1991) [b]

[b]Reprinted with permission from "The clinical science vortex: A developing theory of antisocial behavior." In D. Pepler and K. Rubin (Eds.), *The Development and Treatment of Childhood Aggression.* Copyright 1991 by Lawrence Erlbaum Associates.

psychometric status seemed somewhat dubious, but dropping it would have left only interview data to define the construct, so it was retained.

The data from the separation and clinical samples have been reviewed by Forgatch (1991). As shown in Figure 5.3B, the data for separated families provided support for the configural invariance of the Parental Monitoring construct. Again, the highest loading for the construct was on the interviewer-impressions composite rating, and the lowest was on the parent telephone report. In fact, the magnitude of the factor loadings seemed invariant across the three samples.

The findings for the clinical sample are shown in Figure 5.3C. Together with the findings from the other two samples, the composite interviewer-impressions rating serves as a core indicator for the latent construct. Needless to say, we are pleased that this particular indicator and the child interview worked so well for the at-risk samples.

Discipline

We assume that effective discipline is defined by an interrelated set of skills: (1) accurately tracking and classifying problem behaviors, (2) ignoring trivial coercive events, and (3) using an effective back-up consequence when punishment is necessary. Parents with problem children usually have difficulty in all three of these areas.

Tracking and Classification

Parents with problem children are dramatically different from parents with nonproblem children in the way they track their children's behaviors. A series of laboratory studies carried out at OSLC suggests that parents with problem children tend to be overly inclusive in their schemata for classifying deviant child behavior (Holleran, Littman, Freund, & Schmaling, 1982; Lorber, 1981; Schmaling & Patterson, 1984). In these studies, parents were asked to observe videotapes of children's behavior and indicate whether a specific event was normal or deviant. Significant differences were found between parents with problem children and parents with normal children in all three studies. Parents of problem children were more likely to classify as deviant those behaviors that were classified as normal by our clinical staff and others. In all three studies, this tendency toward overinclusiveness correlated significantly with rates of coercive behaviors observed in the home. We believe this bias in tracking relates to the significantly higher rates of start-up that characterize parents in clinical samples.

Ignoring Trivial Coercive Events

It is important for parents to ignore the relatively trivial coercive behaviors that occur on a daily basis in most homes. When a child initiates a coercive interaction in normal families, other family members go on talking or attending to one another roughly half the time (Patterson, 1982). When parents in a normal family intervene in coercive exchanges, they are most likely to issue a "stop" command or to threaten punishment. Approximately 30% of the time they simply *natter* (i.e., nag or scold irritably). Parents with problem children are less likely to ignore behaviors that others would classify as deviant (Patterson, 1982). They are much more likely to natter in response to children's coercive behaviors, and they also tend to react aversively to behaviors that others would classify as neutral (Patterson, 1982; Taplin & Reid, 1977).

Patterson (1984) found that the mean likelihood of a coercive interaction between mothers and their normal sons was .049, and for fathers and normal sons it was .033; the comparable values for parents interacting with problem children were .065 and .068, respectively ($p < .001$). However, the data indicate that *not all aversive parental reactions function as punishments*, at least in terms of suppressing ongoing behaviors. Sometimes, nattering and irritability actually may serve as stimuli that elicit further coercive behaviors from the child. An effective punishment is an aversive behavior that weakens a response and suppresses its immediate recurrence. Nattering and punishment are both perceived as aversive, but nattering has little or no corrective impact. Effective, nonviolent punishment is certainly perceived as aversive by the child, but it also effectively weakens the child's antisocial behaviors. When it is used correctly, punishment also suppresses ongoing coercive child behavior.

Patterson (1982) found that boys in normal and clinical samples were very likely to direct *single* coercive behaviors at their sisters and then stop (.79 and .82, respectively); when interacting with their mothers, they were somewhat less likely to stop after just one coercive action (.74 and .67, respectively). If the other family member reacted aversively to the aversive initiation of the child, the probability that the child would continue his aversive behavior increased consistently. This increase was particularly dramatic when the target child was interacting with male siblings, but the trend was consistent across family members. Nattering makes things worse, and the effect seems to be amplified in clinical samples.

Back-Up Consequences

If normal parents fail to use consequences to back up their commands and requests, their children become increasingly noncompliant. Gradually, the parents have to use more directives, and eventually threats, to obtain compliance. High rates of child noncompliance are a natural covariate for high rates of parental start and stop commands. For example, "Stop teasing your sister," and "Hang up your coat," probably have a familiar ring to most parents. In normal families, children comply with these requests most of the time (Reid, Taplin, & Lorber,

1981). We think one of the primary reasons for this is that parents with antisocial children do not back up their commands and requests. They also fail to reinforce compliance when it does occur. As a result, even intense demands for children to stop doing something are met with noncompliance. The children in these families have learned that they do not have to comply with commands. In a desperate attempt to regain control, the parents may resort to extreme measures. Reid, Patterson, and Loeber (1982) found that approximately one-third of the children referred for treatment of antisocial problems also had been physically abused according to records at community agencies.

Social Interactional Family Therapy (SIFT) emphasizes the importance of teaching parents to ignore trivial deviant behaviors. A parent is taught to focus on a few problem behaviors at a time. Every time these behaviors occur, the child is told to stop. If the child does not comply within several seconds, a nonviolent punishment is imposed such as time out, a 10-minute work detail, or losing points (Forgatch, Fetrow, & Lathrop, 1985; Patterson & Forgatch, 1987). These punishments serve as back-up consequences for parental commands and requests. Carefully controlled experimental studies have demonstrated the effectiveness of this approach (cf. review in Patterson, 1982). The back-up punishments gradually alter the effectiveness of parental start and stop commands. Parental nattering and periodic physical assaults on the child are no longer necessary.

Empirical Literature

The ground-breaking studies by the Gluecks have established that parents of delinquent youths tend to be both explosive and inconsistent in their punishment (Glueck & Glueck, 1950). The covariation between ineffective parental discipline and antisocial child behavior is a consistent finding in most of the studies that followed (Lefkowitz, Eron, Walder, & Huesmann, 1977; McCord, 1979, 1980; McCord, McCord, & Howard, 1961; Sears, Maccoby, & Levin, 1957; West & Farrington, 1973).

Olweus (1980) systematically modeled the relation between discipline and antisocial child behavior. The criterion for antisocial behavior consisted of peer nomination for status as an antisocial child. Maternal negativism and permissiveness also played key roles in the Olweus model. Retrospective data from parents about their prior childrearing practices showed that threats and violent outbursts directly contributed to antisocial child behaviors for a sample of boys in grade 6. The effect was replicated for a sample of boys in grade 9.

The coercion model (Patterson, 1982) and social control theory (Hirschi, 1969) are based on the assumption that reinforcers for antisocial behavior are readily available. For various reasons, it is difficult to eliminate these reinforcers. If coercive behaviors are permitted, they are likely to be maintained and strengthened, either by the reactions of the victims or by the built-in utility of avoiding unpleasant experiences. This may partially explain why the trait scores for aggression have such a high level of stability, as reported by Loeber (1982) and Olweus (1980).

The permissive-parenting approach allows these reinforcers to occur routinely. It is not surprising to find that permissive parenting is significantly correlated with elevated risk for antisocial child behavior; Schuck (1974) found this to be the case in his reanalysis of the data from Sears et al. (1957) and Yarrow, Campbell, and Burton (1968). This theme was reiterated in the path analyses of retrospective data by Olweus (1980). It is also in accord with the findings reported by Baumrind (1966, 1971, 1978, 1979).

Measurement of the Discipline Construct

It is extremely difficult to measure what constitutes effective discipline. For example, if good discipline practices are used consistently in normal families, discipline confrontations occur infrequently. The problem is, how do you study events that seldom occur? In the at-risk sample, the parents were contacted by telephone six times over a two-week period. During each brief interview, the parents were asked to describe their children's antisocial behaviors and the type of punishment (if any) that was used. The parents of nonaggressive boys reported a discipline confrontation about once every six days. Parents of moderately aggressive boys reported one confrontation every four days, and parents of highly aggressive boys reported one every three days. These data suggest that major discipline confrontations are relatively uncommon events. We suspect, however, that most families have a much higher incidence of relatively minor confrontations, for example, "Stop teasing your brother." Typically, these exchanges do not lead to a major conflict.

The most frequent parental reactions to the problem behaviors reported in the daily telephone interviews were ignoring (18%), commanding or requesting (15%), giving a time out (10%), and scolding or nattering (8%). These figures are similar to those reported in mothers' diaries regarding confrontations with preschool children (Goodenough, 1931). The diary data showed that mothers ignored their boys' outbursts 30% of the time, and put them in bed, in the bedroom, or in a chair 11% of the time.

Suitable technology is not currently available to measure "good" discipline in a family in which things are going well. Because only one or two significant discipline confrontations occur per week in these families, it is almost impossible to collect enough sequential data to estimate the reduction in future child noncompliance that would result from the contingent use of nonviolent punishment by an already skillful parent. Unfortunately,

we only seem to be able to measure discipline when it is *not working*. What are the steps that lead to this end result? One way to study this would be to look for the telltale signs associated with a breakdown in discipline. Is there a high probability of parental nattering? Do the parents threaten and physically strike the child? Presumably, if the parents backed up their house rules and requests with effective punishments, it would not be necessary for them to resort to these other practices.

Our experience with assessing such action–reaction patterns suggests that self-report measures do not provide reliable data. Do parents tend to distort what the child does (e.g., Reid, Kavanagh, & Baldwin, 1987) or do they distort their *reactions* to what the child does? In keeping with the programmatic studies of social cognition by Nisbett and Wilson (1977), our impression is that these sequences of events are so complex and occur so rapidly that parents simply are not tracking them accurately as they occur. Our solution is to use a dual approach in measuring discipline: We ask parents to describe what they do and we train observers to code sequences that define certain aspects of discipline exchanges.

Our first attempt to measure the Discipline construct was based on data from the Planning Study sample (Patterson & Stouthamer-Loeber, 1984). Both observation and self-report data were used as potential indicators. We spent months developing items that could be used in interviews, questionnaires, and telephone reports. The items were tailored to assess various discipline practices, and there were separate item pools for parents and children. Global rating scales were created that could be filled out by the observers after they had collected the sequential microsocial data on family interactions. The global ratings described the observers' impressions of the parents' consistency and follow-through in discipline confrontations.

After investing considerable effort in developing these indicators, it was gratifying to find out that they were internally consistent (i.e., reliable). Our satisfaction was short-lived, however, because we soon discovered that the convergence among the indicators was weak. In fact, in the first modeling study only one indicator functioned properly; this was the observers' global ratings of consistency and follow-through (Patterson, Dishion, & Bank, 1984). Because the discipline concept was central to the model, this was a matter of serious concern.

Before we started the assessment for the OYS, we renewed our efforts to develop better indicators for the Discipline construct. We created entirely new sets of interview items for parents and children (Capaldi & Patterson, 1989). Again, these new *a priori* scales were internally consistent. We also developed items that could be used during the daily telephone interviews that sampled the last 16 hours of interaction. Unfortunately, none of the *a priori* scores survived the requirement of

Table 5.1

Convergent Matrix of Indicators for the Discipline Construct

Cohort I	Cohort II			
	Observer Impressions	Nattering	Explosive Discipline	Mother Interview
Observer Impressions	—	.34[a]	.38	.04
Nattering	.60	—	.41	.08
Explosive Discipline	.37	.41	—	.08
Mother Interview	.23	.31	.18	—

[a]Given the sample sizes involved, any correlation above .21 would be significant at $p = .05$.

convergent validity (i.e., they did not correlate with the observer-impressions indicator). In a subsequent cross-check, the new scores also failed to covary with the Child Antisocial construct for Cohort I.

We examined home observation data for sequences that might reveal important features of discipline exchanges. Two variables that seemed particularly promising survived the requirement for convergent validity: *nattering*, which described the likelihood that the parent would scold and express disapproval when interacting with the child, and *explosive discipline*, which was the likelihood that the parent would use threats or hit when the child acted coercively toward another family member.

The data for the three most promising indicators are summarized in Table 5.1 for both cohorts. It is immediately apparent that the three scores based on the home observation sessions form a reasonably tight cluster for the Discipline construct. Observer global impressions (an indicator left over from the Planning Study) correlated very well with the two variables derived from the microsocial data also collected by observers. Even though global ratings and microsocial ratings may represent different methods, it is important to note that the three variables represent only one agent, the observers. The parent-interview scale did not covary with the other indicators for Cohort I, and the findings were only borderline for Cohort II.

The results of the principal components factor analyses (constrained to a single solution) are summarized in Figure 5.4A. With the exception of the parent-interview indicator (mother report of discipline strategies), the factor loadings were quite stable from Cohort I to Cohort II. Based on these findings, the interview indicator has been dropped from all other studies.

Generalizability. The next issue involved the generalizability of the factor structure across samples. For example, would a similar structure apply to families with younger boys or families with girls? Would the same set of indicators be effective in defining discipline when assessing a clinical sample or families from metropolitan ghettos?

Figure 5.4B summarizes the findings from a study of separated families with boys 6 to 8 years of age (Baldwin & Skinner, 1989). The pattern of factor loadings was highly consistent with that obtained for the OYS cohorts. The Discipline construct loaded most heavily on nattering and observer impressions. Again, the loading was essentially nonsignificant for the interview-based indicator.

Figure 5.4C summarizes the findings from a baseline study of 71 families with antisocial boys and girls referred for treatment (Forgatch, 1991); the children were 5 to 12 years old. For this sample, only two of the original indicators survived. The construct loaded most heavily on nattering and next on observer impressions.

The findings are encouraging. A pattern of factor scores for three of the indicators holds across three samples. The nattering indicator showed the strongest loading, followed by observer impressions and explosive discipline. This leads us to believe that the Discipline construct may be generalizable across a wide range of samples.

Testing the Parent Training Model

As a rough guess, the minimum sample size required to test the parenting model is 150. For this reason, we combined the data for the two cohorts. The correlations based on the combined data for the 10 indicators that define the parent training model are summarized in Table 5.2.

The convergence for the Parental Monitoring construct was moderate; the median correlation was only .25. As noted earlier, the convergence for the Discipline and Child Antisocial constructs was quite good. Because the correlation within the constructs seemed higher than the between-construct correlations, there should be no problem getting a good fit of the clinical model to the data set.

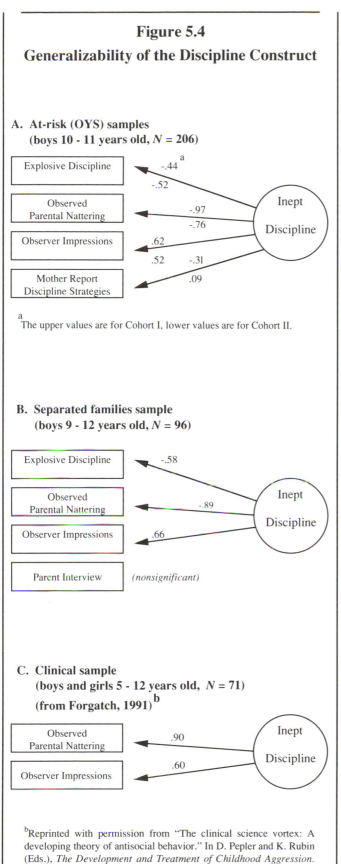

Figure 5.4

Generalizability of the Discipline Construct

A. At-risk (OYS) samples
(boys 10 - 11 years old, N = 206)

Explosive Discipline	-.44[a]
	-.52
Observed Parental Nattering	-.97
	-.76
Observer Impressions	.62
	.52 -.31
Mother Report Discipline Strategies	.09

Inept Discipline

[a] The upper values are for Cohort I, lower values are for Cohort II.

B. Separated families sample
(boys 9 - 12 years old, N = 96)

Explosive Discipline	-.58
Observed Parental Nattering	-.89
Observer Impressions	.66
Parent Interview	*(nonsignificant)*

Inept Discipline

C. Clinical sample
(boys and girls 5 - 12 years old, N = 71)
(from Forgatch, 1991)[b]

Observed Parental Nattering	.90
Observer Impressions	.60

Inept Discipline

[b]Reprinted with permission from "The clinical science vortex: A developing theory of antisocial behavior." In D. Pepler and K. Rubin (Eds.), *The Development and Treatment of Childhood Aggression.* Copyright 1991 by Lawrence Erlbaum Associates.

As shown in Figure 5.5, the results of the SEM provided strong support for the assumptions underlying the parent training model. The Parental Monitoring and Discipline constructs both made significant contributions to the Child Antisocial construct. Their contributions also were of roughly equal magnitude. The path coefficient of -.32 showed that children whose parents were ineffective at monitoring were at risk for higher levels of antisocial behavior even after the contribution of inept discipline had been partialed out.

Similarly, inept discipline made a significant contribution even after the contribution of ineffective monitoring was partialed out. In the model, discipline practices made both direct and indirect contributions to antisocial behavior. The indirect path was mediated by the impact of ineffective discipline on monitoring practices.

The chi-square value showed a good fit between the predicted and the obtained covariance structure. The model accounted for 30% of the variance in the criterion; in this sense, it is a satisfactory performance model. Our confidence in this model is further bolstered by its subsequent replication in two additional samples by Forgatch (1991), who was able to identify two other samples assessed at OSLC in which essentially the same measures were used to define each of the three constructs. Her findings, summarized in Figure 5.6, show an acceptable fit for the model to each of the data sets. For the sample of boys 9 to 12 years of age from single parent families, the path coefficient of .32 was comparable to the .34 obtained for the OYS sample. Notice that the relative contribution of monitoring (.59) seemed to play a greater role in single families than in OYS families.

Does the model also generalize to samples that include both boys and girls? Will it generalize if the sample includes much younger children who are referred for extreme antisocial behavior? The analysis by Forgatch showed that the answer to all three questions is an emphatic yes! The model showed a solid fit to the data set for the clinical sample of children 5 to 12 years of age. Notice, however, two structural changes. The path coefficient from Discipline to Child Antisocial is an impressive .48, while the relative contribution of monitoring is considerably less.

It is very gratifying to conclude that we have a performance model that works. The parent training model consistently accounts for 30% to 50% of the criterion variance. Most satisfying of all, it replicates across widely different settings. Recent data collected on a sample of normal families living in a suburb of Rome, Italy, strongly suggests that the parent training model will generalize across the two cultures (Pastorelli, 1991). This is particularly gratifying, because building a robust parent training model was our first priority in designing the OYS. It seems that the costly effort to build multiagent, multimethod indicators has paid off handsomely.

Table 5.2
Convergent and Discriminant Correlations for the Parent Training Model

	Child Antisocial				Discipline			Monitoring		
	Parent Report	Teacher Report	Child CBC	Peer Report	Observer Impres.	Observed Nattering	Abuse Cluster	Child Interview	Interv. Impres.	Par. Rpt. (hours)
Parent Report	1.00									
Teacher Report	.403	1.00								
Child CBC	.312	.243	1.00							
Peer Report	.367	.368	.196	1.00						
Observer Impres.	-.183	-.286	-.070	-.337	1.00					
Observed Nattering	.263	.195	.131	.221	-.435	1.00				
Abuse Cluster	.224	.185	.082	-.158	-.341	.471	1.00			
Child Interview	-.145	-.112	-.116	-.099	.080	-.129	-.059	1.00		
Interviewer Impres.	-.263	-.280	-.172	-.287	.251	-.189	-.264	.386	1.00	
Parent Report (hrs.)	-.148	-.071	-.116	-.095	.037	-.056	-.078	.147	.229	1.00

[a] No additional parameter estimates or constraints.

Figure 5.5
The Parent Training Path Model

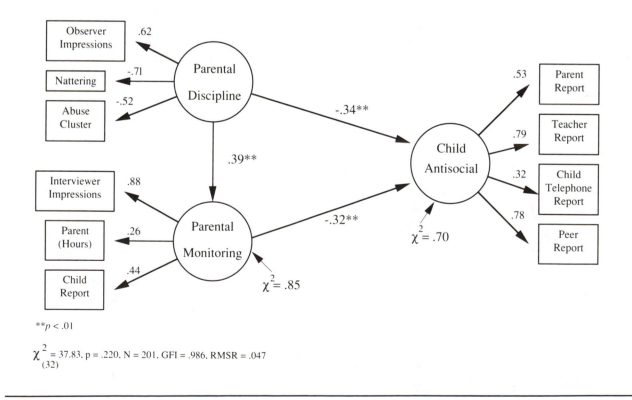

**p < .01

$\chi^2_{(32)} = 37.83$, p = .220, N = 201, GFI = .986, RMSR = .047

Figure 5.6

Two Replications of the Parent Training Model (from Forgatch, 1991)

A. Parenting model for divorced parents sample (boys 9 - 12 years old, *N* = 96)

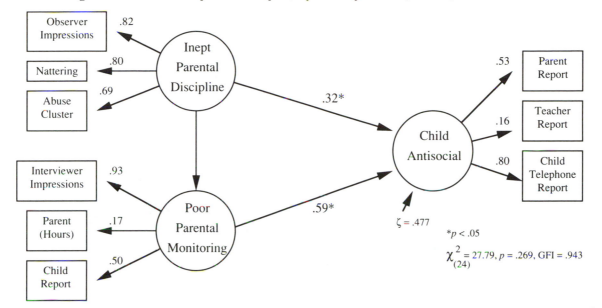

B. Parenting model for clinical sample (boys and girls 5 - 12 years old, *N* = 71)

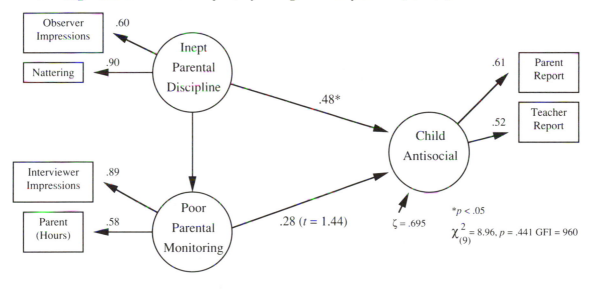

Reprinted with permission from "The clinical science vortex: A developing theory of antisocial behavior." In D. Pepler and K. Rubin (Eds.), *The Development and Treatment of Childhood Aggression*. Copyright 1991 by Lawrence Erlbaum Associates.

Causal Status of Parenting Practices

The next problem to be considered is that correlational models do not establish causal connections no matter how often they are replicated. We can use longitudinal data, but this provides only a weak test for causal status. For example, if parenting practices had a causal effect, then we would expect prior measures of parenting to correlate with *future* measures of antisocial behavior. However, correlating Discipline measured at Time 1 with Child

71

Figure 5.7

Figure 5.7

Cross-Lag Test for the Effect of Discipline (OYS Cohort I only, *N* = 101)

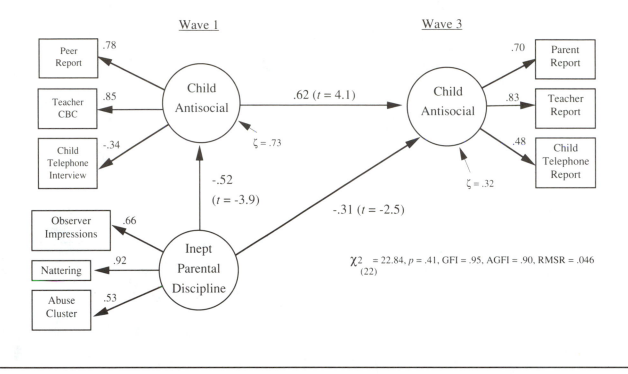

Antisocial measured at Time 2 would not be convincing because we already know that they correlated with each other at Time 1 and probably at Time 2 as well (and, in fact, they are). Thus, correlating Time 1 Discipline with Time 2 Child Antisocial adds little to what we already know. It would be more convincing to demonstrate that Time 1 Discipline contributes to Time 2 Child Antisocial *after* the contribution of Time 1 measures of Child Antisocial have been partialed out. This is modeled in Figure 5.7. The findings showed that changes in Child Antisocial correlated significantly (-.31) with prior measures of Discipline. Ineffective discipline covaried with increases in antisocial behavior measured two years later. Notice that the path for parenting practices is relative to the (residual) stability coefficient of .62 for child behavior. Some of the stability of the child antisocial trait is accounted for by the prior measure of parenting practices. Estimating the stability for the trait by itself would yield path coefficients in the .8 to .9 range (Patterson & Yoerger, 1991). In a way, knowing why parenting practices change over time helps explain why traits are so stable.

These findings offer some support for the causal status of parenting practices. However, Stoolmiller and Bank (in preparation) argue that regression models of this type cannot be used as even a weak test of causal status. As they point out, there are built-in limitations in both the logic and the statistical assumptions underlying this ap-

plication of regression models. They propose instead that changes in intraindividual growth curves should be used as a more sensitive means of demonstrating that one variable such as discipline may impact future outcomes. In our current studies, we will employ latent growth models as an alternative. But in either case, the support for causal status is a weak one and is therefore viewed as an intermediate step toward a more satisfying solution.

Experimental Tests

The prime function of building multivariate models based on longitudinal data is to identify which sets of variables are worthy of experimental manipulation. The strategy is carefully outlined in Forgatch (1991). Our approach to family therapy emphasizes the importance of teaching effective parenting practices. The experiments would involve randomly assigning some parents to experimental groups, where they receive the usual training in family management skills, and assigning other parents to alternative groups. In our first study of this type, Forgatch and Toobert (1979) randomly assigned mothers of normal preschool children to an experimental group and a waiting list control group. The mothers in the experimental group listened to an audiotape describing time out as an effective discipline procedure. The data showed a significant increase in child compliance for the experimental group as compared to the control group.

Unfortunately, there was no direct test of maternal discipline, so the changes in child behavior could not be correlated directly with measured changes in maternal discipline practices. Therefore, the findings are not a direct test of the correlational model. Forgatch (1991) also described a clinical intervention that showed that measured improvements in parental discipline and monitoring covaried with reductions in children's antisocial behavior. However, because the random assignment design was compromised in that study, it was not a strong test of the hypothesis.

Dishion, Patterson, and Kavanagh (1991) carried out the first strong test of the coercion model. The study employed a random assignment design and used adequate measures of changes in parent practices. The sample consisted of preadolescent boys and girls at risk for substance abuse. The parents in the experimental group were trained in the use of contingency management techniques, while the families in the comparison groups were assigned to one of two placebo conditions (peer group meetings or instructional materials alone). Teachers' ratings showed a significant reduction in antisocial behavior for the children in the parent training condition compared to children in the placebo groups. Parents in the experimental group showed significant improvements in observed discipline practices, while parents in the placebo groups did not. Changes in antisocial behavior (with Time 1 measures partialed out) correlated significantly with parental discipline measured at termination. Currently, Dishion is replicating this study. Forgatch will begin an additional replication in 1992 using a sample of recently separated single mothers and their young sons.

Thus far, the findings are consistent with the hypothesis that parental discipline practices may be causally related to children's antisocial behaviors. As yet, we have not carried out a strong test of the other four parenting constructs. Needless to say, it will take dozens of replications and extensions of such experiments before we can conclude that these parenting practices are primary determinants. Furthermore, the data from these studies will not directly address the issue of how the coercion process begins in the first place. That will require yet another series of studies that would begin at the infant and toddler stages. However, some of these studies have been completed, and because they consistently support the family training model, it appears that we now have something that is more than just a web of correlations.

Summary

This chapter has advanced the idea that the thousands of interchanges within families have a cumulative and substantial impact on the child's generalized antisocial trait. We discussed and evaluated a performance model that indicates a direct relation between parenting practices, the reinforcement contingencies within family interactions, and children's antisocial behaviors.

To create a bridge from the microsocial interactions in the family to the child's antisocial trait, we must understand how negative exchanges within the family disrupt the parent's ability to monitor the child and provide effective discipline for antisocial acts that require intervention. The more deviant the child is, the more heated these confrontations become. The parent who cannot handle these unpleasant interchanges begins to back off, even when the child engages in more serious problem behaviors.

The basic training model operationalizes a process in which all family members end up the losers. The SEM study by Eddy (1991a) supports the idea that parental discipline is the key to understanding antisocial behavior in preschool children. For the antisocial behaviors of fourth-grade boys, the model was expanded to include parental monitoring. The path coefficients across three samples of older children were significant for both parenting practices.

The underlying assumption is that parenting behavior directs socialization. In reality, parents have no choice in the matter. If parents fail to take responsibility for their children's social development, the children are at risk for conduct problems, poor peer relations, low self-esteem, school problems, and depression. We acknowledge the reciprocal influence that children have on parents and the wide range of individual differences among children and parents. Nevertheless, all families depend on the guidance and executive functions provided by their caretakers. The basic well-being of the family requires a certain level of attention, care, and skill on the part of parents. These family management skills are the focus of behavioral family therapy.

Chapter 6

Positive Parenting and Children's Prosocial Skills

Historical Perspective

Maccoby (1966) emphasized the necessity for compliance training as a first step in the process of socialization. She argued that children with inadequate compliance skills are at a serious disadvantage in learning the positive social skills that are essential for success in school and for building relationships with peers. We are in complete accord with this position. Failure to achieve an adequate level of compliance places the child at risk for antisocial symptoms and social failure. On the other hand, a reasonably compliant child is ready to be socialized. Compliance, or the lack of it, determines the outcome of socialization for the child.

In the mid-1960s, we were attempting to treat both antisocial symptoms and social skill deficits. We developed procedures for training social skills directly in the classroom and schoolyard (Patterson, Cobb, & Ray, 1972; Patterson, Shaw, & Ebner, 1969). At the same time, home observation data revealed that the levels of conflict and hostility were so intense in families with antisocial children that it overshadowed concerns about deficits in prosocial skills. Many parents appeared to be concerned, caring, and even loving toward their children for brief periods, but those interludes were disrupted by frequent explosions during family interactions. It was obvious that it would be very difficult for an adult to provide *consistent* warmth and encouragement to a 5-year-old who is generating an aversive or hostile response every three minutes. Systematic observations showed that the main difference between normal and clinical samples was that the latter sample was characterized by higher rates of aversive behaviors. The rates of prosocial interactions such as playing, laughing, and touching seemed comparable for normal and clinical families.

The treatment we developed for these families focused on decreasing coercive behaviors (particularly noncompliance) and increasing four or five prosocial behaviors that were important to other family members. Both clinically and empirically, we could see that the parents who were able to learn effective discipline and behavioral support techniques experienced less depression and greater satisfaction with their children (Patterson, 1980, 1982). Interesting enough, the observation data also showed significant reductions in aversive child behavior, but *no increases* in prosocial child behavior! This led us to assume that there was some problem with our method of coding prosocial family interactions. The three revisions of our coding systems for family interaction were designed to provide, among other things, a more sensitive measure of positive social behaviors. In the early 1980s, we began developing new assessment procedures to measure positive parenting skills. A decade later, we still have not developed adequate measures of prosocial skills, but we remain committed to the task. The following is a summary of our efforts to understand positive parenting and its impact on prosocial child behavior.

We believe that the trust that develops between the parent and young child is largely based on the moment-

Figure 6.1
A Hierarchical View of Socialization

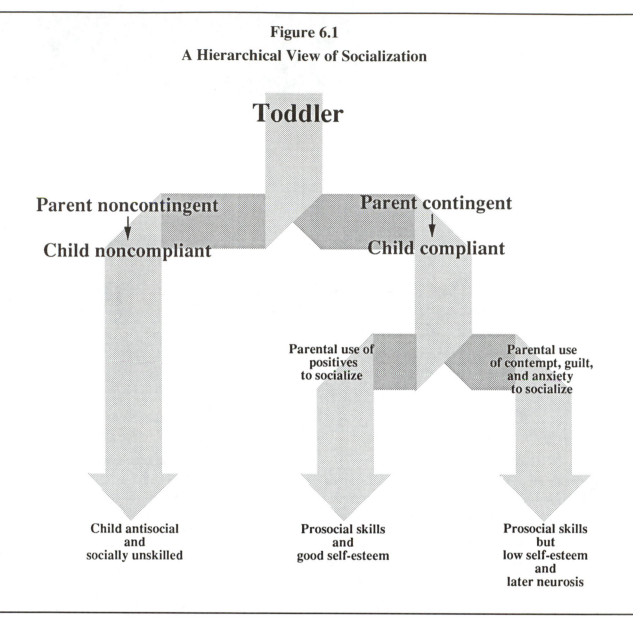

by-moment predictability in their interactions. Such pre-dictability can be established only through clear limits and expectations, consistent and effective discipline, and caring supervision. In this environment, children do not have to worry whether a specific behavior will lead to anger or approval; most of the time, children know which behaviors will lead to conflict and which will produce the encouragement and warmth that both they and their parents enjoy.

The core issue seems to be whether the parents are *contingent* consistently enough to reduce coercive behaviors and increase prosocial skills. The data presented here show that the two sets of contingent reactions are related. If parents are not contingent, the child develops antisocial symptoms *and* is unskilled in the critical areas of work and relationships.

A Two-Stage Hierarchical Model

Figure 6.1 summarizes our position regarding the effect of parenting practices on child behavior. The parameters for the first level are clear. Snyder and Huntley (1990) demonstrated that the parent who is most likely to obtain reasonable levels of child compliance is someone who (1) uses clear requests and commands, (2) responds positively when the child does comply, and (3) provides negative consequences for noncompliance. The multivariate information analyses showed that these three variables accounted for roughly 40% of the variance in measures of child compliance. Whiting and Edwards (1988) carried out observation studies of seven cultures and found that, on the average, 2- to 3-year-old boys complied 74% of the time; the comparable rate for girls was 71%. The vast majority of parents and children in our society are able to clear this first hurdle, but most of the children who remain noncompliant will become both antisocial and unskilled. We also suspect that many of them will be identified later as hyperactive or immature.

The second stage of the hierarchical model is purely speculative. Given that the child is reasonably compliant, there are at least two major paths that parents can follow in socializing their children. The *nurturant path* (Maccoby & Martin, 1983) emphasizes contingent and noncontingent positive consequences, modeling, and a high degree of parental involvement (i.e., time spent with the child). On the other hand, the *anxiety-inducing path* is characteristic of families in which the parents are extremely aversive; unlike parents with antisocial children, however, these parents almost invariably "win" in conflict exchanges. No matter how much the children achieve or excel, it is never quite good enough for the parents. If the children try to assert their autonomy, they are treated with contempt and defeated. Although these children may have good social skills and may be competent in the world of work and academics, the cumulative effect of the abrasive exchanges with their parents is low self-esteem and an accompanying risk for adult neurosis. We have not tested either of these paths to socialization. As already noted, the main obstacle has been the lack of instruments to sensitively describe the parent–child exchanges that differentiate the paths. Also, the anxiety-inducing path consists of low baserate events, which means it would be necessary to identify and study an at-risk sample.

What Are Prosocial Skills?

The first problem we encountered was in defining children's social skills. Hops (1983) carefully reviewed the literature and found that different methods of measurement produce different factors for defining children's social skills. It is only a slight exaggeration to say that there were as many dimensions of social skills as there were measures. More specifically, there seemed to be no way to observe and then obtain valid scores for social skills. Thus, it did not seem possible to study social skills in the same direct manner as that used to study antisocial behavior.

For the sake of expediency, we selected two areas of social skills that seemed crucial to the child's long-term adjustment: academic performance and peer relationships. Both areas have been the subject of many respected empirical studies and appropriate measurement devices were readily available. The advent of Harter's (1983) more effective technique for measuring children's self-esteem led us to include it in our social skills constructs.

We assume that latent constructs measuring parental positive reinforcement, dyadic problem solving, and parental involvement will covary with the measures of children's prosocial skills. In the next section, data are presented that describe the convergence for the positive parenting constructs. The relation of parenting practices to child behavior is then examined using bivariate and multivariate analyses.

Dyadic Problem Solving Construct

It seems to be a law of nature that for two or more people to live together, at least one person must be adept at resolving the almost daily round of interpersonal conflicts and reaching the compromises that are necessary in all groups, including families. In some families, this is accomplished by decree; a "commander-in-chief" makes the decisions, and there is no avenue for appeal. Other families resolve issues by following a democratic process of discussion and compromise. Still others, including the majority of the families who come to OSLC for treatment, prepare for war at the mere hint of a problem or disagreement. The task for a therapist who is working with such families is to teach them basic problem-solving skills. Foremost among these skills is the ability to control negative affect while defining the problem or brainstorming a list of alternatives. The outcome of a problem-solving exchange depends on the contributions of *all* parties. For this reason, we have included the term *dyadic* in the construct name. This dyadic problem-solving process is not the same as the quiet rationality of individual problem solving because either person can sidetrack or facilitate the outcome. It makes a considerable difference whether the participants are parents and children, spouses, friends, or strangers. But there also seems to be a modest trait that is stable across dyads. For example, in a study by Forgatch, single mothers interacted with their children in one problem-solving exchange and then in a later session with one of their confidantes. The correlation for problem-solving outcome across the two settings was .27 ($p < .01$).

Forgatch (1984) analyzed videotapes of families attempting to solve their own problems. The analyses underscored the key role played by negative affect during problem solving. Frequent conflict resulted in a poor outcome. For example, regressing problem-solving outcome against the conditionals that described the exchanges among family members showed that these variables accounted for 26% of the variance. The two variables of particular importance were the likelihood of family members moving from positive to negative exchanges and from neutral to positive exchanges. Additional analyses showed that families with antisocial children were more likely to shift from positive to negative exchanges than from negative to positive. More recently, Forgatch and Fetrow (1990) replicated and extended these analyses for a sample of single mothers. It is interesting to note that irritable mothers tended to select irritable confidantes for their videotaped dyadic problem-

Table 6.1
Convergent Correlations of Indicators for Dyadic Problem Solving

Cohort I	Cohort II		
	Coder Impressions	Parent Solution Given Interaction with Child	Total Positive Solutions by Family
Coder Impressions	—	.436	.353
Parent Solution Given Interaction with Child	.422	—	.452
Total Positive Solutions by Family	.345	.458	—

solving sessions. The contribution of maternal irritability to a poor outcome was highly significant, but the contribution of confidante irritability was only marginal.

From a social interactional perspective, family problem-solving skills typically include the following steps (Forgatch & Patterson, 1989):

(1) The problem should be clearly stated in neutral terms; (2) the other person paraphrases to show that he or she has heard the problem correctly; (3) brainstorm a list of possible solutions; (4) choose a solution through a process of negotiation (compromise), and write a contract that describes the terms of the agreement, the positive consequences for following the agreement, and the negative consequences for violating it.

In building the construct, we assumed that socially competent parents would be better at conducting family problem-solving sessions. It was our impression that directing a group effort to solve emotionally charged problems represented a high order of skill. We also assumed that families in which the parents were less effective at problem solving would be characterized by higher levels of future stress and perhaps higher levels of marital conflict as well.

Measurement of the Problem Solving Construct

We videotaped family problem-solving sessions for both the Planning Study and the OYS and coded them later. The duration of the sessions ranged from 15 to 30 minutes. Families were first asked to plan a weekend activity and then to solve two problems that were selected from a list of current issues they had identified in an earlier interview.

The coders were trained to record the sequence of family problem-solving exchanges using a code developed by Forgatch, Fetrow, and Lathrop (1985). They also coded the affective tone for each interchange and filled out a set of ratings at the end of the session. The ratings included items that described various aspects of

the final solution reached by the family. These ratings formed an internally consistent scale. The second potential indicator was based on the mean of a single item rated by each of the family members at the end of the session, "How well do you think the problem was solved?"

A third indicator was based on the home observers' global ratings of the problem-solving exchanges that occurred during the observations. This indicator showed excellent convergence with ratings by the coders and parents. We did not include the observer-impressions score in the present analysis because those ratings had extremely high method-variance loadings. This type of data is as "volatile" as mothers' ratings in terms of causing models to fail (see Chapter 8). The details of the itemetric and psychometric analyses are presented in Capaldi and Patterson (1989).

Empirical Findings

The correlations among the three indicators for Cohorts I and II are summarized in Table 6.1. Because all three variables were derived from a common procedure (videotapes of family interactions during the task), the median convergence among the constructs was quite high (.422 and .436). Our confidence in the latent construct was considerably enhanced by the fact that we have obtained similar factor structures across different samples when using these indicators.

The findings from the principal components factor analyses for the Dyadic Problem Solving construct are summarized in Figure 6.2A. Notice the factor invariance reflected in Cohorts I and II. Coder impressions of satisfactory outcomes had the highest loadings. The construct also loaded significantly on the number of positive solutions observed during the sessions and on the likelihood of a parental solution given that they were interacting with the child.

The data in Figure 6.2B are from the longitudinal study of single mothers by Forgatch and Ray (1991). The latent construct loaded significantly on two of the three in-

Figure 6.2
Robustness of the Dyadic
Problem Solving Construct

A. Oregon Youth Study Sample

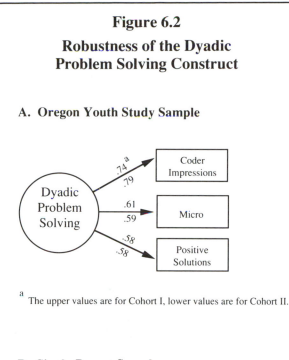

[a] The upper values are for Cohort I, lower values are for Cohort II.

B. Single-Parent Sample

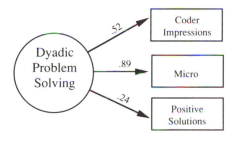

dicators. Notice that the configuration of loadings was quite different from that of the OYS.

Validity. The Planning Study samples provided some information about the validity of an earlier version of the Dyadic Problem Solving construct (Patterson & Stouthamer-Loeber, 1984). The correlation of the construct score with a composite measure of academic skills was .17 (N.S.) for the fourth-grade sample, .28 ($p < .05$) for the seventh-grade sample, and .30 (N.S.) for the tenth-grade sample. The Dyadic Problem Solving construct correlated -.23 ($p < .05$) with child depression and -.22 ($p < .05$) with child antisocial behavior for the adolescent samples in the Planning Study. The findings showed a low level relation between ineffective problem solving and child adjustment problems.

Our recent analysis of the Dyadic Problem Solving construct indicates that it may play a central role in certain kinds of family processes. Effective problem-solving skills are apparently related to several parental characteristics, including intelligence. For the OYS samples,

parental IQ data (as measured with the WAIS) (The Psychological Corporation, 1955) correlated .44 with the construct score. The most detailed examination of the functions, or validities, of the construct were conducted in the single-mother study (Patterson & Forgatch, 1990b). We found that problem-solving skills directly determined future levels of stress and indirectly determined future levels of maternal depression. By using latent growth model analyses of longitudinal data, we demonstrated that prior measures of mother–confidante problem-solving outcomes accounted for significant variance in individual growth curves for stress. Preliminary inspections of comparable data from the OYS have indicated that these relations do not apply to intact families.

For the single-mother sample, problem-solving outcome seems to be significantly related to the characteristics of both members of the dyad and to the type of problem being discussed (Forgatch & Fetrow, 1990). We are confident that the Dyadic Problem Solving construct will be useful in our efforts to analyze family process.

Positive Reinforcement Construct

Parental skill in tracking and reinforcing the occurrences of subtle prosocial child behaviors builds a foundation for the development of prosocial skills. Bijou and Baer (1967) have reviewed the details of this process and the empirical studies supporting the contribution of these contingencies to the socialization process.

During the preschool years, the greatest number of reinforcers are provided by the person who has the most contact with the child. Therefore, the primary caregiver is the most important source of reinforcement. Positive exchanges with the primary caregiver make a significant contribution to the child's prosocial development. For example, Hartup's (1983) review of the research indicated that parents have a stronger influence on the child's commitment to achievement goals (e.g., plans for college and future work roles) than do peers.

We assumed that the younger the child, the more likely the parents are to react contingently with praise and approval to prosocial behaviors. By the time the child is 10 years old, only a small fraction of family interactions involve parental praise and approval for prosocial behaviors, which presents measurement problems similar to those we encountered in assessing low baserate events for the Discipline construct.

We decided to assess both contingent and noncontingent positive parental reactions. The goal was to demonstrate empirically that the two types of reactions were, indeed, related. Parents who show high rates of positive behavior during daily interactions with their children also are likely to reinforce the behaviors necessary for the development of academic and peer relational skills. Of course, we knew that some parenting styles would not fit this simple descriptive model — for example, parents who were noncontingent "gushers" — but we were confident that the issue could be resolved empirically.

Who Reinforces or Punishes What?

From a reinforcement theory perspective, parents' contingent reactions are the key to understanding the socialization process. With this in mind, it is surprising to discover that almost nothing is known about the variables that determine when one person is likely to reinforce or punish another person. This lack of information has forced us to rely on our clinical experience as a basis for the speculations outlined in this section.

"He's such a bad child — it's difficult for me to reinforce him." We often hear variations on this statement in our treatment sessions with parents of antisocial children. Typically, the parents recount the troubles that led them to reject the child and that gradually eroded their warm feelings toward him or her. As the coercion process gains momentum, the child becomes increasingly disruptive and disciplinary confrontations begin to occur more often. The child's abrasive interpersonal style leads to rejection by both parents and peers. Incidentally, the child is similarly influenced; the frequent disciplinary confrontations, abrasiveness, and aversive exchanges lead him or her to reject both parents and peers. In clinical observations, there appears to be a bidirectional relation between the child's deviant behavior and parental rejection. Patterson (1986a) found strong correlational support for the relation between parental rejection and child deviancy. However, Patterson and Dishion (1985) showed that the relation was more likely to be unidirectional, with child antisocial behavior as the determinant for parental rejection.

Parental rejection is accompanied by reductions in positive reinforcement and involvement. Therefore, there should be a negative correlation between measures of the Child Antisocial construct and the Positive Reinforcement construct: the more deviant the child, the less reinforcement from the parents. A significant correlation would also provide support for the idea that children act out because they do not receive parental support.

"I prefer to reinforce behaviors that are similar to my own." Fagot and Patterson (1969) advanced the hypothesis that each socializing agent (e.g., parent, teacher, peer, or sibling) is more likely to reinforce the child's behaviors that resemble the agent's own repertoire of behaviors. For example, female siblings would be more likely to reinforce female-preferred behaviors and male siblings would be more likely to reinforce male-preferred behaviors. Although this idea is somewhat unsatisfying, we have not been able to reject it.

Support for the hypothesis is based on data from a single setting (nursery school) and from the reinforcing reactions of the adults who work in that setting. Fagot and Patterson (1969) found that female nursery school teachers were most likely to reinforce female-preferred behaviors. In fact, this seemed to be the case whether the child was a boy or a girl. Female peers also reinforced female-preferred behaviors; only male peers reinforced male-preferred behaviors. The overall findings have been replicated and extended by several investigators (e.g., Robinson, 1976). In her review of the growing body of literature, Fagot (1978a, 1978b) noted that observations of teachers consistently support the selective-reinforcement hypothesis. When the reinforcing agents were asked what they thought they were doing, however, a different picture emerged. Again, it seems that our global assessments of what we think we are doing are not consistent with our behavior at the molecular, action–reaction level of social interaction.

Few home observation studies have attempted to test the differential-reinforcement hypothesis. Margolin and Patterson (1975) analyzed the data for a small sample of intact normal families that contained both boys and girls. The findings showed a trend that parents were more likely to react positively to the same-sex child, but this was significant only for fathers and sons. Taplin and Reid (1977) conducted a baseline analysis of families with antisocial boys and found that fathers were more likely to react positively to the boys' prosocial behavior (.16) than were mothers (.14). However, neither investigative team tried to determine whether the parents were reinforcing sex-preferred behaviors.

"Nothing the child does is good enough." We believe that parents differ in their schemata regarding what is "good" or "bad" child behavior. Parents with problem children seem to have a narrowly defined schemata for classifying good child behavior, and there is little in the ongoing behavior of the child that they feel merits reinforcement. In laboratory studies, the band width of the parental schema is partly determined by the nature of the interactions with the child. Again, the more coercive the child, the narrower the schema for classifying child behaviors as good (Hess, Holloway, Price, & Dickson, 1982; Schmaling & Patterson, 1984).

Parents with problem children are reluctant to reinforce anything less than outstanding performances. This is evident from self-report data in case after case. The general tenor of the parents' comments indicates that they believe reinforcement will weaken the child in some way, and that it therefore should be used sparingly. In addition, their remarks seem to reflect a sense of injustice about reinforcing the child (e.g., "Why should I reinforce him for doing something he's supposed to do anyway?").

Hess et al. (1982) found that parents with antisocial children were significantly less sensitive to children's prosocial behavior than were parents with normal children. They were underinclusive in the sense that they classified as neutral or even negative certain child behaviors that were classified by others as prosocial. In a second laboratory study employing a similar signal detection design, Schmaling and Patterson (1984) showed that having mothers view videotapes of positive parent-child interactions increased their inclusiveness for categorizing prosocial behaviors. The mothers' observed reactions to their children in the home covaried in the predicted manner with their schematization in the laboratory: Mothers who were more inclusive for children's prosocial behaviors were more likely to react positively in the home (.43, $p < .10$) and when the child had initiated a positive response to her (.53, $p < .05$).

To understand how reinforcement concepts apply to the socialization process, it is necessary to identify the variables that determine or predict parental skill in using positive reinforcement. Unfortunately, this is one of the least explored areas in the literature on social reinforcement. We know that problem children receive less reinforcement, but we do not know whether this is a result of the deviant behavior or part of the process that produces it.

It is helpful to know that we tend to be more reinforcing to those who are most like ourselves, but it is difficult to accept this hypothesis because it is based solely on studies of nursery school children. The hypothesis that seems to have the most potential is that the band width for the range of behaviors that are reinforced expands and contracts as a function of the abrasiveness or supportiveness of the ongoing exchanges. For example, when we fall in love, even trivial behaviors may be schematized as worthy of approval. By the same token, as we slip into a pattern of conflict with our spouse, any minor irritant warrants a negative response.

Finally, it seems that people who are more socially competent are also more reinforcing. Data from OYS samples show that the parental Social Competence construct correlates .34 ($p < .01$) with the parental Positive Reinforcement construct. This supports our assumption that a socially unskilled person is most likely to use coercion to maximize immediate self-gratification and a socially competent person is most likely to use positive reinforcement and negotiation to achieve long-term goals.

Measurement of the Positive Reinforcement Construct

Our approach has been to tailor the assessment devices to include parent and child reports about positive reinforcement as well as observation data that describe interaction sequences. The details of the analyses and psychometric properties for each of the indicators are described in Capaldi and Patterson (1989). One set of scales was obtained by conducting traditional interviews with the parent and the child. Another method was to call the parents and the child separately (six times each) and ask for specific examples of reinforcement that had occurred within the preceding 16 hours.

The third assessment approach was to observe parent–child interaction sequences in the home. This approach, however, may have its limitations. Most of the prosocial behaviors that are observed during brief exchanges in the home are already well established and are maintained by lean schedules of parental reinforcement. The most effective approach would be to have the parent select several prosocial behaviors that would become the focus of assessment and then observe the parent and child interacting in a setting in which the parent tries to teach or strengthen those behaviors. For example, in the longitudinal study by Hess and his colleagues, parents were asked to teach their preschool children to stack blocks (Hess, Holloway, Price, & Dickson, 1982). Sigel and his colleagues used paper-folding and storytelling tasks (Sigel, 1982). These may be ideal settings for measuring parental reinforcement sequences because the target events occur more often. It is difficult to measure a parent's contingent reactions to a child's prosocial behaviors by observing relatively unstructured interactions in the home. The frequency of child behaviors that a parent is likely to target for approval or praise is simply too low. In normal families, for example, mothers use approval once every 11 minutes and fathers use it about half as often (Patterson, 1982).

The Planning Study. In the analyses based on the Planning Study sample, the Positive Reinforcement construct became a conglomerate that included measures of positive reinforcement, general support, and parental involvement. In the more recent studies, contingent reinforcement and support have become one construct, and parental involvement has become a separate construct.

For the Planning Study sample, three indicators were developed that showed significant convergence in defining the Positive Reinforcement construct (Patterson, 1986a; Patterson & Stouthamer-Loeber, 1984). The first indicator consisted of three variables from the home observation data: (1) the likelihood of maternal approval given that she interacted with the target child, (2) maternal positive affect while interacting with the target child, and (3) a measure of maternal distance (involvement). Each conditional probability value was standardized, and the values were combined to form the indicator. The second indicator was based on child-interview reports of parental positive reinforcement for prosocial behavior. The third indicator was a composite of the observers' global ratings following their sessions in the home; the ratings described parents talking to the child about his or her day and the extent to which they seemed to promote the child's interests.

Current studies. In current analyses, the Positive Reinforcement construct was defined as a combination of

Table 6.2

Convergent Matrix of Indicators for the Positive Reinforcement Construct

Cohort II	Cohort I				
	Observer Impressions	Parent Interview	Interviewer Impressions	Parent Daily Report	OCPR[a]
Observer Impressions	—	.20	.32	.34	.20
Parent Interview	.21	—	.31	.17	.12
Interviewer Impressions	.32	.24	—	.46	.11
Parent Daily Report	.19	.13	.33	—	.16
OCPR[a]	.39	.18	.17	.35	—

[a]Observed contingent positive reaction.

parental contingent and noncontingent positive reactions to the child. Five indicators were used to define this construct. One consisted of observed child–parent interaction sequences, two were based on traditional interviews with the parent, one was based on the parents' daily telephone reports about reinforcing exchanges, and one was based on observers' global impressions about reinforcing parent–child exchanges.

The observer-impressions indicator consisted of nine items that formed an internally consistent scale (e.g., parental reinforcement of academic, work, and social skills).

The parental interview consisted of 14 items that described how often the parents let their child know they were pleased with what he was doing (e.g., chores, schoolwork, general demeanor around the house). Some items also sampled their beliefs about giving rewards and reinforcement for good behavior (e.g., "Children are supposed to do as they are told" and "You spoil a child by rewarding him for what he is supposed to do"). A 10-item variation of the parent-interview scale was formed from the child-interview items. Even though it was possible to obtain a reliable subscale, the child interview score did not converge with the other indicators.

The interviewer impressions consisted of just two items: "Seemed to enjoy parenting" and "How would you rate this parent on positive reinforcement?"

The six daily telephone calls to parents consisted of two items each. One item asked whether the parent had used praise or compliments for anything the child had done in the last three days. The other item asked whether the parent had given the child a hug or a kiss because he or she was pleased with him.

The observation indicator summarized the following four variables, each of which described the likelihood of a specific parental reaction to the target child: (1) approval, given an interaction; (2) approval, given that the child did something prosocial; (3) positive affect, given an interaction with the child; and (4) positive affect, given that the child did something prosocial.

Empirical Findings

The correlations among the five indicators are summarized in Table 6.2. The median correlations for Cohort I was .20; for Cohort II it was .21. The convergence is marginal at best. In both samples, the convergence is weakest for the parent-interview indicator.

We have collected the relevant data for several other samples, but the indicator scores have not yet been calculated for the Positive Reinforcement construct. Figure 6.3 summarizes the results of the principal components factor analyses separately for Cohorts I and II. All five indicators show significant factor loadings for both cohorts. The latent construct loads most heavily on the interviewer-impressions and observer-impressions indicators. Notice, however, that the factor loadings shift considerably from one cohort to another. Because the patterns of factor loadings do not meet the requirements for configural invariance, it appears that we need to develop stronger indicators for this construct. On the bright side, Capaldi and Patterson (1989) showed that the distribution for the composite score is almost perfectly normal. The kurtosis and skewness indices were nonsignificant, so the composite score should be suitable for the usual correlational analyses.

Validity. We were able to gather preliminary validity data from the Planning Study samples. The earlier definition for the construct included a mixture of positive reinforcement and parental involvement. The correlation of this conglomerate construct with a composite measure of academic achievement was .28 (N.S.) for the fourth-grade sample, .39 ($p < .05$) for the seventh-grade sample,

Figure 6.3

Robustness of the
Positive Reinforcement Construct

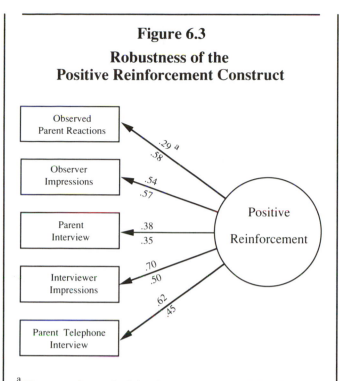

[a] The upper values are for Cohort I, lower values are for Cohort II.

and .30 ($p < .05$) for the tenth-grade sample. For the adolescent samples, the construct correlated .23 ($p < .05$) with the measure of child self-esteem.

The analyses based on OYS data showed that the positive reinforcement composite score was only marginally related to the criterion scores for which it was designed. For example, the correlations with the Academic Achievement construct score were .22 ($p < .05$) for Cohort I and .18 (N.S.) for Cohort II. The correlations with Self-Esteem were in the expected direction but were nonsignificant: .16 for Cohort I and .14 for Cohort II.

Judging from the precarious factor structure and the marginal validity values, we still have a lot of work to do on this construct. Of course, the problem may lie in the concept itself, but we cannot assume this is the case until the underlying measurement problems have been solved.

Parental Involvement Construct

Even if it is properly measured, the Positive Reinforcement construct by itself will not reflect certain critical dimensions of family life. One possible example of this is the parent who reinforces contingently but spends so little time with the child that the impact on the child's behavior is minor. We developed the Parental Involvement construct to assess the time parents spend with their children. This construct was expected to correlate signifi-

cantly with child prosocial behaviors such as achievement, peer relations, and self-esteem.

In distressed families, the frequent irritable exchanges and conflicts make it unpleasant for family members to be together. Because a car trip to the beach or the mountains can be an agonizing experience for everyone, there are few such trips. Birchler, Weiss, and Vincent (1975) and Jacobson, Elwood, and Dallas (1981) found that distressed married couples share fewer activities than do nondistressed couples. A similar pattern seems to characterize families of antisocial boys. Fagan, Langner, Gersten, and Eisenberg (1977) and West and Farrington (1977) found that children whose families spend a substantial amount of leisure time together were at lower risk for delinquency than were those whose families spend little time together. We therefore hypothesized that high scores on the Child Antisocial construct would covary with low scores on the Parental Involvement construct.

We think of the Parental Involvement construct as an indirect measure of parental support, which should play a key role in determining preadolescent self-esteem (Harter, 1983). Engaging in activities that are mutually enjoyable is a noncontingent aspect of the parent–child relationship that makes a significant contribution to the child's self-esteem.

Measurement of the
Parental Involvement Construct

In the first wave of analyses, we tailored appropriate sets of interview items to the construct. This resulted in separate and reliable scales for the parents and the child. We also developed brief telephone interviews that estimated the amount of time the parents and the child spent together. The third method we explored was a checklist of family activities that was filled out separately by the parents and the child. The details of the itemetric and factor analyses for the construct have been reviewed by Capaldi and Patterson (1989).

Although it was generally possible to construct scales that were internally consistent, only four of the six indicators survived the first factor analysis: (1) child interview, (2) child telephone interview items, (3) parent and child checklist, and (4) reports of shared family activities.

The child interview consisted of a single item describing how often the child discussed his or her plans for the coming day with his parents. The child telephone interview included items such as "In the last 24 hours, have your parents taken you on an activity?" and "Did your parents talk to you about your plans for the coming day?" The activities checklist simply counted the number of activities with the entire family (such as sports, scouting, shopping, or eating at home) that had occurred during the last week. The checklist consisted of 28 typical activities for normal families.

Table 6.3
Convergent Matrix of Indicators for the Parental Involvement Construct

Cohort II	Cohort I			
	Parent: Activities with Child	Child Report: Activ. with Parent	Child Interview	Child Phone Interview
Parent: Activities with Child	—	.50	.25	.17
Child Report: Activities with Parent	.33	—	.32	.41
Child Interview	.07	.12	—	.48
Child Phone Interview	.07	.25	.40	—

Empirical Findings

The bivariate correlations among the four most promising indicators are summarized in Table 6.3. The parent and child questionnaire data for shared activities form a common factor, but the other two indicators based on child reports are only marginally related. The median convergence for Cohort I was only .19; for Cohort II it was .37.

We have collected data for a younger sample and a clinical sample, but it has not been analyzed yet. Judging from the results of the principal components factor analyses shown in Figure 6.4, we suspect that the child reports were weighted too heavily in the definition of the latent construct. One alternative would be to define the factor by using only the two questionnaire indicators; then the perceptions of the parent and the child would be equally weighted. The patterns for the factor loadings are an indication that we have at least achieved a configural factor invariance; the rank orders of the factor scores are perfectly correlated. The distribution of the composite scores does not deviate significantly from normality (Capaldi & Patterson, 1989).

Validity. The details of the validity findings are discussed in a separate section of this chapter and in the section on modeling studies in Chapter 7. At this point, it seems that the Parental Involvement construct only marginally served the functions we had intended. The construct related in the expected direction to the measures of achievement and peer relations, but the correlations were nonsignificant in all instances. However, there were significant correlations between the measure of self-esteem and the Parental Involvement construct for both cohorts; the correlations were .21 ($p < .05$) for Cohort I and .44 ($p < .001$) for Cohort II. The comparable correlation for the adolescents in the Planning Study sample was .34 ($p < .001$). In each study, children with parents who were more involved described themselves as having higher self-esteem. The findings supported Harter's (1983) original speculations about the origin of good self-esteem in children. However, the correlations may reflect a significant contribution from shared method; child self-report was used for both of the self-esteem indicators and for three of the four indicators for the Parental Involvement construct. Mismatching the indicators by dropping child report from the Parent Involvement construct would be a good strategy to follow in testing this hypothesis.

Figure 6.4
Robustness of the Parental Involvement Construct

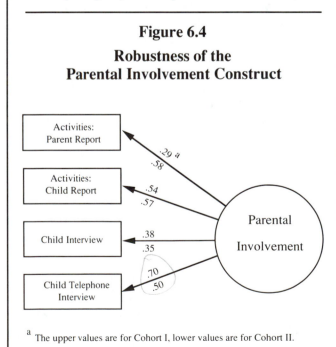

a The upper values are for Cohort I, lower values are for Cohort II.

Further Analyses of Family Management Constructs

Three questions are examined in this section. First, are there five family management constructs, or is there actually a single dimension that ranges from "good parent-

Table 6.4

Intercorrelations Among Family Management Constructs

Cohort II	Cohort I				
	Parental Monitoring	Discipline	Positive Reinforc.	Parental Involvement	Problem Solving
Parental Monitoring	—	.27**	.29***	.27**	.05
Discipline	.17*	—	.25**	.25**	-.02
Positive Reinforcement	.19*	.46***	—	.34***	.21*
Parental Involvement	.33***	.16	.34***	—	.09
Problem Solving	.14	.24**	.30***	.25**	—

*p < .05   **p < .01   ***p < .001

ing" to "bad parenting"? If the latter is true, then all of the constructs should be highly correlated. In other words, parents who are effective at monitoring and discipline also would be effective at problem solving, positive reinforcement, and involvement. Of course, the question implies that it is possible to differentiate one parenting skill from another; this issue is addressed by using confirmatory factor analyses.

The second question is more difficult. It addresses the unique contribution of the five family management constructs. Is the structure of socialization (see Figure 6.1) hierarchical? If it is, then the association of discipline and monitoring with child noncompliance may be all that is required to differentiate children who are socially skilled from those who are unskilled. This assumption is tested by regressing each of the prosocial skill constructs against the battery of family management constructs. If the structure is hierarchical, putting Parental Monitoring and Discipline into the regression analyses first would account for most or all of the variance. The pattern should hold if the criterion variables consisted of deviant or prosocial child behaviors.

Finally, what is the relation between parenting practices and child outcomes? This question is examined from a broader perspective. Canonical correlation analysis is used to search for the simplest parameters of this complex relation.

Intercorrelations Among Family Management Skills

We assume that socially unskilled adults are at serious risk for disruptions in all five family management skills. If this is the case, the intercorrelation among the construct scores would be positive and significant. Parents who are ineffective in discipline confrontations are at risk for inept monitoring, positive reinforcement, and problem solving,

as well as inadequate involvement with their children.

The correlations among the constructs are summarized in Table 6.4. The findings are in accord with the hypothesis of a general lack of parenting skill. The correlations among the scores are positive and significant for all relations. The Discipline and Positive Reinforcement constructs are the most closely related for both cohorts, and Problem Solving is least related to other measures of parenting skill. The median intercorrelation was .25 for both cohorts.

Differentiating One Construct from Another

The consistency of positive intercorrelations between construct scores raises the question of whether these scores reflect more than a lack of social or parenting skills and, if so, in what sense. This is a variation on the classic problem of how to differentiate one trait or concept from another (Campbell & Fiske, 1959).

The investigator must demonstrate that the multimethod indicators correlate more highly *within* constructs than *between* them. We tested the hypothesis that the family management constructs reflect differentiated skills in two phases. In the first phase, we attempted to differentiate the Discipline and Parental Monitoring constructs because of their shared contribution to measures of deviant child behavior. In the second phase, we attempted to differentiate the Positive Reinforcement, Problem Solving, and Parental Involvement constructs by using a confirmatory analysis. This method requires the investigator to specify *beforehand* how many constructs there are and how they will load on each indicator. Then the models can be compared. For example, we could specify that the indicators really define only a single construct: "Bad Parenting." We could then compare it to a model that specifies two factors (e.g., ineffective discipline can be

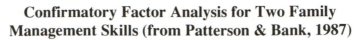

Figure 6.5

**Confirmatory Factor Analysis for Two Family
Management Skills (from Patterson & Bank, 1987)**

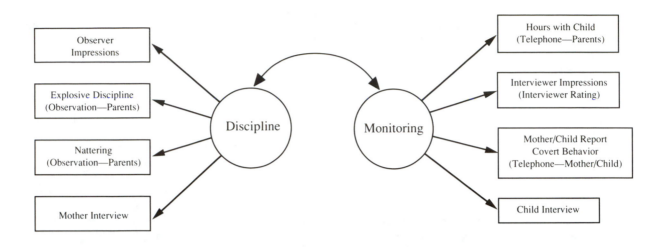

Reprinted with permission from "When is a nomological network a construct?" In D. R. Peterson and D. B. Fishman (Eds.), *Assessment for Decision.* Copyright 1987 by Rutgers, The State University.

differentiated from ineffective monitoring). A chi-square test can be used to determine which model provides the best fit to the data.

Patterson and Bank (1987) compared single- and two-factor models for the Discipline and Parental Monitoring constructs. Figure 6.5 shows these two constructs and the indicators used in the analyses. The confirmatory factor analysis tested two hypotheses. One hypothesis was that there were two constructs, Parental Monitoring and Discipline. Even though they are significantly related, they also can be differentiated from each other. The second hypothesis was that the two constructs were more similar than they were different. The two-factor model provided a significantly better fit than did the single factor describing poor parenting in general. We concluded that, although both constructs may relate to an underlying lack of social or parenting skills, they are also discriminatively different. This means there is some utility in continuing to measure the two skills separately.

We also used a confirmatory factor analysis to test the hypothesis that the three positive parenting constructs were significantly related and discriminatively different at the same time. We combined data from the two cohorts for this analysis. The constructs and their indicators are shown in Figure 6.6. The individual indicators loaded significantly on their respective constructs. The correlation between Positive Reinforcement and Parental Involvement was substantial (.57). The overall goodness-of-fit test revealed an adequate fit of the three-

factor model to the data: chi-square (44) = 50.67, $p < .23$. In this case, a significant chi-square indicates a *difference* between the model and the data set in the covariance structures. We also found that the three-factor model provided a significantly better fit to the data than did a single positive parenting construct, as indicated by the difference of the chi-square indices for the two models: chi-square (2) = 65.2, $p < .001$. There are three different concepts concerning positive parenting skills, and our measures can differentiate one from the others.

Validity of the Parental Monitoring and Discipline Constructs

We demonstrated in Chapter 5 that the Parental Monitoring and Discipline measures covaried as expected with measures of antisocial behavior. In this section, we consider a wider array of child adjustment measures. The data are presented that serve as a basis for comparison with measures of positive parenting skills.

We expected both parenting skills to relate significantly to various forms of antisocial behavior and to other forms of deviancy. Because many antisocial boys are at risk for depression and drug sampling, we included measures of these two behaviors that were based on parent, teacher, and interviewer reports. We also included composite measures of academic and peer-relational skills as well as self-esteem (based on two self-report instruments) to put the contributions into perspective.

The correlations between the Discipline and Parental

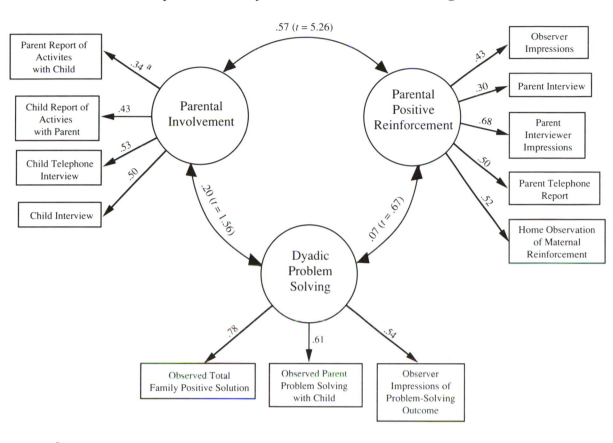

Figure 6.6
Confirmatory Factor Analysis for the Positive Parenting Constructs

.57 (t = 5.26)

Parent Report of Activites with Child — .34 a

Child Report of Activies with Parent — .43

Child Telephone Interview — .53

Child Interview — .50

Parental Involvement

Parental Positive Reinforcement

Observer Impressions — .43

Parent Interview — .30

Parent Interviewer Impressions — .68

Parent Telephone Report — .50

Home Observation of Maternal Reinforcement — .52

.20 (t = 1.56)

.07 (t = .67)

Dyadic Problem Solving

Observed Total Family Positive Solution — .78

Observed Parent Problem Solving with Child — .61

Observer Impressions of Problem-Solving Outcome — .54

a All factor loadings are statistically significant at the .05 level.

$\chi^2_{(44)} = 50.67, p = .23$

Monitoring constructs and the six criterion (composite) measures of child behavior are summarized in Table 6.5. The findings are profoundly satisfying, particularly the replicated findings for the Discipline construct. Disrupted monitoring and discipline were significantly associated with increases in antisocial behavior for both cohorts. The replicated relation to child depression was equally robust. The levels of significance and even the magnitudes of the correlations were stable across cohorts. We believe that the robustness of these findings vindicates the extraordinary expenditure of time required to design the assessment battery and collect the data necessary to define the constructs. We doubt that single (reliable) measures of any of these indicators would produce the same results. We plan to investigate our implicit assumption that multi-agent, multimethod assessment is more likely to replicate.

The contribution of the Discipline construct to drug sampling, academic skill, and peer-relational skills was surprisingly robust; in fact, the order of magnitude of the correlations was almost as great as that for the antisocial criterion. Parents who were inept in their discipline practices were more likely to have antisocial sons who sampled multiple drugs, were failing in school, and had poor peer-relational skills. On the other hand, parents who were ineffective at monitoring were at risk primarily for having antisocial and depressed sons. The contribution of disrupted monitoring to other measures of child adjustment did not replicate from one cohort to the other.

Positive Parenting and Child Behaviors

The correlations between the six criterion measures of child behavior and the three measures of parenting practices are summarized in Table 6.6. There is little cause for celebration here. Only one finding for the Positive Reinforcement construct even approached replication, and that variable accounted for less than 4% of the variance in the measure of academic skill. Because the Parental Involvement construct covaried significantly with the self-esteem

Table 6.5

Correlations Between Parental Monitoring and Discipline and Child Behaviors

Child Behaviors	Parenting Skill			
	Monitoring		Discipline	
	Cohort I	Cohort II	Cohort I	Cohort II
Problem Behaviors				
Antisocial Behavior	-.38***	-.25**	-.44***	-.45***
Drug Sampling	-.33***	-.18	-.31**	-.27**
Skills				
Academic Skills	.36***	.15	.29**	.32**
Peer Relations	.30**	.16	.36***	.45***
Mood				
Self-Esteem	.35***	.18	.15	.18
Depression	-.23*	-.23*	-.28**	-.38***

*p < .05   **p < .01   ***p < .001

measure for both cohorts and replicated the findings from the Planning Study, it appears to be a robust finding. Only one finding was replicated for the Dyadic Problem Solving construct. For both cohorts, ineffective problem solving was associated with higher levels of antisocial child behavior, although the magnitude of the relation was slight in both cases.

Our attempts to build constructs that sample the positive aspects of parenting behavior have not been particularly successful. However, the heart of the problem may be in the concept rather than in our approach to measurement. Reinforcement, involvement, and problem-solving skills may not play the critical roles we thought they did. Nevertheless, we suspect that the impact of positive

Table 6.6

Correlations Between Positive Reinforcement, Problem Solving, and Parental Involvement and Child Behaviors

Child Behaviors	Parenting Skill					
	Positive Reinforcement		Parental Involvement		Dyadic Problem Solving	
	Cohort I	Cohort II	Cohort I	Cohort II	Cohort I	Cohort II
Problem Behaviors						
Antisocial Behavior	-.08	-.25**	.01	-.16	-.19*	-.18*
Drug Sampling	-.08	-.13	-.21*	-.11	-.13	-.24**
Skills						
Academic Skills	.23*	.18*	.08	.07	.16	.18*
Peer Relations	.03	.16*	.13	.18	.04	.18*
Mood						
Self-Esteem	.18*	.14	.28**	.45***	.27**	.08
Depression	-.04	-.23**	-.15	-.26**	-.09	-.04

*p < .05   **p < .01   ***p < .001

Table 6.7

Multivariate Analyses for the Relation Between Family Management Skills and Child Behaviors

Child Behaviors	Parenting Skill[a]					
	Parental Monitoring	Discipline	Positive Reinforcement	Problem Solving	Parental Involvement	R^2
Problem Behaviors						
Antisocial Behavior	-.33	-.44	.11	-.22	.19	.36
	-.17	-.41	.01	-.06	-.03	.24
Drug Sampling	-.26	-.24	.14	-.14	-.12	.19
	-.13	-.22	.05	-.18	.00	.12
Skills						
Academic Skills	.29	.22	.09	.14	-.09	.21
	.10	.28	.01	.10	-.04	.12
Peer Relations	.25	.32	-.14	.06	.02	.19
	.06	.47	-.13	.07	.12	.24
Mood						
Self-Esteem	.28	.04	-.02	-.25	.18	.22
	.02	.16	-.08	-.05	.46	.23
Depression	-.25	-.33	.15	-.11	-.03	.22
	-.13	-.36	.00	.12	-.19	.22

[a] Standard partial betas for Cohort I (upper row) and Cohort II (lower row).

parenting is easier to identify early in the socialization process. In a sample of 100 reasonably compliant 6-year-old boys, for example, positive reinforcement, involvement, and problem-solving variables should make substantial contributions to measures of prosocial child behaviors. For the present, it seems that the parent's approach to establishing child compliance is the best predictor of a child's prosocial skills.

Multivariate Studies of Positive Parenting

The impact of parents on children's prosocial behaviors is mediated by their success in training the child to be reasonably compliant. DeBaryshe, Patterson, and Capaldi (1990) showed that parental discipline contributed directly *and* indirectly to child achievement. The bivariate correlations we have presented so far seem to support this simplistic picture, but it may be prudent to adopt an analytic strategy that allows for a more complex set of relations. To address these issues, we designed the multiple-regression and canonical analyses described in this section.

First, we regressed each family management skill on each of the six measures of child behavior. Table 6.7

summarizes the findings separately for each cohort. The first five columns list the standardized partial beta coefficients for the five parenting variables, and the last column lists the amount of variance (R^2) accounted for in the dependent variable.

The findings reiterate the theme established by the bivariate correlations. For five of the child adjustment measures, the primary contributions were made by measures of parental discipline and monitoring. Notice that this method of estimating the variance yields a range of 24% to 32% for the Child Antisocial construct, which is in keeping with our goal of accounting for 30% of the variance for key criterion variables. For the remaining child adjustment criteria, the range is considerably lower (12% to 24%). Most of the models used to understand peer relations, self-esteem, depression, and achievement must include more than family management measures alone.

For the sample of 10-year-olds, criterion estimates of drug sampling probably would be quite skewed (i.e., very few of them are sampling drugs at this age). Presumably, young antisocial boys are most at risk for such behavior. Even so, the Discipline and Parental Monitoring constructs accounted for a moderate but significant amount of variance. As the boys grow older, we expect the monitoring variable and a measure of deviant peer group involvement to account for increasing amounts of variance in this criterion.

The same assumptions would apply to measures of child depression. At best, the extreme scores describe a small group of boys who have recurring dysphoric moods, and it is likely that few of them are clinically depressed. A logical assumption would be that inept discipline or monitoring practices contribute *directly* to this problem. As we shall see in Chapter 8, the antisocial disposition produces certain reactions from the social environment that contribute to the dysphoric mood (Patterson & Capaldi, 1991b).

Parenting skills alone account for a modest, but significant, share of the variance in children's academic achievement. As demonstrated by DeBaryshe et al. (1990) and Patterson (1991a), however, including measures of the amount of time the child spends on task generates a model that accounts for more than 40% of the variance in achievement.

The child's estimate of his own self-esteem is significantly related to the Parental Involvement construct for both cohorts. Although this finding is of theoretical interest, additional variance could be accounted for by including measures of the child's peer relationships and academic achievement (Bank & Patterson, in press).

In sum, the current findings show that parenting skills make both direct and indirect contributions to all six measures of child adjustment.

Canonical Analyses

One conclusion that can be drawn from the multiple-regression analyses is that a *single primary dimension* cuts across the matrices of both parent and child behaviors. The data indicate that parental discipline and monitoring practices, as well as all measures of child behaviors (with the possible exception of self-esteem), should load on a single dimension. This dimension would be analogous to the first stage of the hierarchical model presented in Figure 6.1. If this dimension were removed, then some other residual dimension (i.e., parental involvement, problem solving, or positive reinforcement) might make its debut. It is conceivable, for example, that a first-dimension loading on monitoring and discipline would load on a few prosocial and all deviant child behaviors, but a second residual might load only on positive parenting and some selected positive child behaviors.

We used data from the Planning Study to carry out the first canonical correlation analysis. Cohort I served as a replication sample. Four child behavior measures defined one matrix and four family management scores defined the other. This function weighted a set of variables in one matrix in such a way that they were maximally related to a set of differentially weighted variables in the second

matrix. We carried out the canonical correlation to examine the relation between the two sets of variables; the square of this correlation is an estimate of the variance shared by the two canonical variates (Pedhazur, 1982). The first canonical variate extracted would be analogous to the first stage in the hierarchical model.

The findings for these analyses are summarized in Table 6.8. The table lists the structural coefficients for each independent and dependent measure on the derived canonical dimensions. We interpreted them as correlational coefficients (i.e., the correlation of each variable with the dimension). Together, the two dimensions accounted for 65% of the variance in indices of the child's behavioral adjustment.

The first dimension was a powerful one. In both studies, the highest loadings for the parenting matrix were for discipline and monitoring. This was in keeping with the hierarchical model. Notice, however, that both positive reinforcement and problem solving had significant structural coefficients loading on this same dimension.

When the first dimension was removed, parental problem solving loads on a canonical dimension that included elements of stealing and academic achievement. This dimension may describe the relatively socialized child who is engaging in some problem behaviors. The family management variables that load on this dimension were problem solving and positive reinforcement. Unfortunately, it did not replicate in an analysis of the OYS cohorts (see Table 6.9).

The analysis of the OYS sample incorporated an expanded list of child adjustment constructs, including some that were not available in the Planning Study. The clandestine and overt indicators of the child's antisocial behavior were merged; this decision was based on the results of the Planning Study canonical correlation and the confirmatory factor analyses (see Chapter 3). The child adjustment constructs included Depression, Self-Esteem, Peer Relations, and Drug Sampling; the family management construct Parental Involvement was the independent variable. The canonical correlation analyses were carried out on the two cohorts separately to ensure a conservative interpretation of the resulting dimensions. This analysis is summarized in Table 6.9.

The first canonical dimension describes a generalized disruption in family management, which results in an antisocial and poorly adjusted boy. Again, discipline and monitoring practices seem to be at the heart of the problem, and the primary outcome appears to be the child's undersocialized, antisocial disposition. Notice that the constructs representing the boys' affective, academic, and peer-relational adjustment were heavily loaded on this first dimension. The first dimension accounted for 40% of the variance for the data from *both* cohorts.

For both cohorts, the second dimension seemed to describe the origins of self-esteem. This analysis indi-

Table 6.8

Structural Coefficients for Canonical Correlation Analyses Relating Family Management Skills to Child Behavior Constructs (Planning Study Sample)

	Canonical Dimension	
	1	2
Family Management Skill		
Parental Monitoring	-.88	-.24
Discipline	-.74	.28
Positive Reinforcement	-.72	.37
Problem Solving	-.46	.64
Child Behaviors		
Total Fighting	.89	-.25
Total Stealing	.85	.50
Academic Skills	-.55	.48
Social Skills	-.74	.28

$R_1 = .64$ $\qquad\qquad (R_1)^2 = .41^a$
$R_2 = .49$ $\qquad\qquad (R_2)^2 = .24$

[a] Variance accounted for in dependent variables.

Table 6.9

Structural Coefficients for Canonical Correlation Analyses Relating Family Management Constructs to Child Adjustment Constructs (Cohorts I and II)

	Canonical Dimension			
	1		2	
	Cohort II	Cohort I	Cohort II	Cohort I
Child Adjustment				
Antisocial Behavior	.75	.83	.25	.45
Drug Sampling	.48	.53	.30	-.27
Academic Skills	-.49	-.63	-.32	-.07
Peer Relations	-.75	-.59	-.11	-.10
Self-Esteem	-.55	-.58	.69	.55
Child Depression	.69	.58	-.18	.26
Family Management				
Parental Monitoring	-.55	-.76	-.05	.24
Discipline	-.83	-.71	-.29	-.30
Positive Reinforcement	-.27	-.30	-.17	.21
Problem Solving	-.36	-.36	-.33	.18
Parental Involvement	-.52	-.27	.74	.84
Dependent Variable				
Canonical Correlation	.63	.63	.36	.33
Variance	.40	.40	.13	.11

cated that a second process describing the boys' adjustment was primarily determined by the parents' level of involvement with the child. The second canonical dimension accounted for 11% of the variance in the dependent variables for Cohort I and 13% of the variance for Cohort II. A third dimension, which was evident in both cohorts, accounted for only a minuscule amount of variance and did not generate an identifiable pattern of structural coefficients.

The existence of a second dimension supports the idea of a hierarchical structure. The findings have promoted our interest in pursuing the topic using samples of younger boys and setting aside those in the sample who are noncompliant. What is particularly interesting about this dimension is that it relates to children's self-esteem, but not to depression. However, it is too early to say that a child's sense of self-worth is determined by how involved the parents are or that sadness is determined by how well the child gets along with his or her normal peer group.

Summary

We were admittedly surprised by the results of some of the analyses we have presented in this chapter. We had expected our measures of positive parenting to carry much more weight. Perhaps this is due to the fact that we put less time into developing measures of positive parenting. But it seems that we simply underestimated the importance of the parenting skills that control child compliance. The parent who is contingent with both rewards and punishment resolves the compliance issue and prepares the child to learn other social skills.

It would be an oversimplification to say that as long as the compliance issue is resolved, it makes no difference what socialization practices the parents follow. Some parents obtain compliance, but at great cost to the child. They not only use aversive events contingently and often, but also present them in such a way that the child is defenseless. We feel strongly that these parents should be studied in their own right.

The data we have presented also provide a provocative glimpse of at least one topic that lies beyond issues of child compliance. It seems that the covariation between child self-esteem and parental involvement is separate from compliance issues. A child may be compliant and still have low self-esteem. On the other hand, noncompliance and antisocial behavior are apparently related to low self-esteem. In that we consider self-esteem an epiphenomena, we have not put much effort into carrying out a functional analysis.

For the moment, we rest our case for prosocial parenting skills. We are puzzled by the fact that the practices associated with child compliance work as well as they do. We are not convinced that the limitations are due to measurement problems, although this is a possibility. Our hunch is that the problem lies in the metaphors about parenting used by ourselves and also by developmental psychologists. In the mean time, the models continue to account for 20% to 50% of the variance in children's prosocial behavior.

Chapter 7

The Analysis of Context

We have been describing the family as if it functioned in splendid isolation. Thus far, our search for variables that control the behavior of family members has been confined to the family itself. Although this perspective has been convenient, it is far too simplistic. The purpose of this chapter is to consider the relation between child adjustment and contextual variables such as stressors, socioeconomic status, and parental personality traits. Our position is that the effect of contextual variables on child adjustment is largely, but not entirely, mediated through family management practices. Not all children living with depressed or antisocial parents become maladjusted, nor do all children living in ghettoes become delinquent. Presumably, each contextual variable such as a depressed parent or social disadvantage identifies a significant subset of parents who are ineffective in their use of family management skills. The contextual variables can be thought of as risk factors, while effective parenting skills serve as protective factors (Garmezy, 1983).

Bronfenbrenner (1977) and others have emphasized that family interactions are embedded in an *ecological matrix*. In other words, the performance of parenting skills is the outcome of a large number of contextual variables. *Context* refers to broad macrovariables (e.g., culture, school, neighborhood, social disadvantage), and it can include variables such as daily stress level or certain parental personality traits. As Bronfenbrenner has pointed out, the interplay among these contextual variables is likely to be extremely complex. In fact, he suggests that the interaction between levels of social experience (e.g.,

parents' work, family interaction patterns), which either directly or indirectly impact the child, may be the most useful for understanding the developmental process. Although there have been a few exemplary research studies, the literature is somewhat sparse (Bronfenbrenner, 1986). Most of our knowledge about the impact of social systems on the development of antisocial behavior patterns is based on bivariate effects.

Figure 7.1 summarizes the relation between three sets of variables: child adjustment, family management practices, and contextual factors. In analyzing contextual effects, we have explored only the limited set of variables shown in Figure 7.1 (parental social disadvantage, grandparental discipline practices, parental psychopathology, marital adjustment, transitions, and stress). Certainly this is not an exhaustive list. We studied these particular variables because they were frequently encountered in our clinical contacts with families of antisocial children, and we could develop a reasonable method of assessment for them.

We believe that the relation between context and family management practices is bidirectional and asymmetric, with the largest effect going from context to family management practices. This would imply, for example, that adding more depressed or socially disadvantaged parents to a sample would result in a corresponding increase in the number of parents with ineffective family management skills. Under certain conditions, however, changes in parenting practices or child adjustment may significantly alter some of the contextual variables. It is

Figure 7.1

A Context for Parenting Practices

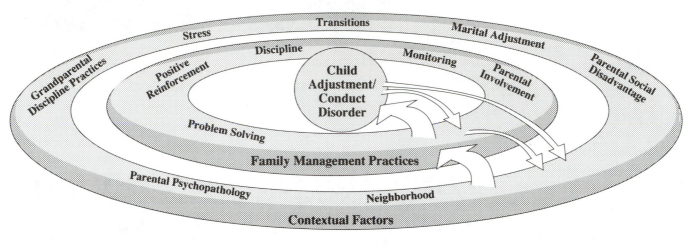
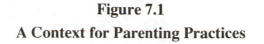

hypothesized that improvements in parenting practices will produce rapid improvements in measures of child adjustment. In addition, the child's behavior may have some effect on parenting practices. An analysis of longitudinal data from the OYS showed a path coefficient of -.36 between the level of antisocial child behavior measured at grade 4 and changes in parental discipline practices over the next two years (Patterson, Bank, & Stoolmiller, 1990). Patterson, Forgatch, and Bank (1990) found a similar effect in a study of boys from separated families; higher levels of boys' antisocial behavior were associated with increased maternal stress a year later.

We do not believe that *all* disruptions in process are due to forces outside the family. It must be that the disrupting force is often the outcome of a process within the family, such as the increasingly bitter conflicts between husband and wife that precede a separation. Unfortunately, we have not been able to make a strong case for marital conflict as a significant within-family disruptor of family processes. Even so, we suspect that such variables will be identified in future studies.

In a sense, the contextual variables are a way of talking about what determines interfamily and intrafamily differences in family management practices. Some of the variables seem to explain how parenting skills can become disrupted when the problem-child-to-be is only a toddler (e.g., social disadvantage, grandparents' discipline practices, and parental psychopathology). Other contextual variables, such as stress (e.g., unemployment) and transitions (e.g., divorce, pubescence), may help us understand why the process seems to begin much later in some families (Patterson, 1991a). In either case, a model of children's antisocial behavior must specify the variables that determine both *initiation* and *maintenance* of

the process. We believe that contextual variables may be most useful in explaining why the disruption process starts.

The central idea presented in Figure 7.1 is that the effect of context on the child's adjustment is mediated through family management variables. We believe that contextual variables must operate selectively in terms of which parenting practices are affected, but we have little information on how this works.

The logical relations implied in mediational models are described in Figure 7.2. This same logic is expressed in each of the structural equation studies that we cite as tests for the mediation hypothesis. We assume that each contextual variable has a significant, but relatively low-level correlation with some measure of child adjustment (e.g., antisocial behavior, academic achievement, depression). We further assume that context is significantly correlated with one or more measures of family management variables. Presumably, this second correlation is higher than the first one. The third hypothesis about the mediational model is the critical one: If the effect of the family management variable is partialed out, the residual contribution of the contextual variable should be marginal or nonsignificant (i.e., in a modeling sense, the variables form a simplex).

The underlying assumption of the coercion model is that family management practices are immediate and modifiable determinants of child adjustment. In a similar vein, contextual variables are assumed to be primary covariates for family management practices. When the term *determinant* is applied to family management variables, it refers to the expected outcome of an experimental manipulation. However, many of the connections between contextual variables and parenting practices are

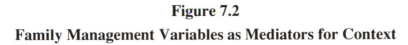

Figure 7.2

Family Management Variables as Mediators for Context

relatively ambiguous. It is also conceivable that some variables function causally. For example, an increase in stress is accompanied by an increase in parental irritability; this, in turn, impairs the mothers' effectiveness in discipline confrontations. In what sense could a parental personality trait or social disadvantage be thought of as *causal* variables? An increase in maternal depression could covary with changes in maternal discipline, as shown in the latent growth model described in Forgatch and Stoolmiller (1991). If a parent obtains a higher-paying job that is accompanied by greater social advantage, do his or her parenting skills improve? Kohn and Schooler (1983) made an argument for this possibility. They showed a correlation between the kind of job a person has and the quality of his or her childrearing techniques.

We take the more conservative position that the connection between family management variables and contextual variables such as parental pathology, grandparental discipline practices, and social disadvantage is merely correlational. These three contextual variables are useful in that they identify a significant subset of parents whose family management skills are inadequate. Future studies may show that some of these variables have causal status, in which case we will revise our position accordingly.

Most of the current research literature supports that idea that contextual variables disrupt parenting practices (Belsky & Pensky, 1988; Emery, 1982; Furstenberg & Seltzer, 1986; Rutter, 1983). In one form or another, each of these investigators mentions disrupted parenting practices in conjunction with certain parental traits, stressors, and marital conflict. There has been little progress in specifying the relations *among* the disrupting variables and their connection to parenting practices. As Belsky (1984) and others have pointed out, such correlations are modest at best and often are not replicated.

In the sections that follow, two categories of contextual variables are discussed separately: first, those that might have causal status, and second those that seem to identify at-risk families. In each section, the work we have com-

pleted on building constructs is presented as are the bivariate correlations with the family management and child adjustment variables. The modeling studies that have been completed thus far also will be examined.

Contextual Determinants

The three contextual variables that we think might have some causal status are measures of stress (excluding family conflict variables), marital adjustment, and transitions. Changes in these variables are likely to be accompanied by shifts in parenting practices. It is thought that such variables will be useful in explaining why some families become disrupted.

Over a period of time, many families experience changes in one or more of these contextual variables. Therefore, longitudinal designs seem appropriate for studying the various effects. In a separate section of this chapter, we will examine the longitudinal data relating changes in contextual variables to shifts in family process.

Stressors

From a social interactional perspective, it is hypothesized that the impact of stressors on child adjustment is mediated by their immediate effect on patterns of social interaction. The children who are most at risk are those from families in which patterns of social exchange are most often disrupted by outside stressors (Patterson, 1983). The general model is illustrated in Figure 7.3.

A decade of work was devoted to understanding stress itself before the concept was applied to family process. Selye's (1956) studies on the physiological reaction to noxious stimuli and the adaptation syndrome generated a profound interest in the effect of stressors on human behavior. Holmes and Masuda (1974) demonstrated the feasibility of assessing life changes as a special class of noxious events. A large number of investigators immediately used the resulting scale to collect retrospective data. For example, a psychiatric patient might be asked to describe the life history events that preceded his or her

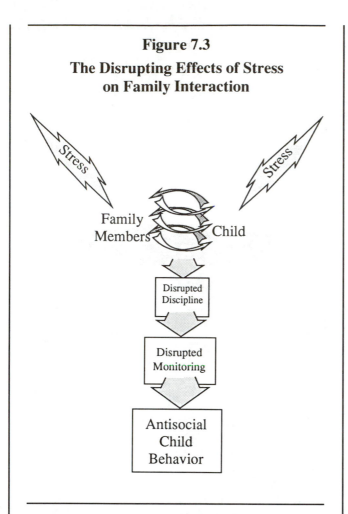

Figure 7.3

The Disrupting Effects of Stress on Family Interaction

Stress

Stress

Family Members ⟷ Child

Disrupted Discipline

Disrupted Monitoring

Antisocial Child Behavior

illness. Reviews of such studies suggested that the kind of stress, as well as the amount and intensity, covaried with a wide spectrum of psychiatric problems. Patients who attempted suicide seemed to be characterized by the highest levels of prior stress, with depression and schizophrenia following in close order (Paykel, 1974). Dohrenwend and Dohrenwend (1974) and others noted that most of the evidence for the covariation was retrospective.

The next decade of research consisted of more carefully designed laboratory studies that generally showed poststress performance decrements on a wide variety of tasks (Cohen, 1980). Some laboratory studies identified a link between stress and effects on the immune system (Rogers, Dubey, & Reich, 1979). At a more speculative level, models were proposed that examined the impact of stress and crises on family life (McCubbin, Joy, Cauble, Comeau, Patterson, & Needle, 1980). The data base for many of those studies consisted mainly of self-report measures for both the dependent and independent variables. Gradually, the questions began to focus more on the individual differences among children and families in the patterning of risk and protective factors (Garmezy, 1983). In the past 10 years, researchers such as Conger, McCarty, Yang, Lahey, and Kropp (1984) and Hetherington, Cox,

and Cox (1978, 1979) have developed more precise data-collection procedures for studying the impact of stress on family life (e.g., observations in the homes of stressed families).

Observing family members over an extended period of time makes it possible to use *intrasubject* designs to examine the covariation between self-reported stressors and observed parent–child interactions. In the OSLC studies, mother–child dyads were observed in the home for 15 to 20 sessions. For each dyad, the covariation was determined across days between stressors and observed maternal reactions to the children. Mothers from several of the dyads were observed to be most irritable in their interactions with their children on the days that they reported the highest levels of stress (Patterson, 1982, 1983). In this original study, the data also indicated that several of the mothers became more distant on high-stress days. Unfortunately, the stress-distancing hypothesis has not been examined in recent studies. Snyder and Huntley (1990) carried out a more systematic study of five mother–child dyads. Each dyad was observed for eight sessions. A disaggregated time-series analysis showed that maternal self-reported stress accounted for 16% of the variance in the observation-based variable of maternal start-up. Wahler and Dumas (1983) replicated the covariation of maternal irritability and stress.

Whether stressors impinge upon the parents or the children, the effect on parenting practices is presumably the same. The family member experiencing stress becomes more irritable, which disrupts parenting practices. This, in turn, places the child at risk for adjustment problems. The effect of stress on child adjustment is mediated first by an increase in irritable exchanges and second by disruptions in parenting practices. This is an example of a mediational model at a microsocial level.

Stress construct. Our initial attempts to build the Stress construct led to an intense debate about the nature of stress itself. What is the procedure for measuring stress? Is it reasonable to think of stress as a factor-defined construct? One of our colleagues, Rick Viken, made a convincing argument that a factor structure is not a reasonable way to think about concepts such as stress. For example, a person with health problems does not necessarily experience a high incidence of *other* negative life events such as deaths in the family, loss of employment, or high rates of daily hassles. One group of staff members took the position that stress is actually a generalized state. This means that individuals who experience high rates of daily hassles are also at risk for developing problems in other areas, such as finances and health. The underlying assumption for those of us who adopted this position was that there are some individuals who are generally lacking in social skills. At any given time, these individuals are likely to have multiple problems, such as social disadvantage or the antisocial trait. Both the lack of skills and the antisocial trait place the parent at risk for high levels of future stress.

Each of these positions leads to a different prediction about the magnitude and significance of the correlations among the indicators designed to measure stress. In general, we have found that the amount of structure obtained varies widely from one sample to another. As yet, we have not been able to identify a pattern that allows the investigator to predict whether a significant factor structure will be obtained.

Data that sampled both molar and molecular self-reports about stress were collected in the Planning Study. One of the more molecular variables was *daily hassles* (Dohrenwend & Shrout, 1985; Lazarus, DeLongis, Folkman, & Gruen, 1985). The details of the instrument are described in Dishion, Capaldi, and Patterson (1990). Also included was a broad-brush measure of negative life events based on the work of Holmes and Rahe (1967), as revised by Sarason, Johnson, and Siegel (1978). Interview-based estimates of current medical problems and financial status provided two additional indicators.

In building the construct, we were sensitive to the problem of confounded measurement (e.g., between self-reports of stress and distress) (Depue & Monroe, 1986; Dohrenwend & Shrout, 1985; Gersten, Langner, Eisenberg, & Simcha-Fagan, 1977; Lazarus et al., 1985). To minimize the issue of confounded measurement, the potential indicators were designed to include some relatively objective measures of stressful life circumstances (e.g., low income, number of children in family). Items that referred to family conflict or to child problems were dropped.

Aside from differences in correlational structure among indicators, it is obvious that the samples differ markedly in their mean levels of stress. Forgatch, Patterson, and Skinner (1988) found an average of 11.9 daily hassles for intact families in the OYS. This was significantly less than the mean of 16.5 for recently separated single mothers. In the intact OYS families, the mean number of major life events was 4.9 for Cohort I and 5.1 for Cohort II. As might be expected, the mean number was significantly greater for recently separated mothers (9.1). The mean number of family health problems was 1.1 for Cohort I and 1.3 for Cohort II.

Principal components factor analyses, constrained to a single solution, were carried out separately for mothers and fathers from the at-risk sample in the OYS. The data collected when the boys were in grade 4 are summarized in Figure 7.4. The findings were analyzed separately for both mothers of intact families and single mothers.

The data for mothers showed that the four indicators (daily hassles, negative life events, financial problems, and family health problems) defined a factor that accounted for approximately 40% of the variance in the matrix. The factor structure seemed comparable for single

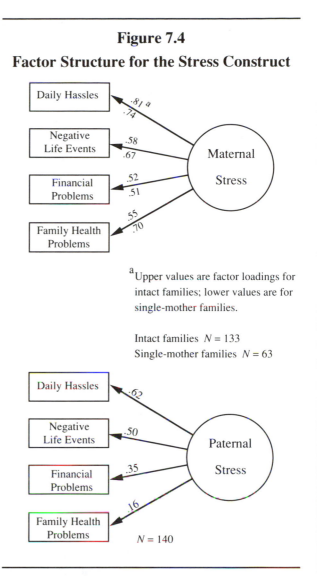

Figure 7.4

Factor Structure for the Stress Construct

[a]Upper values are factor loadings for intact families; lower values are for single-mother families.

Intact families $N = 133$
Single-mother families $N = 63$

$N = 140$

mothers and mothers from intact families in the sense that the construct loaded most heavily on daily hassles and least on financial problems for both samples. We found a heavier loading of the Stress construct on family health problems for the single-mother sample.

The findings from a sample of recently separated mothers showed a configuration of factor loadings that was different from those of either OYS sample (Patterson & Forgatch, 1990b). The highest factor loadings were for negative life events (.84) and daily hassles (.84). The financial and health indicators also showed strong loadings (.78 and .71, respectively).

The factor structure for stress seemed different for mothers and fathers. First, the factor scores for fathers were appreciably lower than those for mothers. In fact, the findings might be interpreted as supporting Viken's hypothesis (i.e., for fathers, it may be more appropriate to think of the stress concept as a risk score than as a factor). The configuration of factor scores for fathers was also different from the configuration for mothers. For example, for fathers the construct did not load significantly on health problems and loaded only marginally on financial problems.

As yet, we have not systematically examined the factor-invariance problem for the Stress construct, but we do not expect to find the structures invariant across samples. In fact, we have some doubt as to whether the data for fathers support the idea of a factor structure at all. In the section that follows, an alternative strategy is briefly outlined that uses stress as a risk score.

Risk score. For "barely defined" constructs, we often combine the information to form a simple risk score (Bank, Dishion, Skinner, & Patterson, 1990). A risk score can be formed by dichotomizing the variates. This approach is similar to the one used by Rutter (1979). The risk score is the number of variables that score above the median for that family. The summary score is not the algebraic sum of actual indicator scores; it is just the number of factors that are not going well. We have not determined whether there is some unique advantage to such a score or, for that matter, whether there is some flaw in logic that undermines its utility. Nevertheless, knowing that one family is subject to two or three times more stressors than another is clinically useful. In our own modeling studies, we use either the risk score or a latent construct depending on how well the indicators converge.

Figure 7.5 shows the distribution of families that had high scores on one to six stressors. Only 6% of the families had only a single stressor. Most families seemed to have several stressors impinging on them at any given time, and more than half of these families were characterized by four or more stressor indices!

Bivariate analyses of the Stress and Marital Conflict constructs. We hypothesized that: (1) high levels of stress would covary significantly with disruptions in family management procedures, and (2) there would be a direct effect of stress on child adjustment. The hypotheses were tested by calculating bivariate correlations separately for mothers and fathers from intact families in the OYS sample assessed at grade 4; the findings are summarized in Table 7.1. We examined the correlations separately for the sample of single mothers from the OYS because we expected the effects to vary as a function of family structure.

The findings did not offer much support for the first hypothesis. For intact families, there were *no* significant correlations between stress and any of the family management composite scores for either fathers or mothers. There was only modest support for the assumed relation between child adjustment and stress; the correlation was .236 for mothers and .241 for fathers. We must conclude that for intact families there is little support for the hypothesis that stress covaries directly with either family management variables or child adjustment variables. Recent analyses by Conger (1991) replicated for the OYS

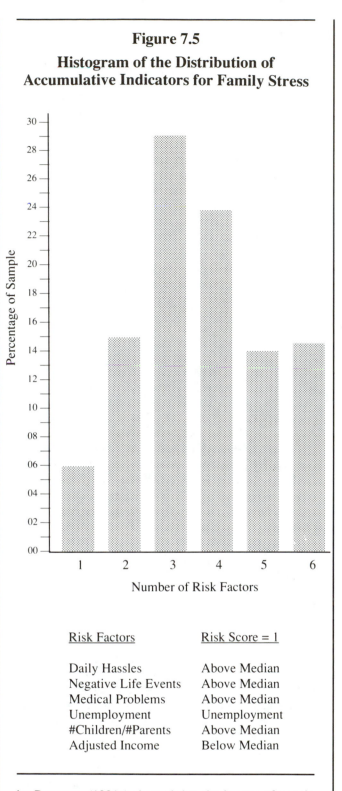

Figure 7.5

Histogram of the Distribution of Accumulative Indicators for Family Stress

Risk Factors	Risk Score = 1
Daily Hassles	Above Median
Negative Life Events	Above Median
Medical Problems	Above Median
Unemployment	Unemployment
#Children/#Parents	Above Median
Adjusted Income	Below Median

by Patterson (1991a) showed that the impact of certain stressors for intact families (a drop in income, severe illness, or a death in the family) on child adjustment is mediated by parental depression. In other words, stress disrupts parenting practices only to the extent that the parents become depressed.

The data for single mothers offered strong support for

Table 7.1

Covariations of Stress and Marital Adjustment Scores with Family Management and Child Adjustment Scores

Family Variable	Stress[a]			Marital Adjustment[b]	
	Mothers (N = 130)	Fathers (N = 130)	Single Mothers (N = 62)	Mothers (N = 130)	Fathers (N = 130)
Family Management					
Discipline	-.052	-.095	-.385***	.16	.12
Parental Monitoring	-.116	-.142	-.053	.21*	.16
Problem Solving	-.134	-.154	.020	.10	.13
Parental Involvement	.044	.050	-.084	.23*	.07
Positive Reinforcement	-.044	.099	-.115	.11	.08
Child Adjustment					
Antisocial Behavior	.236**	.241**	.495***	-.15	-.10
Achievement	-.127	.120	.327**	.13	-.10
Depression	.162	-.089	-.236*	-.13	-.14

*p < .05   **p < .01   ***p < .001

[a]Composite is a risk score.

[b]Only the Dyadic Adjustment score was used here.

a mediational stress model. Forgatch et al. (1988) demonstrated this effect in a study of separated families with boys 6 to 8 years of age. She found a path coefficient of .54 from the stress risk score to the Discipline construct. The comparable coefficient for the sample of families with older boys was nonsignificant.

High levels of stress in single-mother families were associated with notable disruptions in discipline practices for mothers with younger boys. It is interesting that the effect of stress on parenting practices varies as a function of the age of the child and intact or single status of the parent(s). Although it is too early to say whether the Depression construct will play a key role in mediating the effects for both single and intact families, it seems likely.

Marital Adjustment

Belsky and Pensky (1988) view the relationship between parents as pivotal to family functioning. This is in keeping with the consensus that marital discord is related to child adjustment problems. Several developmental psychologists (Belsky, 1984; Olweus, 1980) and family investigators (Caspi & Elder, 1988; Rutter, 1980) have suggested that the marital relationship is a *prime determinant* for the quality of parent–child interactions. In their large-scale survey, Rutter, Tizard, and Whitmore (1970) showed that variables such as marital discord, broken homes, and conduct problems for boys tend to be intercorrelated. In a review of relevant studies, Rutter (1979) reiterated these relations as they applied to both conduct disorders in children and delinquency in adolescents. The findings led him to speculate that marital discord seemed to be more disruptive than divorce to the adjustment of boys (Rutter, 1980). In the 1979 review, he cited a study of children who had been removed from their parents' homes because of extreme family discord. A follow-up of the children showed that of those who had been placed with a family characterized by marital harmony, 19% were described as having a conduct disorder; 53% of those placed with families with marital discord had conduct problems.

However, Emery (1982) noted that the association between marital satisfaction and child adjustment problems is much stronger for clinical samples than it is for normal samples. Oltmanns, Broderick, and O'Leary (1977) compared clinical and nonclinical samples and found a strong association between parental ratings of conduct disorders and marital satisfaction *only* for the clinical group. Emery and O'Leary (1984) used a nonclinical sample to examine the same covariation and found the magnitude to be in the .2 range. They cited several other studies of nonclinical samples in which the findings were similar.

Although there may be a *modest* correlation between marital conflict and child conduct problems, we believe that the magnitude of this relation is often overestimated. These correlations often reflect little more than shared method variance. For example, many studies have used parent self-report data as *both* the dependent and independent variable! This makes it impossible to distinguish shared method variance from the variance attributed to the substantive association between the two variables. For either clinical or normal samples, to what extent are the covariations between ratings of marital discord and child adjustment magnified by a reliance on parental self-report data? It is reassuring that Emery (1982) did find three studies with a significant covariation between self-reports of marital satisfaction and teachers' ratings of child adjustment. Nevertheless, Rickard, Forehand, Atkeson, and Lopez (1982) found no relation between marital adjustment and observed rates of deviant child behavior.

Johnson and Lobitz (1974) reported significant covariations between parental ratings of marital adjustment and observed rates of deviant child behavior. We were unable to replicate this finding in our analyses based on comparable data from the Planning Study. Teachers in this study did, however, report somewhat higher rates of lying, stealing, and truancy for the children of unhappily married parents than for children of happily married parents. The rates of police contacts and self-reported delinquency also were much higher for the children of unhappily married couples than for children of happily married couples.

The careful update of the studies by Eddy (1991a) leaves little doubt that shared method variance has fueled most of the enthusiasm for marital conflict as a determinant for child adjustment problems. When this problem is removed, there is at best a *low-level* positive relation between marital adjustment and child adjustment.

Marital Adjustment construct. The latent construct, Marital Adjustment, was defined initially by using both self-report and observed measures of marital satisfaction. We based our self-report measure on the one developed by Locke and Wallace (1959). Our observation measure provided molecular data describing spouse-to-spouse interactions in the home. Two indicators were derived from the observation data: (1) the proportion of positive spouse-to-spouse interactions, and (2) the proportion of negative spouse-to-spouse interactions.

Figure 7.6 summarizes the findings from the principal components factor analyses constrained to a single solution. The findings were based on the combined data for mothers and fathers from intact families in the OYS samples. The latent construct loaded most heavily on the aversive-exchange indicator and least on the self-reported dyadic-adjustment scores. In fact, the convergence was marginal because the correlation between positive ex-

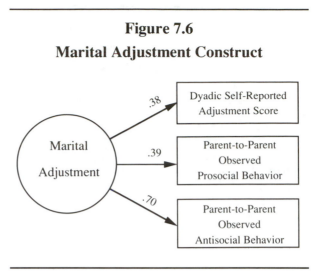

Figure 7.6
Marital Adjustment Construct

changes and the self-report indicators was of borderline significance. As might be expected, there also were high correlations with other constructs that included negative microsocial variables (e.g., a .5 correlation with parental nattering from the Discipline construct).

Our doubts about the adequacy of this definition were confirmed when we attempted to repeat the analyses separately for mothers and fathers, and the construct simply disappeared like the Cheshire cat. Then we attempted to define the construct with just the self-report scale and the observed positive exchanges. When analyzed separately for mothers and fathers, the correlation between these two indicators was less than .1.

Bivariate correlations. We were forced to rely solely on the self-report scale for measuring marital adjustment. We are currently searching for other indicators that will converge. Consequently, we used only the Marital Adjustment construct score in the correlations with the family management and child adjustment constructs. We used the data from intact families to calculate the correlations separately for mothers and fathers.

The findings summarized in Table 7.1 offer little support for either of the hypothesized relations between family variables and marital adjustment. For fathers, none of the correlations of marital satisfaction with family management or child adjustment variables were significant. For mothers, higher levels of marital adjustment covaried significantly with effective monitoring (.21) and parental involvement (.23). In the normal course of events, fluctuations in marital adjustment contribute very little to our understanding of parenting practices or child adjustment. Perhaps the extreme levels of marital conflict that precede separation serve as disruptors. The OYS data suggest that marital conflict plays a very limited role in disrupting measures of parenting practices. It goes without saying that these correlations would be much larger if parent report data were used.

Transitions

We originally thought that each transition from intact family to divorce to remarriage would be accompanied by increasing levels of stress. We also assumed that these increments in stress would disrupt family management practices and lead, in turn, to child adjustment problems. The data show that this is only partly correct. Certain parental traits contribute to poor child adjustment and place the family at risk for transitions. The antisocial mother is at greatest risk for transitions as well as for disruptions in parenting practices.

In our first exploration of the transition hypothesis, we took the position that the *cumulative effect* of family transitions would covary in a linear fashion with child adjustment problems (Capaldi & Patterson, 1991). We expected that transitions such as divorce and remarriage would be associated with increasing levels of child problems (e.g., depression, peer rejection, academic failure, and antisocial acts). The data clearly showed a linear relation. Furthermore, the SEM showed that the effect of the number of transitions on child adjustment was completely mediated by the measure of maternal antisocial behavior. In other words, the more antisocial the mother, the greater the likelihood that her parenting practices would be disrupted. Unpublished data from the study showed that a higher incidence of pathology was associated with increases in the frequency of transitions for both mothers and fathers. As shown in Figure 7.7, parents from intact families showed the fewest indicators of pathology, and parents from families subjected to multiple transitions showed the most.

Patterson and Capaldi (1991a) examined the longitudinal data from the OYS to obtain a quasi-experimental test of the parental pathology hypothesis. Over a two-year interval, 24 families experienced one or more transitions. The prediction that antisocial mothers were at risk for further transitions was confirmed. As expected, antisocial mothers also were characterized by disruptions in discipline practices *prior* to the transition. The transitions were followed by interruptions in monitoring practices. If the transition involved a loss of support, it also was accompanied by an increase in maternal depression. The relation between transitions and disruptions in family management skills is shown in Figure 7.8.

Both the correlational data and the longitudinal data are consistent with the hypothesis that certain parents are more at risk than others for generating transitions. These same traits place them at risk for disruptions in effective parenting skills both before and after the transitions. The adjustment problems of children in these families seem to be more a function of the parental traits associated with frequent transitions than of the turmoil that accompanies the transitions.

In the Oregon Divorce Study, it was shown that

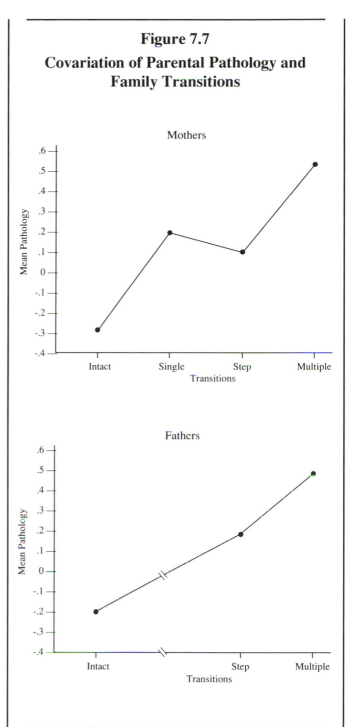

Figure 7.7

Covariation of Parental Pathology and Family Transitions

repartnering was associated with disruptions in parenting practices and child adjustment problems (Forgatch & Ray, 1991). Even though stress is a salient feature of the divorce process, it does not seem to play a major role in child adjustment. We think that the major variables are parent pathology and the repartnering process. Additional studies are needed to determine how much variance the three variables and their interaction terms account for in measures of parenting practices during separation and divorce.

Figure 7.8
Covariation of Transitions with Disrupted Parenting Practices

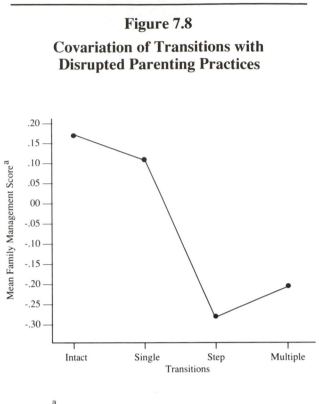

[a] The mean of discipline and monitoring (Z) scores.

Static Contextual Variables

This section reviews some of the findings for the at-risk sample that relate to enduring contextual variables such as family history, parental social disadvantage, and parental pathology.

From One Generation to the Next

We estimate that one-half of the antisocial children who are referred to OSLC for treatment represent second- and third-generation problems. The parents seem to be as antisocial as the children. And, according to all reports, the grandparents were cut from the same mold. Generally speaking, the parents seem to be unskilled in many critical areas, including parenting skills. What is being transmitted from one generation to the next? Is there some heritable antisocial trait, or is it the impact of a generally disruptive interactional style on parenting practices that is passed on across generations? The latter explanation seems most likely to us. Like Caspi and Elder (1988), we believe that what is passed from parent to child is an abrasive interpersonal style that places the individual at serious risk for disrupted parenting practices. Although the abrasive style could have significant genetic determinants, not all such individuals are ineffective in discipline confrontations.

Data from several longitudinal studies have shown strong links between what happens in one generation and what happens in the next. Two hypotheses have consistently received support in the literature. One, that the antisocial trait is transmitted from one generation to another. This requires that grandparental traits covary significantly with parental traits, which in turn covary with grandchildren's traits. In the second hypothesis, faulty discipline practices are transmitted from one generation to the next. This implies that the relation between the antisocial trait in one generation and another is mediated by discipline practices. Needless to say, the two hypotheses are not necessarily antithetical; it would be possible to find significant trait correlations across three generations, and the same data set also could support a mediational hypothesis. It is our impression, however, that a mediational model will account for more variance than a direct transmission (trait-to-trait) model.

Direct transmission. Elder and his colleagues provided support for the trait hypothesis (e.g., Elder, Caspi, & Downey, 1983). The families involved in their longitudinal study endured the Great Depression of the 1930s. In keeping with the direct transmission hypothesis, the *retrospective* ratings of grandmothers' irritability correlated .34 with ratings of mothers' irritability; the comparable correlation for fathers was .36. The grandchildren were interviewed as adolescents. The grandchildren's ratings of their mothers' being ill-tempered correlated with the grandchildren being less productive and more negativistic, rebellious, and deceitful. Robins, West, and Herjanic (1975) replicated the findings. They found that the grandparents' antisocial behavior was significantly correlated with the antisocial behavior of their grandchildren. These analyses established a positive link for antisocial traits across the second and third generations and from the first generation to the third.

McCord's (1986) follow-up of the Cambridge–Somerville sample showed that the aggressiveness and criminality of the parents were important variables for differentiating between delinquent and nondelinquent samples. This is consistent with findings from several other investigators that show a relation between parental criminality and adolescent delinquency (cf. review by Rutter & Giller, 1983; Wilson & Herrnstein, 1985).

Discipline as a mediating mechanism. The mediational hypothesis is based on two assumptions: (1) antisocial parents use ineffective discipline techniques, and (2) inept discipline allows the antisocial trait to develop in the next generation. The mediational hypothesis therefore suggests a significant path between the parental antisocial trait and ineffective discipline practices and another between ineffective discipline and antisocial behavior in children.

The data from the longitudinal studies by Elder and his colleagues provide support for several components of the

Figure 7.9

Discipline as a Mediator for Across-Generation Effects (from Patterson & Dishion, 1988)

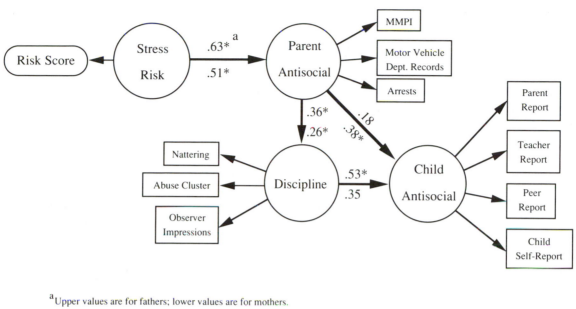

[a] Upper values are for fathers; lower values are for mothers.

*p < .05

mediational hypothesis (Elder, Liker, & Cross, 1984). First, they established a significant relation between grandparental discipline and parental irritability. Then they showed a significant relation between parental irritability and explosive discipline in the second generation. The findings from the longitudinal study by Huesmann, Eron, Lefkowitz, and Walder (1984) also support the mediational hypothesis. They studied a large sample of families living in semirural New York. The families were assessed repeatedly over a 22-year period. The data showed significant correlations between the punitiveness and aggressiveness of the grandparents and the antisocial behavior of their grandchildren.

Several sets of findings from the OYS support the mediational hypothesis. Parents in the at-risk samples were asked to fill out a retrospective account of the discipline practices used by their parents. The Assessing Environments III questionnaire (Berger, Knutson, Mehm, & Perkins, 1988; Zaidi, Knutson, & Mehm, 1988) was administered to mothers and fathers. The questionnaire was scored for the six scales developed by Knutson and his colleagues and for one scale of our own — harsh discipline — that was developed from the same pool of items. The seven scales were correlated with the five family management constructs separately for mothers and fathers. Eleven of the 70 correlations were significant. Most of the significant correlations were with the family management construct of Discipline.

Both mothers and fathers with poor family manage-

ment skills tended to report that their grandparents used harsh discipline and that they were relatively isolated from the rest of the community. The latter finding was in accord with the study by Wahler, Leske, and Rogers (1977) that showed that families of antisocial boys tend to be isolated. When the antisocial trait score for fathers was regressed against the physical punishment scales for grandparents and perception of discipline, the multiple correlation was .37 (p < .001) (Patterson & Dishion, 1988). Fathers who remembered their parents using harsh and punitive discipline were more likely to be antisocial. The comparable correlation for mothers was .21 (p < .05). Attempts to use the complete set of retrospective variables in similar analyses failed to establish significant correlations with parental depression, social competence, substance abuse, marital conflict, and stressors.

The next test of the model was based on SEM for the data collected from intact families at grade 4 (Patterson & Dishion, 1988). The hypothesis was tested that discipline practices mediated the impact of the parental antisocial trait on the child antisocial trait. The findings are summarized in Figure 7.9.

Support for the mediational hypothesis first required a significant path from the Parental Antisocial construct to the Discipline construct. As shown in Figure 7.9, the path coefficients were significant for both fathers and mothers. It also required a significant path from Discipline to Child Antisocial, and this was the case for both parents. By implication, the direct path from Parental Antisocial to

103

Child Antisocial was nonsignificant. The models for both parents are consistent with the hypothesis that the transmission of the antisocial trait from one generation to another is *in part* a function of the fact that antisocial parents are significantly less effective in their discipline practices. This relation is a modest one; the antisocial trait accounts for 13% of the variance in the Discipline construct for fathers and 7% for mothers. The findings for mothers were consistent with both the direct effects and mediational effects hypotheses. The path from the maternal antisocial trait to the child antisocial trait was significant, which supports a direct effects hypothesis. This, in turn, may provide support for the concept of a heritable component.

The available studies support several assumptions about across-generation effects. The findings support the stability of antisocial trait measures across two or three generations. The findings also indicate that discipline practices remain relatively consistent across at least two generations and that discipline practices may be more important as a mediating variable for fathers than for mothers.

Heritability and across-generation effects. Scarr (1985a) made a convincing case for the contribution of genetic factors to both specific measures (e.g., intelligence) and general measures of parenting skills. It is also conceivable that, to some extent, antisocial boys inherit a responsiveness to certain kinds of reinforcers or perhaps a hyporesponsiveness to punishment. This is a complex set of assumptions. Furthermore, the findings from some of the behavioral genetic studies are inconclusive. For example, reviews of the data from twin and adoptee studies failed to show that genetic factors contribute to adolescent delinquency (Cloninger & Gottesman, 1987; Rowe & Plomin, 1981). However, such studies consistently support a heritable component for *adult* criminal behavior (Pollock, Mednick, & Gabrielli, 1983). It is not clear why there would be a genetic link for offenses committed by adults but not for adolescents, particularly when the latter are viewed as antecedents for the former. It is our guess that heritable factors are involved in chronic adolescent delinquency, but not in transitory delinquency. Perhaps the next generation of studies in behavioral genetics will be able to determine exactly which aspects (if any) of preadolescent antisocial behavior are inherited.

Family history of parents as a risk factor. We assumed that a child whose parents both had positive experiences with their own parents would be least at risk for adjustment problems. The child would be at some risk if only one parent had positive childhood experiences; for that child, a separation could mean living with a marginally skilled parent. The child would be most at risk if both parents came from disrupted families.

Berger et al. (1988) and Zaidi et al. (1988) collected retrospective data from a sample of families applying for services at a child psychiatric clinic. Their data showed that if *both* the mother and father of the child referred for psychiatric diagnosis had experienced punitive parenting or acrimonious family interactions or both as children, then the likelihood that the child would be diagnosed as antisocial was 81%. If only the mother reported having these experiences, the likelihood was 50%; if only the father reported such childhood experiences, the likelihood was 63%. In a study of black families, Robins et al. (1975) found that one or both paternal grandparents were antisocial in 31% of the families; the comparable figure for families with delinquents was 53%.

Only a limited set of findings pertains to increased risk as a function of the number of parents with a family history of ineffective parenting skills. The available studies imply that higher risk is associated with having two parents who did not learn effective family management skills from their parents. This suggests that having even one parent with effective family management skills significantly reduces the risk of child adjustment problems.

Neighborhood

One of the earliest findings from sociological studies of crime and delinquency was that in any given city the density of criminal activity varied significantly from one area to the next (Wilson & Herrnstein, 1985). Subsequent studies showed that crime rates varied as a function of whether the setting was rural or urban, as well as with the ethnicity, age, and sex of the child.

From a social interactional perspective, certain areas of the city may have a higher percentage of families in which the parents are unskilled in their use of family management practices. The availability of deviant peers at an early age and the disruptive effects of extreme poverty are important variables that might explain why one neighborhood is characterized by higher rates of antisocial behavior than another. In contrast, some sociologists have suggested that these variables reflect a shared subcultural value system that condones and legitimizes violence (Wolfgang & Ferracuti, 1967). Therefore, the *beliefs* about violence serve as prime determinants for crime. Our position is that the beliefs are *accompaniments* rather than determinants of criminal behavior.

The best way to identify the determinants would be to study what is happening to the families that live in these areas. Sampson (1987) examined the race-specific rates of robbery and homicide by both adults and juveniles living in 150 cities: SEM showed a strong relation between unemployment, economic deprivation, and disruption in the homes. The effects were independent of race, age, city size, or welfare benefits. For example, it was the scarcity of employed black men that increased the risk for families headed by single black women. Disruptions in black families in turn related to high rates of robbery and homicide.

Of course, not all families headed by single women living in ghettoes produce chronic delinquents. The mediating factor would be how well those mothers monitor and discipline their children. We believe it is the interaction of *neighborhood* and *parental skill* that determines the outcome. We have noticed that the risk of delinquency is four or five times higher in some neighborhoods within the Eugene–Springfield (Oregon) metropolitan area. The risk score is based on the proportion of adolescent boys who have arrest records. Our approach to predicting delinquent behavior is to calculate the neighborhood risk factor for each boy in the sample and then give his family a rating for the effectiveness of parental discipline and monitoring. It is our guess that it will be the interactive term (the setting score multiplied by the discipline score) that will account for the most variance.

This perspective suggests that our society places some families at extreme risk. Approximately one-third of all families live in areas that require a *very high degree* of parenting skills just to keep their children out of the juvenile court system. There is no sense in which it is fair for our society to expose these families to such adverse conditions.

If the families that drift into these risk areas tend to be relatively unskilled, each successive generation could contain increasing numbers of antisocial individuals. The assumption is that antisocial parents are least likely to escape from the ghetto. This is in keeping with Kellam's (1990) findings from the Woodlawn studies that highly skilled people tended to move to the more attractive sections of the city.

Social Disadvantage

In their reviews of the literature, Rutter and Giller (1983) and Wilson and Herrnstein (1985) concluded that there is a modest correlation between social status and *serious* crimes by adolescents. In their large-scale survey study, Elliott, Ageton, Huizinga, Knowles, and Canter (1983) showed that families of lower social status were at greater risk for producing an adolescent who commits serious crimes. A team of preeminent epidemiologists has outlined a method for testing the hypothesis that combines representative sampling with multiagent, multimethod assessment procedures (Kellam, 1990). The idea is to intensively assess a stratified random subsample; the data then could be used to determine values for the key parameters in the model. These values would be extremely useful in assessing the generalizability of a model-based sample such as ours.

Our working assumption is that family management skill is the variable that accounts for the covariation between social disadvantage and delinquency. Presumably, there is a higher incidence of irritable parents in samples of socially disadvantaged families, and the irritability is associated with less effective discipline. Radke Yarrow, Richters, and Wilson (1988) showed that mothers of lower social status were observed to be three times as negative with their older children than were middle-class mothers. In our own observation studies of at-risk families, we have found a significant relation between parental aversiveness and measures of occupation and education. Presumably, a higher percentage of families in the lowest social status group are characterized by ineffective discipline and monitoring practices. As we noted earlier, these families may be doubly disadvantaged in that they also live in areas with a large number of deviant peers.

We used data from the OYS to calculate the correlation between social advantage and both parenting practices and child adjustment. Social advantage is defined by occupation (Hollingshead, 1975) and level of education. We carried out analyses separately for mothers from intact families, fathers from intact families, and single mothers. The data presented in Table 7.2 show that social disadvantage makes the most significant contribution of any listed contextual variable to disruptions in parenting practices. This was closely followed by the impact of the parental antisocial trait and, to a lesser extent, substance abuse. In general, the pattern of findings was similar for both groups of mothers.

Effects of Parental Traits on Family Management Practices

This section examines the hypothesis that various forms of parental pathology, such as depressive or antisocial traits, covary with disruptions in family management practices. We also hypothesize that parental pathology contributes indirectly to a wide spectrum of child adjustment problems. Children whose parents have psychiatric problems have been shown to have a high incidence of adjustment problems (Rutter, Izard, & Read, 1986). Furthermore, studies of children with psychiatric problems have generally found that the parents have disproportionately high incidences of psychopathology (Patterson, 1980; Wolking, Dunteman, & Bailey, 1967).

Although the idea that parental personality traits covary directly with the personality traits of their children is appealing, such correlations usually are of very low magnitude. Because the relation between parental traits and child traits seems to be mediated by parenting skills, the most productive approach is to identify *which* parental personality traits are associated with disruptions in family management skills and then establish the magnitude of the correlation with child traits. This approach makes it possible to account for much more variance in measures

Table 7.2
Covariation of Parental Traits with Family Management and Child Adjustment Constructs

Parent Traits	Family Management					Child Adjustment		
	Monitor-ing	Disci-pline	Problem Solving	Positive Reinf.	Parental Involv.	Anti-social	Depres. Mood	Achieve-ment
Intact Families								
Fathers								
Antisocial[a]	-.136	-.220**	-.184	-.276***	-.081	.208**	.256**	-.166
Sub. Abuse[a]	-.133	-.211**	-.059	-.068	-.112	.151	.189	-.114
Social Disad.	.116	.418***	.261**	.313***	.061	-.298***	.295***	.261**
Depression	-.101	-.074	-.144	-.024	-.003	.194*	.261**	-.032
Mothers								
Antisocial[a]	-.254**	.154	.141	.140	.131	.233**	.289***	.189
Sub. Abuse[a]	-.105	-.068	-.183	-.038	-.149	.162	.212**	.080
Social Disad.	.071	.272***	.272***	.318***	.106	.129	-.167	.181
Depression	-.202*	-.188	-.106	-.045	-.107	.105	.179	.172
Single Mothers								
Antisocial[a]	.068	-.241*	-.058	-.043	-.085	.031	-.076	-.280**
Sub. Abuse[a]	-.154	-.312**	-.101	-.055	.020	.384***	.200	-.161
Social Disad.	.029	.274*	.113	.278**	.186	-.152	-.144	.294**
Depression	.038	-.150	.004	.054	-.098	.284*	.212*	.030

*p < .05   **p < .01   ***p < .001

[a]The composite is analyzed as a risk score.

of child adjustment than merely knowing the parental trait score.

The Antisocial Parent

This section examines the hypothesis that a parent with an antisocial disposition is most likely to use ineffective discipline techniques. Data are presented on the correlation between the parental antisocial trait and family management practices. A separate section examines the hypothesis that discipline mediates the relation between the antisocial traits of parents and children. Transmission of the antisocial trait across generations is discussed in detail in Chapter 3.

Based on the findings from clinical studies of families with antisocial children referred for treatment, it appears that many of the parents also are antisocial. In accord with this impression, both mothers and fathers from referred families scored significantly higher than parents of normal children on the MMPI scales of psychopathic deviance and hypomania (Patterson, 1980, 1982). Hathaway and Monachesi (1953) showed in their lon-

gitudinal study that these two scales were significant predictors of delinquency for adolescent boys and girls.

Robins and Earls (1986) cited studies showing that antisocial individuals tend to marry one another. Because there are more antisocial males than females, the intermarriage matching is probably not balanced for the two sexes; that is, most antisocial women are married to antisocial men, but most antisocial men are not married to antisocial women because there are not enough to go around. In the present context, it seems reasonable to assume that the risk for disrupted discipline must be significantly higher when both parents are antisocial.

Building the Parental Antisocial construct. An effort was made to use heteromethod, heteroagent measures to define the Parental Antisocial construct. Parents' self-reports on the MMPI provided two scale scores: psychopathic deviance and hypomania. These scores were combined to form one indicator. A second indicator was based on Motor Vehicles Division records of all traffic violations. The third indicator was based on state records of arrests for reasons other than traffic violations.

Figure 7.10
Parental Antisocial and Depression Constructs

A. Antisocial

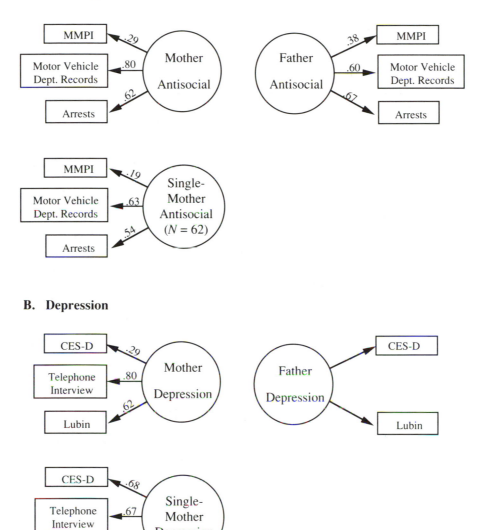

B. Depression

The findings from a confirmatory factor analysis of parents from intact families and single-mother families are summarized in Figure 7.10A. For all parents, the data from state records had the highest loadings, and self-report data had the lowest. The factor loadings for the mothers' samples rest on a rather shaky data base. For all samples, the distributions for both state records were skewed and highly kurtotic (i.e., most of the data entries were zeros). In the sample of 62 single mothers, for example, only six had arrest records. This was not a problem for the sample of fathers.

The findings summarized in Table 7.2 show that the Parental Antisocial construct correlated significantly with the Child Antisocial construct and depressive behaviors. The correlations were significant for both mothers and fathers from intact families. In keeping with the mediational hypothesis, the parents' trait scores also covaried significantly with their parenting practices. The patterns were different for mothers and fathers. For fathers, the antisocial trait covaried with disruptions in discipline and

107

positive reinforcement; for mothers, it correlated only with monitoring.

We identified a unique pattern of findings for antisocial single mothers. The mothers' trait score correlated significantly with children's achievement problems and with disrupted discipline practices. Forgatch (1989) replicated these findings for the Discipline construct in a study of recently separated mothers. For families with boys 9 to 12 years old, the path coefficients for the Maternal Antisocial construct were .43 to Parental Monitoring and .34 to Discipline. The path coefficients to Child Conduct Disorder from Parental Monitoring and Discipline were .62 and .42 respectively. In a comparable analysis of families with younger boys, the path coefficients from the Maternal Antisocial construct were .57 to Parental Monitoring and .26 to Discipline; the corresponding path coefficients to Child Conduct Disorder were .24 and .37, respectively.

The Depressed Parent

Investigators seem to agree that children with depressed parents are at significant risk for adjustment problems (Hops, Sherman, & Biglan, 1990; Radke Yarrow, 1990). These investigators showed that maternal depression was associated with significant increases in children's school difficulties, emotional problems (including depression), and a wide variety of DSM-III diagnoses. Significant differences were found between depressed and nondepressed parents in their observed interactions with their children. Hops and his colleagues hypothesized that older children (particularly girls) with depressed mothers were most at risk for dysphoric moods. Their analyses of the clinical samples also showed that both maternal depression and marital adjustment made significant, independent contributions to children's depressed mood.

Building the Parental Depression construct. We used a battery of measures to assess parental depression: the Lubin forms C and D (Lubin, 1963), CES-D (Radloff, 1977), home observer ratings of sadness, and three telephone interviews to assess daily sadness. Capaldi and Patterson (1989) described the details of the psychometric analyses. The results of the principal components factor analyses for the sample of mothers are summarized in Figure 7.10B.

Only three of the potential indicators survived the analyses. For mothers, the convergence among the three indicators was in the moderate range (.26 to .51). For all three samples, the latent construct loaded more heavily on the self-report questionnaires than it did on the telephone interview indicator. Only the CES-D and Lubin variables showed significant convergence for the fathers (.43). The correlation between the composite depression scores for mothers and fathers was modest but significant (.27)

The contributions of parental depression to parenting

practices and child adjustment are summarized in Table 7.2. There seems to be a direct correlation between the parental trait and the child trait that is of at least borderline significance for all three sets of parents. Depressed fathers (.261), mothers (.179), and single mothers (.212) seem to have depressed sons. Depressed fathers and single mothers are also more likely to have antisocial sons.

With one exception, parental depression does not seem to covary significantly with disruptions in parenting practices. Forgatch (1989) studied the families of recently separated mothers and found that Maternal Depression was significantly related to disruptions in Parental Monitoring (path coefficient of .76). This relation held for the sample of families with younger boys (ages 6 to 8), but not for families with older boys.

The Substance-Abusing Parent

Zucker and his colleagues (e.g., Zucker, 1976) conducted programmatic studies and literature reviews and found a strong relation between parental alcoholism and both substance abuse and delinquency problems for the child. These researchers also found a strong interrelation among variables such as parental alcoholism, depression, divorce, and antisocial behavior (Zucker, 1987). Zucker theorizes that the alcoholic is so ineffective in employing parenting skills that the preschool child is at grave risk for becoming antisocial, being rejected by peers, and failing in school. These children also may be at risk for substance abuse as adolescents. Zucker's well-conceived longitudinal study using random assignment to prevention or nonprevention groups is now in progress.

Dishion, Reid, and Patterson (1988) analyzed data from the at-risk sample and found that parents who reported heavy use of marijuana, illicit drugs, and alcohol contributed both directly and indirectly to their sons' early drug exploration. Parental substance use contributed directly (the path coefficient was .54) and indirectly (through ineffective monitoring) to child drug exploration; this, in turn, contributed to involvement with deviant peers.

Building the Substance Abuse construct. This construct was essentially based on self-report data obtained from parents through interviews and questionnaires. During the interview, the parents were asked separately for information about how frequently they used marijuana and prescription drugs (for sleep, pain, anxiety, etc.). They also were asked about their use of hard drugs such as cocaine, methamphetamine, and morphine. The MAST was used to estimate the degree of problems caused by alcohol consumption. The correlation of all five variables with the corrected total scores was .20 or greater. The alpha values were borderline (.58 for fathers and .62 for mothers).

The exploratory factor analysis consisted of a principal components analysis constrained to a single solution. The

Figure 7.11
Parental Substance Abuse Construct

Intact Families (*N* = 130)

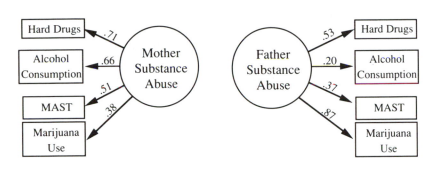

Single-Mother Families

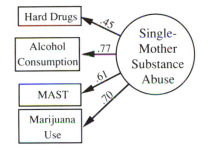

results presented in Figure 7.11 show considerable shifts in the factor loadings among the three samples. An examination of the score distributions for the four indicators reveals that all of them are quite skewed and kurtotic. Very few parents were willing to admit to hard drug use or heavy alcohol consumption. This means it is risky to apply correlational analyses to these data. Of course, it may be that we should not think of these three samples as replications in any sense. Nevertheless, we are concerned about the fact that the indicator converged significantly for one sample and *non*significantly for another sample (e.g., the fathers' construct loaded only .20 on alcohol).

In keeping with Zucker's (1987) hypothesis, the findings summarized in Table 7.2 show that fathers' and single mothers' substance abuse covaried significantly with disrupted discipline. The Substance Abuse constructs showed only limited correlations with child adjustment. For single mothers, there was a correlation of .384 (*p* < .001) with Child Antisocial; for mothers of intact families, there was a borderline correlation with Child Depressed Mood (.21, *p* < .001).

The Avoidant Parent

Although we often encounter avoidant parents in our clinical work, we do not have adequate measures to back up our clinical impressions with relevant data. In spite of this, it is included in our discussion because of its potential usefulness to other investigators and clinicians.

Our impression is that many parents of antisocial boys consistently *avoid confrontations*. They seem to avoid all unpleasant interactions with people in general and family members in particular. These parents try to convince themselves and their therapists that deviant child behaviors either are not really deviant or that there is nothing they can do about them. If the parents do not consider the behavior to be deviant, then they do not have to confront it. Probably, being defeated hundreds of times during earlier confrontations with the child has taught the parent to avoid trying to change his or her behavior. This may be compounded by defeats experienced in many other aspects of life.

The avoidant individual generally seems to have a

Table 7.3
Regression for Each Family Management Composite Against Parental Traits

Dependent Variable	Significant Independent Variable	R Value	Significant Independent Variable	R Value	Significant Independent Variable	R Value
	Intact Families				**Single Mothers**	
	Fathers		*Mothers*			
Parental Monitoring	—[a]	—	Antisocial	.257*	—	—
Discipline	Social Disadv.	.381***	Depression	.326***	Stress	.431***
Problem Solving	Social Disadv.	.251**	Social Disadv.	.272**	—	—
Positive Reinforcement	Antisocial	.360***	Social Disadv.	.318***	Social Disadv.	.278*
Parental Involvement	—	—	—	—	—	—

*$p < .05$ **$p < .01$ ***$p < .001$

[a]Blanks indicate no significant correlations for this dependent variable.

nonassertive life-style. Clinically, many of these parents have a gentle schizoid quality such that much of their life seems to revolve around avoiding or escaping unpleasant interpersonal interactions. This is not necessarily the same as depression, schizophrenia, anxiety, or any other specific personality trait. These people simply withdraw from aversive confrontations. Of course, this means they are the preferred prey for the coercive child, spouse, neighbor, or irritable grocery clerk.

Multiple-Regression Analyses

It is likely that some of the information contained in the parental-trait composite scores is redundant. For example, depressive or antisocial traits may reflect a second-order factor (e.g., social competence). Thus, all of the contextual variables would be expected to intercorrelate. Table 7.3 summarizes the relevant findings separately for mothers, fathers, and single mothers. Approximately half of the correlations among contextual variables for each group were significant. This is far more than what would be expected by chance. Depending upon personal biases, the findings could be interpreted as supporting either the second-order factor hypothesis (i.e., social competence) or an independent variable definition of contextual effects (i.e., most of the correlations are relatively modest).

We were interested in studying the unique contribution of each contextual variable to family management skills. All of the contextual variables except the marital adjustment score were regressed against each separate measure of family management skills. For each analysis, the social disadvantage composite was introduced first and then followed by all of the other trait measures. Except for

parental involvement, the parental traits accounted for approximately 6% to 10% of the variance in family management skills in intact families. For all three samples, discipline and positive reinforcement were the family management practices that seemed to most sensitively reflect parental traits.

The contextual variables that seemed to account for unique variance in family management practices for intact families were measures of social disadvantage and antisocial behavior, and to a lesser extent, maternal depression. For single mothers, the measures of social disadvantage and stress accounted for the most variance.

Some Speculations and Models

This section reviews the findings from modeling studies that have directly tested the mediation assumption. Most of these studies have examined the contributions of social disadvantage and the parental antisocial trait to family process.

Social Disadvantage and Child Adjustment

The findings from three studies have consistently supported the hypothesis that the effect of social disadvantage on child adjustment is mediated through family management practices. One of the most dramatic findings was reported by Laub and Sampson (1988). They reanalyzed data from the well-known longitudinal study by the Gluecks (e.g., Glueck & Glueck, 1959) and showed that the effects of contextual variables such as parental criminality and alcoholism, broken homes, and over-crowding on delinquency were mediated through mater-

Figure 7.12

Tests of Mediational Hypothesis for Social Disadvantage and Parenting Practices

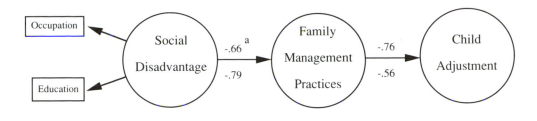

a The upper values are from Larzelere & Patterson, 1990; the lower values are from Bank, Forgatch, & Patterson (1991)

nal supervision, parental discipline, and parental attachment. The effects of context were entirely *indirect* and were mediated through parenting practices.

Larzelere and Patterson (1990) used longitudinal data from the OYS as a first test of the mediational model. They measured social disadvantage (defined by education and occupation) at grade 4 and parental discipline and monitoring practices at grade 6. The findings are summarized in Figure 7.12. The path coefficient from context to parenting practices was -.66; the path coefficient from parenting practices to delinquent activity (self-report and court records) measured a year later was -.76. The direct path from social disadvantage to delinquency was nonsignificant. The model offered strong support for the indirect contribution of social disadvantage to child adjustment.

The replication study was based on data from 90 boys 6 to 8 years of age from families with recently separated or divorced parents (Bank, Forgatch, & Patterson, 1991). The expanded measure of social disadvantage included occupation, education, WAIS vocabulary score, and income. As shown in Figure 7.12, the path coefficient from social disadvantage to maternal discipline was -.79. Again, more extreme social disadvantage was correlated with greater disruptions in parenting practices. The path coefficient from parenting practices to child antisocial (based on mother, teacher, and child reports) was -.56. There was no significant direct path from social disadvantage to child adjustment.

The findings consistently indicate that many of the parents in samples of socially disadvantaged families are ineffective. We also hypothesize that chronic unemployment and poverty can *directly* disrupt parenting practices. In a classic anthropological study, Turnbull (1972) offered some of the strongest support for this hypothesis. The forced resettlement of the Ik resulted in near starvation and a total disintegration of the family. The effects of chronic unemployment on black families living in ghettoes are equally dramatic (Sampson, 1987).

Parental Antisocial Trait

Are there hierarchical structures that could be imposed on contextual variables or is the effect of each variable on family management practices independent of all others? Our clinical experience suggests that the parental antisocial trait may be a candidate for a key position in a hierarchy of contextual effects.

Antisocial parents tend to generate many of the contextual variables described in the coercion model. For the antisocial mother or father, a weekend drinking spree at a local tavern may result in a brawl or a traffic accident. These individuals fail to keep careful records and ignore notices about unpaid bills. This life-style creates a steady stream of low-level daily hassles. Not paying bills on time may result in eviction from a rental home or having a car repossessed. Health problems and repeated divorce and remarriage also tend to be features of this life-style.

The general hypothesis is that certain forms of parental pathology place the family at significant risk for future transitions, high levels of stress, and continued social disadvantage. Aldwin and Revenson (1986) collected survey data that were consistent with this hypothesis. They regressed stress scores collected at Time 2 on stress scores and symptom scores for Time 1. The symptoms contributed significantly to the variance accounted for in stress measured at Time 2.

The hypothesis is also supported by findings from the large-scale longitudinal study reported by Gersten et al. (1977). These researchers found statistically reliable correlations among parental stress, parental traits, and family environment variables. They concluded that these correlations reflected the confound between parental distress and stress more than the etiological role of stress in disrupting families. Indeed, the parents' level of prior disturbance was more related to later stress than vice versa.

Three modeling studies have examined the role of parental antisocial traits as mediators for the effect of other contextual variables on parenting practices. All of the studies were based on data from the OYS, so we cannot say how robust the findings might be. As shown in Figure 7.13A, the first set of findings showed that the contribution of an enriched measure (i.e., income was added) of social disadvantage to maternal discipline was entirely *indirect* (Bank & Patterson, 1989). The effect of this contextual variable was mediated through the measure of maternal antisocial trait. After the information contained in the measure of antisocial trait was partialed out, social disadvantage offered no additional information. The findings were replicated by Bank, Forgatch, and Patterson (1991) in a study of older boys from divorced families. It is important to note that these findings were not replicated for a sample of families of antisocial children referred for treatment (Patterson, 1990). In that analysis, parental antisocial trait made a nonsignificant contribution to discipline practices after the measure of social disadvantage was partialed out.

Figure 7.13B describes the effect of the number of divorce and remarriage transitions on parental supervision (Capaldi & Patterson, 1991). Again, the effect on parenting practices was entirely indirect. Antisocial parents are characterized by more transitions. If the measure of antisocial trait is partialed out, however, the transition variable adds no new information.

The findings described in Figure 7.9 show a comparable mediating effect of parental antisocial traits for stress. Extremely antisocial mothers and fathers had high stress scores. When regressed against discipline practices, however, the contribution of stress was nonsignificant after the antisocial trait scores were partialed out.

The findings strongly suggest that the parental antisocial trait may play a major role in the hierarchy of contextual variables. It seems that this particular trait relates to current and future shifts in family context. For example, the parental antisocial trait scores covaried significantly with both social disadvantage and stress for the OYS samples. In addition, the trait scores mediated the effect of these contextual variables on parenting practices. An earlier study also demonstrated that maternal antisocial trait scores covaried with marital adjustment (Patterson & Bank, 1989).

Several qualifiers should be considered in evaluating these findings. For example, it seems that parental antisocial traits may *not* play such a central role in clinical samples. Furthermore, broadening the definition of social disadvantage to include measures of social skills places it in the role of mediator, while the maternal antisocial trait becomes an indirect contributor to disrupted discipline. Obviously, before we can become comfortable with these ideas, more analyses must be carried out on the role of antisocial traits using data from additional samples.

Our current position is that parental antisocial personality traits play a central role in family disruption and the development of child adjustment problems. The findings presented by Lahey, Hartdagen, Frick, McBurnett, Connor, and Hynd (1988) support this position. These researchers argued that the well-established correlation between divorce and boys externalizing problems is entirely mediated by parental antisocial traits. They stated that antisocial parents are more likely to divorce *and* to have ineffective parenting skills.

The Amplifier Hypothesis

Intuitively, the idea that major shifts in stressors may amplify existing negative parental traits has considerable appeal. As yet, however, we have not used our longitudinal data set to test this idea. Prolonged unemployment might increase the frequency and, indirectly, the intensity (because of escalation processes) of irritable exchanges for antisocial parents. What is of particular interest in the present context is the increase in irritability during discipline confrontations. An adequate test would require that prior measures of the parental antisocial trait show a significant increase following a major stressor and *concomitant* increases in disrupted discipline.

The amplifier hypothesis was first brought to our attention by Elder and his colleagues (Caspi & Elder, 1988; Elder et al., 1984; Elder, Van Nguyen, & Caspi, 1985). Their findings provided a strong test of the hypothesis by showing that fathers who were irritable prior to the Great Depression became increasingly irritable when faced with severe economic stress. These changes were followed by disruptions in discipline and, in turn, by increases in antisocial child behavior. Elder, Downey, and Cross (1986) found that the impact of an irritable (antisocial) father on a socially disadvantaged family can be mitigated by an affectionate and skilled mother.

The retrospective follow-up study of Vietnam veterans by Robins (1981) also provided support for the assumption that stress may amplify adjustment problems for antisocial individuals. Antisocial veterans were more at risk for drug addiction during their war experience and also for depression, alcoholism, illicit drug use, and psychiatric care three years after the experience.

Some alternatives. There are several plausible alternatives to a mediational model. Bronfenbrenner's (1977) interactional terms offer a promising way to formulate analyses. For example, it seems reasonable to expect that if single-mother stress and substance abuse are related to disrupted discipline, then the contribution of high scores on *both* variables would be more than additive (i.e., there would be an interaction effect). We have only explored this possibility once, when the data for maternal stress and substance abuse were analyzed as potential interactive terms. We carried out three separate analyses of variance using all 2x2 combinations of disruptor and parental trait for the Discipline construct. None of the analyses produced a significant interaction term, but a single

Figure 7.13
Effects of Context on Parenting Practices

A. Social Disadvantage (adapted from Bank & Patterson, 1989)

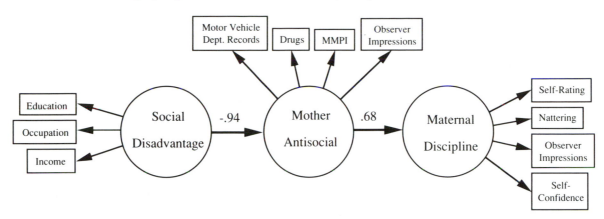

B. Transitions (from Capaldi & Patterson, 1991) [a]

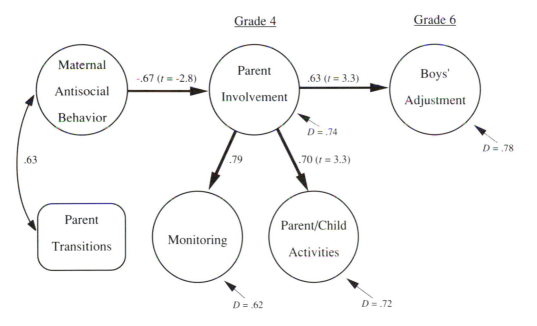

[a]Reprinted with permission from "Relation of parental transitions to boys' adjustment problems: I. A linear hypothesis. II. Mothers at risk for transitions and unskilled parenting." *Developmental Psychology*, 27(3), 489-504. Copyright 1991 by the American Psychological Association.

analysis is hardly a systematic test for this point of view. We plan to carry out programmatic studies along these lines in the near future.

Summary

We have considered the impact of two types of contextual variables on family processes. Our intent has been to use the classification more as a heuristic for organizing the discussion than as a strong hypothesis. We defined one set of variables as those that seem, *a priori*, to be relatively static. They include social disadvantage, grandparental discipline, parental antisocial traits, and substance abuse. Presumably, such contextual variables might determine early start-up for the coercion process, particularly in conjunction with a temperamentally difficult toddler.

Other contextual variables are more dynamic. They include transitions, stress, and marital adjustment. Changes can occur in these variables at any point in the family's history. Transitions include the onset of adolescence, divorce, remarriage, unemployment, or a prolonged illness. The assumption is that dramatic changes in any of these variables will be followed by disruptions in one or more family management practices. Our working hypothesis was that each of these contextual variables had an *indirect* effect on child adjustment. The findings suggest that family management variables serve as mediators for the effect of context on child adjustment.

We have tried to establish a multiagent, multimethod definition for each contextual variable. The convergent validities seemed satisfactory for social disadvantage and minimally adequate for substance abuse and depressive traits. There was only marginal convergence for the Stress and Parental Antisocial constructs, so risk scores were used as alternatives. An unsatisfactory factor structure was obtained for the Marital Adjustment construct.

Bivariate correlations indicated that the risk score for stress served as an important disruptor for single-mother families but not for intact families. The marital adjustment score based on self-report data seemed to make little or no contribution to measures of parenting practices and child adjustment. There was a linear relation between frequency of transitions and both child adjustment and family management practices.

The bivariate correlations underscored the potential contribution of both social disadvantage and parental antisocial behavior to discipline and positive reinforcement. These covariations held for intact families and single-parent families. The antisocial and social disadvantage scores also covaried significantly with one or more measures of child adjustment (depression, antisocial behavior, and achievement) for mothers and fathers from intact families and for single mothers.

There was a strong indication that the effect of contextual variables such as transitions, stress, and social disadvantage on parenting skills might be *indirect*. Several studies showed that the effect of these variables on parenting skills became nonsignificant when the parental antisocial trait scores were first partialed out.

We made a case for a hierarchical structure organizing the impact of contextual variables on family process. The parental antisocial trait was identified as the primary organizing variable; families with one or more antisocial parents are at risk for disruptions in family management practices and for increases in stress, marital conflict, social disadvantage (including downward social mobility), future divorce, and remarriage.

Chapter 8

The Effects of Being Antisocial

A child's antisocial behavior sets into motion a tidal wave of reactions from his social environment. From the day the problem child walks into school, these reactions begin to change his life. Up to that point he has been at home, where other family members are much like him. At school, however, he learns a hundred times over that he is different from his peers. He begins to fail at academics almost immediately, and within a few weeks he begins to be rejected by normal children. After a few months, it is clear that he is slipping behind the others in schoolwork. Anger and sadness soon follow, and the child begins to search for a social environment in which he can fit in. This chapter describes how these changes take place.

Characteristics of the Stage Model

In the initial chapters of this book, we showed how the antisocial trait results from the reinforcement contingencies found in interactions with family members. The contribution of contextual variables to child adjustment was explored in Chapter 7. In this chapter, the trait concept is examined in the broader context of the effects produced by the trait behaviors. We are not suggesting that the antisocial trait is a causal variable that produces certain effects directly; rather, the behaviors that make up the trait elicit *both* short-term and long-term reactions from the social environment. The immediate response of the social environment to the child's antisocial behavior is to provide reinforcing consequences that include avoiding responsibilities and immediate self-gratification. Over the

long-term, however, the reaction of the social environment is disastrous for the antisocial child. These consequences are quite predictable: rejection by normal peers and serious risk for academic failure. For convenience, we have labeled these two dramatic reactions from the social environment as *stages*.

As we noted in Chapter 1, stages are probabilistic relations between events. Given the recent unfortunate history of stage concepts in developmental psychology, it might have been wise to select some other metaphor. What we intend to convey here is simply that once antisocial behaviors develop, certain outcomes are likely to occur in a predictable sequence.

Figure 8.1 portrays a series of events that form a kind of action–reaction sequence. The child's antisocial *actions* produce a set of reliable *reactions* from the social environment. In this case, the reactions — rejection by family and peer group and academic failure — constitute massive failures that severely disrupt the socialization process. When accompanied by obdurate antisocial acts, these failures place the child on a developmental path that is very different from that of the normal child. This path does not move the child toward the adult world of intimate relationships, family, and work, but to a growing commitment to a deviant peer group, antisocial attitudes, and increasing sadness. We call this set of reactions stage 3.

We suspect that longitudinal studies of preschool children will show that many of the action–reaction components occur almost simultaneously. For example, the coercive reactions of the preschool child would covary

115

Figure 8.1

A Concatenation of Actions and Reactions

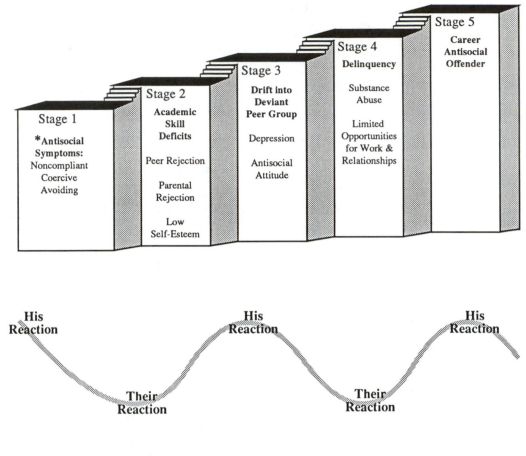

*The defining characteristics for that stage.

with the initial stages of rejection by parents, which would be accompanied by sadness and low self-esteem on the part of the child. Critical changes may take place within weeks or months rather than years. However, the important feature of the stage model is the action–reaction sequence itself. We believe that the characteristics of each stage are causal variables for events in subsequent stages (e.g., antisocial behaviors determine academic failure and peer rejection, academic failure determines involvement with deviant peers, etc.).

In contrast with other traits, the trait for antisocial behavior provides information about profound disruptions in key dimensions that define the developmental process. It is a special kind of marker variable that identifies a dynamic process fueled by action–reaction sequences. The behaviors that make up the antisocial trait seem to have the destructive power of a tidal wave, disrupting each stage of social development in the life

course of the child. Unlike the unstoppable force of the tidal wave, however, the process that moves the child from one stage to the next *can* be interrupted. The child's parents can be trained to use more effective discipline techniques, the child can learn skills for relating to peers, and academic difficulties can be remediated. The stage model is not intended to convey a sense of inevitability. Patterson and Bank (1989) describe the stage model as a "concatentation of actions and reactions unfolding over time" (p. 167). Although a little awkward, this is a better description of the stage model.

The phase model for alcoholism described by Zucker (1987) is analogous in many ways to our concept of stages. His formulation traces the progression from preschool years, starting with difficult temperament, poor socialization practices, and heavy use of alcohol by parents. In middle childhood this is followed by difficulties in school, involvement in a deviant peer group, and early experimentation with alcohol. The progression moves on to increasingly apparent skill deficits, social failure, and alcohol abuse. Zucker currently is conducting a longitudinal study to test these hypotheses. Because the study began when the children were very young, it should provide a direct test of many of the ideas presented here.

If the process begins in the preschool years, it is assumed that the child would move through each stage in the sequence. A similar sequence should be observed for children who begin the process in the second or third grade. We cannot be sure about this because the appropriate data are not yet available. If the child begins the process during early adolescence, we hypothesize that the sequence would be quite different (Patterson, DeBaryshe, & Ramsey, 1989). The key assumption is that late starters will have at least a marginal level of social skills; this makes a considerable difference in the stage sequence because the late starters are trained to use antisocial behaviors by a deviant peer group rather than by family members. We also hypothesize that late starters are the antisocial individuals most likely to drop out of the delinquency process. This volume is dedicated to the study of early starters: those boys who are most at risk to become antisocial adult offenders.

In the sections that follow, we use structural equation models based on OYS data collected for both cohorts at grade 4 to examine each of the predicted action–reaction sequences that define the stage model.

Progression

The stage concept was described in earlier chapters as a progression from frequently occurring minor problem behaviors to infrequent but more serious deviant acts. In the present context, it is assumed that relatively innocuous preschool behaviors such as noncompliance and temper tantrums are precursors of the more extreme forms of antisocial behavior exhibited by adolescents (i.e., index crimes). The ultimate goal is to use the coercion progression to identify chronic offenders. A small group of chronic offenders is involved in more than half of all the crimes committed by a given cohort; they also make a substantial contribution to the incidence of index crimes. In keeping with the early and late starter notion, we assume that the progression only applies to the early starters.

The second key assumption is that the action–reaction sequence is transitive. A systematic test of the progression and transitivity concepts would require a longitudinal study starting in the preschool years. Then we could demonstrate that some boys move through each stage in sequence and calculate the likelihood that a boy in any given stage arrived there via the preceding stages. In fact, the transitivity assumption *requires* such a progression. If the boys who become involved with deviant peers are not rejected by normal peers (stage 2) or are not antisocial

(stage 1), then the sequence is not transitive and the *a priori* model is faulty.

Using data from grades 4 and 6 from Cohort I of the OYS, Patterson and Bank (1989) examined the coercion progression. They made a set of arbitrary decisions for setting the at-risk cutoff points for each stage and calculated the transitional probabilities for moving from antisocial to peer rejection, to involvement with deviant peers, to police offenses. The findings support the transitivity assumption. First, the majority (60% to 80%) of the boys in any given stage also went through the preceding stage. For each stage, the conditional probability was higher than the baserate value. Even though the boys were only 12 years old at the time of the study, 11 of them already had been arrested at least once. Eighty percent of the offenders were involved with a deviant peer group. Even more powerful support for the transitivity hypothesis was provided by the finding that 64% of the delinquent youths went through *every one of the prior stages* in the progression. In fact, most of the boys who were false-negative errors had only missed a single stage. The hit rate was 87% with a false-positive error of 59% and false-negative error of 36%.

The findings for the symptom progressions described in Chapter 4 indicated that the coercion model accounted for roughly two-thirds of the boys who are stealers. According to that analysis, most coercive boys go on to become stealers. The data for the delinquency progression presented in Patterson and Bank (1989) were drawn from a different sample and essentially replicated that finding. Roughly two-thirds of the boys who were delinquent went through all of the prior stages in the progression; the coercion model seemed to fit most delinquents who were early starters.

It would be interesting to try to build a model for the offenders who do not fit the coercion model. In our staff discussions, we refer to this group as "sneaky aggressors." Our clinical speculations are that this model should contain composite measures of parental distance (coldness) combined with *overly effective* punishment. In the cases we have treated, these boys tend to be stealers who seldom win in direct confrontations with their parents. Their acts of theft and vandalism seem to represent an indirect attack on parental status and authority.

Career offenders typically represent 5% to 7% of a normal sample, depending on the definition used (West & Farrington, 1973; Wolfgang, Figlio, & Sellin, 1972). Evidence clearly shows that this group is responsible for more than 50% of the criminal activity both in the United States (Elliott, Huizinga, & Ageton, 1985) and abroad (West & Farrington, 1973).

Because of the high-risk nature of the OYS sample, we thought that at least 10% to 15% of the boys would have three or more police arrests by the time they graduate from high school. Recently analyzed OYS data showed that by age 16, 14% of the boys had three or more police contacts and 42% reported three or more delinquent acts for that year. It seems, then, that by the time the cohorts graduate from high school, a combination of court and self-report records should identify a substantial group of early starter, chronic offenders.

Stationarity

It appears that similar reinforcement contingencies maintain antisocial acts at each stage in the progression. In this general sense, it could be said that the underlying process is unidimensional. Nevertheless, some developmental shifts are likely, as indicated by the variables associated with these contingencies. Patterson (1988, 1990) and Patterson and Bank (1989) have discussed the nature of these shifts in detail.

A developmental account of the coercion model emphasizes the fact that it is not stationary: The contribution of determinants varies as a function of trials and developmental stages (Patterson, 1990). Two shifts in the contribution of causal variables are thought to be salient; one is the contribution of peers, and the other is a shift in the parenting skills that are most relevant.

From a developmental perspective, measures of parental discipline practices should be the primary determinants for the performance of antisocial behavior during the preschool years. Fagot and Eddy (1990) recently offered strong support for this hypothesis in their analyses of both boys and girls. Baldwin and Skinner (1989) demonstrated that parental discipline also made a significant contribution in a sample of boys 6 to 8 years of age from recently separated families.

Presumably, parental monitoring of deviant behavior would contribute little or nothing to our understanding of antisocial behavior in samples of preadolescents, because monitoring plays a minor role until children are spending a considerable amount of time unsupervised by adults (Patterson & Stouthamer-Loeber, 1984). Baldwin and Skinner (1989) could not obtain convergence for monitoring indicators based on data for younger boys. For 10-year-olds in the OYS, Patterson and Bank (1989) found that the monitoring indicators converged and the Monitoring construct made a significant but modest contribution (.32) to the Child Antisocial construct when the contributions of Parental Discipline had been partialed out.

Data from the Planning Study showed that for boys between the ages of 13 and 16 there was a twofold increase in the amount of unsupervised time they were allowed *and* in the frequency of police contacts (Patterson & Stouthamer-Loeber, 1984). There also should be a significant increase in the contribution of parental monitoring. In analyses of the OYS longitudinal data, Patterson (1990) controlled for factor invariance in the indicators used in the models for 10- and 12-year-olds.

The findings were consistent with the developmental hypothesis.

The developmental hypothesis includes the assumption that stages may differ in the *kinds* of determinants for antisocial behavior. For example, parenting practices should account for most of the variance in the early stages. As the child enters grade school, interactions with peers should provide additional reinforcement for antisocial behavior. By early adolescence, the deviant peer group begins to contribute to the process. As yet, we have not conducted a systematic study of this aspect of the stationarity hypothesis.

Limited Shopping

The abrasive exchanges between the antisocial boy and key persons in his social environment produce a kind of dyadic avoidance. Gradually, the boy becomes a spectator to many of the normal socialization experiences. This is not to say that he never participates in organized activities with normal peers or that he never has contact with popular members of his peer group. Instead, he misses an occasional experience each day. What he misses most are the subtle exchanges with normal peers that teach cooperation. Youniss (1980) and others have pointed out that *parents cannot teach this*. The antisocial boy does not learn when or how to accept negative feedback through experiences with peers. Because the antisocial boy spends less time participating in organized sports, he quickly falls behind in skills such as throwing a baseball, catching a football, and all of the other activities that are status-related for boys of this age (Hops, 1983). Walker, Shinn, O'Neill, and Ramsey (1987) collected observation data in the schoolyard at recess for a subgroup of boys in the at-risk sample when they were in grade 5. The antisocial boys played alone 4.4% of the time, and normal boys played alone 2.7% of the time. The antisocial boys only spent 32% of the time in structured activities; the comparable figure for normal boys was 52%.

The "limited shopping" situation becomes more pronounced at each stage. What seems to happen is an accumulation of missed opportunities (see Figure 8.2). As the boy's antisocial behavior becomes more noticeable, he is more at risk for associating with other deviant children. As the process continues, the antisocial boy and his deviant friends are increasingly likely to select settings in which they can associate with other problem children. Increasingly large portions of his life become opportunities for further deviancy training. The problem child selects the people and the settings that define the context in which he lives. This, in turn, functions as a feedback loop that locks him into the process.

The coercive style of the antisocial boy means it is extremely unlikely that his father or other adults will teach

Figure 8.2
The Relation Between Traits and Contexts

A. Simple and Linear

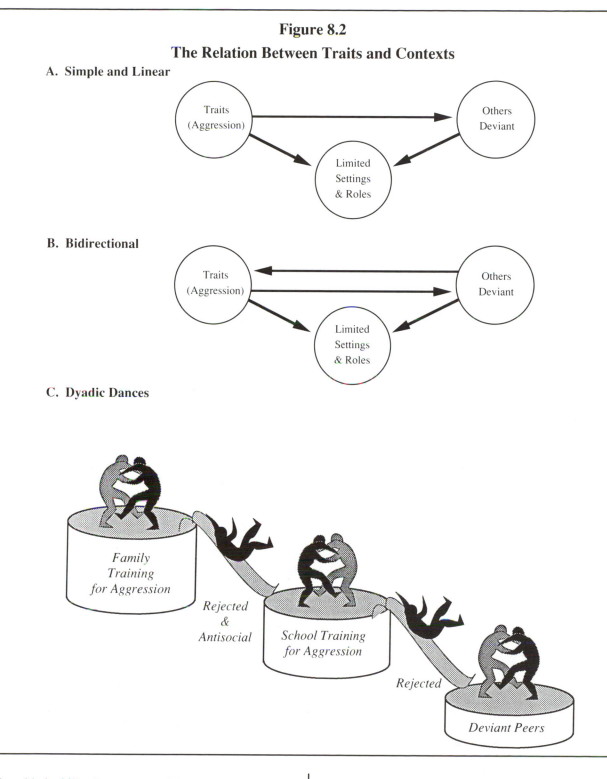

B. Bidirectional

C. Dyadic Dances

him athletic skills. Consequently, it is also highly unlikely that he will become a member of an athletic team or that he will win acceptance from peers who value athletic skills.

The antisocial child perceives himself as the victim of a cruel and unjust world. Observations conducted in the home and in school show that his perceptions are ab-solutely correct. He is not treated fairly by others. He receives more punishment and ridicule than do other members of his family (Patterson, 1982). Compared to his normal peers, he is more likely to be picked on and less likely to be selected for group activities (Shinn, Ramsey, Walker, Stieber, & O'Neill, 1987).

Not only does the problem boy miss out on valuable

social experiences, but also many of his experiences are qualitatively different from those of normal peers. He is more likely to interact with children who are younger than himself and to select deviant children. In his analyses of peer-nomination data from the OYS at grade 4, Dishion (1988) showed that the antisocial child selected more rejected children as "Kids I like as friends." As shown in Figure 8.2A, the child's antisocial behaviors severely limit the settings and roles available to him; his social contacts are more likely to be with deviant peers, who provide further reinforcement for antisocial acts. This bidirectional model is illustrated in Figure 8.2B.

As shown in Figure 8.2C, the developmental model for antisocial behavior can be depicted as a sequence of dyadic dances that begins with family members, shifts to the normal peer group, and finally moves to the deviant peer group. Each dance contributes to the antisocial process. In Chapter 7, we noted that contextual variables are important determinants for the antisocial trait. In a very real sense, *the effect of the antisocial trait is to alter the context*. Patterson, Bank, and Stoolmiller (1990) have provided further support for this idea.

One implication of the limited shopping hypothesis is that there are fewer opportunities for experiences that might lead the antisocial child to a more productive path. The longer the child remains in the process, the greater the cumulative omissions and the less likely that intervention efforts will be successful. Each omission is a tiny blank spot on the child's map of social experiences. Over a period of years, these blank spots lead to an attitude about social realities that is fundamentally different from that of normal adolescents. If asked about the omissions, the child probably would say, "Who cares?" The repeated failures, low self-esteem, and recurring depressed moods, however, all reduce the likelihood that these oversights in basic socialization will be redressed.

The shopping hypothesis could be tested in a longitudinal design by simply listing the activities in which the child engages, those he avoids, and those from which he drops out. Early academic failure and rejection by peers would relate to later avoidance and dropout behaviors. No provision was made in the current study for a systematic test of the limited shopping hypothesis.

Stage 1: Family Training for Antisocial Behavior

In a way, this entire volume provides a detailed description of what occurs during stage 1. The family members inadvertently provide contingencies that reinforce coercive behaviors and fail to provide support for most prosocial behaviors. As the problem behaviors become more frequent and more extreme, they generalize to other settings such as the school and the neighborhood. This, in turn, sets the stage for certain highly predictable reactions by peers and adults who are confronted by these problem behaviors.

Stage 2: Reactions from the Social Environment

This section examines five hypotheses that describe the stage 2 effects: (1) The antisocial behaviors learned at home are accompanied by parental rejection, (2) parental rejection is accompanied by low child self-esteem, (3) the antisocial behaviors practiced at home generalize to the school setting, (4) the reactions to antisocial acts in school include rejection by peers, and (5) the child's antisocial disposition leads to academic failure. These hypotheses are tested using SEM based on the data collected for both cohorts at grade 4.

Parental Rejection

We hypothesize that there is a bidirectional relation between child deviance and parental rejection. The path with the largest magnitude should describe the impact of child deviant behavior on parental rejection. It seems likely that parental rejection increases at about the same rate as the child's coercive behavior.

One of our first impressions in working with the families referred to OSLC for treatment was that many of the parents simply did not like their children. McCord (1978) found significant correlations between the parents' early lack of affection and later incidence of serious crimes. Parents who were less affectionate also tended to provide less supervision for their children. The covariation between lack of parental warmth and delinquent children has been noted consistently across studies (Loeber & Dishion, 1983), beginning with the classic studies by Glueck and Glueck (1950, 1959).

Parents' reports during treatment sessions indicated that rejection of the child began relatively early. Sometimes it seemed to begin because the child was difficult to control as an infant or toddler. In other cases, the early rejection was related to a chaotic life-style characterized by poverty and high levels of stress. Some parents seemed immature and tentative in their commitment to parental responsibility. We believe these uncommitted parents would perform poorly on measures of family management practices. The combination of an unskilled parent and a temperamentally difficult toddler would define a sample at very high risk for later antisocial behavior.

Building a satisfactory construct for parental rejection has been difficult. To date, we have developed three indicators based on mother and father interviews, but the convergence tends to be moderate. Borderline results have been obtained by including child reports. Patterson (1986a) used the parental rejection composite from the

Planning Study sample to test the relation between parental rejection and child deviance. The assumption was that the child's coercive exchanges with family members lead to the parents not liking the child. Evidently, both parents share the same perception of the child; the correlation between mothers' and fathers' rejection scores was .67 ($p < .001$). The first analysis focused on home-based variables. These consisted of the observed day-to-day abrasive exchanges of the problem child with siblings and parents. The multiple-correlation coefficient produced by regressing parental rejection on these variables was .69 ($p < .001$). The second analysis focused on variables that presumably indicate to the public that the parents have failed (e.g., academic problems). The multiple-correlation coefficient for this set of variables was .49 ($p < .001$).

As expected, there were significant correlations between parental rejection and measures of antisocial behavior. For example, in the Planning Study sample the correlation between court records of police offenses for boys in grade 7 and the composite measure of rejection was .26 ($p < .05$) for mothers and .32 ($p < .05$) for fathers. For the at-risk sample, the antisocial composite at grade 4 correlated .51 ($p < .001$) with the composite measure of parental rejection.

Patterson and Dishion (1988) used parent interviews and interviewer impressions to define parental rejection. The data from Cohort I of the OYS showed factor loadings of .62 (parent interview) and .55 (interviewer impressions) for the two indicators measured at grade 4, and .86 and .65, respectively, when measured two years later. The path coefficient from the Child Antisocial construct to the Parental Rejection construct was .74 ($p < .05$). The longitudinal data showed that changes in antisocial behavior over the two-year interval correlated .41 with changes in parental acceptance. The implication was that parental rejection increased as the child became more antisocial.

We have not yet made a systematic study of the hypothesized bidirectional relation between parental rejection and child deviant behavior. As the findings now stand, they are consistent with the hypothesis that the covariation between the two constructs is significant.

Self-Esteem

We do not assume that high or low self-esteem is a significant determinant for social behavior. We currently view self-esteem as a convenient gauge of how well the child fits into the social environment (i.e., the extent to which the child is evaluated as competent by family members and peers).

We hypothesize that measures of both child deviance and parenting skills will covary significantly with measures of child self-esteem. Presumably, the child's self-report data reflect his awareness that he is not getting along well with others in his family or at school. The accompanying hypothesis is that this is indirectly the result of ineffective parenting practices.

Prosocial behavior and self-esteem. Harter (1983) reviewed the extensive literature on child self-esteem and related topics. As she noted, William James defined *self-esteem* as the ratio of successes to pretensions (i.e., potentialities). For our purposes, it is assumed that a simple tally of the child's successes and failures would provide an adequate account of self-esteem. The more social successes at home and school, the higher the child's self-esteem.

A consistent relation has been reported between high self-esteem and academic achievement for children, adolescents, and adults (see reviews by Purkey, 1970, and Connell & Harter, 1984). A large body of findings also demonstrates the covariation between deviant behavior and lower self-esteem. Feshbach (1970) cited several studies that showed a covariation between low self-esteem and aggressive behavior in children. Loney (1974) reviewed studies that showed significant covariation between hyperactivity and low self-esteem.

We suspect that most, if not all, forms of deviant child behaviors are accompanied by lower self-esteem and that these problem behaviors elicit negative reactions from significant others. We also assume that certain parenting skills covary significantly with the full range of maladaptive child behaviors. This suggests that parenting behaviors make a significant contribution to child self-esteem. Harter (1983) cited several reviews of the literature on this topic and noted that although there is some support for the idea, the number of relevant studies is surprisingly small. The strongest support for the effect of childrearing practices on child self-esteem was provided by the Blocks in their longitudinal study (Block, 1985). Ratings of 14 parenting behaviors were obtained for a sample of families with boys who were 3 to 4 years of age. They found a significant correlation between these ratings and the boys' descriptions of self-concept at age 14. In general, positive parenting behaviors for both mothers and fathers were associated with better self-esteem.

Findings from the OYS. The first problem in testing these hypotheses was to develop an adequate definition for the criterion construct. Two self-report measures were used to define child self-esteem. The details of the psychometric analyses are summarized in Capaldi and Patterson (1989). An itemetric analysis of Kaplan's (1975) Child Perception Scale identified four items with an alpha value of .69. The scale measured the child's global sense of worth (e.g., "At times I feel that I'm a failure"). A similar analysis for a checklist of child skills produced 10 items with an alpha value of .76 that described the child's general sense of competence in specific areas (e.g., "How well do you do in math?"). As shown in Figure 8.3, the latent construct loaded most

Figure 8.3
The Deviancy Model of Self-Esteem

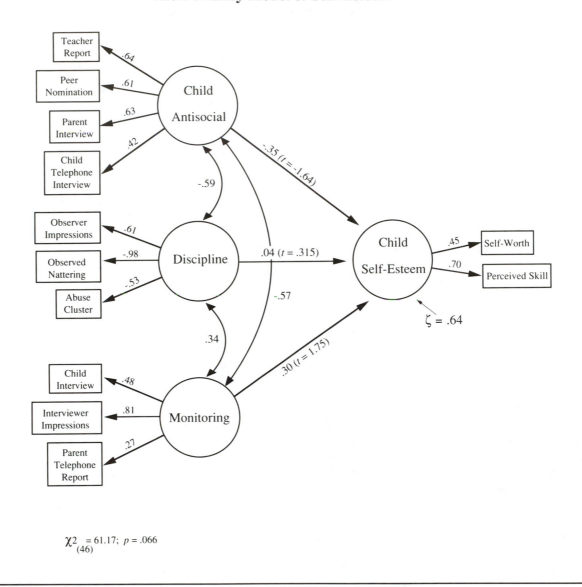

$\chi^2_{(46)} = 61.17;\ p = .066$

heavily on the measure of child-perceived skill (.70) and to a lesser extent on the child's sense of self-worth (.45).

The correlations among the 12 indicators that define the deviance model for self-esteem are summarized in Table 8.1. Note that the convergence for both the Child Self-Esteem and Parental Monitoring constructs were rather modest. Because the discriminative correlations tended to be of relatively low magnitude, this did not pose a major problem in obtaining a fit for the model.

The *a priori* model specified that the child's antisocial behavior should make a direct contribution to low self-esteem. Presumably, the contribution of discipline and monitoring practices would be indirect, mediated through the Child Antisocial construct. We were not sure

whether parenting practices would contribute anything more, but we included them in the model to explore this further. The findings offered moderate support for the deviance model of self-esteem. As we expected, the more antisocial the child, the lower his self-esteem. The path coefficient of .35 was of borderline significance. Self-report data from poorly monitored children also indicated low self-esteem. The model accounted for 36% of the variance in child reports of self-esteem. The chi-square value showed an acceptable fit between the covariance structures that were predicted and those obtained. The findings supported the idea that inadequate monitoring and deviant child behavior are associated with low self-esteem.

Table 8.1

Matrix for Convergent and Discriminant Correlations for Self-Esteem Deviancy Model

	Child Self-Esteem		Child Antisocial				Good Discipline			Good Monitoring		
	Child Report: Worth	Child Report: Skill	Teacher Report	Peer Report	Parent Report	Child Phone Report	Observer Impres.	Nattering	Abuse Cluster	Child Report: Rules	Interviewer Impres.	Parent Report: Hours
Chld Rpt: Worth	1.00											
Chld Rpt: Skill	.315	1.00										
Teacher Rpt	-.094	-.224	1.00									
Peer Rpt	-.106	-.219	.640	1.00								
Parent Rpt	-.243	-.170	.414	.370	1.00							
Chld Phone Rpt	-.231	-.302	.244	.201	.321	1.00						
Observer Imp	.099	.090	-.285	-.334	-.181	-.070	1.00					
Nattering	-.127	-.257	.409	.391	.338	.185	-.592	1.00				
Abuse Cluster	-.060	-.040	.273	.211	.141	.103	-.489	.515	1.00			
Chld Rpt: Rules	.154	.268	-.113	-.151	-.170	-.116	.082	-.099	.056	1.00		
Int Impressions	.163	.287	-.278	-.326	-.284	-.159	.254	-.297	-.143	.377	1.00	
Par Rpt: Hours	-.012	.008	-.071	-.092	-.191	-.112	.036	.044	.040	.150	.233	1.00

The second model was based on a more developmental approach. We assumed that measures of positive parenting skills would contribute directly to the development of high self-esteem in children. Three positive parenting constructs were used to test this hypothesis: Problem Solving, Parental Involvement, and Positive Reinforcement. The details of the psychometric analyses for these three constructs are provided in Capaldi and Patterson (1989). The Positive Reinforcement construct was based on three indicators: observer impressions, observed likelihood of the mother reacting positively when she was interacting with the target child, and parent daily telephone reports. The Parental Involvement construct consisted of two indicators: parent and child questionnaire reports of daily activities. The Problem Solving construct was based on three indicators: the sum of three variables that described outcomes of videotaped family problem-solving interactions, total positive solutions, and the likelihood that a parent would respond to any child behavior with a problem-solving behavior.

As shown in Figure 8.4, the developmental model was a modest success. Among the positive parenting constructs, Problem Solving seemed most significantly related (.66) to child self-esteem. Given that the family was effective in solving its own problems, the child was more likely to report high self-esteem. The developmental model provided an acceptable fit to the data and accounted for 54% of the variance in the Child Self-Esteem construct.

Despite our concerns about the adequacy of the measures for the criterion construct, both the developmental and the deviance models worked surprisingly well. When we combined the best components of each model, the effects of the Problem Solving construct on Child Self-Esteem were no longer significant. Efforts to develop a school-based model using the Academic Achievement and Peer Relations (peer-nomination) constructs produced an acceptable fit, although the model accounted for only 11% of the variance in the criterion measure and the path coefficients were of borderline significance.

Self-esteem reported at grade 4 seems to lend itself to a rather simple model. Deviance is associated with low self-esteem. We were surprised that although other models make significant contributions to self-esteem, all of them seem secondary to the deviance model. We thought that the models for adolescents' self-esteem would be more complex. However, Bank (1990) showed that antisocial behavior is the prime determinant for low self-esteem in adolescents as well.

Figure 8.4
A Developmental Model of Self-Esteem

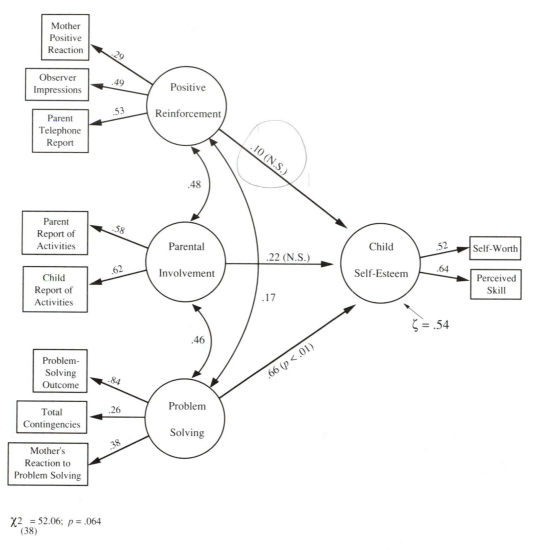

$\chi^2_{(38)} = 52.06;\ p = .064$

Cause or effect? The literature on self-concept is devoted primarily to understanding the development and maintenance of a positive self-evaluation. As Harter (1983) noted, however, a sense of self seems to have at least two components. One consists of an evaluation of *areas of competence* (e.g., social, physical, academic). The focus of the other component is on *affective overtones*. Usually, a measure of self-esteem will include both of these components.

Investigators are divided on the issue of whether one or both of these components have a causal effect on the behavior of the child (Harter, 1983). Some agree with Bandura (1978), who believed that a person's positive statements about competencies lead to expectations about future successes, which in turn facilitate future perfor-

mance. Harter noted that this position has led some investigators to conclude that enhancing the child's self-esteem would lead to higher levels of achievement in the future. For example, Gunnison (1990) described the findings from a task force supported by the state of California. The 26-member commission, headed by Assemblyman J. Vasconcellos, released a report that recommended the enhancement of children's self-esteem as an inoculation against crime, teenage pregnancy, child abuse, and substance abuse!

Harter (1983) cited three longitudinal studies that used SEM to evaluate the causal status of self-esteem measures as determinants of future academic achievement (Bachman & O'Malley, 1977, 1980; Calsyn & Kenny, 1977; Rubin, Maruyama, & Kingsbury, 1979). All three studies found that the best predictor of future achievement was past achievement. The contribution of self-esteem measures to these predictions was not significant. Entwisle, Alexander, Pallas, and Cadigan (1987) replicated these negative findings in their longitudinal study of first-grade children.

Bank (1990) arrived at a similar conclusion in his analysis of longitudinal data from the OYS. Self-esteem measured at age 10 did not make a contribution to antisocial behavior measured at age 12 after the prior measure of antisocial behavior had been partialed out. In general, these findings are consistent with the hypothesis that self-esteem reflects the child's sense of competency and feelings about how well he is doing. However, when we take into account objective measures of how well he is doing at the present time, the child's sense of competency adds nothing to our ability to predict what he will do in the future. Low self-esteem means there is a problem, but the problem is not caused by the impaired sense of self-worth.

Some investigators have suggested that it is not what we do but *how others react to our actions* that leads to negative self-evaluations of competence or worth. For example, self-evaluation may not change following aggressive actions, because individuals who behave immorally do not necessarily evaluate themselves less positively. An extreme example of this has been reported by Lifton (1986), who found that the majority of Nazi doctors who served at Auschwitz were not markedly negative in their self-evaluations following their experiences there. Apparently, doing bad things, or even being caught doing them, does not necessarily lead to low self-esteem. It is not so much what you do but rather how others respond to what you do that determines self-esteem.

Generalization from Home to School

One of the key assumptions of the coercion model is that the effects of reinforcement contingencies provided at home will generalize to other settings, such as the school. Ramsey, Patterson, and Walker (1990) tested this generalization hypothesis. They used home-based indicators to define the Child Antisocial construct for 10-year-olds and school-based indicators to define the same construct a year later. The resulting path coefficient of .73 demonstrated that the trait constructs were generalizable across time and settings. As we noted in Chapter 3, coercion is a style of coping with environmental demands that is highly stable and generalizable across settings.

The stage model stipulates that there are at least two critical outcomes of generalization. There should be evidence of rejection by normal peers within weeks, and academic problems should be apparent within several months. We hypothesized that there would be direct paths between the Child Antisocial construct and all of the outcomes discussed so far (i.e., parental rejection, peer rejection, and academic failure). The findings for the combined cohorts assessed at grade 4 are summarized in Figure 8.5. To identify the model, we set equal factor loadings for the indicator pairs for the latent construct Discipline, Peer Relations, and Parent–Child Relationship.

The findings offer solid support for the generalization of effects that define stage 2. There is a good fit of the theory-driven model to the data. The nonsignificant chi-square value ($p < .30$) showed no reliable difference between the predicted and obtained covariance structures. In addition, all of the path coefficients were significant and relatively large in magnitude. A simple direct-effects model showed that antisocial behaviors related to each of the three outcomes.

The modification indices strongly suggested a direct path from parental discipline practices to the Academic Achievement construct. In a second attempt, the direct path was significant but small in magnitude (.28). The chi-square analysis showed that the second model was a significant improvement over the first.

The use of concurrent data from fourth-grade boys is not the best way to test the stage 2 hypothesis. The ideal design would be a longitudinal study that begins with the measurement of antisocial behavior for an at-risk sample of preschool boys. Peer-nomination data collected at grade 1 and academic achievement and parental rejection data collected at grade 2 or 3 would test the idea of movement from one stage to another *across time*. The current data set is based on the implicit assumption that such movement already has occurred, and what were once cause-and-effect relations are now concurrent covariations. If the concurrent correlations are nonsignificant, the hypothesis would not be confirmed; even if they are significant, the findings could only be described as consistent.

The direct path from antisocial behavior to peer rejection and academic failure is consistent with the hypothesis that a moderate level of child compliance is necessary for socialization (see Chapter 6). White and Carew-Watts (1973) studied the development of social competence in young children and found that competent children tend to be more compliant and come from homes in which clear limits are set. A more generalized form of the hypothesis would be that measures of antisocial behavior correlate negatively with most measures of child social competence (i.e., prosocial behavior). Dishion (1988) provided strong support for this hypothesis in his confirmatory factor analyses of data collected at grade 4. The analyses showed that measures of child social competence could not be clearly differentiated from measures of child antisocial behavior. He found a correlation of -.65 between the two construct scores.

To account for additional variance in the Peer Rejection

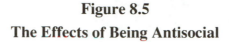

Figure 8.5

The Effects of Being Antisocial

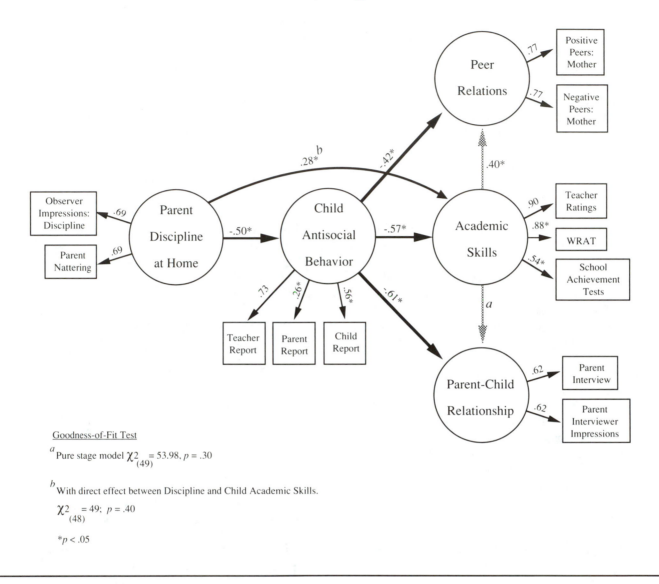

Goodness-of-Fit Test

^{a} Pure stage model $\chi^2_{(49)} = 53.98$, $p = .30$

^{b} With direct effect between Discipline and Child Academic Skills.

$\chi^2_{(48)} = 49$; $p = .40$

*$p < .05$

and Academic Achievement constructs, it would be necessary to identify the mechanisms that produce the link between antisocial behaviors and these two outcomes. Determining *why* antisocial children are rejected requires a new formulation, which leads to a new measurement problem. The sections that follow include a brief discussion of the possible mechanisms, a review of the relevant empirical findings, and, where possible, an application of SEM to the refined model.

Academic Skills

Reviews of the empirical literature consistently reveal a negative correlation between antisocial behavior and academic achievement (Patterson, 1982; Rutter & Giller,

1983; Rutter, Tizard, & Whitmore, 1970; Wilson & Herrnstein, 1985). For example, the large-scale survey of parental report data by Achenbach and Edelbrock (1981) showed that "poor school work" was a problem for 15% of the normal boys; the comparable figure for boys in a clinical sample was 60%.

We assume that several mechanisms contribute to this negative correlation. The noncompliance that is a salient feature of antisocial behavior has a profound impact on the child's academic skills. It is thought that noncompliance correlates negatively with time on task, and that time on task is related to academic achievement. There is a general consensus that proficiency in academic skills such as reading, spelling, and arithmetic is primarily a function of *time spent on task* both in the classroom and at home. Antisocial children spend less time on task in both settings. Because of their noncompliance and abrasive interpersonal style, they learn less in the classroom and on the playground. Critical feedback is not accepted, whether it concerns their performance in sports or academics. The effect of this is that antisocial children are avoided by the individuals who could teach them new skills. Over time, these effects should produce a significant negative correlation between measures of antisocial behavior and academic achievement.

Shinn et al. (1987) investigated the relation between antisocial behavior and time spent on task in the classroom. The study involved classroom observations of 40 antisocial boys and 40 normal boys in grade 5. The subjects were drawn from OYS at-risk samples. It was found that the antisocial boys spent significantly less time on task. Antisocial boys were on task 70.2% of the time; the comparable figure for normal boys was 83.4%. Twice as many of the antisocial boys were receiving remedial education; 18% already had been held back at least one year, compared to 10% of the normal boys.

A connection also has been demonstrated between noncompliance and poor academic achievement. At one level, it seems relatively straightforward: Teachers consistently emphasize child compliance as a prerequisite for learning. This was confirmed by Hirsh and Walker (1983) in a review of teacher-survey studies. The first direct test was by Cobb (1970), who found that observed rates of inattentive, noncompliant, and disruptive classroom behaviors covaried significantly with achievement-test scores. Our data from the OYS showed that the correlations between composite scores for Academic Achievement and Child Antisocial were -.52 ($p < .001$) for grade 7 and -.29 ($p < .05$) for grade 10. Hess and McDevitt (1984) provided longitudinal observation data that showed that noncompliance at age 4 correlated significantly with measures of achievement when the children were tested again at ages 5, 6, and 12.

The family plays an absolutely crucial role in academic performance. Ideally, the parents should provide a home environment that ensures that children do their homework. Most antisocial boys report that they do not have any homework, and their parents often accept the "no homework" story because it is more convenient for them, too. In reality, however, by the time children reach the fourth or fifth grade they are expected to do some homework. Interview data from the combined cohorts showed that 34% of the at-risk boys in grade 4 had homework at least one or two nights per week; only 26% reported having no homework at all. Knorr (1981) showed that the correlation between academic achievement and homework assignments becomes increasingly significant as children move from the elementary grades to the secondary grades. In a longitudinal study, Rutter,

Maugham, Mortimore, Ouston, and Smith (1979) found a correlation of .61 between the amount of homework assigned and the children's achievement-test scores. Foyle (1984) found significant improvements in achievement-test scores for high school youths randomly assigned to homework conditions that involved spending more time doing homework.

A mediational hypothesis. We tested the hypothesis that the effect of antisocial behavior on achievement is mediated by a construct we have labeled Academic Engagement. The construct was designed to sample time spent on task in both the classroom and at home. One indicator was based on the item analysis from the teachers' CBC, which described the child's classroom behaviors (e.g., fidgets, disturbs other pupils). The other indicator, based on separate interviews with the child and the parent(s), rated whether homework was completed or not completed. In wave 1 of data collection, the indicator consisted of items that described the *frequency* of homework, but this measure was not effective. SEM was used to examine the set of relationships associated with the mediational hypothesis.

It was our clinical impression that training parents to track whether homework assignments had been completed led to improvements in academic achievement. We also assumed that reducing the rates of antisocial behavior in the home would increase compliance rates and thus indirectly contribute to more time on task.

SEM for the mediational hypothesis was carried out separately for each cohort in a replication design. The data base was collected at grades 4 and 5. We included data for grade 5 because we had not designed the set of indicators for the measure of time on task when the data were collected for grade 4. The data in Table 8.2 summarize the correlations among the indicators that define the four constructs for the model. To conserve space, only the data from Cohort I have been included. The convergence for each of the four constructs was very good; the median convergent correlations ranged from .320 to .688. We generally use a minimum median of .20.

Presumably, the replication of a finding provides the strongest evidence of the robustness of a model. The findings presented in Figure 8.6 provide strong support for the mediational model for academic achievement.

The mediational hypothesis requires two significant outcomes. First, there must be a significant path coefficient from the Child Antisocial construct assessed at grade 4 to the Academic Engagement construct measured at grade 5. The path coefficients for both cohorts were significant and roughly equal in magnitude (-.54 for Cohort I and -.49 for Cohort II). Boys who were antisocial at grade 4 spent less time on task at grade 5. Second, there must be a significant path from Academic Engagement to Academic Achievement. Again, both path coefficients were significant and roughly equal in magnitude (.64 for

Table 8.2

Convergent and Discriminant Correlations for Mediated Achievement Model (Cohort I)

	Child Antisocial				Good Discipline				Academic Engagement			Academic Achievement	
	Child Ph. Int.	Parent Report	Peer Report	Obser-vation	Nat-tering	Abuse Cluster	Mother Interv.	Obs. Impres.	Teach-er Rep.	Child Interv.	Parent Interv.	Parent Report	School Tests
Child Phone Int	1.00												
Parent Report	-.332	1.00											
Peer Report	-.236	.396	1.00										
Observation	-.293	.424	.331	1.00									
Nattering	-.234	.267	.235	.262	1.00								
Abuse Cluster	-.218	.308	.139	.254	.435	1.00							
Mother Interv	.085	-.422	-.165	-.159	-.303	-.303	1.00						
Obs Impression	.173	-.215	-.310	-.278	-.560	-.337	.164	1.00					
Teacher Report	.104	-.390	-.291	-.233	-.132	-.007	.085	.221	1.00				
Child Interv	.212	-.214	-.012	-.206	-.072	-.062	.088	.246	.510	1.00			
Parent Interv	.119	-.367	-.330	-.184	-.009	-.001	.285	.164	.475	.456	1.00		
Parent Report	.129	-.289	-.278	-.199	-.272	-.309	.191	.288	.410	.403	.441	1.00	
School Tests	.146	-.277	-.421	-.166	-.225	-.263	.115	.233	.451	.337	.436	.688	1.00

Cohort I and .52 for Cohort II).

The modification indices emphasized the need for a path that was not included in our *a priori* hypotheses. There seemed to be a direct path from Discipline to Academic Achievement that made a modest, but significant contribution for both cohorts. What makes this particularly interesting is that the direct path was not significant for these same samples at grade 6 (DeBaryshe, 1989). This implies there might be a developmental shift in the direct contribution of parental discipline to the child's academic achievement.

The chi-square tests showed a good fit between the predicted covariance structures and those obtained. The model accounted for 60% of the variance in Academic Achievement for Cohort I and 45% for Cohort II. This compares favorably with the findings from a large-scale survey study by Dornbusch, Ritter, Leiderman, Roberts, and Fraleigh (1987); they reported that parenting variables accounted for 18% of the variance in grades for a sample of adolescents. When the data for the two cohorts were combined, the chi-square value of 74.84 ($p < .08$) showed a good fit between the predicted covariance structures and those obtained. The GFI of .94 and root mean square of .05 provided further evidence that the model was solid.

Several unpublished findings further increased our confidence in the achievement model. An analysis for Cohort I data showed that the path coefficient from Child Antisocial at grade 4 to Academic Engagement at grade 6 was surprisingly high (.65); the path coefficient from Academic Engagement to Academic Achievement was .68. The direct contribution of Discipline was .06 (N.S.), and the overall fit of the model was acceptable ($p < .069$).

Gauvain and Skinner (1987) provided data from a sample of separated mothers with younger boys (ages 6 to 8) and a sample with older boys (ages 9 to 12). The assessment for two of the key constructs (Academic Engagement and Academic Achievement) was less than satisfactory, so the findings should be accepted with caution. Their data showed some support for the developmental-shift hypothesis. For the younger sample, the direct path from Child Antisocial to Academic Achievement was of borderline significance (.33). The chi-square showed an acceptable fit to the model ($p < .12$). The model for boys 9 to 12 years of age did show a significant path (.27) from Academic Engagement to Academic Achievement. The developmental shift hypothesis is *post hoc*, but it does seem plausible and worth pursuing.

Genetic contributions. The consensus seems to be that children who are high achievers tend to come from homes in which intellectual activities are emphasized and the parents are warm and nurturing. It is assumed these circumstances reflect both environmental and genetic factors.

Figure 8.6

A Mediational Model for Academic Achievement

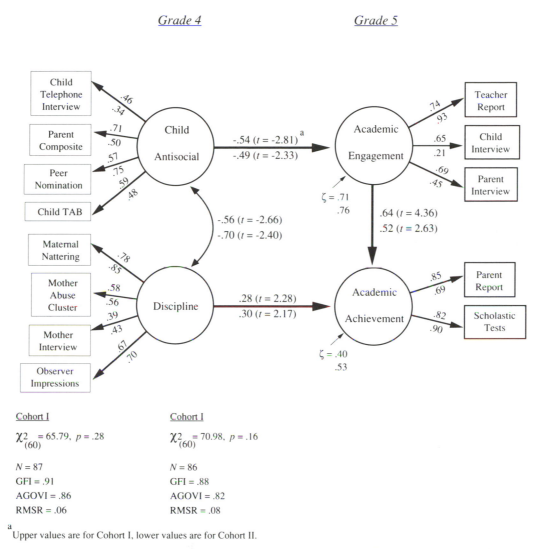

Grade 4   Grade 5

Cohort I

$\chi^2_{(60)} = 65.79$, $p = .28$

$N = 87$
GFI = .91
AGOVI = .86
RMSR = .06

Cohort I

$\chi^2_{(60)} = 70.98$, $p = .16$

$N = 86$
GFI = .88
AGOVI = .82
RMSR = .08

[a] Upper values are for Cohort I, lower values are for Cohort II.

The nurturance hypothesis is supported by the findings from the longitudinal study by Schaefer and Hunter (1983). Low-order positive correlations were found between maternal stimulation, interaction style, and children's verbal skills. Interestingly enough, there were strong negative correlations between these maternal behaviors and maternal irritability. As noted earlier, findings from the OYS are consistent with this position in showing that parents who are involved, reinforcing, and effective at problem solving are also effective disciplinarians. In our analyses, positive parenting constructs tend to correlate with achievement, but when modeled in the context of discipline, they do not make a unique contribution (i.e., the Discipline construct accounts for the variance).

There is also considerable support for the idea that the parents of high achievers emphasize intellectual activities, make books available, and plan for their children to attend college. Hess, Holloway, Price, and Dickson (1982) found that children were better readers if their mothers read to them often. Sigel, McGillicuddy-DeLisi, and Johnson (1980) made a convincing case for the covariation between cognitive development in children and parental beliefs and values regarding the importance of learning. Sigel and his colleagues are in agreement with our position that parents' childrearing practices and belief systems are partially determined by their education and social status. Our model differs from Sigel's in that it considers parental expectations to be the *outcome* rather than the determinant of successful socialization; that is, the child's performance in school gradually leads to parental expectations about the child's advanced education. An unpublished analysis by Moore (personal communication, 1989) showed that parents' expectations about academic achievement did not make a significant contribution to later measures of achievement after current levels of achievement were partialed out.

Scarr (1985b) hypothesized that parents respond differently to their children as a function of the child's genetic makeup. Genetic variation might also relate to the differential reactions of children to parental behaviors. In keeping with this formulation, Scarr (1985a) demonstrated that the best predictors of preschool children's IQs were their mothers' IQs. Bright mothers were more likely to have bright children. However, they also were more likely to create home environments that supported learning.

Our own position is that the parents' family management practices mediate the contribution of genetics and social advantage to child achievement. The children of bright, well-educated parents are at risk for poor achievement if their parents do not use effective discipline and fail to track their homework and school adjustment. DeBaryshe's (1989) SEM for the data collected at grade 6 showed that parental achievement (based on WAIS IQ and education) contributed both directly (.38, $p < .01$) and indirectly to child achievement. The indirect effect was mediated by the relation of parental achievement level to discipline effectiveness. This path was a partial replication of the .33 correlation reported by Scarr (1985a) between maternal IQ and self-reports of discipline practices. Intelligent, well-educated parents are more likely to use effective discipline practices, which is related to children spending more time on task.

Cause or effect? Academic failure is a salient covariate of antisocial behavior. It is not surprising to find that there have been many attempts to reduce delinquency by teaching reading and other academic skills. The implication is that antisocial behavior can be cured by improving the child's academic performance.

Large-scale programmatic studies on the effect of remedial programs on delinquents in institutions and community-based treatment centers have failed to demonstrate a significant effect (Cohen, 1973; Cohen & Filipczak, 1971; Cohen, Filipczak, Slavin, & Boren, 1971). Most of the programs have demonstrated significant increases in academic skills, but these increases *were not* accompanied by reductions in antisocial behavior. Wilson and Herrnstein (1985) provided a more detailed review of these studies. In spite of the consistently negative findings, the policy issues for the National Institute for Juvenile Justice and Delinquency Prevention continue to focus on learning problems as causal variables for delinquency (Dunivant, 1982).

Our position is that teaching academic and social skills

is a useful adjunct to parent training, but these skills are neither necessary nor sufficient for reducing antisocial behavior. On the other hand, reducing antisocial behavior is probably a necessary (but not *sufficient*) condition for the child's long-term adjustment. The assumption is that a minimum degree of social, academic, and work-oriented skills are required to be successful in our culture. The evidence is lacking, but we suspect that youths might still be at risk for marginal adjustment as adults after their antisocial behavior has subsided.

Peer Rejection

This section explores the bidirectional relation between antisocial behavior and rejection by normal peers. It is our impression that the rejection occurs soon after the antisocial boy is introduced to the peer group. Over a period of years, this rejection solidifies his antisocial status.

Observational studies of preschool children have consistently shown a relation between antisocial behavior and rejection by normal peer groups (Hartup, 1982; Roff, 1961, 1972). The consistency of the findings led investigators to search for an explanation. Is the lack of social skills a critical factor or is the risk of rejection the result of the antisocial child's abrasive and negative style of interaction? The studies related to these questions are briefly reviewed in this section.

Determinants for rejection. In methodical studies of preschool children's social interactions, Gottman (1977) differentiated socially isolated children from rejected children. The findings showed that rejected children were more likely to be aversive in their interactions with peers. Asher (1983) showed that rejected children, rather than isolated children, were most at risk for later adjustment problems.

The next question addressed the contribution of inept entry behaviors to the peer-rejection process. The observation studies by Putallaz and Gottman (1981) showed that unpopular children tend to exert negative control and call attention to themselves when entering a peer group. On the other hand, popular children tend to be quite skilled at entering a group. They use strategies to maximize acceptance by unfamiliar peers; for example, they quickly identify the theme of the group's activity and enter in a nonegocentric way. Similar findings were obtained in observation studies of children's behavior at recess for a subgroup of the OYS sample. The data for grade 5 showed that 70% of the antisocial boys and only 6% of the normal boys were observed initiating an aggressive interchange with peers (Shinn et al., 1987).

A common interpretation of these studies is that aggressive children want to have the same social experiences as well-liked children, but they lack the necessary skills. However, Asarnow and Callan (1985) have suggested that the use of aggressive strategies may involve more than just skill deficits. They examined the social problem-solving skills of rejected and popular children in grades 4 and 6. Using interviews and role-playing activities, they assessed the children's skill in dealing with aggressive and prosocial interactions with peers. It was found that rejected children were more aggressive, less appropriately assertive, and less likely to generate alternative solutions than were popular children. The skill-deficit hypothesis suggests that if aggressive children were given the right skills, they would be eager to use them to obtain reinforcement from peers, but the data did not support that assumption. Instead, when asked to evaluate prosocial and aggressive strategies for solving social dilemmas involving peers, rejected children gave prosocial solutions *negative* evaluations. When these children were asked to role-play a prosocial solution, they made more negative self-statements. Are cognitions the determinants for the antisocial reactions or are they merely attendant phenomena that accompany the acts? Clinically, it appears that antisocial boys fail to use the social skills they do have. Time after time, their immediate reactions are coercive. This happens often enough that the negative events overshadow the much larger class of episodes in which their reactions are appropriate (or at least neutral).

The data collected for the at-risk sample at grade 4 were used to test the hypothesis that measures of child deviance and social skills both make a unique contribution to a composite measure of peer relations. Three indicators provided by teachers, peers, and parents defined the Peer Relations construct. The peer and teacher indicators loaded most heavily on this construct; they also made significant contributions to the same latent construct in the Planning Study (Patterson, Dishion, & Bank, 1984). The correlation between child antisocial behavior and social competence was high (-.65). Confirmatory factor analyses showed that social competence and antisocial behavior represented different poles of the same underlying dimension. The Peer Rejection composite score was regressed against the composite scores measuring Child Antisocial and Social Skills. The data for the combined cohorts at grade 4 showed that both variables made significant contributions. Adding the Discipline and Parental Involvement composites did not account for additional variance. Apparently, the child who is both unskilled and antisocial is at greatest risk for rejection by peers.

Cause or effect? Does rejection by peers cause aggression or is it the result of being aggressive? Dodge (1980) found that aggressive children tend to mistakenly attribute hostile intentions to the peer group members who reject them. He assumed that this attributional bias increased the likelihood that the child would respond aggressively when he or she was provoked by peers. Later studies indicated that aggressive behavior led to rejection, but that

rejection did not lead to aggression. Coie and Kupersmidt (1983) showed that when new groups were formed, the coercive behaviors of some children led to their rejection. The pattern was apparent after only two or three sessions. Dodge (1983) replicated these findings.

The omission of crucial socialization experiences that build the foundation for intimate relationships represents a major risk factor for children who remain in the coercion process for extended periods of time. Patterson and Bank (1989) provided a test for the causal lagged hypothesis. They used SEM for data from Cohort I collected at grades 4 and 6 and found that the antisocial boys who also were rejected by normal peers were at serious risk for antisocial behavior at grade 6. The path coefficient from the earlier measure of Peer Rejection to the later measure of Child Antisocial was .46 after the earlier measure of antisocial behavior was partialed out.

The findings are generally consistent with the bidirectional effects hypothesis. The effect of antisocial behavior on the normal peer group seems relatively immediate, but the effect of rejection on later aggressiveness seems lagged over a long period of time.

Stage 3: Later Effects of Being Antisocial

As noted in earlier chapters, the longer the child remains in the coercion process, the more likely he is to engage in extreme forms of antisocial behavior (e.g., physical assault, theft, fire setting). Spending more time in the process also implies a higher overall frequency of antisocial acts. If the process continues into early adolescence, the youth encounters a powerful support system — the deviant peer group. But the ongoing academic difficulties and rejection by peers are accompanied by recurring episodes of dysphoric mood. This section reviews the stage 3 outcomes that represent further shifts in the child's behavior: involvement in a deviant peer group, depressed mood, and the development of an antisocial attitude. If our impressions about the stage sequences are correct, then the primary determinants for the outcomes at stage 3 can be found in the outcomes at stage 2.

Deviant Peers

From a social interactional perspective, social exchanges among peers represent a powerful socialization mechanism. We hypothesize that if the peer group is deviant, the training includes direct, substantial contributions to antisocial and delinquent behavior. The vehicle for the training is similar to that provided by family members. The studies relating to this hypothesis are reviewed in the section that follows.

Burgess and Akers (1966) reformulated Sutherland's (1947) theory of differential association to make it more compatible with reinforcement theory. Sutherland's position was that criminal behavior is learned by association with members of one's intimate group. Members of the deviant peer group were thought to provide training in specific techniques, foster the acquisition of values and attitudinal systems that promote criminal behavior, and offer reinforcers for performing deviant acts. From this perspective, the deviant behavior was the outcome of a set of expectations about the relative likelihoods of reward and punishment outcomes for prosocial and deviant behaviors. The emphasis on expectations or anticipation of contingencies is analogous to the positions taken by Bandura (1981, 1985) and Wilson and Herrnstein (1985) that cognitions about contingencies are mediating mechanisms. This is in contrast to the social interactional position, which assumes that the contingencies actually *experienced* by the youth are what determine the outcome. In their synthesis of the strain, control, and cognitive social learning theories, Elliott, Huizinga, and Ageton (1982) have taken a very strong position on the role of the peer group in training for deviancy:

> For the most part, neither the family nor the school is seen as a deviant training context…. With few exceptions, both are quite conventional in their normative orientations and types of behavior modeled and reinforced…. The primary deviant learning context is the adolescent peer group. (pp. 34–35)

Elliott and Huizinga (1985) used a path analysis of their longitudinal data set to show that only current involvement with deviant peers contributed significantly (the path coefficient ranged from .2 to .3) to current levels of self-reported delinquency. The other major contributor to current levels of antisocial behavior was the level of self-reported delinquency for the previous year (the path coefficient was .5).

The coercion model differs from the model developed by Elliott et al. (1982) in several important respects. First, we assumed that the determinants for early starter delinquents are found primarily in the home and secondarily in interactions with members of the peer group. With the onset of adolescence, this pattern changes considerably; the contribution of the deviant peer group becomes more direct and significant, and the contribution of family variables becomes more indirect and less significant. Second, the coercion formulation describes in detail the way in which family members may inadvertently but *directly* reinforce the child for antisocial behavior. Third, membership in a deviant peer group is thought to be preceded by a breakdown in parental family management skills. It seems likely that Elliott and his colleagues would agree with the general hypothesis, but they might express it differently (e.g., involvement with deviant peers is the result of inadequate bonding with the parents).

Only a few observational studies have directly tested the assumption that deviant peers reinforce deviant behaviors. Buehler, Patterson, and Furniss (1966) col-

lected observational data in a correctional setting. The findings showed that deviant peers were much more likely to reinforce delinquent responses than to punish them. On the other hand, they were more likely to punish behavior that conformed with social norms. The findings suggest that some correctional institutions may actually function as training centers for deviant behavior. Sanson-Fisher and Jenkins (1978) also conducted an observational study in a correctional setting. They found that the peer group provides rich schedules of positive reinforcement for deviant behavior in that setting.

Collecting data to test this hypothesis in noninstitutional settings has been difficult. Dishion, Andrews, and Patterson (1990) designed a procedure appropriate for 13- to 14-year old boys in the OYS. Each boy was asked to bring a friend to the laboratory for a videotaped discussion. The findings showed that antisocial boys were more likely to select antisocial peers, and these antisocial dyads were significantly more likely to engage in antisocial talk. In addition, the observed rates of antisocial talk were significantly related to both self-reported and official records of delinquency. The findings are consistent with the hypothesis that deviant peers may play an important role in promoting antisocial behavior.

Many studies have shown strong covariations among variables such as association with deviant peers, antisocial behavior, antisocial attitudes, and substance use during adolescence. Using questionnaire data from a very large sample of adolescents, Huba and Bentler (1983) found a longitudinal relation between earlier involvement with peers, peer pressure to use substances, and later substance use. Similarly, Jessor (1976) and Jessor and Jessor (1975) used questionnaires completed by adolescents in high school settings to show a predictive relation between friends' approval of substance use and later initiation into marijuana and alcohol use. West and Farrington (1973, 1977), showed that involvement with a deviant peer group during adolescence is highly related to court recidivism and adult criminality.

In keeping with the social interactional position, several studies have demonstrated that family and peer group variables make a unique contribution to adolescent substance abuse. Kandel (1973) compared the influence of parents and peers on marijuana use by independently interviewing adolescents, their parents, and their best friends. These data revealed that peers exert a more powerful influence on concomitant marijuana use during adolescence. Using the Planning Study sample of adolescents, Dishion and Loeber (1985) examined the contribution of parental monitoring practices and association with deviant peers. They found that deviant peers and poor monitoring were both significant determinants for adolescent marijuana use. Associating with deviant peers made the only significant contribution to the regression equation for alcohol use. Parental alcohol use did not contribute to the regression equation for alcohol or marijuana use when both deviant peers and poor parental monitoring were included. It appears that involvement with deviant peers is partially determined by parental monitoring practices.

Patterson and Dishion (1985) used the data for boys in grades 7 and 10 from the Planning Study sample to examine the relation of family variables and the child's social skills to involvement with deviant peers. The findings showed that the unskilled and hostile child is most at risk for involvement with deviant peers; the path coefficient was .74. Snyder, Dishion, and Patterson (1986) reviewed the Planning Study data from a somewhat broader perspective. This time, the data were analyzed to identify developmental shifts in the relations among composite scores for attitudes, social skills, and family variables as they related to involvement with deviant peers at grades 4, 7, and 10. It was assumed that the primary determinants would be the child's antisocial behavior, lack of social skills, and inadequate parental monitoring. Snyder and his colleagues found that all three variables covaried significantly with the Deviant Peers construct scores for all three grades. A multiple-regression analysis suggested that there may be some interesting developmental shifts in the relative contribution of these variables to involvement with deviant peers. For the younger samples (grades 4 and 7), the variance in the Deviant Peers construct was primarily accounted for by the Hostile–Unskilled and Antisocial Attitudes constructs. In the older sample (grade 10), however, Parental Monitoring accounted for most of the variance. In a risk-type analysis, 50% of the children who were hostile–unskilled, involved with deviant peers, had poor academic skills, and whose parents had poor monitoring skills had at least one police contact.

Thus far, the antisocial behavior and lack of social skills variables have been combined to form a single construct. We used data from the combined cohorts at grade 4 to test our hypothesis that separate measures of deviant behavior and social skills would each make a unique contribution to involvement with deviant peers. The measure of social skills included indicators based on reports from teachers, peers, parents, and observers. The standard partial betas were .18 for antisocial, -.18 for social skills, and -.25 for monitoring. The multiple correlation coefficient of .56 was significant ($F = 18.3$, $p < .001$). The findings provided strong support for the hypothesis.

Dishion, Patterson, and Skinner (1989) used data from the combined OYS cohorts to model the relation between the Peer Rejection, Parental Monitoring, and Deviant Peers constructs at grades 4 and 6. At grade 4, the two determinants accounted for 96% of the variance in the composite score for the Deviant Peers construct. As

Gollob and Reichardt (1987) pointed out, such a cross-sectional analysis probably overestimates the variance accounted for. The analysis is based on the assumption that the autoregressive effect (correlation with scores at Time 1) is zero, which is unlikely. When the stability data were taken into account at grade 6, the path coefficients were -.37 for Parental Monitoring, -.27 for Peer Rejection, and a residual .42 for stability.

The data now available strongly support the idea that some combination of the child antisocial trait, measures of social skills, and parental monitoring account for substantial variance in measures of involvement with deviant peers. It is unclear whether involvement with deviant peers and rejection by normal peers occur simultaneously. Correlational analyses (not reported here) showed that the Deviant Peer construct correlated at least as well with stage 1 variables as it did with stage 2 variables. This leads us to believe that it might be best to collapse stages 2 and 3 into a single stage (i.e., both stages describe effects of being antisocial that emerge at about the same time).

Depressed Mood

We hypothesize that antisocial children are at risk for recurring bouts of depression in response to rejection by normal peers and academic failure. This implies that the cascade of effects that accompany antisocial behavior are an important path to sadness or depressed mood for children. It seems obvious that there are multiple paths to depressive disorders in children. Garber (1984) considered two types of childhood depression. The self-esteem type was associated with feeling disliked and having low social competency. Our formulation, which is discussed in a section that follows, is most similar to this. Garber's second alternative was the *guilt type*, which was characterized by an unspecified feeling of "being bad." A possible third path would be grieving for a lost loved one.

Only a small percentage of young children display all of the symptoms associated with clinical depression; the most common symptom is sadness. We decided to study sadness because we felt that it would occur at a reasonably high rate in the OYS samples.

Literature review. Research on childhood depression has gained considerable momentum during the last decade. Publications such as *Depression in Young People* (Rutter, Izard, & Read, 1986) demonstrate that the research has moved beyond the sphere of clinical case studies. The new generation of studies are more sophisticated in their approach to measurement and design problems, as reflected in the programmatic work of Lewinsohn (e.g., Lewinsohn, Clarke, Hops, & Andrews, 1990; Clarke, Lewinsohn, & Hops, 1990), Forehand (e.g., Forehand, McComb, & Brody, 1987), and Kazdin (e.g., Kazdin & Petti, 1982).

Estimates of the number of depressed children vary

according to how depression is defined. In a review of the literature on child psychopathology, Rutter (1983) estimated that between 2% and 40% of the adolescent community samples meet the DSM-III diagnostic criteria for depression. In recent years, several large-scale epidemiological studies have shown that clinical depression among teenagers is a significant problem, affecting up to 3% of the general high school population at any one point in time (Kashani, Holcomb, & Orvaschel 1986; Lewinsohn, Hops, Roberts, & Seeley, 1988). By age 18, up to 20% of all teenagers have had at least one episode of clinical depression (Lewinsohn et al., 1988). These rates make depression *the most frequently reported mental health problem for this age group*.

Clinical observers have commented on the relation between conduct disorders and children's depressed mood. For example, Puig-Antich (1982) cited a clinical study of adolescent suicide that identified antisocial behavior as a strong component for 75% of the sample. In Puig-Antich's study of 43 children with major depression, 37% were described as also having a conduct disorder. The overlap led some earlier writers to describe the mix of conduct disorder and depression as "masked depression," based on the implicit assumption that depression causes the child to act out. Our position is that antisocial behavior leads to social failure, which produces a depressed mood. Angst and Clayton (1986) found evidence to support this assumption in their longitudinal study. They evaluated several thousand young army recruits and found significantly higher incidences of depression and suicide for those who reported themselves to be aggressive. This study does not rule out the possibility that a more detailed assessment would have shown that depression preceded the reported aggressiveness.

Regardless of speculations about cause and effect, there is substantial evidence that the two sets of symptoms covary significantly. Kandel (1982) reported a correlation of .18 between self-reports of depressed mood and delinquency. In a follow-up study, adolescents who reported being depressed also reported more depression at age 24 to 25, and they were at greater risk for theft and crime convictions (excluding traffic violations). Sas and Jaffe (1986) cited two studies that showed a covariation between delinquency and depressive symptoms; they also presented data from referrals to an outpatient clinic that showed a similar covariation. Interestingly, the adolescents who were extremely delinquent tended to be depressed at follow-up.

The general consensus is that child adjustment problems covary with parental diagnoses for depression. In the study by Billings and Moos (1983), the likelihood of child adjustment problems given one depressed parent was .26. If the depressed parent also was highly stressed, the likelihood of child problems was .38. Patterson (1980) cited several studies in which mothers of antisocial boys referred to clinical settings had significantly higher levels of self-reported depression than did mothers of normal boys. Socially aggressive boys whose mothers had received training in effective parenting practices showed reductions in observed rates of antisocial behavior; this was accompanied by a significant reduction in maternal depression. Holmes and Robins (1986) collected *retrospective* data from samples of adults who were depressed, alcoholic, and nondisturbed controls. They found that 57% of the patients in the clinical group reported that their parents had major psychiatric problems such as depression, schizophrenia, alcoholism, and drug abuse. In their review of the empirical findings from 34 studies, Forehand et al. (1987) found a negative correlation between parental depressive states and measures of child functioning in 55% of the studies.

We have reason to believe that the magnitude of the direct relation between parental depression and child pathology may be exaggerated. A significant proportion of the variance in maternal ratings of child behavior apparently is determined by the mother's general level of distress. As pointed out by Dawes (1985) and others, global ratings of this kind reflect a positive or negative "tilt" that reflects how individuals feel about themselves at any given time. We suspect that parents' ratings of child behavior covary more with their current levels of distress, as measured by self-reported depression or marital conflict, than with observed child behaviors.

It is conceivable that the problem lies in the observation data and not in parental tilt, but this does not appear to be the case. Griest, Wells, and Forehand (1979) found that mothers' reports of child deviance covaried with the mothers' self-reported depression but *not* with observed rates of specific child behaviors. This was followed by a more systematic test by Brody and Forehand (1986) that showed that observed levels of child deviance *and* maternal depression contributed to maternal ratings of child deviance. These findings are in keeping with those reported by Patterson & Capaldi (1991a) and with Dawes's (1985) tilt hypothesis.

Kazdin and his colleagues have carried out systematic studies of the problems associated with measuring children's depression (Kazdin, 1981, 1987; Kazdin, Esveldt-Dawson, Sherick, & Colbus, 1985). As Kazdin and Petti (1982) pointed out, some contemporary child self-report instruments provide adequate test–retest stabilities (in the .70 range) for time intervals as brief as a week or a month, but the self-report data have consistently failed to demonstrate discriminant validity. Using an adolescent sample, Fauber, Forehand, Long, Burke, and Faust (1987) found significant correlations between self-reported depression and both parent and teacher ratings of the adolescent's social competence, but the correlation between self-reported depression and observed problem-solving competency was not significant.

Figure 8.7

A Dual Failure Model for Child Depressed Mood

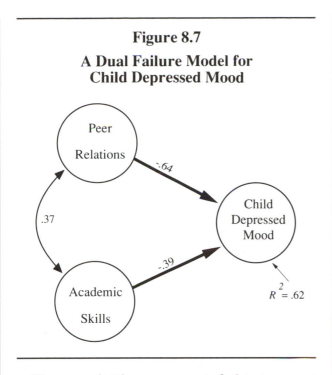

We assume that the measurement of a latent construct for child, adolescent, or adult depression must include more than just self-report measures (e.g., ratings of mood by friends and other family members, judgments about emotion based on facial expression and vocal intonation). It seems doubtful that a measure of depression defined by self-report could survive a multitrait, multimethod analysis (see Forgatch, Patterson, & Skinner, 1988).

Obtaining satisfactory convergence for measures of depression in younger children is difficult. The study of normal preadolescent children by Reynolds, Anderson, and Bartel (1985) showed good convergence among reports from parents and teachers but low correlations with child self-report. Patterson and Capaldi (1991a) used the data for the grade 4 at-risk sample to analyze five indicators for Child Depressed Mood that included ratings from the mother, father, teacher, observer, and child. All of the indicators were primarily designed to assess sadness or dysphoric mood. The latent construct for depressed mood did not load significantly on the child self-report for either cohort.

A model for children's depressed mood. We have developed what might be called a social failure model to explain children's depressed mood. As shown in Figure 8.7, the chief components are failures in peer relations and academic skills. Many studies provide empirical support for the contribution of these two components to child depressed mood. Reynolds and Coats (1982) asked several hundred adolescents what they thought produced their mood swings; 41% of those with depressed moods reported family problems as the primary cause, 19% reported academic difficulties, and 19% reported

problems with friends. Weinberg and Rehmet (1983) found that the majority of children admitted to a school for learning problems had a depressive disorder. Kellam (1990) also found a covariation between depression and academic achievement. Children (especially boys) who had learning problems in grade 1 were more likely to self-report depression as adolescents.

Results. Patterson and Capaldi (1991b) tested several models for child depressed mood using a replication design for the OYS assessments at grade 4. They found good support for the contribution of peer rejection to sadness for both cohorts. Academic failure also contributed to depressed mood, but it was unclear whether the relation was direct or indirect (i.e., mediated through disrupted peer relations). The Self-Esteem construct was tested in the model, but a weak contribution that was found for Cohort I was not replicated for Cohort II. A Venn diagram analysis of the relation between self-esteem and depressed mood showed that *almost all* (83%) of the depressed children had low self-esteem. However, most children with low self-esteem were not perceived as being sad (25%). Based on these results, we decided not to include the Self-Esteem construct in the model for this age group.

Patterson and Stoolmiller (1990) tested the generalizability of the dual failure model. They examined the data for Cohorts I and II at grade 4 and the data for a sample of boys 9 to 12 years old from recently separated families. A mismatching strategy was used to form the model (Bank, Dishion, Skinner, & Patterson, 1990). The result was that none of the indicators were matched for constructs believed to be causally related. The analyses demonstrated invariance for the factor structures for both cohorts. The findings also demonstrated significant across-sample invariances for the estimates of the path between peer rejection and depressed mood and for the covariation between peer rejection and academic failure. The path coefficient of .64 is our best estimate of the contribution of peer rejection to sadness. The path from academic skills to sadness was *not* invariant across samples; our rough estimate for the path coefficient is .39.

One obvious alternative to the dual failure model is to simply use measures of parental depression to predict child depressed mood. Patterson and Capaldi (1991b) found correlations between these constructs of .35 for Cohort I and .08 for Cohort II. However, the dual failure model still seems to be the most promising. The findings from three samples suggest that the general model accounts for approximately 60% of the variance in adults' ratings of child sadness. We are interested in finding out how early the child's depressed mood begins in the antisocial process. Are antisocial preschool boys sad? From a clinical standpoint, it seems that antisocial behavior and depression must occur together; the problem in modeling this effect is to find measures of sadness that can be used with preschool children.

Antisocial Attitudes

Antisocial attitudes are an important concomitant of antisocial behavior. The primary prerequisites for the development of antisocial attitudes are antisocial behavior and, later on, involvement with a deviant peer group.

Most criminological models for delinquent behavior attribute central *causal* status to attitudes and beliefs about conformity. Hirschi, the major proponent of this view, holds that disruptions in the attachment of the child to his or her parents lead to a failure to internalize conventional beliefs about work, school, and the validity of societal norms (Hirschi, 1969; Hirschi & Hindelang, 1977). The most recent evaluation of these variables was carried out by Elliott et al. (1985) for a national probability sample. Consistent with the model, they found low correlations between self-reported delinquency and antisocial attitudes and values.

Our assumption is that attitudes and beliefs *accompany* delinquent behavior but do not function as determinants for it. Research has failed to demonstrate a causal connection between attitudes and behavior. After reviewing the empirical studies of the 1960s, social psychologists began to comment on the lack of connection between attitudes and behaviors. Festinger (1964) noted that although it is possible to produce significant changes in *attitudes*, these manipulations are not related to changes in *behaviors*. Bem (1967) later concluded that attitudes are, in fact, derived from behavior. Calder and Ross (1973) concluded that behavior is a useful predictor of future attitudes and beliefs, but that attitudes and beliefs do not predict behavior.

We assume that the child's antisocial behavior and ongoing failures will correlate significantly with self-reported deviance and antisocial attitudes toward authority (e.g., school, teachers, police). We tested for this by using the data for the combined cohorts to regress a composite measure of antisocial attitudes against composite measures of child social behavior, child antisocial behavior, and parental discipline. All three variables made significant contributions in accounting for variance. The multiple correlation value of .57 ($F = 32.7$, $p < .001$) strongly supported the hypothesis that attitudes covary with behavior.

The child behaviors that are outcomes of stage 1 correlated with antisocial attitudes at approximately the same magnitude as stage 2 variables. Like the findings for the Deviant Peers construct, this suggests that many of the products of this process can be predicted *directly* from the primary stage 1 product, antisocial behavior. Again, it appears that stages 2 and 3 should be collapsed into a single stage.

Antisocial Behavior and Delinquency

Early Starters

Throughout this book, we have repeatedly stated that the coercion model describes the developmental history that characterizes chronic delinquents and antisocial adults. The implication is that juvenile forms of antisocial behavior are related to later delinquency.

The published findings suggest that boys who start their antisocial careers during early adolescence may be at the greatest risk for becoming chronic offenders (Farrington, 1983; Glueck & Glueck, 1959; Loeber, 1982; Wadsworth, 1979). Comparison studies of prison populations have shown that, on the average, recidivists were arrested for the first time at the age of 14 or 15. One-time offenders usually were arrested for the first time at a later age (Gendreau, Madden, & Leipciger, 1979; Mandelzys, 1979; Mannheim & Wilkins, 1955). Farrington, Gallagher, Morley, St. Ledger, and West (1988) studied the average number of convictions as a function of age of onset. In a sample of delinquents 16 to 18 years old, the group of early starters (those who began between the ages of 10 and 12) averaged almost twice as many convictions as did the late starters (those who began between the ages of 13 and 15). It also was reported that the early starters continued committing crimes at higher rates as adults. In fact, these findings were the inspiration for our initial formulation about early and late-starter delinquents (Patterson, Capaldi, & Bank, 1990).

The hypothesis is that boys who score high on the Child Antisocial construct at grade 3 or 4 are at the greatest risk for committing police offenses at an early age. These early starters also should be at risk for becoming chronic-offender adolescents. The analyses of official records for the OYS sample showed that, at wave 5 (ages 14 to 15), approximately 23% of the boys already had committed one or more police offenses (Patterson, 1990). In keeping with the early starter hypothesis, 84% of the delinquent boys scored above the mean on the Child Antisocial construct at grade 4. By the age of 14 or 15, approximately 42% of the boys identified as antisocial at grade 4 already had one or more contacts with police. In fact, 25% of the boys with high scores had committed three or more offenses by this age. The findings offer strong support for the hypothesis that antisocial behaviors in younger boys are prototypes for crimes committed later.

Patterson, Capaldi, and Bank (1990) used SEM to examine the relation between the Child Antisocial construct measured at grade 4 and the Delinquency construct measured at grade 8. The path coefficient of .66 was highly significant. The model accounted for 44% of the variance in the measure of delinquency. In that same study, it seemed that the severity of earlier antisocial behavior might make a unique contribution to delinquency. When antisocial behavior was measured at grades 4 and 6, the earlier measure contributed both directly and indirectly to the later measure of delinquency. The total amount of variance accounted for was 60%.

These findings offer strong support for the assumption that identification of at-risk samples at grade 4 may be accurate enough to warrant the implementation of prevention programs. In fact, NIMH recently approved funding for OSLC to study the *prevention* of conduct disorders in children. The coercion model will be tested by simultaneously starting prevention programs in grades 1 and 5.

Late Starters

Our models suggest that one-third to one-half of all delinquent acts are committed by youths who are *not* products of the coercion process (Patterson, DeBaryshe, & Ramsey, 1989). We call this group the late starters. Presumably, the late starters are fundamentally different from early starters in three important respects: (1) They do not begin their delinquent behavior until mid-adolescence; (2) they have at least marginal social skills; and (3) when assessed at grade 4, they would not be classified as antisocial. The stealing, vandalism, truancy, and substance abuse are by-products of associating with a deviant peer group and are not direct outcomes of a coercive interpersonal style of interaction. Because of the late start, these boys are more socialized than early starters and have developed skills for relating to peers and meeting academic requirements. Although some of them may become chronic offenders by late adolescence, we hypothesize that they tend to drop out of the antisocial process and become involved in the world of work and family.

We will have a better understanding of the developmental sequence for late starters after the OYS samples graduate from high school. At that time, we can test the hypothesis that the boys who commit their first offenses after age 15 have tested below the mean on the Child Antisocial construct at grade 4 and have experienced family transitions (divorce, moving, early pubescence) that disrupted parental monitoring. Presumably, the disruption in monitoring will be followed by involvement with deviant peers and increased risk for delinquent behavior and substance abuse. Finally, we expect that a disproportionate number of late starters (as compared to early starters) will drop out of the criminal process altogether between the ages of 18 and 25.

Summary and Implications

In this chapter, we have reviewed the empirical underpinnings for the idea that children's antisocial behaviors produce predictable outcomes. The findings showed that antisocial behaviors covaried with peer rejection, parental rejection, academic failure, low self-esteem, depressed mood, and antisocial attitudes. We have argued that some of these relations might be bidirectional (e.g., the covariation between antisocial acts and rejection by both parents and peers). We have attempted to build a case for the causal status of antisocial acts by reviewing the limited number of studies available. Although it is too early to make any definitive statements, the data seem to be consistent with our position.

The stage model of antisocial behavior outlined in Chapter 1 is a convenient way to organize an extensive array of covariations. The findings reviewed in this chapter indicate that we probably will need to modify the sequence for longitudinal studies that start with preschool samples. The findings are consistent with the idea that the antisocial acts in stage 1 are accompanied almost immediately by parental rejection, low self-esteem, and sadness. Stage 2 is defined by a separate set of outcomes that seem to occur later: peer rejection, academic failure, and antisocial attitudes. Stage 3 is characterized by involvement with deviant peers, substance abuse, and delinquency. The stage model is an outline of the ripple effects produced by antisocial behavior over time.

We are astounded by the stability of the constructs we have developed to describe parenting practices and child behavior. Our analyses have shown that there is a parallel continuity between both the Discipline and the Parental Monitoring constructs and child behavior. It is also apparent that additional factors become involved in the coercion process by early adolescence. In fact, certain secondary effects (e.g., rejection by peers and academic failure) may serve as feedback loops that keep the process going. If this is the case, then the model that is emerging will be more dynamic than we had imagined a decade ago. The shopping hypothesis that we have added to the coercion model is further evidence of our search for dynamic mechanisms. It also is a way to represent the active role played by the child in selecting the settings and people that contribute to the process.

In retrospect, we can see that we should have spent more time studying younger children. We also are convinced that we should have made more provisions for actually observing the interactions of the target child with members of his peer group. We have added two such assessment probes to the OYS; in both cases, the payoffs have been dramatic in terms of generating information and advancing our understanding of antisocial children.

The findings we have presented more than justify the endless months of building and rebuilding the assessment battery to achieve a closer fit to the concepts in the coercion model. A surprising number of the constructs and models have been replicated across different samples. For example, both the basic training model and the dual failure model have been replicated across at least three samples. This is a good beginning. The hypothesis that early forms of antisocial behavior are prototypes of later delinquency also has been confirmed for both cohorts, so we can bring this phase of the OYS to a close. Now we can focus on building a developmental (i.e., process) model for changes in antisocial behavior.

Chapter 9

Closing Remarks

We have now completed the journey that began a decade ago. Our search for a theory of children's aggressive behavior has taken us down many twisting pathways. Some of these paths turned out to be digressions, but others were more productive. Through it all, the data we had at the time were our guide. What has been surprising about this process is how frequently the data forced us to change both our thinking and the theory. It is deeply satisfying to find that the resulting theory outlined in this volume seems to have many practical implications.

Our field studies in homes and classrooms convinced us that the social environment provided payoffs for the child's aggressive behavior. We assumed that problem children were aggressive because it worked for them. Our initial goal was simple: investigate how parents, siblings, and peers reinforce problem children for being aggressive. As we collected the observation data, however, it became apparent that problem children also changed the people with whom they interacted. We are still trying to understand the nature of these complex bidirectional effects. Once the data revealed the nature of the reinforcers for aggressive behavior, a new question emerged: Why do some families provide more of these contingencies than others? In an attempt to answer this question, we have spent 10 years trying to define and measure the five family management skills described in this volume.

Our modest success in applying family management concepts has led to a new set of questions. What is the relation between child adjustment outcomes and contextual factors such as poverty, divorce, and maternal depres-

sion? Are socially disadvantaged parents or depressed mothers less effective in their use of parenting skills? Do disrupted parenting practices explain the low-level but consistent correlations between social disadvantage and antisocial behavior in children? Our excitement grew with each successful application of the mediational model. A series of studies showed that variables such as divorce or stress only contribute to children's antisocial behavior if they disrupt the parents' family management skills. The implication was that contextual variables could be used to define samples of at-risk families, which then could be targeted for prevention programs. Studies of context have suggested that antisocial children are most likely to come from families in which the parents are socially disadvantaged, antisocial, divorced or separated, or experiencing high levels of stress. We suspect that teenage parents also should be included in this group. The coercion model shows that prevention programs should focus on helping these parents improve their family management skills to reduce the risk of future child adjustment problems.

We have found that these same contextual variables also relate to parental resistance to participation in therapy sessions. During treatment, the socially disadvantaged, depressed, or antisocial parent often responds by saying "I won't" or "I can't." This has a profound impact both on the behavior of the therapist and on treatment outcome (Patterson & Chamberlain, 1988; Patterson & Chamberlain, in press). As the therapist tries to change the behavior of the parent, the highly resistant parent changes the behavior of the therapist! These at-risk families seem to

Figure 9.1
Bootstrapping a Theory

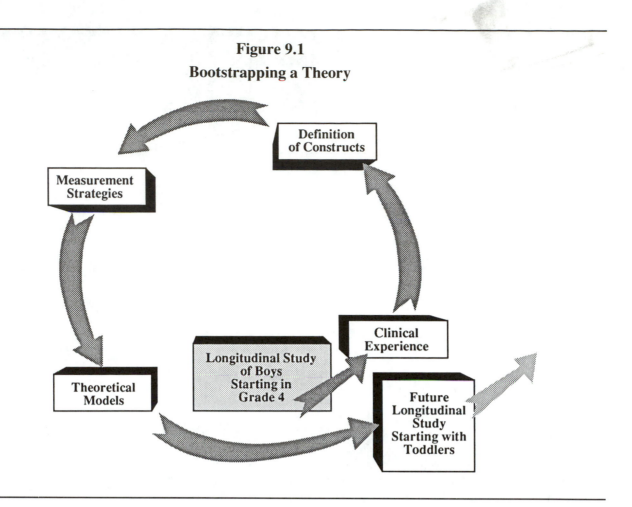

have two strikes against them. They are most likely to have problem children and least likely to benefit from treatment if they receive it.

Our early field studies showed that antisocial boys were socially unskilled. In fact, we used the phrase "arrested socialization" to describe this characteristic lack of skills (Patterson, 1982). At the time, we overlooked the fact that the most consistent skill deficits were peer rejection and academic problems. We did not understand that it was the antisocial child's abrasive style of relating to the social environment that actually produced these problems. Now we see the cascade of effects as an orderly sequence that flows from the child's antisocial behavior (Patterson & Yoerger, 1991). We hypothesize that each addition to the pattern leads to the next problem in the sequence. Although problems such as peer rejection, depression, and academic failure have different features, they are outcomes of the same set of causes.

The antisocial boy is likely to have a wide spectrum of problems by the time he is 9 or 10 years old. Typically, he has been rejected by normal peers for several years, and his poor school performance and low self-esteem have become more profound. The model suggests that the usual parent training intervention is not sufficient by itself for these older boys; the treatment must also include specific academic and social skills training (Patterson, Dishion, & Chamberlain, 1991). The follow-up studies by Forehand and Long (1991) show that even successful treatment of younger oppositional boys does not insulate them from the risk of later academic failure.

The knowledge we have gained from the series of modeling studies we have completed to date can be applied in several ways. It can be used to design longitudinal studies that would begin with toddlers or, better yet, newborns. Improved versions of our measures could be used to find out how the coercion process starts in families. Does infant temperament interact with a lack of parental skill to set the process in motion? Do children's antisocial behaviors move through a progression and become increasingly severe over time? We need to know the answers to these questions. As illustrated in Figure 9.1, we have completed the first cycle of the bootstrapping process. Now we are ready to begin our second round of studies.

Now that we have a solid empirical base for understanding children's antisocial behavior, we are in a position to address the problem of delinquency in a new way. The multiple causation models that have prevailed for the last three or four decades have stressed that all of the variables listed in the causal wheel (see Chapter 1) must be taken into account to understand, treat, or prevent juvenile delinquency. We agree that social disadvantage, neighborhood, involvement with deviant peers, academic failure, peer rejection, antisocial attitudes, and having criminal parents all are significantly related to delinquency. Our theory of children's antisocial behavior organizes each of these variables into an orderly pattern, although only a few of them are thought to be direct determinants of delinquency. A breakdown in family management practices seems to set the process in motion for the early starters. For the late starters, the deviant peer group provides the training for delinquent acts and a lack of parental monitoring serves as an indirect determinant. The context studies show that variables such as social disadvantage are indirect determinants.

Reorganizing the causal variables for delinquency into an understandable sequence of effects is important primarily because of the implications it has for prevention trials. The general consensus is that there is little hope of changing the life course of a young, chronic offender adolescent. The obvious alternative is to design prevention programs for at-risk samples so that these problems can be addressed before the child reaches adolescence. This conclusion is in accord with the position taken by NIMH, which has recently funded several prevention centers across the country. We are proud of the fact that the center for the prevention of conduct disorders has just been established at OSLC, with John B. Reid as director. It should not be surprising that the design for the prevention studies includes major components of the coercion model and assessment procedures developed for the OYS. In five years we should know whether a community-wide prevention program beginning as early as first grade can alleviate these behaviors. R. Tremblay and his colleagues in Montreal have mounted a similar prevention program beginning as early as kindergarten. The Eugene and Montreal designs include random assignment, pre- and post-treatment assessment, and intensive follow-up. Parent training is one of the key components in both interventions. Another prevention center has been established at Johns Hopkins University under the direction of S. Kellam and J. Anthony. This center will focus on developing classroom interventions for children's social and academic skills. These investigators are collecting data on very large samples using a random assignment design and long-term follow-up. Components from the coercion model also have been included in the study. At OSLC, T. Dishion has started a series of prevention trials for preadolescents at risk for substance abuse. M. Forgatch, also at OSLC, has been awarded funds to begin a long-term prevention project that will focus on recently separated young mothers with young sons. The two studies at OSLC were designed to directly test the causal status of the key components of the coercion model. Both studies are using assessment batteries based on those developed for the OYS.

The first three waves of data from the OYS (assessments at grades 4, 6, and 8) have been collected and stored in the computer. Our next task is to study this massive stockpile of data to learn more about the relation between child adjustment outcomes and the changes that take place in families. The new studies will help us understand how antisocial behavior is involved in the process. For example, how is it that the form of antisocial behavior changes over time? Are the determinants for antisocial behavior the same in childhood as they are in midadolescence? Is the process maintained by feedback loops? The first two papers addressing these questions have made significant contributions to our understanding of these important issues (Patterson & Bank, 1989; Patterson, in preparation).

Perhaps it comes as no surprise that this book moves through cycles of macro (big picture) and micro (action–reaction patterns) perspectives as we have tried to integrate the findings from the OYS with our earlier work. It is like climbing to the top of a mountain to get your bearings and then plunging into the valley below to explore the details. Now that we have arrived at the end of this journey, the question we encounter at the top of the mountain is: How do you explain dyadic interactions in families? Our answer, of course, is a logical extension of our current social interactional perspective... *(see next page)*

"It's elephants all the way down!"

Appendix

Appendix 1
Sample Characteristics and
Assessment Procedures

The Community

The first modeling studies were based on data from the Planning Study conducted in 1979–1980 (Patterson & Dishion, 1985; Patterson, Dishion, & Bank, 1984). The sample consisted of normal families with boys in grades 4, 7, and 10. The longitudinal OYS began in 1983 with a cohort of families with boys in grade 7 who were living in high-crime areas; a second cohort entered into the study in the fall of 1984.

Both studies were conducted in Oregon in the adjacent cities of Eugene and Springfield. At that time, the combined population of the Eugene–Springfield metropolitan area was approximately 150,000 (U.S. Department of Commerce, 1983). Eugene was classified in Group II of the census of cities (population of 100,000 to 249,999), and Springfield was in Group IV (population of 25,000 to 49,999). Approximately 30% of U.S. residents live in cities with populations of 25,000 to 250,000.

Employment in the Eugene–Springfield area consists of jobs in the trades (28%), followed by government services and education (25%), manufacturing (primarily lumber-related) (17%), and then construction, utilities, finance, realty, and services (Lane Council of Governments, 1978). The population is predominantly white (95.6%).

Recruitment

Capaldi and Patterson (1987) reviewed previous longitudinal studies and noted that other investigators had some difficultly recruiting families. For example, Elliott, Ageton, Huizinga, Knowles, and Canter (1983) reported only a 73% participation rate when the assessment battery involved interviewing just the target child! Huesmann, Lagerspetz, and Eron (1984) had a 59% participation rate in a study that included limited participation by parents. Because the assessment battery for our studies was expected to take 15 to 20 hours, our first task was to develop a procedure that would persuade families to participate in the study.

The Planning Study

The Eugene-Springfield area has three school districts, two of which agreed to participate in the Planning Study (Stouthamer-Loeber & Loeber, 1982). We began by ex-

plaining the purpose of the study to district administrators and other influential people in the community. Then a research proposal was submitted to each district's formal review committee. Twenty-two of the 28 schools that were contacted agreed to participate.

A slightly different procedure was used to contact families in each of the two school districts. In the first district, the school administration mailed a letter to families that explained and endorsed the study. One week later, the families received a letter from OSLC that described the study and informed them that a staff member would call to find out if they were willing to participate. When they were contacted by telephone a few days later, the families agreed to sign up, refused, or requested more information. Consent forms were immediately mailed out to the families who agreed to be involved in the study, and a staff member visited the homes of the families who wanted more information. We were unable to contact 11% of the families in the first district, because they either did not have a telephone or were not available when the staff member called.

Based on our recruiting experience in the first school district, we made some changes in our procedures before we contacted families in the second district. This time, the school administration did not write a letter to the families. Instead, a letter was sent directly from OSLC indicating that the family would receive a telephone call in a few days to schedule an appointment during which the project would be explained. The home visitors brought consent forms with them rather than mailing them to families who agreed to participate. We were unable to contact approximately 7% of the families. The rate of completion for the total population canvassed in the two districts was 21.3%.

Although our recruitment efforts for the Planning Study were not very successful, the experience proved to be valuable in developing strategies for the OYS. In addition, our relationship with the school districts was well established by the time the OYS began, which made our work easier. For example, the one school district that declined to participate in the Planning Study agreed to be involved in the OYS. We attribute this change to: (1) The regular progress reports that were sent to the reluctant school district over the course of the Planning Study and (2) invitations were extended to its administrators to attend the planning sessions we held with the superintendents of the participating districts.

Table 1

Subject Recruitment for OYS Cohorts I and II

Recruitment Characteristic	Cohort I	Cohort II
On list from school	153	155
Ineligible[a]	20	11
Declined participation[b]	30	40
Signed up and started assessment	103	104
Dropped out during assessment[c]	1	0
Percentage of eligible who completed assessment	76.7%	72.2%

[a] The reasons for ineligibility are provided in Table 2.

[b] This included some families who signed up and changed their minds before starting assessment and families who were unable to participate after signing up because of problems such as severe illness of a parent.

[c] The father in this family was deaf and had not fully understood the requirements of the study when they were explained during the home visit.

The OYS

The first step in the recruitment process for the OYS was to examine the arrest data for the students in each school. Then we divided the number of arrests by the number of families with boys in grade 4 at that school, and the 10 schools with the highest arrest rates were randomly ordered. Our plan was to recruit from that group of schools until we obtained a sample of at least 100 families. It was necessary to recruit from six schools to obtain a sample of 103 families for Cohort I. The process was repeated for Cohort II, and we obtained a sample of 104 families by recruiting from seven schools.

We assumed that the home visitor played a critical role in recruiting families. The home visitor contacted each family immediately after the school principal mailed a letter introducing OSLC and the OYS. The purpose of this telephone contact was to arrange for a home visit during which the project could be explained in detail. The success of our recruiting efforts depended on the skills of the home visitor in carrying out these two social contacts with the family.

Because the function of the home visitors was to "sell" the project to the families, they needed to have many of the characteristics of effective salespeople. OSLC clinical staff members were instrumental in creating a battery of role-playing assessment procedures, which were designed to select outgoing, warm, and self-confident individuals. After the home visitors had been hired, they were trained in skills related to building and maintaining rapport with families. The hiring and training procedures we used seemed to have been effective in establishing excellent relations with the families in the study.

The families were paid for the initial home visit, and the home visitors were paid according to an incentive system that provided a $15 bonus for recruiting a family and another $15 if the family completed the assessment battery; the visitors received an additional $10 bonus for recruiting a family that did not have a telephone.

Several changes were made in the recruitment procedures to increase the likelihood that families would agree to participate in the study (Capaldi & Patterson, 1987). For example, payments to subjects for all phases of participation were considerably increased. In the Planning Study, the stipend was $40 per family. The stipend was increased to $272 for two-parent families in the OYS. The assessment battery was also significantly revised after the Planning Study. A concerted effort was made to develop an assessment battery that was extensive, but which still could be *comfortably* completed in the allotted time. In the earlier study, some of the interviews with the parents and child had taken three to four hours to complete.

As shown in Table 1, the rate of completion was 76.7% for Cohort I and 72.2% for Cohort II. Thirty-one percent of the families were considered to be ineligible. When this number is added back into the denominator, it provides a more conservative estimate that 67% of the sample was actually recruited. This participation rate is comparable to the rate reported in other longitudinal studies that used much less extensive assessment batteries (Elliott et al., 1983; Huesmann et al., 1984).

In research of this kind, it is useful to collect data on the families who did not participate in the study. These data are summarized in Table 2. Thirty-one families were considered to be ineligible for the reasons listed. A majority of the families who refused to participate either said they were too busy or indicated that they were not interested in the research. A few families declined for

Table 2

Reasons for Subject Ineligibility and Subject Refusal in the OYS Cohorts

	Number of Subjects	
	Cohort I	Cohort II
Reason for Ineligibility		
Did not speak English	6	0
Moving out of town/out of state	5	5
Moved before contact	3	4
Parent losing custody	2	0
Moved from study school	2	0
Brother in study	1	0
Mother and son mentally incapable	1	0
In another study at OSLC	0	1
Not currently living with parent	0	1
Reason for Refusing to Participate		
Too busy	8	10
Not interested	11	14
Privacy and/or religious concerns	4	10
Asked school not to release name	3	2
Just separated, busy finding a job	2	1
Felt that taxes should not be spent on research	1	0
Boy was starting new speech program	1	0
Father said son didn't deserve to participate	0	1
Mother's illness	0	2

religious reasons or because they felt the research would be too intrusive. The remaining reasons were idiosyncratic to individual families.

The data-collection design for the first five years of the OYS is shown in Table 3. Our plan is to have yearly contacts with the families, with an alternating pattern of full and partial assessments. A full assessment refers to an intensive evaluation of family functioning, which includes home observations of family interaction, repeated telephone calls, and more intensive interviews regarding the parents' family management practices. Partial assessments focus on the child's behavior at home and school based on short interviews with the child and parent(s) and ratings by teachers. So far, we have completed full assess-

Table 3

Minimum Assessment Probes for the OYS

	Years			
	1983–1984 (9–10 years)[a]	1984–1985 (9–10 years)	1985–1986 (11–12 years)	1986–1987 (11–12 years)
Cohort I	Full[b]	Partial	Full	Partial
Cohort II	None	Full	Partial	Full

[a] Indicates age of boys in sample.

[b] *Full assessment* included interviews with parent(s) and child, home observations, teacher ratings, telephone interviews, and questionnaires. *Partial assessment* included short inteviews with parent(s) and child, and questionnaires.

Table 4

Demographic Characteristics of Planning Study and OYS Samples

	Planning Study Sample (%)	Cohort I (%)	Cohort II (%)	Comparative Statistics (%)
Family Socioeconomic Status				**National Youth Survey**[a]
Lower (Categories 1 and 2)	30	34	28	42
Working (Category 3)	26	23	26	29
Middle (Categories 4 and 5)	42	22	26	23
Unemployed	3	22	20	—
Family Income				**Western U.S.**[b]
0,000 – 4,999	2	11	16	12
5,000 – 9,999	11	21	20	15
10,000 – 14,999	11	16	17	15
15,000 – 19,999	15	14	14	14
20,000 – 24,999	22	17	14	13
25,000 – 29,999	11	8	10	—
30,000 – 39,999	17	13	6	—
40,000+	11	3	3	—
25,000+	39	24	19	32
Family Structure				
Stepparent	—	25	20	—
Single Parent	28	31	40	—
1–2 Children	76 (84)[c]	52	58	—
3–4 Children	21 (16)	37	32	—
5–6 Children	3 (0)	12	11	—
Mean age of mother (years)	39 (37)	34	36	—
Mean age of father (years)	41 (38)	36	37	—
Child Achievement				
WRAT Reading	109.4[d] (112.2)	106	108.7	—
Standard Deviation	14.6 (10.7)	13.8	17.0	—

Note: All figures except those for "Child Achievement" are rounded to the nearest whole number.

[a]From *Explaining Delinquency and Drug Use* by D. S. Elliott, D. Huizinga, and S. S. Ageton, 1985, Beverly Hills, CA: Sage.

[b]From *1980 Census of Population: Vol. 1. Characteristics of the Population, Chapter C. General Social Economic Characteristics, Part 1: United States Summary* (Report No. PC80-1-C1) by the United States Department of Commerce, Bureau of the Census, 1983, Washington, DC: United States Government Printing Office.

[c]Figures in parentheses are for the subsample of fourth-grade boys in the Planning Study.

[d]Mean standard score.

ments for both cohorts at grades 4, 6, and 8. The empirical analyses in this volume are based primarily on the full assessments completed at grade 4 for both cohorts and secondarily on some of the data collected in the Planning Study.

Demographic Characteristics of Samples

Table 4 summarizes the demographic characteristics of the samples from the Planning Study and both OYS

Table 5

**Mean *T* Scores on Teacher CBC Items and Scales for OYS Participants and Refusers
(from Capaldi and Patterson, 1987)**

	Cohort I		Cohort II	
	Study (*N* = 103)	Nonstudy (*N* = 31)	Study (*N* = 104)	Nonstudy (*N* = 36)
Items				
School performance	43.8	48.4	46.7	47.0
Working hard	46.9	49.2	47.1	49.4
How much learning	47.0	49.0	47.9	48.8
Scales				
Social withdrawal	60.0	59.4	60.1	58.8
Unpopular	58.8	57.7	58.0	57.7
Self-destructive	59.2	58.3	58.4	57.3
Obsessive-compulsive	57.6	56.8	57.2	56.1
Inattentive	59.4	57.4	58.5	57.3
Nervous-overactive	58.3	57.3	57.2	56.4
Aggressive	58.5	57.5	58.4	57.7

cohorts. For comparison purposes, data are also supplied from the more representative National Youth Survey (Elliott, Huizinga, & Ageton, 1985) and from the 1980 United States census (U.S. Department of Commerce, 1983). The description of family socioeconomic status is based on parent occupations using the categories described in Hollingshead (1975).

A comparison of the characteristics of the national probability sample and the OYS cohorts reveals a tendency for the latter to oversample lower income levels and undersample higher income levels. This bias probably results from the recruitment procedures, which produced a substantial influx of unemployed parents. It is also apparent that the Planning Study sample consisted of more middle-class families than did the national probability sample or the OYS cohorts.

Considerable differences were evident in the kinds of family structures represented in our samples. The at-risk samples contained more large families (three to six children) than the Planning Study sample. They also had more single parents; this is of particular interest in studying delinquency because of the consistent, moderately predictive relation between large family size and male adolescent delinquency across longitudinal studies of antisocial children (Loeber & Dishion, 1983). It is also noteworthy that 20% to 25% of the families in the OYS sample included a stepparent, usually a stepfather. In effect, whether they were living with a single parent or a stepparent, more than half of the boys in the sample were from disrupted homes.

The samples also differed in the children's performance on the reading section of the Wide Range Achievement Test (WRAT) (Jastak, Bijou, & Jastak, 1976). As shown in Table 4, the children's reading achievement scores were slightly higher in the Planning Study sample than in the OYS sample, which is within one standard deviation of the average for this test (M = 100, S.D. = 10).

Sample Bias

The review of the literature by Capaldi and Patterson (1987) noted two characteristics of families with aggressive members that are relevant for the design of longitudinal studies. These families are less likely to agree to participate in studies, more likely to drop out, and tend to be more mobile than are nonaggressive families. Capaldi and Patterson tested the hypothesis that the families who refused to participate had target boys who were no more deviant than boys from families who agreed to participate. The teacher version of the Child Behavior Checklist (CBC) (Achenbach & Edelbrock, 1979) was collected anonymously for most of the boys whose families declined to participate in the full study. The mean *T* scores for the boys in the participating and nonparticipating samples are summarized in Table 5. The general trend was for participants to be slightly *more* pathological than their nonparticipating peers on all scales. These data support the conclusion that the selection and recruitment procedures used in the study did not necessarily discourage participation by families with more extreme problems. If anything, the financial inducements (or perhaps other variables) led to the recruitment of a slightly higher proportion of families with aggressive children. It is also worth noting that the OYS samples were roughly one standard deviation above the mean for normal samples on most of the clinical scales. The sample was truly "at risk" at least as perceived by teachers.

Overview of the Assessment Battery

The details of the assessment battery used across assessment waves for the OYS are presented in Dishion, Capaldi, and Patterson (1990). Generally, in both the Planning Study and the OYS, assessments consisted of three phases based on the setting in which the data were collected: at school, during an interview at OSLC, and at home. In the OYS, all three phases occurred within approximately one month of each other and required roughly 23 hours to complete. It would have been possible to evaluate most of the models described in Chapter 8 with much less data. A more extensive data set was required to complete the measurement studies necessary to understand how to operationalize the key theoretical constructs (e.g., antisocial behavior, school failure, depression, peer rejection, self-esteem, and substance abuse).

School Phase

The school phase involved collecting information such as teacher ratings, peer nominations, school records, and achievement-test scores. The only contact we had with the children in the school setting was when peer-nomination data were collected. The nominations required 15 to 20 minutes of class time and were administered by the OSLC research staff at the convenience of the participating teachers. The children included in the administration groups were those whose parents had provided signed consent to the research project.[1] The ideal size of the administration groups was from 9 to 15 children, and the number of nominees selected was adjusted to represent 20% to 30% of the administration group. For a group of 10, for example, children were asked to select three children who best fit the description on each page of the nomination form. Classrooms were occasionally combined to increase the number of children, but only under

the advisement of teachers regarding the degree to which the children were mutually acquainted.

The teachers were asked to complete their ratings at the same time the peer nominations were scheduled, and the rating forms were retrieved when the peer data were collected. Some variation was noted in the measures collected in each study; the information is summarized in Table 5.

Interview Phase

The second phase of data collection was conducted at OSLC, where the study child and his parent(s) were interviewed separately. In the Planning Study, the assessment was designed to take 3 hours to complete, but it often took as long as 4 hours. The OYS interview lasted 2.5 hours on the average. Children and parents were given a 5- to 10-minute break in the middle of the interview session. In both studies, if there were two parents in the family, they were interviewed separately.

The child and his parent(s) completed separate questionnaires as part of the interview. The children were reassured that their answers to all questions would be kept completely confidential and would not be shared with their parents. The interviews developed in the Planning Study were revised for the OYS. Also, slightly different sets of questionnaires were used in each study.

During the interview, the study child and his parents participated in a videotaped problem-solving session that took 25 minutes to complete. The session consisted of three tasks. First, they were asked to spend 5 minutes planning an activity that they could do together sometime during the next week. For the next task, the child was asked to suggest a problem that he would like to work on with his parents. The family was asked to spend 10 minutes trying to solve the problem. During the last 10 minutes, the parent(s) suggested a problem to work on. Families had been asked beforehand to complete a questionnaire about current issues and problems. The interviewer helped the family select an issue that was listed as controversial (i.e., "hot") to work on. After the session, family members were asked to reach a consensus on how well they thought they had done in solving the problem.

Different coding systems were developed for each study to assess the problem-solving sessions; the coding systems are described in detail in Forgatch and Weider (1980) for the Planning Study and in Forgatch, Fetrow, and Lathrop (1985) for the OYS. The coding systems were designed to describe the sequence of family interactions in terms of affective valence, nonverbal behavior, and content of verbal interactions regarding the family problem. The staff members who coded the videotaped

[1] In the Planning Study, families were given the option of joining only the school phase of data collection. This was not the case in the OYS; only those children who were involved in all phases of assessment were included in the administration groups.

sessions also made global ratings of the family members' problem-solving skills.

Home Phase

Two sets of data were collected in the home. One set consisted of a series of six telephone calls to the child and his parent(s). The other involved a series of three home observations by trained observers.

Telephone interviews. The telephone reports were structured interviews that lasted 5 to 10 minutes per respondent. If possible, the parent and child were interviewed separately during each call. Typically, the parent who was the primary caretaker was selected for the interview; almost invariably this was the mother.

The concept of using telephone interviews was originally developed during earlier treatment outcome studies (Patterson, Cobb, & Ray, 1972). It has been found that the data from five or six telephone interviews provide a stable estimate of children's antisocial behavior (Chamberlain, 1980; Chamberlain & Reid, 1987). It has also been shown that the data are highly correlated with observed rates of social aggression in the home (Jones, 1974; Patterson, Chamberlain, & Reid, 1982) and that the findings are generalizable across days of the week, times of the day, and interviewers (Dishion, 1982).

A standard format has been adopted for administering the telephone interviews (Jones, 1974). The interaction should be conducted in a matter-of-fact style with a minimum of personal conversation. Items were added to the telephone interviews in both studies to assess a wide range of parent and child behaviors. Again, the children were assured that the information they provided would remain confidential. The questions were phrased so that only yes/no responses were required. Typically, the same interviewer completed the entire set of calls to a given family, except in those instances in which two interviewers were randomly assigned to a family to assess inter-interviewer reliability.

Home observations. The training process for observers required two to three months to complete. The procedures employed closely resembled those recommended by Reid (1978, 1982). The details are provided in Dishion, Gardner, Patterson, Reid, Spyron, and Thibodeaux (1983). All observers participated in regular retraining sessions throughout the course of the study. They were also required to accompany one another at regular intervals to collect reliability data. A low agreement with the calibrating observer resulted in automatic suspension from further data collection and intensive retraining. A persistent failure to meet and maintain an acceptable reliability level would mean suspension of salary, although this was never necessary.

Specific rules were adopted for the home observation sessions to facilitate the coding of family members'

behavior and to prevent interruptions. Generally, the rules were consistent with those developed for the Family Interaction Coding System (FICS) described in Reid (1978). Before each observation, the family was asked to comply with these rules: (1) All family members must be present, (2) no guests during the observation, (3) family activities are limited to two rooms, (4) no television allowed, and (5) no telephone calls out and responses to incoming calls should be as brief as possible.

The MOSAIC (Measurement of Social Adjustment in Children) observation code (Toobert, Patterson, Moore, & Halper, 1980) was used in the Planning Study to assess family interactions. This code is an intensive system for quantifying both prosocial and antisocial family interactions. Unlike the FICS in Reid (1978), the MOSAIC describes behavior in real time. It provides information relating to 62 content categories, ratings of affective valence for each interaction episode, and regular encoding of settings. However, we discovered that one of the problems with using such a complicated coding system is that it is difficult to achieve intercoder reliability. Low basecrates for many of the content codes also presented a problem.

A new code, the Family Process Code (FPC) (Dishion et al., 1983), was developed for the OYS. The FPC retained the multidimensional features of the MOSAIC, but the number of code categories was reduced to improve interobserver reliability. The new categories were designed to systematically sample the verbal, nonverbal, physical behavior, and vocal aspects of family interactions. The reactions were also categorized as negative, positive, or neutral. Like the MOSAIC, the FPC included ongoing ratings of emotional valence.

Because of a lack of funds, less than 50% of the families in the Planning Study were observed. In the OYS, each parent and target child was observed for 15 minutes; in single-parent families the target child was observed for 30 minutes. The order in which family members were targeted was randomly determined prior to each observation.

The decision rule for Cohort II was changed to increase the sampling of the target child's behavior during interactions with siblings. In Cohort I, only the target child and the parent(s) were targeted in observations. In Cohort II, siblings were included as a focus. The codes for siblings reflected age and sex categories (i.e., older male or female and younger male or female). The sibling selected for targeting was randomly determined. Details of the targeting procedure are provided in Dishion et al. (1983).

After the observation sessions, the parent(s) spent approximately 30 minutes completing questionnaires about recent events that had affected the overall mood of the family. This session usually required a total of approximately 90 minutes.

Staff

The first task in running a study of this kind is to develop an organizational structure that can handle an avalanche of yearly assessments. We were fortunate to have Deborah Capaldi as the supervisor for the OYS. Deborah and her staff worked in teams to generate a continuous flow of high-quality data. The team leaders who were responsible for this remarkable achievement were Lynn Crosby (observations), Karen Gardner (interviews), Margaret Lathrop (family problem solving), and Becky Fetrow (telephone interviews).

Summary

The recruitment and data-collection procedures outlined in this appendix are the result of a long and tedious process. Our mixed success in recruiting families for the Planning Study provided a foundation for developing a recruitment strategy that encouraged families to cooperate with the intensive assessments included in the OYS. Ultimately, the success of the OYS will be determined by the strategies we have adopted. The OYS data that we have analyzed so far suggests that most of our initial decisions were good ones.

References

Achenbach, T. M., & Edelbrock, C. S. *Child Behavior Checklist*. Bethesda, MD: National Institute of Mental Health, 1979.

Achenbach, T. M., & Edelbrock, C. S. Behavioral problems and competencies reported by parents of normal and disturbed children aged four through sixteen. *Monographs of the Society for Research in Child Development*, 1981, *46*(1, Serial No. 188).

Aldwin, C., & Revenson, T. Vulnerability to economic stress. *American Journal of Community Psychology*, 1986, *14*, 161–175.

Allport, G. W. *Personality: A psychological interpretation*. New York: Holt, Rinehart & Winston, 1937.

American Psychiatric Association. *Diagnostic and statistical manual of mental disorders* (3rd ed.). Washington, DC: American Psychiatric Association, 1987.

Angst, J., & Clayton, P. J. *Premorbid personality of depressed unipolar disorders, suicides, and sociopaths*. Paper presented at the annual meeting of the International Society for Research on Aggression, Evanston, Illinois, 1986.

Asarnow, J. R., & Callan, J. W. Boys with peer adjustment problems: Social cognitive processes. *Journal of Consulting and Clinical Psychology*, 1985, *53*, 80–87.

Asher, S. R. Social competence and peer status: Recent advances and future directions. *Child Development*, 1983, *54*, 1427–1434.

Bachman, J. G., & O'Malley, P. M. Self–esteem in young men: A longitudinal analysis of the impact of educational and occupational attainment. *Journal of Personality and Social Psychology*, 1977, *35*, 365–380.

Bachman, J. G., & O'Malley, P. M. *The young in transition series: A study of change and stability in young men*, Vol. 1: *Research in Sociology of Education and Socialization* (pp. 127–160). Greenwich, CT: JAI Press Inc, 1980.

Baldwin, D. V. *Perturbations in family interactions: Stationarity and sequential parent responses to aversive child behaviors at home*. Unpublished manuscript, 1987.

Baldwin, D. V., & Skinner, M. L. Structural models for antisocial behavior: Generalization to single-mother families. *Developmental Psychology*, 1989, *25*, 45–50.

Bandura, A. *Aggression: A social learning analysis*. Englewood Cliffs, NJ: Prentice-Hall, 1973.

Bandura, A. The self-system in reciprocal determinism. *American Psychologist*, 1978, *33*, 344–358.

Bandura, A. In search of pure unidirectional determinants. *Behavior Therapy*, 1981, *12*, 30–40.

Bandura, A. Model of causality in social learning theory. In M. J. Mahoney & A. Freeman (Eds.), *Cognition and psychotherapy* (pp. 81–99). New York: Plenum, 1985.

Bank, L. *A functional analysis of self-esteem using longitudinal data*. Unpublished manuscript, 1990.

Bank, L., Dishion, T. J., Skinner, M. L., & Patterson, G. R. Method variance in structural equation modeling: Living with "glop." In G. R. Patterson (Ed.), *Depression and aggression in family interaction* (pp. 247–279). Hillsdale, NJ: Lawrence Erlbaum Associates, 1990.

Bank, L., Duncan, T., & Fisher, P. *The development of disruptive behavior disorders*. Paper presented at the third biennial conference of the Society for Community Research and Action, Tempe, Arizona, June 1991.

Bank, L., Forgatch, M. S., & Patterson, G. R. *Parenting practices: Mediators of negative contextual factors in divorce*. Manuscript submitted for publication, 1991.

Bank, L., & Patterson, G. R. *Use of structural equation models in combining data from different levels of assessment*. Paper presented at the conference of the Rocky Mountain Psychological Association, Reno, Nevada, April 1989.

Bank, L., & Patterson, G. R. The use of structural equation modeling in combining data from different types of assessment. In J. Rosen & P. McReynolds (Eds.), *Advances in psychological assessment* (Vol. 8). New York: Plenum, in press.

Bank, L., & Patterson, G. R. *Studies of self-esteem*. Eugene, OR: Oregon Social Learning Center, in preparation.

Barker, R. G. The stream of behavior as an empirical problem. In R. G. Barker (Ed.), *The stream of behavior: Explorations of its structure and content* (pp. 1–22). New York: Appleton-Century-Crofts, 1963.

Bates, J. E., & Bayles, K. Attachment and the development of behavior problems. In J. Belsky & T. Nezworski (Eds.), *Clinical implications of attachment* (pp. 253–294). Hillsdale, NJ: Lawrence Erlbaum Associates, 1988.

Baumrind, D. Effects of authoritative parental control on child behavior. *Child Development, 1966, 37,* 887–907.

Baumrind, D. Current patterns of parental authority. *Developmental Psychology, 1971, 4,* 12.

Baumrind, D. Parental disciplinary patterns and social competence in children. *Youth and Society, 1978, 9,* 239–272.

Baumrind, D. *New directions in socialization research*. Paper presented at the annual meeting of the Society for Research in Child Development, San Francisco, California, April 1979.

Belsky, J. The determinants of parenting: A process model. *Child Development, 1984, 55,* 83–96.

Belsky, J., & Pensky, E. Developmental history, personality, and family relationships: Toward an emergent family system. In R. A. Hinde & J. Stevenson-Hinde (Eds.), *Relationships within families: Mutual influences* (pp. 193–217). Oxford: Clarendon Press, 1988.

Bem, D. Self-perception: An alternative interpretation of cognitive dissonance phenomenon. *Psychological Review, 1967, 74,* 183–200.

Bentler, P. M. Multivariate analysis with latent variables: Causal modeling. *Annual Review of Psychology, 1980, 31,* 419–455.

Bentler, P. M., & Bonnett, D. G. Significance tests and goodness of fit in the analysis of covariance structures. *Psychological Bulletin, 1980, 88,* 588–606.

Berger, A. M., Knutson, J. F., Mehm, J. G., & Perkins, K. A. The self-report of punitive childhood experiences of young adults and adolescents. *Child Abuse and Neglect, 1988, 12,* 251–262.

Bernal, M. E., Delfini, L. F., North, J. A., & Kreutzer, S. L. Comparison of boys' behavior in homes and classrooms. In E. J. Mash, L. A. Hamerlynck, & L. C. Handy (Eds.), *Behavior modification and families*, Vol. 1: *Theory and research* (pp. 204–227). New York: Brunner/Mazel, 1976.

Bien, N. Z., & Bry, N. H. An experimentally designed comparison of four intensities of school-based prevention programs for adolescents with adjustment problems. *Journal of Community Psychology, 1980, 8,* 110–116.

Bierman, K. L., Miller, C. L., & Stabb, S. D. Improving the social behavior of rejected boys: Effects of social skill training with instructions and prohibitions. *Journal of Consulting and Clinical Psychology, 1987, 55,* 194–200.

Bijou, S. W., & Baer, D. M. (Eds.). *Child development: Readings in experimental analysis*. New York: Appleton-Century-Crofts, 1967.

Billings, A. G, & Moos, R. H. Comparisons of children

of depressed and nondepressed parents: A social environmental perspective. *Journal of Abnormal Child Psychology,* 1983, *11,* 463–486.

Birchler, G. R., Weiss, R. L., & Vincent, J. P. Multimethod analysis of social reinforcement exchange between maritally distressed and nondistressed spouse and stranger dyads. *Journal of Personality and Social Psychology,* 1975, *31,* 349–360.

Blechman, E. A. Family problem-solving training. *American Journal of Family Therapy,* 1980, *8,* 3–22.

Block, J. *Some relationships regarding the self emanating from the Block and Block longitudinal study.* Paper presented at the SSRC Conference on Selfhood, Center for the Advanced study in the Behavioral Sciences, Palo Alto, California, October 1985.

Blumstein, A., Cohen, J., Roth, J. A., & Visher, C. A. (Eds.). *Criminal careers and career criminals* (Vols. I and II). Washington, D.C.: National Academy Press, 1986.

Bohman, M. Some genetic aspects of alcoholism and criminality: A population of adoptees. *Archives of General Psychiatry,* 1978, *35,* 269–276.

Brody, G. H., & Forehand, R. Maternal perceptions of child maladjustment as a function of the combined influence of child behavior and maternal depression. *Journal of Consulting and Clinical Psychology,* 1986, *54,* 237–240.

Bronfenbrenner, U. Toward an experimental ecology of human development. *American Psychologist,* 1977, *32,* 513–531.

Bronfenbrenner, U. Ecology of the family as a context for human development: Research perspectives. *Developmental Psychology,* 1986, *22,* 723–742.

Bronfenbrenner, U. Interacting systems in human development. Research paradigms: Present and future. In N. Bolger, A. Caspi, G. Downey, & M. Moorehouse (Eds.), *Persons in context: Developmental processes* (pp. 25–49). New York: Cambridge University Press, 1988.

Buehler, R. E., Patterson, G. R., & Furniss, J. M. The reinforcement of behavior in institutional settings. *Behavior Research and Therapy,* 1966, *4,* 157–167.

Burgess, R., & Akers, R. L. A differential association-reinforcement theory of criminal behavior. *Social Problems,* 1966, *14,* 128–147.

Buss, D. M., & Craik, K. H. The act frequency approach to personality. *Psychological Review,* 1983, *90,* 105–126.

Cadoret, R. J. Psychopathology in adopted-away offspring of biological parents with antisocial behavior. *Archives of General Psychiatry,* 1978, *35,* 176–184.

Cairns, R. B. *Social development: The origins and plasticity of interchanges.* San Francisco, CA: W. H. Freeman and Company, 1979.

Calder, G. J., & Ross, M. *Attitudes and behavior.* Morristown, NY: General Learning Press, 1973.

Calsyn, R. J., & Kenny, D. A. Self-concept of ability and perceived evaluation of others: Cause or effect of academic achievement? *Journal of Educational Psychology,* 1977, *69*(2), 136–145.

Campbell, D. T., & Fiske, D. W. Convergent and discriminant validation of the multitrait and multimethod matrix. *Psychological Bulletin,* 1959, *56,* 81–105.

Capaldi, D. M., & Patterson, G. R. An approach to the problem of recruitment and retention rates for longitudinal research. *Behavioral Assessment,* 1987, *9,* 169–177.

Capaldi, D. M., & Patterson, G. R. *Psychometric properties of fourteen latent constructs from the Oregon Youth Study.* New York: Springer-Verlag, 1989.

Capaldi, D. M., & Patterson, G. R. The relation of parental transitions to boys' adjustment problems: I. A linear hypothesis, and II. Mothers at risk for transitions and unskilled parenting. *Developmental Psychology,* 1991, *27,* 489–504.

Caspi, A., Bem, D. J., & Elder, G. H., Jr. Continuities and consequences of interactional styles across the life course. *Journal of Personality,* 1989, *57,* 375–406.

Caspi, A., & Elder, G. H. Emergent family patterns: The intergenerational construction of problem behaviour and relationships. In R. A. Hinde & J. Stevenson-Hinde (Eds.), *Relationships within families: Mutual influences* (pp. 218–240). Oxford: Clarendon Press, 1988.

Caspi, A., Elder, G. H., & Bem, D. J. Moving against the world: Life course patterns of explosive children. *Developmental Psychology,* 1987, *23,* 308–313.

Chamberlain, P. *Standardization of a parent report measure.* Unpublished doctoral dissertation, University of Oregon, Eugene, 1980.

Chamberlain, P., & Reid, J. B. Parent observation and

report of child symptoms. *Behavioral Assessment,* 1987, *9,* 97–109.

Clarke, G. N., Lewinsohn, P. M., & Hops, H. *Leader's manual for adolescent groups: The adolescent coping with depression course.* Eugene, OR: Castalia Publishing Company, 1990.

Cloninger, C. R., & Gottesman, I. I. Genetic and environmental factors in antisocial behavior disorders. In S. A. Mednick, T. E. Moffitt, & S. A. Stack (Eds.), *The causes of crime: New biological approaches* (pp. 92–109). New York: Cambridge University Press, 1987.

Cobb, J. A. *Survival skills and first grade academic achievement.* Unpublished manuscript, 1970.

Cohen, A. K. *Delinquent boys.* New York: The Free Press, 1955.

Cohen, H. L. Behavior modification and socially deviant youth. In C. Thoreson (Ed.), *Behavior modification in education,* (pp. 291–314). Chicago, IL: University of Chicago Press, 1973.

Cohen, H. L., & Filipczak, J. *A new learning environment.* San Francisco, CA: Jossey-Bass, 1971.

Cohen, H. L., Filipczak, J., Slavin, J., & Boren J. *PICA: Programming interpersonal curricula for adolescents.* Paper presented at the annual meeting of the American Psychological Association, Washington, D.C., September 1971.

Cohen, S. After-effects of stress on human performance and social behavior: A review of research and theory. *Psychological Bulletin,* 1980, *88,* 82–108.

Coie, J. D., & Kupersmidt, J. B. A behavioral analysis of emerging social status in boys' groups. *Child Development,* 1983, *54,* 1400–1416.

Conger, R. *Impact of life stressors and adult relationships on adolescent adjustment.* Paper presented at the annual meeting of the Society for Research in Child Development, Seattle, Washington, April 1991.

Conger, R. D., McCarty, J. A., Yang, R. K., Lahey, B. B., & Kropp, J. P. Perception of child, childrearing values, and emotional distress as mediating links between environmental stressors and observed maternal behavior. *Child Development,* 1984, *55,* 2234–2247.

Connell, J. P., & Harter, S. A model of children's achievement and related self-perceptions of competence, control, and motivational orientation. In J. Nicholls (Ed.), *Advances in motivation and achievement* (Vol. 3, pp. 219–250). Greenwich, CT: JAI Press, 1984.

Cook, T. D., Campbell, D. T. *Quasi-experimentation: Design and analysis issues for field settings.* Boston, MA: Houghton-Mifflin, 1979.

Coyne, J. X. Depression and the response of others. *Journal of Abnormal Psychology,* 1976, *85,* 186–193.

Cronbach, L. J. Coefficient alpha and the internal structure of tests. *Psychometrika,* 1951, *16,* 297–334.

Cronbach, L. J., & Gleser, G. C. *Psychological tests and personnel decisions.* Urbana, IL: University of Illinois Press, 1965.

Crowe, R. R. An adoptive study of psychopathy: Preliminary results from arrest records and psychiatric hospital records. In R. R. Fieve, D. Rosenthal, & H. Brill (Eds.), *Genetic research in psychiatry* (pp. 95–103). Baltimore, MD: Johns Hopkins University Press, 1975.

Dawes, R. M. Shallow psychology. In J. S. Carroll & J. W. Payne (Eds.), *Cognition and social behavior* (pp. 3–11). Hillsdale, NJ: Lawrence Erlbaum Associates, 1976.

Dawes, R. M. *Plato vs. Russell: Hoess and the relevance of cognitive psychology.* Paper presented at the annual meeting of the American Psychological Association, Los Angeles, California, 1981.

Dawes, R. M. *The distorting effect of theory-based schemas on responses to questionnaire items eliciting summaries or global judgment based on retrospective memory.* Unpublished manuscript, Carnegie-Mellon University, Pittsburgh, PA, 1985.

DeBaryshe, B. D. *A model for academic achievement in sixth-grade boys.* Unpublished manuscript, 1989.

DeBaryshe, B. D., Patterson, G. R., & Capaldi, D. *A performance model for academic achievement in early adolescent boys.* Manuscript submitted for publication, 1990.

Dengerink, H. A., Schnedler, R. S., & Covey, M. K. The role of avoidance in aggressive responses to attack and no attack. *Journal of Personality and Social Psychology,* 1978, *36,* 1044–1053.

Depue, R. A., & Monroe, S. M. Conceptualization and measurement of human disorder in life stress research: The problem of chronic disturbance. *Psychological Bulletin,* 1986, *99,* 36–51.

Dishion, T. J. *Generalizability of parent telephone report data* (Technical Report). Eugene, OR: Oregon Social Learning Center, 1982.

Dishion, T. J. *A developmental model for peer relations: Middle childhood correlates and one-year sequelae.* Unpublished doctoral dissertation, University of Oregon, Eugene, 1988.

Dishion, T. J., Andrews, D. W., & Patterson, G. R. *The microsocial peer interactions of adolescent boys and their relation to delinquent behaviors.* Paper presented at the conference of the Society for Research in Child and Adolescent Psychopathology, Costa Mesa, California, January 1990.

Dishion, T. J., Capaldi, D. M., & Patterson, G. R. *Assessment battery for family variables in the Oregon Youth Study* (Technical Report). Eugene, OR: Oregon Social Learning Center, 1990.

Dishion, T. J., Gardner, K., Patterson, G. R., Reid, J. B., Spyrou, S., & Thibodeaux, S. *The Family Process Code: A multidimensional system for observing family interaction* (Technical Report). Eugene, OR: Oregon Social Learning Center, 1982.

Dishion, T. J., & Loeber, R. Adolescent marijuana and alcohol use: The role of parents and peers revisited. *American Journal of Drug and Alcohol Abuse,* 1985, *11*(1 & 2), 11–25.

Dishion, T. J., Patterson, G. R., & Kavanagh, K. An experimental test of the coercion model: Linking theory, measurement and intervention. In J. McCord and R. Trembley (Eds.), *The interaction of theory and practice: Experimental studies of intervention.* New York: Guilford Press, 1991.

Dishion, T. J., Patterson, G. R., & Skinner, M. *Some models for peer group involvement.* Unpublished manuscript, 1989.

Dishion, T. J., Reid, J. B., & Patterson, G. R. Empirical guidelines for a family intervention for adolescent drug use. *Journal of Chemical Dependency Treatment,* 1988, *1,* 189–224.

Doane, J. A., Falloon, I. R. H., Goldstein, M. J., & Mintz, J. Parental affective style and the treatment of schizophrenia: Predicting course of illness and social functioning. *Archives of General Psychiatry,* 1985, *42,* 34–42.

Dodge, K. A. Social cognition and children's aggressive behavior. *Child Development,* 1980, *51,* 162–170.

Dodge, K. A. Behavioral antecedents: A peer social status. *Child Development,* 1983, *54,* 1386–1399.

Dodge, K. A., Bates, J. E., & Pettit, G. S. *Mechanisms in the cycle of violence.* Paper presented at the annual convention of the Association for Advancement of Behavior Therapy, San Francisco, California, November 1990.

Dodge, K. A., Pettit, G. S., McClaskey, C. L., & Brown, M. M. Social competence in children. *Monographs of the Society for Research in Child Development,* 1986, *51,* (2, Serial No. 213).

Dohrenwend, B. P., & Shrout, P. E. "Hassles" in the conceptualization and measurement of life stress variables. *American Psychologist,* 1985, *40,* 780–785.

Dohrenwend, B. S., & Dohrenwend, B. P. *Stressful life events: Their nature and effects.* New York: John Wiley & Sons, 1974.

Dollard, J., Doob, L. W., Miller, N. E., Mowrer, O. H., & Sears, R. R. *Frustration and aggression.* New Haven, CT: Yale University Press, 1939.

Domjan, M., & Burkhard, B. *The principles of learning and behavior* (2nd ed.). Monterey, CA: Brooks/Cole, 1986.

Dornbusch, S. M., Ritter, P. L., Leiderman, P. H., Roberts, D. F., & Fraleigh, M. J. The relation of parenting style to adolescent school performance. *Child Development,* 1987, *58,* 1244–1257.

Duncan, O. D. *Introduction to structural equation models.* New York: Academic Press, 1975.

Dunivant, N. Learning disabilities and juvenile delinquency: A summary report. *State Court Journal,* 1982 (fall) 12–15.

Dunst, C. J., & Lingerfelt, B. Maternal ratings of temperament and operant learning in two- to three-month-old infants. *Child Development,* 1985, *56,* 555–563.

Dwyer, J. H. *Statistical models for the social and behavioral sciences.* New York: Oxford University Press, 1983.

Eddy, J. M. *The coercion model of antisocial behavior: Generalization to five-year-old children and their parents.* Paper presented at the annual meeting of the Society for Research in Child Development, Seattle, Washington, April 1991a.

Eddy, J. M. *The stability in parental definitions of the antisocial trait at different ages of the child.* Unpublished manuscript, 1991b.

Elder, G. H., Caspi, A., & Downey, G. Problem behavior in family relationships: A multigenerational analysis. In A. Sorensen, F. Weinert, & L. Sherrod (Eds.), *Human development: Interdisciplinary perspective* (pp. 93–118). Hillsdale, NJ: Lawrence Erlbaum Associates, 1983.

Elder, G. H., Downey, G., & Cross, C. E. Family ties and life chances: Hard times and hard choices in women's lives since the 1930s. In N. Datan, A. L. Green, & H. W. Reese (Eds.), *Life span developmental psychology: Intergenerational relations* (pp. 151–183). Hillsdale, NJ: Lawrence Erlbaum Associates, 1986.

Elder, G. H., Liker, J. K., & Cross, C. E. Parent-child behavior in the Great Depression: Life course and intergenerational influences. In P. B. Baltes & O. G. Brim (Eds.), *Life span development and behavior* (Vol. 6, pp. 109–158). New York: Academic Press, 1984.

Elder, G. H., Van Nguyen, T., & Caspi, A. Linking family hardship to children's lives. *Child Development,* 1985, *56,* 361–375.

Elliott, D. S., Ageton, S. S., Huizinga, D., Knowles, B. A., & Canter, R. J. *The prevalence and incidence of delinquent behavior: 1976–1980. National estimates of delinquent behavior by sex, race, social class, and other selected variables.* (National Youth Survey Report No. 26). Boulder, CO: Behavioral Research Institute, 1983.

Elliott, D. S., & Huizinga, D. *Defining patterned delinquency: A conceptual typology of delinquent offenders.* Paper presented at the meeting of the American Society of Criminology, San Francisco, California, November 1980.

Elliott, D. S., & Huizinga, D. *The dynamics of deviant behavior: A national survey continuation grant application.* Progress report of the National Youth Survey, National Institute of Mental Health, Department of Health and Human Services, July 1985.

Elliott, D. S., Huizinga, D., & Ageton, S. S. *Explaining delinquency and drug use.* (National Youth Survey Report No. 21). Boulder, CO: Behavioral Research Institute, 1982.

Elliott, D. S., Huizinga, D., & Ageton, S. S. *Explaining delinquency and drug use.* Beverly Hills, CA: Sage Publications, 1985.

Elliott, D. S., & Voss, H. L. *Delinquency and dropout.* Lexington, MA: Lexington Books, 1974.

Emery, R. E. Interparental conflict and the children of discord and divorce. *Psychological Bulletin,* 1982, *92,* 310–330.

Emery, R. E., & O'Leary, K. D. Marital discord and child behavior problems in a nonclinical sample. *Journal of*

Abnormal Child Psychology, 1984, 37, 1097–1126.

Entwisle, D. R., Alexander, K. L., Pallas, A. M., & Cadigan, D. The emergent academic self-image of first graders: Its response to social structure. *Child Development,* 1987, *58,* 1190–1206.

Epstein, S. The stability of behavior: I. On predicting most of the people much of the time. *Journal of Personality and Social Psychology,* 1979, *37,* 1097–1126.

Eron, L. D., Walder, L. O., & Lefkowitz, M. M. *Learning of aggression in children.* Boston, MA: Little, Brown & Co, 1971.

Fagan, O. S., Langner, T. S., Gersten, J. C., & Eisenberg, J. *Violent and antisocial behavior: A longitudinal study of urban youth.* Interim report of the Division of Epidemiology, New York: Columbia University of Public Health, 1977.

Fagot, B. I. Reinforcing contingencies for sex role behavior: Effect of experience with children. *Child Development,* 1978a, *49,* 30–36.

Fagot, B. I. The influence of sex of child and parental reactions to toddler children. *Child Development,* 1978b, *49,* 459.

Fagot, B. I., & Eddy, J. M. *The relation of parental discipline practices to preschool aggression for boys and girls.* Unpublished manuscript, 1990.

Fagot, B. I., & Patterson, G. R. An *in vivo* analysis of reinforcing contingencies for sex-role behaviors in the preschool child. *Developmental Psychology,* 1969, *1,* 563–568.

Falloon, I. R. H. Prevention of morbidity in schizophrenia. In I. R. H. Falloon (Ed.), *Handbook of behavioral family therapy* (pp. 316–349). New York: Guilford Press, 1988.

Farrington, D. P. The family backgrounds of aggressive youths. In L. Hersov, M. Berger, & D. Shaffer (Eds.), *Aggression and antisocial behaviour in childhood and adolescence* (pp. 73–93). Elmsford, NY: Pergamon Press, 1978.

Farrington, D. P. *Stepping stones to adult criminal careers.* Paper presented at the conference on the Development of Antisocial and Prosocial Behavior, Voss, Norway, July 1982.

Farrington, D. P. Offending from 10 to 25 years of age. In K. T. Van Dusen & S. A. Mednick (Eds.), *Prospective studies of crime and delinquency* (pp. 17–37). Boston, MA: Kluwer-Nijhoff, 1983.

Farrington, D. P., Gallagher, B., Morley, L., St. Ledger, R. J., & West, D. J. *Cambridge study in delinquent development: Long-term follow-up*. Final report to the Cambridge University Institute of Criminology, Cambridge, England, September 1988.

Fauber, R., Forehand, R., Long, N., Burke, M. & Faust, J. The relationship of young adolescent Children's Depression Inventory (CDI) scores to their social and cognitive functioning. *Journal of Psychopathology and Behavioral Assessment*, 1987, *9*, 161–172.

Fawl, C. I. Disturbances experienced by children in their natural habitats. In R. G. Barker (Ed.), *The stream of behavior*. New York: Appleton-Century-Crofts, 1963.

Feshbach, S. Aggression. In P. H. Mussen (Ed.), *Carmichael's manual of child psychology* (pp. 159–259). New York: John Wiley & Sons, 1970.

Festinger, L. Behavioral support for opinion change. *Public Opinion Quarterly*, 1964, *28*, 404–417.

Fiske, D. W. The limits for the conventional science of personality. *Journal of Personality*, 1974, *42*, 1–11.

Fiske, D. W. Construct invalidity comes from method effects. *Educational and Psychological Measurement*, 1987, *47*, 285–307.

Forehand, R., & Long, N. Prevention of aggression and other behavior problems in the early adolescent years. In D. Pepler and K. H. Rubin (Eds.), *The development and treatment of childhood aggression* (pp. 317–330). Hillsdale, NJ: Lawrence Erlbaum Associates, 1991.

Forehand, R., McComb, A., & Brody, G. H. The relationship between parental depressive mood states and child functioning. *Advances in Behavioral and Research Therapy*, 1987, *9*, 1–20.

Forgatch, M. S. *A two-stage analysis of family problem solving: Global and microsocial*. Unpublished doctoral dissertation, University of Oregon, Eugene, 1984.

Forgatch, M. S. Patterns and outcome in family problem solving: The disrupting effect of negative emotion. *Journal of Marriage and the Family*, 1989, *51*, 115–124.

Forgatch, M. S. The clinical science vortex: A developing theory of antisocial behavior. In D. Pepler and K. H. Rubin (Eds.), *The development and treatment of childhood aggression*. Hillsdale, NJ: Lawrence Erlbaum Associates, 1991.

Forgatch, M. S., & Fetrow, B. *The contribution of single mother irritability to dyadic problem solving out-comes*. Unpublished manuscript, Oregon Social Learning Center, 1990.

Forgatch, M. S., Fetrow, B., & Lathrop, M. *Solving problems in family interactions* (Training Manual). Oregon Social Learning Center, 1985.

Forgatch, M. S., & Patterson, G. R. *Parents and adolescents living together*, Part 2: *Family problem solving*. Eugene, OR: Castalia Publishing Company, 1989.

Forgatch, M. S., Patterson, G. R., & Duncan, T. *Developmental model for maternal depression in divorce: Still single versus repartnered mothers*. Unpublished manuscript, 1990.

Forgatch, M. S., Patterson, G. R., & Skinner, M. A mediational model for the effect of divorce on antisocial behavior in boys. In E. M. Hetherington (Ed.), *The impact of divorce, single parenting, and stepparenting on children* (pp. 135–154). Hillsdale, NJ: Lawrence Erlbaum Associates, 1988.

Forgatch, M. S., & Ray, J. *Stress, divorce, parenting, repartnering, and child adjustment*. Paper presented at the annual meeting of the Society for Research in Child Development, Seattle, Washington, April 1991.

Forgatch, M. S., & Stoolmiller, M. *An application of latent growth modeling to the covariation of maternal depression and parenting practices in two samples*. Paper presented at the annual meeting of the Society for Research in Child Development, Seattle, Washington, April 1991.

Forgatch, M. S., & Toobert, D. J. A cost effective parent training program for use with normal preschool children. *Journal of Pediatric Psychology*, 1979, *4*, 129–145.

Forgatch, M. S., & Weider, G. B. *PANIC: Parent adolescent negotiation interaction code* (Training Manual). Oregon Social Learning Center, 1980.

Fowles, D. C. Biological variables in psychopathology: A psychobiological perspective. In H. E. Adams & P. B. Sutker (Eds.), *Comprehensive handbook of psychopathology* (pp. 77–110). New York: Plenum, 1984.

Foyle, H. C. *The effects of preparation and practice homework on student achievement in tenth grade American history*. Unpublished doctoral dissertation, Kansas State University, Manhattan, 1984.

Freedman, D. A. *Structural equation models: A case study* (Technical Report No. 22). Berkeley: University of California, Department of Statistics, 1983.

Furstenberg, F. F., & Seltzer, J. A. Divorce and child development. In *Sociological studies of child development* (Vol. 1, pp. 137–160). Greenwich, CT: JAI Press, 1986.

Garber, J. The developmental progression of depression in female children. In D. Cicchetti & K. Schneider-Rosen (Eds.), *Childhood depression* (pp. 29–58). San Francisco, CA: Jossey-Bass, 1984.

Garmezy, N. Stressors of childhood. In N. Garmezy & M. Rutter (Eds.), *Stress, coping, and development in children* (pp. 43–84). Baltimore, MD: The Johns Hopkins University Press, 1983.

Gauvain, M., & Skinner, M. *Models of academic achievement in the crisis and support sample* (Technical Report). Oregon Social Learning Center, 1987.

Gendreau, P., Madden, P., & Leipciger, M. Norms and recidivism for social history and institutional experience for first incarcerates: Implications for programming. *Canadian Journal of Criminology,* 1979, *21,* 1–26.

Gersten, J. C., Langner, T. S., Eisenberg, J. G., & Simcha-Fagan, O. An evaluation of the etiologic role of stressful life-change events in psychological disorders. *Journal of Health and Social Behavior,* 1977, *18,* 228–244.

Gewirtz, J., & Boyd, E. Experiments on mother-infant interaction underlying mutual attachment acquisition: The infant conditions the mother. In T. Alloway, P. Pliner, & L. Krames (Eds.), *Attachment behavior* (pp. 109–143). New York: Plenum, 1977.

Glueck, S., & Glueck, E. *Unraveling juvenile delinquency.* Cambridge, MA: Harvard University Press, 1950.

Glueck, S., & Glueck, E. *Predicting delinquency and crime.* Cambridge, MA: Harvard University Press, 1959.

Glueck, S., & Glueck, E. *Delinquents and nondelinquents in perspective.* Cambridge, MA: Harvard University Press, 1968.

Goldsmith, H. H. Genetic influences on personality from infancy to adulthood. *Child Development,* 1983, *54,* 331–355.

Goldstein, H. S. Parental composition, supervision, and conduct problems in youths 12–17 years old. *Journal of the American Academy of Child Psychiatry,* 1984, *23,* 679–684.

Gollob, H. F., & Reichardt, C. S. Taking account of time lags in causal models. *Child Development,* 1987, *58,* 80–92.

Goodenough, R. L. *Anger in young children.* Minneapolis, MN: University of Minnesota Press, 1931.

Gottman, J. M. Toward a definition of social isolation in children. *Child Development,* 1977, *48,* 513–517.

Gottman, J. M. *Marital interaction: Experimental investigations.* New York: Academic Press, 1979.

Gottman, J. M. Analyzing for sequential connection and assessing interobserver reliability for the sequential analysis of observational data. *Behavioral Assessment,* 1980, *2,* 361–368.

Gottman, J. M. *Time series analysis: A comprehensive introduction for social scientists.* New York: Cambridge University Press, 1981.

Gottman, J. M. How children become friends. *Monographs of the Society for Research in Child Development,* 1983, *48*(3, Serial No. 201).

Gottman, J. M. Chaos and regulated change in families: A metaphor for the study of transitions. In P. A. Cowan and E. M. Hetherington (Eds.), *Family transitions* (pp.247–272). Hillsdale, NJ: Lawrence Erlbaum Associates, 1991.

Gottman, J. M., & Levenson, R. W. Why marriages fail: Affective and physiological patterns in marital interaction. In J. C. Masters & K. Yarkin-Levin (Eds.), *Boundary areas in social and developmental psychology* (pp. 67–106). Orlando, FL: Academic Press, 1984.

Gray, J. A. The neuropsychology of anxiety. *British Journal of Psychology,* 1978, *69,* 417–434.

Griest, D. L., Wells, K., & Forehand, R. An examination of predictors of maternal perceptions of maladjustment in clinic referred children. *Journal of Abnormal Psychology,* 1979, *88,* 277–281.

Gunnison, R. Self-esteem seen as a social vaccine. Eugene, OR: *The Register-Guard,* pg. 1, January 24, 1990.

Guttman, L. A. A basis for scaling qualitative data. *American Sociological Review,* 1944, *9,* 139–150.

Hahlweg, K., Reisner, L., Kohli, G., Vollmer, M., Schindler, L., & Revensdorf, D. Development and validity of a new system to analyze interpersonal communication: Kategoriensystem fur partnerschaftliche interaktion. In K. Hahlweg & N. S. Jacobson (Eds.), *Marital interaction: Analysis and modification.* New York: Guilford Press, 1984.

Harris, A., & Reid, J. B. The consistency of a class of coercive child behaviors across school settings for individual subjects. *Journal of Abnormal Child Psychology,* 1981, *9,* 219–227.

Harter, S. Developmental perspectives on the self-system. In P. Mussen (Ed.) and E. M. Hetherington (vol. Ed.), *Social and personality development: Handbook of child psychology,* Vol. IV: *Socialization, personality, and social development* (4th ed., pp. 275–385). New York: John Wiley & Sons, 1983.

Hartup, W. W. Symmetrics and asymmetrics in children's relationships. In J. DeWit & H. L. Benton (Eds.), *Perspectives in child study.* Lisse, Netherlands: Zwets & Zeitlinger, 1982.

Hartup, W. W. Peer relations. In P. Mussen (Ed.) and E. M. Hetherington (vol. Ed.), *Social and personality development: Handbook of child psychology,* Vol. IV: *Socialization, personality, and social development* (4th ed., pp. 103–196). New York: John Wiley & Sons, 1983.

Hathaway, S. R., & Monachesi, E. D. *Analyzing and predicting juvenile delinquency with the MMPI.* Minneapolis, MN: University of Minnesota Press, 1953.

Herrnstein, R. J. Relative and absolute strength of response as a function of frequency of reinforcement. *Journal of Experimental Analysis of Behavior,* 1961, *4,* 267–272.

Hess, R. D., Holloway, S., Price, G. G., & Dickson, W. P. Family environment and the acquisition of reading skills: Toward a more precise analysis. In L. M. Laosa & I. E. Sigel (Eds.), *Families as learning environments for children* (pp. 87–113). New York: Plenum, 1982.

Hess, R. D., & McDevitt, T. M. Some cognitive consequences of maternal intervention techniques: A longitudinal study. *Child Development,* 1984, *55,* 2017–2030.

Hetherington, E. M., Cox, M., & Cox, R. The aftermath of divorce. In J. H. Stevens, Jr., & M. Matthews (Eds.), *Mother–child, father–child relations* (pp. 110–155). Washington, DC: National Association for the Education of Young Children, 1978.

Hetherington, E. M., Cox, M., & Cox, R. Family interaction and the social, emotional, and cognitive development of children following divorce. In V. Vaughn & T. B. Brazelton (Eds.), *The family: Setting priorities* (pp. 89–128). New York: Science and Medicine, 1979.

Hineline, P. N. Negative reinforcement and avoidance. In W. K. Honig & J. E. Staddon (Eds.), *Handbook of operant behavior* (pp. 364–414). Englewood Cliffs, NJ: Prentice-Hall, 1977.

Hirschi, T. *Causes of delinquency.* Berkeley, CA: University of California Press, 1969.

Hirschi, T., & Hindelang, M. J. Intelligence and delinquency: A revisionist review. *American Sociological Review,* 1977, *42,* 571–587.

Hirsh, R. H. & Walker, H. M. Great expectations: Making schools effective for all students. *Policy Studies Review,* 1983, *2* (No. 1), 147–188.

Hoffman, D. A., Fagot, B. I., Reid, J. B., & Patterson, G. R. Parents rate the Family Interaction Coding System: Comparisons of problem and nonproblem boys using parent-derived behavior composites. *Behavioral Assessment,* 1987, *9,* 131–140.

Holleran, P. A., Littman, D. C., Freund, R. D., & Schmaling, K. B. A signal detection approach to social perception: Identification of negative and positive behaviors by parents of normal and problem children. *Journal of Abnormal Child Psychology,* 1982, *10,* 549–557.

Hollingshead, A. B. *Four factor index of social status.* Unpublished manuscript, Yale University, Department of Sociology, New Haven, CT, 1975.

Holmes, T. H., & Rahe, R. H. The Social Readjustment Rating Scale. *Journal of Psychosomatic Research,* 1967, *11,* 213.

Holmes, S. J., & Robins, L. N. *The influence of childhood disciplinary experience on the development of alcoholism and depression.* Unpublished manuscript, 1986.

Holmes, T. H., & Masuda, M. Life changes and illness susceptibility. In B. S. Dohrenwend & B. P. Dohrenwend (Eds.), *Stressful life events: Their nature and effects* (pp. 45–72). New York: John Wiley & Sons, 1974.

Hood, R., & Sparks, R. *Key issues in criminology.* London: Weidenfeld & Nicolson, 1970.

Hops, H. Children's social competence and skill: Current research practices and future directions. *Behavior Therapy,* 1983, *14,* 3–18.

Hops, H., Biglan, A., Sherman, L., Arthur, J., Friedman, L., & Osteen, V. Home observations of family interactions of depressed women. *Journal of Consulting and Clinical Psychology,* 1987, *55,* 341–346.

Hops, H., Sherman, L., & Biglan, A. Maternal depression, marital discord, and children's behavior: A developmental perspective. In G. R. Patterson (Ed.), *Depression and aggression in family interaction* (pp. 185–208). Hillsdale, NJ: Lawrence Erlbaum Associates, 1990.

Howard, D. V. *Cognitive psychology: Memory, language, and thought.* New York: MacMillan, 1983.

Huba, G. J., & Bentler, P. M. Causal models of the development of law abidance and its relationship to psychosocial factors and drug use. In W. S. Laufer & J. M. Day (Eds.), *Personality theory, moral development, and criminal behavior* (pp. 165–215). Lexington, MA: Lexington Books, 1983.

Huesmann, L. R., Eron, L. D., Lefkowitz, M. M., & Walder, L. O. Stability of aggression over time and generations. *Developmental Psychology,* 1984, *20,* 1120–1134.

Huesmann, L. R., Lagerspetz, K., & Eron, L. D. Intervening variables in the television violence-aggression relation: Evidence from two countries. *Developmental Psychology,* 1984, *20,* 1120–1134.

Hutchings, B., & Mednick, S. A. Criminality in adoptees and their adoptive and biological parents: A pilot study. In S. A. Mednick & K. O. Christiansen (Eds.), *Biosocial bases of criminal behavior* (pp. 127–141). New York: Gardner Press, 1977.

Jacobson, N., Elwood, R., & Dallas, M. The behavioral assessment of marital dysfunction. In D. H. Barlow (Ed.), *Behavioral assessment of adult disorders.* New York: Guilford Press, 1981.

Jastak, J. F., Bijou, S. W., & Jastak, S. R. *Wide Range Achievement Test.* Wilmington, DE: Guidance Association of Delaware, 1976.

Jessor, R. Predicting time of onset of marijuana use: A developmental study of high school youth. *Journal of Consulting and Clinical Psychology,* 1976, *44,* 125–134.

Jessor, R., & Jessor, S. L. Adolescent development and the onset of drinking: A longitudinal study. *Journal of Studies on Alcohol,* 1975, *36,* 27–51.

Johnson, S. M., & Lobitz, G. K. Parental manipulation of child behavior in home observations: A methodological concern. *Journal of Applied Behavior Analysis,* 1974, *7,* 23–31.

Jones, R. R. *Observation by telephone* (Technical Report). Eugene, OR: Oregon Research Institute, 1974.

Jones, R. R., Reid, J. B., & Patterson, G. R. Naturalistic

observation in clinical assessment. In P. McReynolds (Ed.), *Advances in psychological assessment* (Vol. 3, pp. 42–95). San Francisco, CA: Jossey-Bass, 1975.

Jöreskog, K. G., & Sörbom, D. *LISREL VI: Analysis of linear structural relationships by maximum likelihood and least squares methods* (2nd ed.). Chicago: Natural Education Resources, 1983.

Kandel, D. B. Adolescent marijuana use: Role of parents and peers. *Science,* 1973, *181,* 1067–1070.

Kandel, D. B. Epidemiological and psychosocial perspectives on adolescent drug use. *Journal of the American Academy of Child Psychiatry,* 1982, *21,* 328–347.

Kanfer, F. H. Self-regulation and behavior. In H. Heckhousen, P. M. Gollwitzer, & F. E. Weinert (Eds.), *Jenseits des Rubikon* (pp. 286–299). Heidelberg: Springer-Verlag, 1987.

Kaplan, H. B. Increase in self-rejection as an antecedent of deviant responses. *Journal of Youth and Adolescence,* 1975, *4,* 281–292.

Kashani, J. H., Holcomb, W. R., and Orvaschel, H. Depression and depressive symptoms in preschool children from the general population. *American Journal of Psychiatry,* 1986, *143,* 1138–1143.

Kazdin, A. E. Assessment techniques for childhood depression: A critical appraisal. *Journal of the American Academy of Child Psychiatry,* 1981, *20,* 358–375.

Kazdin, A. E. *Treatment of antisocial behavior in children and adolescents.* Homewood, IL: Dorsey, 1985.

Kazdin, A. E. Assessment of childhood depression: Current issues and strategies. *Behavioral Assessment,* 1987, *9,* 291–319.

Kazdin, A. E., Esveldt-Dawson, K., Sherick, R. B., & Colbus, D. Assessment of overt behavior and childhood depression among psychiatrically disturbed children. *Journal of Consulting and Clinical Psychology,* 1985, *53,* 201–210.

Kazdin, A. E., & Petti, T. A. Self-report and interview measures of childhood and adolescent depression. *Journal of Child Psychology and Psychiatry,* 1982, *23,* 437–457.

Kellam, S. G. Developmental epidemiological framework for family research on depression and aggression. In G. R. Patterson (Ed.), *Depression and aggression in family interaction* (pp. 11–48).

Hillsdale, NJ: Lawrence Erlbaum Associates, 1990.

Knorr, E. L. *A synthesis of homework research and related literature.* Presented to the Lehigh Chapter of Phi Delta Kappa, Bethlehem, Pennsylvania, 1981.

Kohn, M. L., & Schooler, C. *Work and personality: An inquiry into the impact of social stratification.* Norwood, NJ: Ablex Publishing, 1983.

Koller, K. M., & Gosden, S. D. Recidivists: Their past and families compared with first time only prisoners. *Australian and New Zealand Journal of Criminology,* 1980, *13,* 117–123.

Korner, A. F., Zeanah, C. H., Linden, J., Berkowitz, R. I., Kraemer, H. C., & Agras, W. S. The relation between neonatal and later activity and temperament. *Child Development,* 1985, *56,* 38–42.

Lahey, B. B., Hartdagen, S. E., Frick, P. J., McBurnett, K., Connor, R., & Hynd, G. W. Conduct disorder: Parsing the confounded relation to parental divorce and antisocial personality. *Journal of Abnormal Psychology,* 1988, *97,* 334–337.

Lane Council of Governments. *Population, households, and employment.* Eugene, OR: Lane County, 1978.

Langer, E. J. *Rethinking the role of thought in social interaction.* Paper presented at the conference of the Oregon Psychological Association, 1984.

Larzelere, R. E., & Patterson, G. R. Parental management: Mediator of the effect of socioeconomic status on early delinquency. *Criminology,* 1990, *28,* 301–324.

Laub, J. H., & Sampson, R. J. Unraveling families and delinquency: A reanalysis of the Gluecks' data. *Criminology,* 1988, *26,* 355–380.

Lazarus, R. S., DeLongis, A., Folkman, S., & Gruen, R. Stress and adaptational outcomes: The problem of confounded measures. *American Psychologist,* 1985, *40,* 770–779.

Lee, C. L., & Bates, J. E. Mother-child interaction at age two years and perceived difficult temperament. *Child Development,* 1985, *56,* 1314–1325.

Leff, J., & Vaughan, C. *Expressed emotion in families: Its significance for mental illness in families.* New York: Guilford Press, 1985.

Lefkowitz, M. M., Eron, L. D., Walder, L. O., & Huesmann, L. R. *Growing up to be violent: A longitudinal study of the development of aggression.* New York: Pergamon Press, 1977.

Lewinsohn, P. M., Clarke, G. N., Hops, H., & Andrews, J. Cognitive-behavioral treatment of depressed adolescents. *Behavior Therapy,* 1990, *21,* 385–401.

Lewinsohn, P. M., Hops, H., Roberts, R., & Seeley, J. *Adolescent depression: Prevalence and psychosocial aspects.* Paper presented at the annual meeting of the American Public Health Association, Boston, Massachusetts, November 1988.

Lifton, R. J. *The Nazi doctors: Medical killing and the psychology of genocide.* New York: Basic Books, 1986.

Ling, R. G. Review of correlation and causality. *Journal of the American Statistical Association,* 1982, *77,* 489–491.

Lobitz, G. K., & Johnson, S. M. Parental manipulation of the behavior of normal and deviant children. *Child Development,* 1975, *46,* 719–726.

Locke, H. J., & Wallace, K. M. Short marital-adjustment and accord in distressed and nondistressed marital partners. *Journal of Consulting and Clinical Psychology,* 1959, *49,* 554–567.

Loeber, R. The stability of antisocial and delinquent child behavior: A review. *Child Development,* 1982, *53,* 1431–1446.

Loeber, R., & Dishion, T. J. Early predictors of male delinquency: A review. *Psychological Bulletin,* 1983, *94,* 68–99.

Loeber, R., & Dishion, T. J. Boys who fight at home and school: Family conditions influencing cross-setting consistency. *Journal of Consulting and Clinical Psychology,* 1984, *52,* 759–768.

Loeber, R., Dishion, T. J., & Patterson, G. R. Multiple gating: A multistage assessment procedure for identifying youths at risk for delinquency. *Journal of Research in Crime and Delinquency,* 1984, *21,* 7–32.

Loeber, R., & Schmaling, K. B. Empirical evidence for overt and covert patterns of antisocial conduct problems: A meta-analysis. *Journal of Abnormal Child Psychology,* 1985a, *13,* 337–352.

Loeber, R., & Schmaling, K. B. The utility of differentiating between mixed and pure forms of antisocial child behavior. *Journal of Abnormal Child Psychology,* 1985b, *13,* 315–336.

Loney, J. The intellectual functioning of hyperactive elementary school boys: A cross-sectional investigation. *American Journal of Orthopsychiatry,* 1974, *44*(5), 754–761.

Lorber, R. *Parental tracking of childhood behavior as a function of family stress.* Unpublished doctoral dissertation, University of Oregon, Eugene, 1981.

Lorber, R. Felton, D. K., & Reid, J. B. A social learning approach to the reduction of coercive processes in child abusive families: A molecular analysis. *Advances in Behavior Research and Therapy,* 1984, *6,* 29–45.

Lubin, B. Adjective checklists for measurement of depression. *Archives of General Psychiatry,* 1963, *12,* 57–62.

Lykken, D. J. A study of anxiety in the sociopathic personality. *Journal of Abnormal and Social Psychology,* 1957, *55,* 6–10.

Lytton, H. Do parents create, or respond to, differences in twins? *Developmental Psychology,* 1977, *13,* 456–459.

Lytton, H. *Parent-child interaction: The socialization process observed in twin and singleton families.* New York: Plenum, 1980.

Maccoby, E. E. (Ed.) *The development of sex differences.* Stanford, CA: Stanford University Press, 1966.

Maccoby, E. E., & Martin, J. Socialization in the context of the family: Parent-child interaction. In P. Mussen (Ed.) and E. M. Hetherington (vol. Ed.), *Handbook of child psychology,* Vol. IV: *Socialization, personality, and social development* (4th ed., pp. 1–101). New York: John Wiley & Sons, 1983.

Magnusson, D. *Early conduct and biological factors in the developmental background of adult delinquency.* Lecture presented at Oxford University, Oxford, England, September 1984.

Mandelzys, N. Correlates of offense severity and recidivism probability in a Canadian sample. *Journal of Consulting Psychology,* 1979, *35,* 897–907.

Mannheim, H., & Wilkins, L. T. *Prediction methods in relation to Borstal training.* London: Her Majesty's Stationery Office, 1955.

Margolin, G. *A sequential analysis of dyadic communication.* Paper presented at the annual conference of the Association for the Advancement of Behavior Therapy, Atlanta, Georgia, December 1977.

Margolin, G., & Patterson, G. R. The differential consequences provided by mothers and fathers for their sons and daughters. *Developmental Psychology,* 1975, *11,* 537–538.

Margolin, G., & Wampold, B. E. Sequential analysis of

conflict and accord in distressed and nondistressed marital partners. *Journal of Consulting and Clinical Psychology,* 1981, *49,* 554–567.

Martin, J. A. A longitudinal study of the consequences of early mother-infant interaction: A microanalytic approach. *Monographs of the Society for Research in Child Development,* 1981, *46*(3, Serial No. 190).

McCord, J. *A longitudinal study of the link between broken homes and criminality.* Paper presented at the meeting of the National Council on Family Relations, Philadelphia, Pennsylvania, October 1978.

McCord, J. Some child-rearing antecedents of criminal behavior in adult men. *Journal of Personality and Social Psychology,* 1979, *8,* 1477–1486.

McCord, J. Patterns of deviance. In S. B. Sells, R. Crandall, M. Roff, J. S. Strauss, & W. Pollin (Eds.), *Human functioning in longitudinal perspective: Studies of normal and psychopathic populations* (pp. 157–167). Baltimore, MD: Williams & Wilkins, 1980.

McCord, J. Instigation and insulation: How families affect antisocial aggression. In D. Olweus, J. Block, & M. Radke Yarrow (Eds.), *Development of antisocial and prosocial behavior: Research, theories, and issues* (pp. 343–357). Orlando, FL: Academic Press, 1986.

McCord, W., McCord, J., & Howard, A. Familial correlates of aggression in nondelinquent male children. *Journal of Abnormal and Social Psychology,* 1961, *62,* 79–93.

McCubbin, H. I., Joy, C. B., Cauble, A. E., Comeau, J. K., Patterson, J. M., & Needle, R. H. Family stress and coping: A decade review. *Journal of Marriage and the Family,* 1980, *42,* 855–871.

Mednick, S. A., & Christiansen, K. O. *Biosocial bases of criminal behavior.* New York: Gardner Press, 1977.

Mednick, S. A., Gabrielli, W. F., Jr., & Hutchings, B. *Genetic influences in criminal behavior.* Unpublished manuscript, 1982.

Meehl, P. *Clinical versus statistical prediction: A theoretical analysis and a review of the evidence.* Minneapolis, MN: University of Minnesota Press, 1954.

Mischel, W. *Personality and assessment.* New York: John Wiley & Sons, 1968.

Mitchell, S., & Rosa, P. Boyhood behavior problems as precursors of criminality: A fifteen-year follow-up study. *Journal of Child Psychology and Psychiatry,* 1981, *22,* 19–33.

Nisbett, R. E., & Wilson, T. D. Telling more than we can know: Verbal reports on mental processes. *Psychological Review,* 1977, *84,* 231–259.

Oltmanns, T., Broderick, J., & O'Leary, K. Marital adjustment and the efficacy of behavior therapy with children. *Journal of Consulting and Clinical Psychology,* 1977, *45*(5), 724–729.

Olweus, D. Stability of aggressive reaction patterns in males: A review. *Psychological Bulletin,* 1979, *86,* 852–875.

Olweus, D. The consistency issue in personality psychology revisited—with special reference to aggression. *British Journal of Social and Clinical Psychology,* 1980, *19,* 377–390.

Pastorelli, T. *The across cultural replication of the parent training model.* Paper presented at the Oregon Social Learning Center, Eugene, OR, 1991.

Patterson, G. R. Changes in status of family members as controlling stimuli: A basis for describing treatment process. In L. A. Hamerlynck, L. C. Handy, & E. J. Mash (Eds.), *Behavior change: Methodology, concepts, and practice* (pp. 169–191). Champaign, IL: Research Press, 1973.

Patterson, G. R. Interventions for boys with conduct problems: Multiple settings, treatments, and criteria. *Journal of Consulting and Clinical Psychology,* 1974a, *42,* 471–481.

Patterson, G. R. Retraining of aggressive boys by their parents: Review of recent literature and follow-up evaluation. *Canadian Psychiatric Association Journal,* 1974b, *19,* 142–161.

Patterson, G. R. The aggressive child: Victim and architect of a coercive system. In E. J. Mash, L. A. Hamerlynck, & L. C. Handy (Eds.), *Behavior modification and families,* Vol. 1: *Theory and research* (pp. 267–316). New York: Brunner/Mazel, 1976.

Patterson, G. R. *Multivariate prediction/understanding of delinquency* (Grant No. MH 37940). Washington, DC: National Institute of Mental Health, 1979a.

Patterson, G. R. A performance theory for coercive family interaction. In R. B. Cairns (Ed.), *The analysis of social interactions: Methods, issues, and illustrations* (pp. 119–162). Hillsdale. NJ: Lawrence Erlbaum Associates, 1979b.

Patterson, G. R. Treatment for children with conduct

problems: A review of outcome studies. In S. Feshbach & A. Fraczek (Eds.), *Aggression and behavior change: Biological and social process* (pp. 83–132). New York: Praeger, 1979c.

Patterson, G. R. Mothers: The unacknowledged victims. *Monographs of the Society for Research in Child Development,* 1980, *45*(5, Serial No. 186), 1–64.

Patterson, G. R. *A social learning approach,* Vol. 3: *Coercive family process.* Eugene, OR: Castalia Publishing Company, 1982.

Patterson, G. R. Stress: A change agent for family process. In N. Garmezy & M. Rutter (Eds.), *Stress, coping, and development in children* (pp. 235–264). New York: McGraw-Hill, 1983.

Patterson, G. R. Siblings: Fellow travelers in coercive family processes. In R. J. Blanchard & D. C. Blanchard (Eds.), *Advances in the study of aggression* (Vol. 1, pp. 173–215). Orlando, FL: Academic Press, 1984.

Patterson, G. R. A microsocial analysis of anger and irritable behavior. In M. A. Chesney & R. H. Rosenman (Eds.), *Anger and hostility in cardiovascular and behavioral disorders* (pp. 83–100). New York: Hemisphere Publishing, 1985.

Patterson, G. R. Maternal rejection: Determinant or product for deviant child behavior? In W. W. Hartup & Z. Rubin (Eds.), *Relationships and development* (pp. 73–94). Hillsdale, NJ: Lawrence Erlbaum Associates, 1986a.

Patterson, G. R. Performance models for antisocial boys. *American Psychologist,* 1986b, *41,* 432–444.

Patterson, G. R. Family process: Loops, levels, and linkages. In N. Bolger, A. Caspi, G. Downey, & M. Moorehouse (Eds.), *Persons in context: Developmental processes* (pp. 114–151). New York: Cambridge University Press, 1988.

Patterson, G. R. *Developmental changes in antisocial behavior.* Paper presented at the 22nd annual Banff International Conference on Behavioural Sciences, Banff, Alberta, Canada, March 1990.

Patterson, G. R. *Parenting skills for what? Mediational models work better.* Paper presented at the annual meeting of the Society for Research in Child Development, Seattle, Washington, April 1991a.

Patterson, G. R. *Interaction of stress and family structure, and their relation to child adjustment: An example of across-site collaboration.* Paper presented at the annual meeting of the Society for Research in Child

Development, Seattle, Washington, April 1991b.

Patterson, G. R. Changes in a stable world: The chimera effect. Paper to be included in a special edition of the *Journal of Consulting and Clinical Psychology,* in preparation.

Patterson, G. R., & Bank, L. When is a nomological network a construct? In D. R. Peterson & D. B. Fishman (Eds.), *Assessment for decision* (pp. 249–279). New Brunswick, NJ: Rutgers University Press, 1987.

Patterson, G. R., & Bank, L. Some amplifying mechanisms for pathologic processes in families. In M. R. Gunnar & E. Thelen (Eds.), *Systems and development: The Minnesota Symposia on Child Psychology* (Vol. 22, pp. 167–209). Hillsdale, NJ: Lawrence Erlbaum Associates, 1989.

Patterson, G. R., Bank, L., & Stoolmiller, M. The preadolescent's contributions to disrupted family process. In R. Montemayor, G. R. Adams, & T. P. Gullotta (Eds.), *From childhood to adolescence: A transitional period?* (pp. 107–133). Newbury Park, CA: Sage, 1990.

Patterson, G. R., & Brodsky, G. A behaviour modification programme for a child with multiple problem behaviours. *Journal of Child Psychology and Psychiatry,* 1966, *7,* 277–295.

Patterson, G. R., & Capaldi, D. M. Antisocial parents: Unskilled and vulnerable. In P. A. Cowan & E. M. Hetherington (Eds.), *Advances in family research,* II: *Family transitions* (pp. 195–218). Hillsdale, NJ: Lawrence Erlbaum Associates, 1991a.

Patterson, G. R., & Capaldi, D. A mediational model for boys' depressed mood. In J. E. Rolf, A. Masten, D. Cicchetti, K. Neuchterlein, & S. Weintraub (Eds.), *Risk and protective factors in the development of psychopathology* (pp. 141–163). Boston, MA: Syndicate of the Press, University of Cambridge, 1991b.

Patterson, G. R., Capaldi, D., & Bank, L. An early starter model for predicting delinquency. In D. Pepler & K. H. Rubin (Eds.), *The development and treatment of childhood aggression* (pp. 139–168). Hillsdale, NJ: Lawrence Erlbaum Associates, 1990.

Patterson, G. R., & Chamberlain, P. Treatment process: A problem at three levels. In L. C. Wynne (Ed.), *The state of the art in family therapy research: Controversies and recommendations* (pp. 189–223). New York: Science Press, 1988.

Patterson, G. R., & Chamberlain, P. Some antecedents and functions for resistance during parent training: A

neobehavioral perspective. In H. Arkowitz (Ed.), *Why don't people change? New perspectives on resistance and noncompliance.* New York: Guilford Press, in press.

Patterson, G. R., Chamberlain, P., & Reid, J. B. A comparative evaluation of parent training procedures. *Behavior Therapy,* 1982, *13,* 638–650.

Patterson, G. R., Cobb, J. A., & Ray, R. S. Direct intervention in the classroom: A set of procedures for the aggressive child. In F. W. Clark, D. R. Evans, & L. A. Hamerlynck (Eds.), *Implementing behavioral programs for schools and clinics* (pp. 151–201). Champaign, IL: Research Press, 1972.

Patterson, G. R., Crosby, L., & Vuchinich S. *Predicting risk of early police arrest.* Manuscript submitted for publication, 1991.

Patterson, G. R., & Dawes, R. M. A Guttman scale of children's coercive behaviors. *Journal of Consulting and Clinical Psychology,* 1975, *43,* 594.

Patterson, G. R., DeBaryshe, B. D., & Ramsey, E. A developmental perspective on antisocial behavior. *American Psychologist,* 1989, *44,* 329–335.

Patterson, G. R., & Dishion, T. J. Contributions of families and peers to delinquency. *Criminology,* 1985, *23,* 63–79.

Patterson, G. R., & Dishion, T. J. Multilevel family process models: Traits, interactions, and relationships. In R. Hinde & J. Stevenson-Hinde (Eds.), *Relationships within families: Mutual influences* (pp. 283–310). Oxford: Clarendon Press, 1988.

Patterson, G. R., Dishion, T. J., & Bank, L. Family interaction: A process model of deviancy training. In L. Eron (Ed.), special edition of *Aggressive Behavior,* 1984, *10,* 253–267.

Patterson, G. R., Dishion T. J., & Chamberlain, P. *Evaluating treatment outcomes for antisocial boys.* Unpublished manuscript, 1991.

Patterson, G. R., & Duncan, T. *Toddler progressions to deviancy.* Unpublished Technical Report, 1991.

Patterson, G. R., & Forgatch, M. S. *Parents and adolescents living together,* Part 1: *The basics.* Eugene, OR: Castalia Publishing Company, 1987.

Patterson, G. R., & Forgatch, M. S. *Developmental growth models for maternal depression.* Paper presented at the fifth annual Family Consortium Institute, "Stress, coping, and resiliency in children and the family," Monterey, California, June 1990a.

Patterson, G. R., & Forgatch, M. S. Initiation and maintenance of processes disrupting single-mother families. In G. R. Patterson (Ed.), *Depression and aggression in family interaction* (pp. 209–245). Hillsdale, NJ: Lawrence Erlbaum Associates, 1990b.

Patterson, G. R., Forgatch, M. S., & Bank, L. *The relation of contextual variables to samples of divorced families*. Unpublished manuscript, 1990.

Patterson, G. R., & Reid, J. B. Reciprocity and coercion: Two facets of social systems. In C. Neuringer & J. L. Michael (Eds.), *Behavior modification in clinical psychology* (pp. 133–177). New York: Appleton-Century-Crofts, 1970.

Patterson, G. R., & Reid, J. B. Social interactional processes within the family: The study of moment-by-moment family transactions in which human social development is imbedded. *Journal of Applied Developmental Psychology*, 1984, *5*, 237–262.

Patterson, G. R., Shaw, D. A., & Ebner, M. J. Teachers, peers, and parents as agents of change in the classroom. In F. A. M. Benson (Ed.), *Modifying deviant social behaviors in various classroom settings* (Monograph No. 1, pp. 13–47). University of Oregon, Eugene, 1969.

Patterson, G. R., & Stoolmiller, M. *Replications of a dual failure model for boys' depressed mood*. Manuscript submitted for publication, 1990.

Patterson, G. R., & Stouthamer-Loeber, M. The correlation of family management practices and delinquency. *Child Development*, 1984, *55*, 1299–1307.

Patterson, G. R., & Yoerger, K. *The development of antisocial behavior*. Paper presented at the NATO Advanced Study Institute, "Crime and Mental Disorder," Ciocco, Italy, August 1991.

Paykel, E. S. Life stress and psychiatric disorder: Applications of the clinical approach. In B. S. Dohrenwend & B. P. Dohrenwend (Eds.), *Stressful life events: Their nature and effects* (pp. 135–149). New York: John Wiley & Sons, 1974.

Pedhazur, E. J. *Multiple regression in behavioral research: Explanation and prediction* (2nd ed.). New York: Holt, Reinhart & Winston, 1982.

Petrinovich, L. Probabilistic functionalism: A conception of research method. *American Psychologist*, 1979, *34*, 373–390.

Pollock, V., Mednick, S. A., & Gabrielli, W. F., Jr. Crime causation: Biological theories. In S. Kadish (Ed.), *En-cyclopedia of crime and delinquency* (pp. 308–316). New York: The Free Press, 1983.

The Psychological Corporation. (1955). *The WAIS vocabulary test*. New York: Author.

Puig-Antich, J. Major depression and conduct disorder in prepuberty. *Journal of the American Academy of Child Psychiatry*, 1982, *21*, 118–128.

Pulkkinen, L. Finland: Search for alternatives to aggression. In A. P. Goldstein & M. Segall (Eds.), *Aggression in global perspective* (pp. 104–144). New York: Pergamon Press, 1983.

Purkey, W. W. *Self-concept and school achievement*. Englewood Cliffs, NJ: Prentice-Hall, 1970.

Putallaz, M., & Gottman, J. An interactional model for children's entry into peer groups. *Child Development*, 1981, *52*, 986–994.

Quay, H. C. Personality and delinquency. In H. C. Quay (Ed.), *Juvenile delinquency: Research and theory*, (pp. 139–169). Princeton, NJ: Van Nostrand, 1965.

Quay, H. C. *Some speculations about different types of delinquents*. Seminar conducted at the Oregon Social Learning Center, July 1982.

Quay, H. C. *Electrodermal responding, inhibition, and reward-seeking in undersocialized, aggressive, conduct disordered children*. Paper presented at the annual meeting of the American Academy of Child and Adolescent Psychiatry, Chicago, Illinois, October 1990.

Radke Yarrow, M. Family environments of depressed and well parents and their children: Issues of research and methods. In G. R. Patterson (Ed.), *Depression and aggression in family interaction* (pp. 169–184). Hillsdale, NJ: Lawrence Erlbaum Associates, 1990.

Radke Yarrow, M., Richters, J., & Wilson, W. E. Child development in a network of relationships. In R. A. Hinde & J. Stevenson-Hinde (Eds.), *Relationships within families: Mutual influences* (pp. 48–67). Oxford: Clarendon Press, 1988.

Radloff, L. S. The CES-D scale: A self-report depression scale for research in the general population. *Applied Psychological Measurement*, 1977, *1*, 385–401.

Ramsey, E., Walker, H. M., & Patterson, G. R. Generalization of the antisocial trait from home to school settings. *Journal of Applied Developmental Psychology*, 1990, *11*, 209–223.

Raush, H. L. Interaction sequences. *Journal of Person-*

ality and Social Psychology, 1965, *2*, 487–499.

Reed, S. K. *Cognition: Theory and applications.* Monterey, CA: Brooks/Cole, 1982.

Reid, J. B. (Ed.). *A social learning approach*, Vol. 2: *Observation in home settings.* Eugene, OR: Castalia Publishing Company, 1978.

Reid, J. B. Observer training in naturalistic research. In D. P. Hartmann (Ed.), *New directions for methodology of social and behavioral science*, No. 14: *Using observers to study behavior* (pp. 37–50). San Francisco, CA: Jossey-Bass, 1982.

Reid, J. B. Social-interactional patterns in families of abused and nonabused children. In C. Zahn-Waxler, E. M. Cummings, & R. Iannotti (Eds.), *Altruism and aggression: Biological and social origins* (pp. 238–255). New York: Cambridge University Press, 1986.

Reid, J. B., Bank, L., Patterson, G. R., & Skinner, M. L. *The generalizability of single versus multiple methods in structural equation models of child development.* Paper presented at the annual meeting of the Society for Research in Child Development, Baltimore, Maryland, April 1987.

Reid, J. B., & Hendriks, A. F. C. J. Preliminary analysis of the effectiveness of direct home intervention for the treatment of pre-delinquent boys who steal. In L. A. Hamerlynck, L. C. Handy, & E. J. Mash (Eds.), *Behavior change: Methodology, concepts, and practice* (pp. 209–220). Champaign, IL: Research Press, 1973.

Reid, J. B., Kavanagh, K., & Baldwin, D. V. Abusive parents' perceptions of child problem behaviors: An example of parental bias. *Journal of Abnormal Child Psychology*, 1987, *15*, 457–466.

Reid, J. B., Patterson, G. R., & Loeber, R. The abused child: Victim, instigator, or innocent bystander? In D. Bernstein (Ed.), *Response structure and organization* (pp. 47–68). Lincoln, NE: University of Nebraska Press, 1982.

Reid, J. B., Taplin, P. S., & Lorber, R. A social interactional approach to the treatment of abusive families. In R. B. Stuart (Ed.), *Violent behavior: Social learning approaches to prediction, management, and treatment* (pp. 83–101). New York: Brunner/Mazel, 1981.

Reynolds, W., Anderson, G., & Bartel, N. Measuring depression in children: A multimethod assessment investigation. *Journal of Abnormal Child Psychology*, 1985, *13*, 513–526.

Reynolds, W. M., & Coats, K. *Depression in adolescents:* *Incidence, depth, and correlates.* Paper presented at the 10th Congress of the International Association for Child and Adolescent Psychiatry, Dublin, Ireland, July 1982.

Rickard, K.M., Forehand, R., Atkeson, B.M., & Lopez, C. An examination of the effects of marital satisfaction and divorce on parent–child interactions. *Journal of Clinical and Child Psychology*, 1982, *11*, 61–65.

Roberts, G. C., Block, J., & Block, J. A. Continuity and change in parents' childrearing practices. *Child Development*, 1984, *55*, 586–597.

Robins, L. N. *Deviant children grown up: A sociological and psychiatric study of sociopathic personality.* Baltimore, MD: Williams & Wilkins, 1966.

Robins, L. N. Antisocial behavior disturbances of childhood: Prevalence, prognosis, and prospects. In E. J. Anthony & C. Koupernik (Eds.), *The child in his family*, Vol. 3: *Children at psychiatric risk* (pp. 447–460). New York: John Wiley & Sons, 1974.

Robins, L. N. *What effect did Viet Nam have on veterans' mental health?* Unpublished manuscript, 1981.

Robins, L. N. *Conduct disorder in adult psychiatric diagnosis.* Unpublished manuscript, 1984.

Robins, L. N., & Earls, F. A program for preventing antisocial behavior for high risk infants and preschoolers: A research perspective. In R. Hough, V. Brown, P. Gongola, & S. Goldston (Eds.), *Psychiatric epidemiology and prevention: The possibilities* (pp. 73–83). Los Angeles, CA: Neuropsychiatric Institute, 1986.

Robins, L. N., & Ratcliff, K. S. Risk factors in the continuation of childhood antisocial behaviors into adulthood. *International Journal of Mental Health*, 1978–1979, *7*(3–4), 96–116.

Robins, L. N., West, P. A., & Herjanic, B. L. Arrests and delinquency in two generations: A study of black urban families and their children. *Journal of Child Psychology and Psychiatry*, 1975, *16*, 125–140.

Robins, L. N., & Wish, E. Childhood deviance as a developmental process: A study of 223 urban black men from birth to 18. *Social Forces*, 1977, *56*, 448–473.

Robinson, B. E. *Sex-typed attitudes, sex-typed contingency behaviors, and personality characteristics of male caregivers.* Unpublished doctoral dissertation, University of North Carolina at Greensborough, 1976.

Robinson, J. P. Toward a more appropriate use of Guttman scaling. *Public Opinion Quarterly,* 1973, *37,* 260–267.

Rodnick, E. H., & Garmezy, N. An experimental approach to the study of motivation in schizophrenia. In M. R. Jones (Ed.), *Nebraska Symposium on Motivation* (p. 109). Lincoln, NE: University of Nebraska Press, 1957.

Roff, M. Childhood social interactions and young adult bad conduct. *Journal of Abnormal and Social Psychology,* 1961, *63,* 333–337.

Roff, M. A two-factor approach to juvenile delinquency and the later histories of juvenile delinquency. In M. Roff, L. N. Robins, & M. Pollack (Eds.), *Life history research in psychopathology* (Vol. 2, pp. 77–101). Minneapolis, MN: University of Minnesota Press, 1972.

Rogers, M. P., Dubey, D., & Reich, P. The influence of the psyche and the brain on immunity and disease susceptibility: A critical review. *Psychosomatic Medicine,* 1979, *41,* 147–164.

Rosenfeld, H. M., & Baer, D. M. Unnoticed verbal conditioning of an aware experimenter by a more aware subject: The double agent effect. *Psychological Review,* 1969, *76,* 425–432.

Rosenfeld, H. M., & Gunnell, P. K. Pragmatics vs. reinforcers: An experimental analysis of verbal accommodation. In M. Giles & R. St. Clair (Eds.), *Recent advances in language communication and social psychology* (pp. 109–143). London: Lawrence Erlbaum Associates, 1985.

Rowe, D. C., & Plomin, R. The importance of nonshared environmental (E_1) influences on behavioral development. *Developmental Psychology,* 1981, *17,* 517–531.

Rubin, R. A., Maruyama, G., & Kingsbury, G. G. *Self-esteem and education achievement: A causal model analysis.* Paper presented at the American Psychological Association convention, New York, September 1979.

Rutter, M. Protective factors in children's responses to stress and disadvantage. In M. Kent and J. E. Roff (Eds.), *Primary prevention of psychopathology,* Vol. 3: *Social competence in children.* Hanover, NH: University Press of New England, 1979.

Rutter, M. *Changing youth in a changing society.* Cambridge, MA: Harvard University Press, 1980.

Rutter, M. Stress, coping, and development: Some issues and some questions. In N. Garmezy & M. Rutter (Eds.), *Stress, coping, and development in children* (pp. 1–41). New York: McGraw-Hill, 1983.

Rutter, M., & Giller, H. *Juvenile delinquency: Trends and perspectives.* Middlesex, England: Penguin, 1983.

Rutter, M., Izard, C. E., & Read, P. B. (Eds.) *Depression in young people: Developmental and clinical perspectives.* New York: Guilford Press, 1986.

Rutter, M., Maugham, B., Mortimore, P., Ouston, J., & Smith, A. *Fifteen thousand hours.* Cambridge, MA: Harvard University Press, 1979.

Rutter, M., Tizard, J., & Whitmore, K. *Education, health, and behavior.* London: Longmans, 1970.

Sameroff, A. J. Development and the dialectic: The need for a systems approach. In W. A. Collins (Ed.), *Minnesota Symposium on Child Psychology* (Vol. 15, pp. 83–103). Hillsdale, NJ: Lawrence Erlbaum Associates, 1981.

Sameroff, A. J., Seifer, R., & Elias, P. Sociocultural variability in infant temperament ratings. *Child Development,* 1982, *53,* 164–173.

Sampson, R. J. Urban black violence: The effect of male joblessness and family disruption. *American Journal of Sociology,* 1987, *93,* 348–382.

Sanson-Fisher, B., & Jenkins, H. Interaction patterns between inmates and staff in a maximum-security institution for delinquents. *Behavior Therapy,* 1978, *9,* 703–716.

Sarason, I. G., Johnson, J. H., & Siegel, J. M. Assessing the impact of life changes: Development of the life experience survey. *Journal of Consulting and Clinical Psychology,* 1978, *46,* 932–946.

Sas, L., & Jaffe, P. Understanding depression in juvenile delinquency: Implications for institutional admission policies and treatment programs. *Juvenile and Family Court Journal,* 1986, *37*(1), 49–58.

Scarr, S. Constructing psychology: Making facts and fables for our times. *American Psychologist,* 1985a, *40,* 499–512.

Scarr, S. *Personality and experience: Individual encounters with the world.* Paper presented at the Henry A. Murray Lectures in Personality, Michigan State University, East Lansing, April 1985b.

Schaefer, E. S. Children's reports of parental behavior: An inventory. *Child Development,* 1965, *36,* 413–424.

Schaefer, E. S., & Hunter, W. M. *Mother-infant interac-*

tion and maternal psychosocial predictors of kindergarten adaptation. Paper presented at the biennial meeting of the Society for Research in Child Development, Detroit, Michigan, April 1983.

Schmaling, K. B., & Patterson, G. R. *Maternal classification of deviant and prosocial child behavior and reactions to the child in the home*. Paper presented at the annual convention of the Association for the Advancement of Behavior Therapy, Philadelphia, Pennsylvania, November 1984.

Schmauk, F. J. Punishment, arousal, and avoidance learning in sociopaths. *Journal of Abnormal Psychology,* 1970, *76,* 325–335.

Schuck, G. R. The use of causal nonexperimental models in aggression research. In J. DeWit & W. W. Hartup (Eds.), *Determinants and origins of aggressive behavior* (pp. 381–389). The Hague, Netherlands: Mouton, 1974.

Schulsinger, F. Psychopathy: Heredity and environment. In S. A. Mednick & K. O. Christiansen (Eds.), *Biosocial bases of criminal behavior* (pp. 109–125). New York: Gardner Press, 1977.

Schur, E. M. *Radical nonintervention: Rethinking the delinquency problem*. Englewood Cliffs, NJ: Prentice-Hall, 1973.

Sears, R. R., Maccoby, E. E., & Levin, H. *Patterns of childrearing*. Evanston, IL: Row & Peterson, 1957.

Selye, H. *The stress of life*. New York: McGraw-Hill, 1956.

Shinn, M. R., Ramsey, E., Walker, H. M., Stieber, H., & O'Neill, R. E. Antisocial behavior in school settings: Initial differences in an at-risk and normal population. *Journal of Special Education,* 1987, *21*(2), 69–84.

Siddle, D. A. T. Electrodermal activity and psychopathy. In S. A. Mednick & K. O. Christiansen (Eds.), *Biosocial bases of criminal behavior* (pp. 199–211). New York: Gardner Press, 1977.

Sigel, I. E. The relationship between parental distancing strategies and the child's cognitive behavior. In L. M. Laosa & I. E. Sigel (Eds.), *Families as learning environments for children* (pp. 47–86). New York: Plenum, 1982.

Sigel, I. E., McGillicuddy-DeLisi, A. V., & Johnson, J. E. *Parental distancing beliefs and children's representational competence within the family context* (Research Report). Princeton, NJ: Educational Testing Service, 1980.

Skinner, B. F. *Contingencies of reinforcement: A theoretical analysis*. New York: Appleton-Century-Crofts, 1969.

Slovic, P., Fischhoff, B., & Lichtenstein, S. Behavioral decision theory. *Annual Review of Psychology,* 1977, *28,* 1–39.

Snyder, J. J. Reinforcement analysis of interaction in problem and nonproblem families. *Journal of Abnormal Psychology,* 1977, *86,* 528–535.

Snyder, J. J. *The effect of settings on behavior*. Seminar conducted at Oregon Social Learning Center, Eugene, OR, April 1987a.

Snyder, J. J. *Learning and family interaction*. Paper presented at the second annual Summer Institute of the Family Research Consortium, Santa Fe, New Mexico, June 1987b.

Snyder, J. J. Discipline as a mediator of the impact of maternal stress and mood on child conduct problems. *Development and Psychopathology,* 1991, *3,* 263–276.

Snyder, J. J., & Huntley, D. Troubled families and troubled youth: The development of antisocial behavior and depression in children. In P. E. Leone (Ed.), *Understanding troubled and troubling youth* (pp. 194–225). Newbury Park, CA: Sage, 1990.

Snyder, J. J., Dishion, T. J., & Patterson, G. R. Determinants and consequences of associating with deviant peers during preadolescence and adolescence. *Journal of Early Adolescence,* 1986, *6,* 29–43.

Snyder, J. J., & Patterson, G. R. The effects of consequences on patterns of social interaction: A quasi-experimental approach to reinforcement in natural interaction. *Child Development,* 1986, *57,* 1257–1268.

Stoolmiller, M., & Bank, L. *Autoregressive effects in structural equation models: We see some problems*. Eugene, OR: Oregon Social Learning Center, in preparation.

Stouthamer-Loeber, M., & Loeber, R. *Respondent recruitment and respondent loss*. Unpublished manuscript, Oregon Social Learning Center, Eugene, 1982.

Straus, M. A. Wife beating: How common and why? *Victimology,* 1978, *2*(3–4), 443–458.

Sullivan, J. L. Multiple indicators: Some criteria of selection. In H. M. Blalock (Ed.), *Measurement in the social sciences* (pp. 93–156). New York: Aldine de Gruyter, 1974.

Sutherland, E. H. *Principles of criminology* (4th ed.). Philadelphia, PA: J. B. Lippincott, 1947.

Taplin, P. S., & Reid, J. B. Changes in parental consequation as a function of family intervention. *Journal of Consulting and Clinical Psychology*, 1977, *4*, 973–981.

Thomas, A., Chess, J., & Birch, H. G. *Temperament and behavior disorders in children*. New York: New York University Press, 1968.

Toobert, D. J., Patterson, G. R., Moore, D., & Halper, V. *MOSAIC: Measurement of social adjustment in children* (Training Manual). Eugene, OR: Oregon Social Learning Center, 1980.

Turnbull, C. M. (1972). *The mountain people*. New York: Simon & Schuster, 1972.

Tversky, A., & Kahneman, D. Judgment under uncertainty: Heuristics and biases. *Science*, 1974, *185*, 1124–1131.

United States Department of Commerce, Bureau of the Census. *1980 Census of population*, Vol. 1: *Characteristics of the population*. Chapter C: *General social and economic characteristics*. Part 39: *Oregon* (Report No. PC80–1–C39). Washington, DC: United States Government Printing Office, 1983.

Vaughan, C. E., & Leff, J. P. The influence of family and social factors on the course of psychiatric illness: A comparison of schizophrenic and depressed neurotic outpatients. *British Journal of Psychiatry*, 1981, *129*, 125–137.

Vuchinich, S., Bank, L., & Patterson, G. R. The stability and maintenance of antisocial behavior in preadolescent males. *Developmental Psychology* 1991 (in preparation).

Wadsworth, M. E. J. *Roots of delinquency: Infancy, adolescence, and crime*. Oxford: Robertson, 1979.

Wahler, R. G., & Dumas, J. E. *Stimulus class determinants of mother-child coercive exchanges in multi-distressed families: Assessment and intervention*. Paper presented at the Vermont Conference on Primary Prevention of Psychopathology, Bolton Valley Winter/Summer Resort, Vermont, June 1983.

Wahler, R. G., Leske, G., & Rogers, E. S. *The insular family: A deviance support system for oppositional children*. Paper presented at the Banff International Conference on Behavior Modification, Alberta, Canada, March 1977.

Waksman, S. An application of a multitrait-multimethod test to validity data of a social learning treatment for aggressive children. *Journal of Abnormal Child Psychology*, 1978, *6*, 1–10.

Walker, H. M., Shinn, M. R., O'Neill, R. E., & Ramsey, E. A longitudinal assessment of the development of antisocial behavior in boys: Rationale, methodology, and first-year results. *Remedial and Special Education*, 1987, *8*(4), 7–16.

Watson, D., & Clark, L. A. Negative affectivity: The disposition to experience aversive emotional states. *Psychological Bulletin*, 1984, *96*, 465–490.

Watson, D., & Tellegen, A. Toward a consensual structure of mood. *Psychological Bulletin*, 1985, *98*, 219–235.

Watson, J. S. Perception of contingency as a determinant of social responsiveness. In E. B. Thoman (Ed.), *Origins of the infant's social responsiveness* (pp. 33–64). Hillsdale, NJ: Lawrence Erlbaum Associates, 1979.

Weinberg, W., & Rehmet, A. Childhood affective disorder and school problems. In D. P. Cantwell & G. A. Carlson (Eds.), *Affective disorders in childhood and adolescence: An update* (pp. 109–128). Lancaster, England: MTP Press Ltd, 1983.

Welsh, R. S. Severe parental punishment and delinquency: A developmental theory. *Journal of Clinical Child Psychology*, 1976, *5*, 17–21.

West, D. J. *Present conduct and future delinquency*. London: Heinemann, 1969.

West, D. J., & Farrington, D. P. *Who becomes delinquent?* New York: Crane, Russak & Co., 1973.

West, D. J., & Farrington, D. P. *The delinquent way of life*. New York: Crane, Russak & Co., 1977.

White, B. L. & Carew-Watts, J. *Experience and environment: Major influences on the development of the young child*. Englewood Cliffs, NJ: Prentice-Hall, 1973.

Whiting, B. B., & Edwards, C. P. *Children of different worlds: The formation of social behavior*. Cambridge, MA: Harvard University Press, 1988.

Whiting, B. B., & Whiting, J. M. *Children of six cultures: A psycho-cultural analysis*. Cambridge, MA: Harvard University Press, 1975.

Wiggins, J. S. (Ed.) *Personality and prediction: Principles of personality assessment*. Reading, MA: Addison-Wesley, 1973.

Wilson, H. Parental supervision: A neglected aspect of delinquency. *British Journal of Criminology,* 1980a, *20,* 203–235.

Wilson, H. Parenting and poverty. *British Journal of Social Work,* 1980b, *4,* 241–254.

Wilson, J. Q., & Herrnstein, R. J. *Crime and human nature.* New York: Simon & Schuster, 1985.

Wilson, T. D., & Nisbett, R. E. The accuracy of verbal reports about the effects of stimuli on evaluations and behavior. *Social Psychology,* 1978, *41,* 118–131.

Wolfgang, M. E., & Ferracuti, F. *The subculture of violence.* London: Tavistock, 1967.

Wolfgang, M. E., Figlio, R., & Sellin, T. *Delinquency in a birth cohort.* Chicago, IL: University of Chicago Press, 1972.

Wolking, W. D., Dunteman, G. H., & Bailey, J. P. Multivariate analyses of parents' MMPIs based on psychiatric diagnosis of their children. *Journal of Consulting Psychology,* 1967, *31,* 521–524.

Wright, J. C. *The structure and perception of behavioral consistency.* Unpublished doctoral dissertation, Stanford University, 1983.

Yarrow, M., Campbell, J. D., & Burton, R. V. *Childrearing: An inquiry into research and methods.* San Francisco, CA: Jossey-Bass, 1968.

Youniss, J. *Parents and peers in social development: A Sullivan-Piaget perspective.* Chicago, IL: University of Chicago Press, 1980.

Zaidi, L. Y., Knutson, J. F., & Mehm, J. G. *Transgenerational patterns of abusive parenting: Analogue and clinical tests.* Unpublished manuscript, 1988.

Zucker, R. A. Parental influences on the drinking patterns of their children. In M. Greenblatt & M. A. Schuckit (Eds.), *Alcoholism problems in women and children* (pp. 211–238). New York: Grune & Stratton, 1976.

Zucker, R. A. The four alcoholisms: A developmental account of the etiologic process. In P.C. Rivers (Ed.), *Nebraska symposium on motivation,* Vol. 34: *Alcohol and addictive behaviors* (pp.27–83). Lincoln, NE: University of Nebraska Press, 1987.

Author Index

Jones, R. R., 26, 150
Jöreskog, K. G., 19
Joy, C. B., 96

K

Kahneman, D., 57
Kandel, D. B., 132, 134
Kanfer, F. H., 57
Kaplan, H. B., 121
Kashani, J. H., 134
Kavanagh, K., 67, 73
Kazdin, A. E., 53, 133, 134
Kellam, S. G., 16, 105, 135
Kenny, D. A., 124
Kingsbury, G. G., 124
Knorr, E. L., 127
Knowles, B. A., 15, 33, 105, 144
Knutson, J. F., 103
Kohli, G., 49
Kohn, M. L., 95
Koller, K. M., 34
Korner, A. F., 35
Kraemer, H. C., 35
Kreutzer, S. L., 26
Kropp, J. P., 96
Kupersmidt, J. B., 9, 131

L

Lagerspetz, K., 144
Lahey, B. B., 96, 112
Lane Council of Governments, 144
Langer, E. J., 57
Langner, T. S., 83, 97
Larzelere, R. E., 111
Lathrop, M., 66, 78, 149
Laub, J. H., 110
Lazarus, R. S., 97
Lee, C. L., 35
Leff, J. P., 55
Lefkowitz, M. M., 14, 25, 66, 103
Leiderman, P. H., 128
Leipciger, M., 34, 136
Leske, G., 103
Levenson, R. W., 46
Levin, H., xiii, 7, 66
Lewinsohn, P. M., 133, 134
Lichtenstein, S., 57
Lifton, R. J., 125
Liker, J. K., 103
Linden, J., 35
Ling, R. G., 9
Lingerfelt, B., 35
Littman, D. C., 65
Lobitz, G. K., 19, 100
Locke, H. J., 100

Loeber, R., 9, 11, 14, 23, 25, 26, 27, 31, 32, 45, 67, 120, 132, 136, 144, 148
Loney, J., 121
Long, N., 134, 140
Lopez, C., 100
Lorber, R., 10, 45, 65, 66
Lubin, B., 108
Lykken, D. J., 35, 36
Lytton, H., 35

M

McBurnett, K., 112
McCarty, J. A., 96
McClaskey, C. L., 58
Maccoby, E. E., xiii, 7, 66, 75, 77
McComb, A., 133
McCord, J., 63, 66, 102, 120
McCord, W., 66
McCubbin, H. I., 96
McDevitt, T. M., 127
McGillicuddy-DeLisi, A. V., 129
Madden, P., 34, 136
Magnusson, D., 14
Mandelzys, N., 34, 136
Mannheim, H., 34, 136
Margolin, G., 49, 80
Martin, J. A., 23, 77
Maruyama, G., 124
Masuda, M., 95
Maugham, B., 127
Mednick, S. A., 35, 36, 104
Meehl, P., 9
Mehm, J. G., 103
Miller, C. L., 58
Miller, N. E., 52
Mintz, J., 55
Mischel, W., 26
Mitchell, S., 27
Monachesi, E. D., 106
Monroe, S. M., 97
Moore, D., 150
Moos, R. H., 134
Morley, L., 24, 34, 136
Mortimore, P., 127
Mowrer, O. H., 52

N

Needle, R. H., 96
Nisbett, R. E., 57, 58, 67
North, J. A., 26

O

O'Leary, K. D., 99
Oltmanns, T., 99
Olweus, D., 23, 66, 67, 99

177

Subject Index

179

182

and avoidant parents, 109–110
and coercion model, 132
and family management skills, 132
modes of, *122*
and peer rejection, 131–133
and Planning Study, 100
reinforcement of, 132
  See also Antisocial behavior.
Deviant peer hypothesis, 132
Deviant peers, 11, 12–13, 63, 131–133
Deviant Peers construct, 133, 136
  See also Antisocial Attitudes construct; Hostile–
  Unskilled construct; Parental Monitoring construct; Peer Rejection construct.
Diagnostic and Statistical Manual III-R (DSM-III-R), 6,
  134
  categories in, 6
Differential-reinforcement hypothesis, 80
  See also Reinforcement; Reinforcement contingencies; Reinforcement theory; Selective-
  reinforcement hypothesis.
Direct transmission hypothesis of antisocial behavior,
  102
Discipline, 25, 65–66, 69, 102–103, *103*, 105–108
  defined, 65
  and mediational hypothesis of antisocial behavior,
    102–103, *103*
  techniques of, 105–108
    See also Discipline construct; Parental discipline;
    Parental Discipline construct.
Discipline construct, 17, 26, 51, 61, 62, 63, 67–68, 69,
  71–72, 79, 85, *85*, 86, 87, *88*, 89, *89*, 90, 99, 103,
  103, 104, 108, *122*, 125, 128, 129, *129*, 131, 137
  and Academic Achievement construct, 128, *129*
  and action–reaction patterns, 17
  and antisocial trait, 104
  and Child Antisocial construct, 62, 71–72, *103*,
    103–104, *122, 129*
  and child behaviors, *88*
  and Child Conduct Disorder construct, 108
  and Child Self-Esteem construct, *122*
  and Coercive Child construct, 61
  and confirmatory factor analysis, 85–86
  and continuance, 67–68
  and convergent validity, 67–68
  generalizability of, 68, 69
  and Maternal Antisocial construct, 108
  measurement of, 67–68
  and mediational hypothesis of antisocial behavior, 103,
    103, 104
  and Parental Antisocial construct, 103, *103*, 104
  and Parental Monitoring construct, 85, 86–87, *122*
  and Peer Rejection construct, 131
  and Planning Study, 67
  sampling indicators for, 68

and stress risk score, 99
  validity of, 86–87
    See also Discipline; Parental discipline; Parental
    Discipline construct.
Discriminant validity, 31
Disobedience, 33
Double-agent studies, 58
DSM-III-R. *See Diagnostic and Statistical Manual III-R.*
Dual failure model, 135–136
Dyadic dances, *119*, 120
Dyadic problem solving, 77–78, *78*
Dyadic Problem Solving construct. *See* Problem Solving
  construct.
Dysphoric mood, 90, 131

E

Early onset hypothesis, 34, 36, 136–137
  and delinquency, 136–137
Early starters, 117, 136–137
Ecological matrix, 93
Escalation, 11
Escalation hypothesis, 44
Escape–avoidance learning, 29
Escape conditioning, 21, 39, 40, 41, *41*, 42, 48, 54, 55
  and aversive behavior, 40
  and depression, 55
  mechanisms for, 54
  paradigm for, 39
  and positive reinforcement, 42
  sequence for, 41, *41*, 42
  and social exchanges, 40
  and social interaction, 40
Escape contingencies, 39, 48, 56
  and schizophrenic adults, 56
Explosive discipline, 68

F

Factor loading, 17
Family Interaction Coding System (FICS), 44, 150
  and aversive exchanges, 44
Family interaction, 2, 4, 47–48, 58, 93
  and context, 2, 4
  and ecological matrix, 93
  and punishment contingencies, 47, 58
  and reinforcement contingencies, 48, 58
  and sequences for, 58
Family management constructs, 84–89, 85, *85, 91, 106,*
  110
  and child adjustment constructs, *91*
  intercorrelations among, 85, *85*
  and parental traits, *106, 110*
    See also Discipline ; Discipline construct; Family
    management practices; Family management
    skills; Family management variables; Parental In-
    volvement construct; Parental Monitoring con-

and self-esteem, 121–122
and stress, 97
and stage model, 117–118
OSLC. *See* Oregon Social Learning Center.
Overlearned behavior, 56, 57, 58–59
and automatic processing, 57
concept of, 56
Overt antisocial behavior, *28,* 31, 32, *32, 33,* 33, 34
and Child Antisocial construct, *28*
extreme forms of, 33
frequency of, 34
measurement of, 31–32
See also Antisocial behavior; Clandestine antisocial behavior; Clandestine Antisocial construct; Overt Antisocial construct.
Overt Antisocial construct, 32
See also Antisocial behavior; Clandestine Antisocial construct.
OYS. *See* Oregon Youth Study.

P

Parental Antisocial construct, 42, 103, *103,* 104, 106–107, *107,* 108, 114
and Child Antisocial construct, 103, *103,* 104, 107
and Discipline construct, 103, *103,* 104
See also Maternal Antisocial construct; Parental antisocial traits.
Parental antisocial traits, 111–112
Parental characteristics and family problem solving, 79
Parental depression, 108, 134
and child adjustment problems, 108, 134
and parenting practices, 108
See also Child Depressed Mood construct; Child depression; Depression; Depression construct; Maternal depression; Maternal Depression construct; Parental Depression construct.
Parental Depression construct, *107,* 108
and principal components factor analysis, 108
See also Child Depressed Mood construct; Depression construct; Maternal Depression construct.
Parental discipline, 12, 66–67, 73, 89, 116, 118, 128
and academic achievement, 128
and antisocial children, 12
and child adjustment, 89
See also Discipline; Discipline construct; Parental Discipline construct; Parental Involvement construct; Parental monitoring; Parental Monitoring construct.
Parental Discipline construct, 118
and Child Antisocial construct, 118
and Parental Monitoring construct, 118
See also Discipline construct; Parental Involve-

ment construct; Parental Monitoring construct.
Parental Involvement construct, 83–84, *84,* 85, *85,* 86, 87, *87,* 88, *88, 89,* 90, 123, *124,* 131
and Child Antisocial construct, 83
and child behaviors, *88*
and Child Self-Esteem construct, *124*
and confirmatory factor analysis, 86
indicators for, *84*
measurement of, 83
and Peer Rejection construct, 131
and Planning Study, 84, 87–88
and Positive Reinforcement construct, 85, *124*
and Problem Solving construct, 85, *124*
robustness of, *84*
and self-esteem, 83
validity of, 84
See also Discipline construct; Parental Discipline construct; Parental Monitoring construct.
Parental monitoring, 62–63, 64, 69–73, 118, 132–133
and substance abuse, 132–133
See also Discipline; Discipline construct; Parental discipline; Parental Discipline construct; Parental Involvement construct; Parental Monitoring construct.
Parental Monitoring construct, 26, 62, 63, 64–65, *65,* 69, 85, *85,* 86–87, *88, 89, 89,* 90, 108, 118, 122, *122,* 133, 137
and Child Antisocial construct, 63, 118, *122*
and child behaviors, *88*
and Child Conduct Disorder construct, 108
and Child Self-Esteem construct, 122, *122*
and confirmatory factor analysis, 85–86
and Deviant Peers construct, 133
and Discipline construct, 85, 86–87, *122*
generalizability of, *65*
and Maternal Antisocial construct, 108
and Maternal Depression construct, 108
measurement of, 64–65
and Parental Discipline construct, 118
and Planning Study, 64
and principal components factor analysis, 64
validity of, 86–87
See also Parental Involvement construct; Parental Monitoring construct.
Parental pathology, *101,* 105–106
and child adjustment problems, *101,* 105–106
and covariations with family transitions, *101*
Parental rejection, 12, 80, 120–121
and coercive exchanges, 121
and composite scores, 120–121
and reinforcement, 80
Parental Rejection construct, 121
Parental schema and child behaviors, 80–81

Parental substance abuse, 108
  See also Substance abuse; Substance Abuse construct.
Parental traits, 105–106, *106, 110*
  and child adjustment constructs, *106*
  and family management constructs, *106, 110*
  and family management practices, 105–106
  See also Family management skills.
Parental violence and antisocial behavior, 10
Parent–child interactions, 3, 4
Parent–Child Relationship construct, 125
Parent Daily Report (PDR), 29
Parenting constructs, 77, *85, 87*
Parenting practices, 51, 61, 62, 71, 77–78, 94, *94*, 95, *102*, 105, 107–108, 110–111, *111, 113*, 122
  and child adjustment, 94, 105
  and coercive behavior, 62
  and context, *94, 113*
  and contextual variables, 94–95, 110–111
  and covariation with transitions, *102*
  and mediational hypothesis of antisocial behavior, 107–108
  and Oregon Youth Study, 105
  and parental depression, 108
  and poverty and unemployment, 111
  and reinforcement contingencies, 51
  and self-esteem, 122
  and social disadvantage, *111*
  See also Family management practices; Family management skills; Parenting skills.
Parenting skills, 27, 93, 112
  See also Discipline construct; Family management practices; Family management skills; Parental Involvement construct; Parental Monitoring construct; Parenting practices; Positive Reinforcement construct; Problem Solving construct.
Parent interviews, 16
Parent training model, 53, 54, 61–62, *62*, 68–70, *70*, 71, *71*, 72
  and Coercive Child construct, 62
  and Oregon Youth Study, 62
PDR. See Parent Daily Report.
Peer group, 3, 4, 9, 21, 77, 131
  and child adjustment, 3, 4
  and reinforcement, 131
  and substance abuse, 9
  and social interactional theory, 131
  See also Peer rejection; Peer Rejection construct; Peer Relations construct.
Peer rejection, 9, 130–135
  and bidirectional effects, 131
  and coercion process, 131
  and depression, 133–135
  determinants of, 130–131
  and deviant behavior, 131–133

and Discipline construct, 131
and dysphoric mood, 131
skill-deficit hypothesis of, 131
and social interactional theory, 132–133
and substance abuse, 132–133
  See also Peer group; Peer Rejection construct; Peer Relations construct.
Peer Rejection construct, 125, 131, 133
  and Child Antisocial construct, 131
  and Parental Involvement construct, 131
  and structural equation modeling, 131
  See also Peer Relations construct.
Peer Relations construct, 123, 125, 131, *135*
  and Child Depressed Mood construct, *135*
  See also Peer Rejection construct.
Performance theory, 6
Permissive parenting, 67
Philadelphia Cohort Studies of antisocial behavior, 15
Physical abuse, 66
Physical aggression, 47, 50, *51*
  and negative affect, 47
  and transitivity hypothesis, 50
Physical punishment and delinquent behavior, 9
Planning Study, 8, 9, 27, 29, 31, 32, *32*, 33, 63, 64, 67, 78, 79, 81, 84, 87–88, 90, 97, 100, 120–121, 131, 132–133, 144, 147–148, 149–150
  assessment battery for, 149–150
  demographic characteristics of, 147–148
  and deviant behavior, 100
  and Discipline construct, 67
  and family problem solving, 78, 79
  history of, 144
  and marital adjustment, 100
  and measures of antisocial behavior, *32*
  and National Institutes of Mental Health, 8
  and Parental Involvement construct, 84, 87–88
  and Parental Monitoring construct, 64
  and Positive Reinforcement construct, 81
  and stress, 97
  and substance abuse, 132–133
Positive parenting, 87, *87*, 88, 89–90, 92
  multivariate studies of, 89–90
Positive parenting constructs, 87
  See also Parental Involvement construct; Positive Reinforcement construct; Problem Solving construct.
Positive reinforcement, 39, 42, 53, 132
  and avoidance conditioning, 42
  and clandestine antisocial behavior, 39
  and escape conditioning, 42
  and microsocial theory of antisocial behavior, 53
  and Snyder technique, 53
  See also Positive Reinforcement construct.
Positive Reinforcement construct, 79–82, *82*, 83, *83*, 85, *85*, 86, 87, *88, 89*, 123, *124*

and Academic Achievement construct, 83
and Child Antisocial construct, 80
and child behaviors, *88*
and Child Self-Esteem construct, *124*
and confirmatory factor analysis, 86
measurement of, 81–82
and Parental Involvement construct, 85, *124*
and Planning Study, 81
and Problem Solving construct, 85, *124*
robustness of, *83*
sampling indicators for, 81–82, *82*
and Social Competence construct, 81
validity of, 82–83
    See also Positive reinforcement.
Preschool behavior, 61–62, 117
Principal components factor analysis, 7, 17, 18–19, 64, 68, 78, 97, 100, 108–109
and construct building, 17
and Marital Adjustment construct, 100
and Parental Depression construct, 108
and Parental Monitoring construct, 64
and Problem Solving construct, 78
and Stress construct, 97
and Substance Abuse construct, 108–109
Problem solving, 77–78
and maternal irritability, 77–78
and negative affect, 77
Problem Solving construct (*also called* Dyadic Problem Solving construct, 77–78, 79, *79, 85, 85, 88, 88, 89,* 123, *124*
and child behaviors, *88*
and Child Self-Esteem construct, *124*
and Parental Involvement construct, *124*
and Positive Reinforcement construct, *124*
and principal components factor analysis, 78
validity of, 79
Progression hypothesis, 30, *30*
    See also Transitivity hypothesis.
Prosocial behavior, 75–79
and self-esteem, 121
    See also Positive Reinforcement construct; Parental Involvement construct.
Punishment and microsocial theory of antisocial behavior, 53
Punishment contingencies, 47, 58
and family interaction, 58
and social interaction, 47

Q

Quantitative developmental hypothesis of antisocial behavior, 22

R

Rationality, 56–57
Referral ratio of girls to boys, 2

Reinforcement, 80, 81, 131–132
assessment of, 81
and coercion process, 80
of deviant behavior, 132
and gender, 80
and parental rejection, 80
and peer group, 131
and socialization, 81
    See also Differential-reinforcement hypothesis; Reinforcement contingencies; Reinforcement theory; Selective-reinforcement hypothesis.
Reinforcement contingencies, 42, 47–48, 51, 53, 58, 125
and coercion model, 125
and double-agent studies, 58
and family interaction, 48, 58
and parenting practices, 51
and social interaction, 47
    See also Differential-reinforcement hypothesis; Reinforcement; Reinforcement theory; Selective-reinforcement hypothesis.
Reinforcement theory, 80, 131–132
and theory of differential association, 131–132
    See also Differential-reinforcement hypothesis; Reinforcement; Reinforcement contingencies; Selective-reinforcement hypothesis.
Replication and construct building, 17
Representative sampling, 15, 16
Risk score, 98

S

Sample selection, 15, 144–148
Sampling indicators, 17, 18, *18,* 19, 64–65
building of, 18
and construct building, 17
and factor loading, 17
mismatching of, 19
and multiagent, multimethod indicators, *18*
selection of, 17
and structural equation modeling, 17
and test–retest reliability, 17
Schizophrenic adults, 55–56
and avoidance contingencies, 56
and escape contingencies, 56
Selective-reinforcement hypothesis, 80
    See also Differential-reinforcement hypothesis; Reinforcement; Reinforcement contingencies; Reinforcement theory.
Self-esteem, 9, 58, 77, 83, 92, 121, 122, *122,* 123, *123,* 124–125
and academic achievement, 121, 124–125
and academic failure, 9
and antisocial trait, 9
California study of, 124
defined, 121
developmental model of, 123, 124, *124*

190

and confounded measurement, 97
development of, 96–97
and principal components factor analysis, 97
Stress risk score, 98, 99
Stressors. *See* Stress.
Structural equation modeling (SEM), 7, 8, 9, 16, 17, 19,
  31–32, 117, 124, 127, 131, 136–137
advantage of, 7
and Child Antisocial construct, 136–137
and confirmatory factor analysis, 31–32
and LISREL VI, 31–32
and mediational hypothesis of academic achievement,
  127
and multiagent, multimethod indicators, 17
and Peer Rejection construct, 131
and sampling indicators, 19
and self-esteem, 124
and stage model, 117
Structural variables, 48–50, *51, 52,* 61
and coercion process, 48–50
and Family Process Code, 49
progression of, *51*
  See also Continuance; Negative synchronicity;
  Start-up.
Substance abuse, 9, 132–133
and parental monitoring, 132–133
and peer group, 9
and peer rejection, 132–133
and Planning Study, 132–133
  See also Parental substance abuse; Substance
  Abuse construct.
Substance Abuse construct, 108–109, *109*
and Child Antisocial construct, 109
and Child Depressed Mood construct, 109

and principal components factor analysis, 108–109
  See also Parental substance abuse; Substance
  abuse.
Systems theory, 21

T

TAB. *See* Total Aversive Behavior.
Television violence, 6
Temperament and heritability of aggression, 35
Test–retest reliability, 17
Theory of differential association, 131–132
Total Aversive Behavior (TAB), 26, 28
  and Child Antisocial construct, 28
Trait score, 22, 23
Trait stability, 23–25, 26–27
  See also Continuity hypothesis.
Transitions, 101, *102*
  and child adjustment problems, 101
  and covariation with parenting practices, 101, *102*
Transitive progression concept, 30
Transitivity hypothesis, 50, 127
  and coercion process, 50
  and continuance, 50
  and negative synchronicity, 50
  and physical aggression, 50
  and stage model, 117
  and start-up, 50
  See also Progression hypothesis.
Trivial–serious hypothesis, 28–29
Twins studies of criminal behavior, 35–36

U

Unattached parents, 63

About the Authors

Gerald R. Patterson, Ph.D., is one of the most respected researchers and theorists in the field of clinical child psychology. He has been a research psychologist for 25 years, first at the Oregon Research Institute and currently at the Oregon Social Learning Center. Dr. Patterson has devoted his professional career to understanding families with aggressive children. During the course of his programmatic research, Dr. Patterson has addressed a wide range of related topics in the areas of intervention, assessment, evaluation of treatment outcome, and research methodology. More recently, he has been working on the social interactional theory of delinquency and antisocial behavior outlined in this volume. Dr. Patterson is highly regarded for his extensive contributions to the research literature: He is the editor, author, or coauthor of several books, and he has written numerous book chapters and journal articles.

Dr. Patterson is the past president of the Association for Advancement of Behavior Therapy. His most recent awards include the Distinguished Professional Contribution Award from the Clinical Child Psychology section of the American Psychological Association, the Cumulative Contribution to Research in Family Therapy Award from the American Association for Marriage and Family Therapy, and the Distinguished Scientist Award for Applications of Psychology from the American Psychological Association.

John B. Reid, Ph.D., is a senior research scientist and clinician at the Oregon Social Learning Center, where he also serves as the executive director. Dr. Reid has been a research scientist for the past 25 years, and he is regarded as an authority on the prevention of conduct disorders in children and assessment methodology. Dr. Reid is the editor, author, or coauthor of more than 100 journal articles, book chapters, and books on developmental psychopathology, prevention research, assessment methodology, and child abuse. He regularly serves as an editorial consultant for professional journals, and he is both a member and chair on grant-application review committees for the National Institutes of Mental Health (NIMH). Dr. Reid has recently been appointed director of the National Center for the Prevention of Conduct Disorders established by NIMH. Dr. Reid is currently modifying and extending existing intervention techniques so that parents and teachers can collaborate in working with conduct-problem children.

Thomas J. Dishion, Ph.D., is a research scientist and clinical psychologist at the Oregon Social Learning Center. Over the past 10 years, Dr. Dishion has been involved in research on the influence of peers and parents on adolescent delinquency. The focus of his research is on understanding the unique contribution of peers to social development, formulating a model of substance abuse in adolescents, and advancing research methodology. He is the author or coauthor of several dozen journal articles and book chapters. Dr. Dishion is currently implementing and testing the "Adolescent Transitions Program," a prevention program for families with young adolescents who are at risk for substance abuse, severe depression, and conduct problems.